INVISIBLE HERO

Endowed by
TOM WATSON BROWN
and
THE WATSON-BROWN FOUNDATION, INC.

INVISIBLE HERO
PATRICK R. CLEBURNE

Bruce H. Stewart Jr.

MERCER UNIVERSITY PRESS

Macon, Georgia

MUP/H756

First Edition.

978-088146-108-4

Books published by Mercer University Press are printed on acid free paper that meets the requirements of American National Standard for Information Sciences—Permanence of Paper for Printed Library Materials.

Mercer University Press is a member of Green Press initiative (greenpressinitiative.org), a nonprofit organization working to help publishers and printers increase their use of recycled paper and decrease their use of fiber derived from endangered forests. This book is printed on recycled paper.

Library of Congress Cataloging-in-Publication Data

CONTENTS

For General John C. Persons

PREFACE

Patrick Cleburne was a man of extraordinary talent, yet he was unappreciated by his government and is largely unrecognized by posterity. Despite his ability, there have been few works dedicated to his memory. This book is not filled with personal anecdotes; rather, it is a study of his military career and the factors and relationships that governed it. When Cleburne was killed at the battle of Franklin, the South lost a man many consider to be the finest infantry officer in the Western theatre. The battles and campaigns in which he participated are treated in their entirety, with his own command discussed in much greater detail. Careful examination is given to the decisions of his superiors, with particular attention to the impact they had on General Cleburne's performance.

Cleburne's troops repeatedly outperformed any unit on the field, Confederate or Union, only to be turned away for lack of support. Yet, he proved that numerical inferiority was not an insurmountable obstacle. The study of his sector reveals a level of military excellence unmatched by those above him. While he was junior in rank, had he been given the position held by Braxton Bragg, the Confederate fortunes in the West may well have been quite different. This book attempts to reconstruct each battle in an objective light, in order that the reader may be able to clearly see the fortunes of Cleburne's men. Hopefully, this serves to both illustrate his triumphs and expose his failures.

The role played by Patrick Cleburne in the Army of Tennessee is a very poignant one. His is a story not found in the casual imagination of what might have been; it is a four-year saga in which his own president and commanders prevented what should have been.

ACKNOWLEDGMENTS

No serious historical effort can be undertaken without considerable help. I am deeply indebted to the many individuals who have given their time and support to this project. The Late Ollie Keller, Cassie Barrow, and Mauriel and Rick Joslyn of the Patrick Cleburne Society have offered continued assistance in the substantiation of certain details throughout the book. Lee White and Jim Ogden at the Chickamauga-Chattanooga National Military Park gave me great assistance with both of those battles, as well as the action at Ringgold Gap, and allowed me to examine all of their information pertaining to the war record of General Cleburne. Dan Pollock and Bill Scaife of the Civil War Round Table of Atlanta shared their insight surrounding the battles around Missionary Ridge, Ringgold Gap, and Atlanta. At the Carter House Archives in Franklin, Tennessee, Tom Cartwright and David Fraley made their files available for research, which has been a tremendous addition to the work. In addition, they have both offered very specific information concerning the chapters on Spring Hill and Franklin, and the opportunity to study the battlefield at Franklin with them has been invaluable. David Vaughan has been able to guide me through the more technical questions regarding cover design, and John Evans has given expert advice concerning the relationship between Patrick Cleburne and Leonidas Polk. Gordon Jones and Mike Brubaker at the Atlanta History Center provided the archival help which was indispensable. Finally, I would like to express my thanks to the staffs in the state archives of Alabama and Tennessee, as well as the libraries at the Universities of Arkansas and North Carolina. Without their help this book would not have been possible, and I am truly grateful to each and every one.

1

THE STAGE IS SET

Throughout the short history of this country, immigrants have played an important role in its development. In the first half of the nineteenth century, economic deprivations in Europe created a desire for many to seek opportunity in America.[1] Despite a strong work ethic, for the most part immigrants toiled without recognition. The American Civil War brought an end to their obscurity. Without regard for politics they served bravely on both sides of the conflict, and though many different countries were represented, no nation could boast of finer soldiers than Ireland. As the war progressed, one man rose above all other foreign officers. His name was Patrick Cleburne.

Born in 1828, Cleburne began his military career eighteen years later as a private in the British 41st regiment of foot. Ireland stood on the verge of a national crisis. In September 1845 farmers had discovered a blight in the potato crop; although this was a serious problem, they were confident that disaster could be averted with a sound harvest the following year. Relief did not appear. Famine struck in spring 1846 and food became scarce.

The economics of Irish agriculture weighed heavily on the poor. Approximately one-third of the population depended on the potato for their sole means of subsistence. Ironically, other crops fared quite well. Harvests of barley, wheat, and oats were plentiful but the grains were exported to England; those profits brought the peasants little comfort.

Patrick Cleburne was a sensitive man, but he was suddenly confronted by the awful devastation. Thousands perished in their homes, in workshops, or on the streets, where rats and dogs fed on the dead and dying, too weak to escape their fate. It was reported that 500 people died each week in Cork alone.[2] The British government scattered the 41st throughout central and

---

[1] Craig L. Symonds, *Stonewall of the West* (Lawrence: University of Kansas Press, 1997) 9–10. On page 26 he states that "over two million Irishmen emigrated to the United States in the 1850s."

[2] James S. Donnelly, Jr., *The Land and People of Nineteenth Century Cork* (London: Routledge & Keegan Paul, 1975) 85–87.

south central Ireland protecting property and preventing riots. The situation had deteriorated to the point where landlords were being murdered by desperate tenants.[3] This picture of Ireland was not at all the one Cleburne had envisioned.

During the latter part of 1847, Cleburne's company was shifted back and forth between Mullingar and Philipstown. In December he was placed on guard duty. Disregarding his health, he stood long hours exposed to freezing weather. He contracted severe rheumatism and spent seventeen days convalescing in the regimental hospital at Gravesend. An avid reader, he devoted most of his time to history, specifically the exploits of the Duke of Wellington. He studied the campaigns against Napoleon and paid particular attention to Wellington's personal traits and military strategy. Cleburne may well have applied the knowledge gained here to his service in the Confederacy. He also began to read Blackstone's *Commentaries*, which fostered a future interest in the law.[4]

By 1848 the famine had begun to subside, and while the Cleburnes had fared better than most Irish families, they had not escaped the ravages of recent years. Faced with immediate hardship, they began to consider a new life in America. Patrick purchased his discharge from the army and on 5 November, along with his siblings William, Joseph, and Anne, boarded the *Bridgetown* bound for New Orleans. They arrived on Christmas Day but it appears as though Cleburne had no intention of remaining, as he left almost immediately for Cincinnati.

As the steamboat moved up the Mississippi River, Cleburne could not help but notice the contrast between America and Ireland. The river itself was very impressive, and so was the activity along its shores as cargo moved back and forth along the docks. After a nine-day journey he reached Cincinnati; only two days later William, Anne, and Joseph arrived. Anne recorded her observations of the trip: "We were very much delighted the two days we spent sailing up the river. The scenery was beautiful at both sides, woods,

---

[3] Symonds, *Stonewall of the West,* 10, 19.

[4] Isaac W. Avery, "Patrick Ronayne Cleburne," *Kennesaw Gazette,* 15 May 1887, 2; Mauriel P. Joslyn, ed., *A Meteor Shining Brightly* (Macon GA: Mercer University Press, 2000) 13–14.

plantations, pretty thatched cottages with gardens, large orange trees covered with fruit. I never saw anything so pretty before."[5]

Patrick was able to obtain a position in a local pharmacy run by Thomas Salter. While he was gainfully employed, there was little room for advancement. He worked there through the spring, when Salter presented him with an ideal opportunity. A Mr. Freeman of Helena, Arkansas, had recently sold his drugstore to two physicians, and the new owners were too busy with a growing medical practice to properly manage their business operations.

When Freeman expressed a desire to move to Cincinnati, Hector Grant and Charles Nash asked him to watch for a worthy candidate. Despite persistent attempts he was unable to find a suitable replacement. He met Salter, and when he inquired as to Cleburne's interest in the venture he received an enthusiastic response. With nothing more than a recommendation Pat Cleburne headed down river to Helena.

His relationship with Grant and Nash proved to be a fruitful one. Over time, the success of a thriving business raised Cleburne's social standing from that of a shy immigrant to a prominent member of the community. He attended the Episcopal Church and joined both the literary club and the debating society. He formed a chess club and became its first president. Shortly thereafter he applied for membership in the Masonic Lodge, the most prestigious men's club in Helena. He was accepted in 1852 and during the next year was elected Worshipful Master.[6]

Although the Masons were well respected, they did not represent the social elite. That distinction belonged to the planters, and the most important crop in Arkansas was cotton. Production in Phillips County increased five-fold in the 1850s, from 5,165 bales in 1850 to 26,993 in 1860. The value of a typical farm rose as well, from $859 to $2,712 in the same period.[7] A successful operation required a large amount of capital and entailed

---

[5] Anne Cleburne to Isabella Cleburne, n.d., Cleburne family letters file, Carter House Archives, Franklin TN.

[6] Howell and Elizabeth Purdue, *Pat Cleburne Confederate General* (1973; repr., Gaithersburg MD: Olde Soldier Books, 1987) 43.

[7] Carl H. Moneyhon, *The Impact of the Civil War and Reconstruction on Arkansas Persistence in the Midst of Ruin* (Baton Rouge: Louisiana State University Press, 1994) 13–14, 54–55; Diane Neal and Thomas W. Kremm, *Lion of the South: General Thomas C. Hindman* (Macon GA: Mercer University Press, 1993) 22 add that Phillips County was the third largest cotton producing county in the state.

considerable risk. Cleburne never expressed any interest in becoming a cotton planter, and he was somewhat indifferent regarding slavery. It was an accepted practice in Arkansas and most people did not give serious thought to the institution itself.

Cleburne had great respect for both physicians, but he began to grow restless. His interest in law had never really gone away, and since it was clear that in order to pass the bar he would have to dedicate all of his time to his studies, he severed his ties with the pharmacy in 1854. Helena was still a frontier town and quarrels over land deals were unending. As a result, there were five law firms as well as several independent attorneys, which was a quite a large number for such a small town. Cleburne successfully passed the bar and formed a partnership, but his career was unremarkable, perhaps because he was forced to compete with the most prominent lawyers in the state. Without any malicious intent, Thomas Hanly, Charles Adams, and John Preston left little room for a small concern with a limited resume. Despite a lack of accomplishment in this latest endeavor, Cleburne's life in Helena was a good one. He had found a home, he had made many friends, and he was financially secure. Elsewhere, however, trouble loomed. His world was about to be turned upside down.

As the decade came to a close, two events brought sectional differences to a boiling point. On 6 March 1857 the U.S. Supreme Court rendered a decision in the complicated case of *Dred Scott vs. Sanford.*[8] Dred Scott was a slave from Missouri owned by Dr. John Emerson, a surgeon in the United States Army. Emerson had taken Scott with him on a military assignment to Illinois in 1834 and from there to the Wisconsin Territory. In 1838 they returned to Missouri. Five years later Emerson died of consumption[9] and all of his holdings, including the slaves, were left to his wife.[10] In 1846 Scott sued her in an attempt to gain his independence. His lawyer contended that because he had resided in a free state and a free territory, he should be released from bondage. In 1850 the lower court upheld his claim.

[8] The defendant in this case was John F. A. Sanford. A court official mistakenly spelled his surname Stanford, an error that appears in some sources.

[9] Don E. Fehrenbacher, *The Dred Scott Case* (New York: Oxford University Press, 1978) 248 explains that the official diagnosis was consumption, but that the real cause of death may well have been an advanced stage of syphilis.

[10] David M. Potter, *The Impending Crisis, 1848–1861* (New York: Harper & Row, 1976) 267–68.

Mrs. Emerson could not accept the decision and decided to appeal. While the legal battle continued she remarried and moved to Massachusetts, leaving Scott in the control[11] of her brother, John F. A. Sanford. In 1852 the Supreme Court of Missouri reversed the decision and Dred Scott remained a slave. By this time Sanford had also moved east, though he still retained business interests in St. Louis. He had become a resident of New York and was now beyond the jurisdiction of the Missouri judicial system. Any further action in the case must take place in a Federal court. New York was a free state, and Scott brought one more lawsuit. Sanford's position was that because Scott was a Negro, he was not a citizen of Missouri and therefore could not sue.[12]

The case was taken to the US Supreme Court. In a landmark decision, Chief Justice Roger B. Taney delivered a ruling in favor of Mr. Sanford on the grounds that: a) a Negro cannot become a member of the political community created by the Constitution and be entitled to the rights of Federal citizenship; and b) the Missouri Compromise, which prohibited slavery in every part of the national territory, was unconstitutional. Although the court had arrived at a verdict, controversy still raged and the fundamental issues were far from settled. Republicans in the North maintained that no judicial decree could inhibit the power of Congress. The Scott decision denied Congress the power to pass prohibitory legislation; therefore the ruling was invalid. On the other hand, the Democrats in the South believed that the opinion of the court only strengthened their original position and guaranteed the right of a slaveholder to take his property into another territory. Furthermore, everything depended on local law enforcement, and by withholding such protection a free man could be prevented from bringing his slaves from a state into a territory. Both arguments were filled with inconsistency and at times were illogical, but the two sides were unable to reconcile their differences.[13]

---

[11] Potter, *Impending Crisis,* 269. The legal status of Dred Scott at this point is debatable. He may have been sold to Sanford in a legal transfer of ownership, or merely left under Sanford's control, while still being technically owned by Mrs. Emerson. At any rate, the subsequent lawsuit was brought against Sanford under the argument by Sanford's attorneys that the owner was indeed John F. A. Sanford.

[12] Hudson Strode, *American Patriot, 1808–1861* (New York: Harcourt, Brace and Company, 1955) 291–92.

[13] Fehrenbacher, *Dred Scott,* 516–17; William and Bruce Catton, *Two Roads to Sumter* (New York: McGraw-Hill, 1963) 134–36.

While the *Dred Scott* case represented a social and legal dispute, just over two years later a military uprising caused even more alarm. In the fall of 1859 a radical abolitionist from Kansas named John Brown began to plan an invasion of the South. He hoped to incite a slave revolt that would ultimately result in their emancipation. A raiding party of twenty-two men was assembled, five of them Negroes.[14] The initial target was Harper's Ferry, Virginia, the site of the southernmost Federal arsenal. During the night of 16 October they attacked and captured the arsenal, the armory, and the rifle factory.

After seizing several citizens in their sleep and taking them hostage, the marauders continued on to the house of Colonel Lewis Washington, the great-great-nephew of George Washington. Brown captured the colonel, armed his slaves, and told them they were free. Washington and twelve other hostages were then incarcerated in the engine house. It was a strong building, some 35 feet long and 30 feet deep with stone buttressed double doors made of solid oak.[15] Several of the slaves were ordered to guard their master and the other prisoners. Understandably, they could not fully comprehend the instructions to guard their master. Despite Brown's promises of liberty, the slaves' assistance was nonexistent. The Kansan had hoped for an immediate display of aggression but instead received only apathy.

In the meantime, the early morning train had carried reports of the attack to neighboring towns. The local papers had the news out and rumors spread, wildly exaggerating the size of the raiding party. The thought of a slave insurrection had given Southerners great anxiety for generations, but now the nightmare had become reality. John Brown had truly precipitated a crisis. The countryside armed itself, but by the time the first volunteers and militia arrived, several citizens, including the mayor, had already been killed. The surprise attack required military intervention, and quickly. Fortunately, one of the most respected officers in the United States Army[16] was close at hand.

---

[14] Edwin C. Bearss, *Fields of Honor* (Washington, DC: National Geographic, 2006) 5; Strode, *American Patriot*, 337; James McPherson, *Battle Cry of Freedom* (New York: Oxford University Press, 1988) 205.

[15] Clifford Dowdey, *Lee* (Boston: Little Brown & Co., 1965) 118; Allan Nevins, *The Emergence of Lincoln: Prologue to the Civil War, 1859–1861,* 2 vols. (New York: Charles Scribner's Sons, 1950) 78.

[16] Robert E. Lee had served under Winfield Scott in the Mexican War. Scott greatly admired Lee's military skill and on 18 April 1861, Lee would be offered command of all

October 17 found Colonel Robert E. Lee at his family home of Arlington, completing repairs on the property. That morning Lieutenant J. E. B. Stuart arrived with an urgent message from the secretary of war. Colonel Lee was to report at once.

Orders were immediately issued to capture the invaders. At 10:00 P.M. the two men boarded a train and arrived shortly thereafter at Sandy Hook, just over a mile from Harper's Ferry. Lee and Stuart were met by four companies of Maryland militia, along with 90 marines under the command of Lieutenant Israel Green. The troops were placed in position, but Lee believed that a night attack might cause unnecessary casualties. He decided to wait until morning. Around 2:00 A.M. Lee gave Stuart instructions to deliver the terms of surrender.

By 7 o'clock[17] preparations were finished and Lieutenant Stuart approached the engine house. Brown refused the offer and Stuart waved his hat to alert the marines. A detachment of twelve soldiers stormed the building and without firing a shot they were soon inside. The contest lasted only a few minutes, and despite the confusion all thirteen hostages survived unharmed.[18] John Brown was quickly captured and brought to trial in Charlestown, Virginia. On 31 October he was found guilty of treason against the state of Virginia and of inciting slave rebellion. Brown was sentenced to be executed and on 2 December 1859 he was hanged.

While the raid itself was only a small affair, it had enormous repercussions. Northern newspapers even portrayed Brown as a martyr.[19] New York, Philadelphia, and Boston saw an outpouring of admiration. Prominent literary figures of the day added their support. Ralph Waldo Emerson stated that Brown would "make the gallows as glorious as the cross," and Henry

---

United States military forces in the field, with the corresponding rank of major general. While he respected the offer, he could not take up arms against Virginia. He declined and offered his services to the Confederacy.

[17] Douglas S. Freeman, *R. E. Lee,* 4 vols. (New York: Charles Scribner's Sons, 1934–1936) 1:395–98.

[18] Dowdey, *Lee,* 119; Freeman, *R. E. Lee,* 400; Potter, *Impending Crisis,* 371.

[19] John. W. Thomason, Jr., *Jeb Stuart* (1930; repr., New York: William S. Konecky Associates, 1958) 57; Paul M. Angle and Earl S. Miers, *Tragic Years, 1860–1865,* 2 vols. (New York: Simon & Schuster, 1960) 1:33; Freeman, *R. E. Lee,* 402; George Cary Eggleston, *The History of the Confederate War* (New York, Sturgis & Walton Company, 1910) 141.

David Thoreau called him an "angel of light." Louisa May Alcott penned the following tribute: "No breath of shame can touch his shield / Nor ages dim its shine. / Living, he made life beautiful, / Dying, he made death divine."[20]

Certainly it would not be argued today that the intent of these compliments was to instigate civil war. No doubt there were those who strongly opposed slavery and did in fact agree with Brown's motives. However, the public praise of such a man produced tragic consequences. Throughout the South it appeared as though some factions in the North actually condoned murder as a means to effect abolitionist aims. Not only had the possibility of a slave revolt been glorified, but the entire social system had been assailed as well. There had always been economic differences between North and South, but prior to the engagement at Harper's Ferry there was no concerted movement toward dissolution of the country. The attack on Virginia soil put the matter in a very different light.

In this emotionally charged atmosphere, rational consideration of current events began to disappear and a peaceable compromise became much more difficult. The mood of the country turned to antagonism, and the presidential election of 1860 occurred amid a cloud of distrust. On 18 May the National Convention of the Republican Party convened in Chicago. Abraham Lincoln of Illinois was chosen as the party's nominee for president, with Hannibal Hamlin of Maine as his running mate. A cornerstone of the platform was the Homestead Act,[21] which provided for the settlement of unoccupied land at the cost of only a nominal filing fee. In addition, the party supported congressional prohibition of slavery in the Western territories.

While the Republicans spoke with one voice, the Democrats began to split apart. In order to select one candidate, three separate conventions were held. Only nine days earlier the Constitutional Union Party had adopted John Bell of Tennessee. Although he certainly was not the most prominent candidate, his conservative stance had the support of the border states. He was not particularly controversial and the issue of slavery was not addressed.

---

[20] Nevins, *Emergence of Lincoln*, 102; Potter, *Impending Crisis*, 378.

[21] The Homestead Act was eventually signed into law by President Lincoln in 1862. It allowed any individual who was at least twenty-one years of age and the head of a household to receive 160 acres of land, provided that the settler built a home and farmed the land for a period of at least five years. The distribution of free land had been opposed by the Southern states, but after secession the bill was easily passed by the legislature.

Democrats from the Northern states supported Stephen Douglas, and on 23 June a second convention was held. Although Douglas was both well known and popular in the North, he was perceived in the South as a candidate who would not have national appeal. He had a very hands-off approach to slavery, which was unacceptable in the minds of Southern voters. The prevailing view among slaveholding states was that Federal protection in the Western territories was an essential ingredient in the party platform and must be guaranteed. The recent Supreme Court decision in the *Dred Scott* case only reinforced this conviction. The Douglas Democrats constituted the largest group of delegates, yet they had presented a platform that failed to address a very important concern. Southern extremists regarded this omission as an insult. Senator William Yancey of Alabama furiously objected and received an angry rebuttal from George Pugh of Ohio. The delegates from Alabama stormed out of the convention, followed by representatives from Mississippi, Louisiana, South Carolina, Florida, Texas, and Arkansas. The next day Georgia also withdrew. Emotion had defeated reason, and for all intents and purposes the destruction of the party was complete.

The Democrats simply could not reach a consensus. On 28 June yet a third convention was held, this time by the Southern Democrats. John C. Breckinridge of Kentucky emerged as the favorite and the provision that the Federal government must uphold the practice of slavery was formally adopted. The difference of opinion within the party on the importance of this particular issue was unmistakable, and it would determine the outcome of the election.

The political views of 1860 went far beyond social theory. There was a sharp contrast between North and South in the basic utility of slavery itself. With constant innovation over several generations, the manufacturing base of the United States had grown up in the large, industrialized cities in the North. It was a dynamic, rapidly changing society. Farming was widespread, but the economy was well diversified. The agrarian life in the South was largely static, with little incentive to change. This created a heavy reliance on a few crops, such as cotton, tobacco, and rice. In only ten years the production of cotton had doubled, while prices remained constant, reflecting on a national scale what was also occurring in Arkansas. Similar increases were seen in tobacco and sugar. Invention had changed the face of the South as well, but in a very different manner. In 1793 Eli Whitney had invented the cotton gin. World demand seemed insatiable, and while this led to increased production it also stifled the development of other industries. It was a labor-intensive crop, requiring large plantations and numerous slaves. With increasing commercial success, Southern planters felt it necessary to preserve the status quo. The evolution of the economic structures led to two very different conclusions. The North had no need for any type of bondage; the South could not survive without it.

Although this dichotomy was striking, there were economic factors that played an even more important role in the outbreak of war. In a heated campaign of rhetoric, both sides claimed injury by the other. The truth lay somewhere in the middle. In November 1860 Robert Toombs placed his emphasis on foreign trade. Speaking before the Georgia legislature, he asserted that current law protected Northern interests. High tariffs prevented European ships from docking at Southern ports, thereby preventing the South from negotiating more favorable terms with foreign merchants. This objection had considerable merit, but Toombs went even further. In a very weak argument he claimed that the North had diverted money from the South through Federal improvements to Northern harbors. In his view, this money should come not from the national treasury but solely at the expense of the Northern shippers.[22]

According to an editorial from the *Vicksburg Daily Whig*, the North had profited at the expense of the South, depleting the South without actually destroying it. Sparing neither side, the *Whig* continued that the South had allowed it to happen.[23] In perhaps the strongest statement of all, John H. Reagan of Texas contended that the South had been forced to secede, as economic subjugation left it no other choice.[24]

Naturally, there was another point of view. Northern capitalists insisted that the entire country was being sacrificed to the slaveholders and that it was the desire to perpetuate these conditions that led to the demands for more slave states.[25] In an article published on 12 November 1860, the *Boston Herald* maintained that if the South seceded it would strike more profitable shipping

---

[22] *The Rebellion Record*, supplement, 362–68, quoted in Kenneth Stampp, ed., *The Causes of the Civil War* (New York: Touchstone Books, 1986) 64–65.
[23] *Vicksburg Daily Whig*, 18 January 1860, quoted in Dwight Lowell Dumond, ed., *Southern Editorials on Secession* (1931; repr., Gloucester MA: P. Smith, 1964) 13–14.
[24] *Congressional Globe*, 15 January 1861, 391.
[25] Stampp, ed., *Causes of the Civil War*, 67.

contracts with many of these European firms, to the detriment of Northern merchants.

Although these arguments were heavily biased, they clearly illustrate the conflict between protectionist policies in the North and free-trade interests in the South. The Boston *Transcript* summarized the essence of the dispute quite succinctly on 18 March 1861. In the most neutral and accurate assessment of all, the *Transcript* stated that the argument was about the economic interests of each side, while slavery played only a secondary role.

There was a basic disagreement in principle between a strong, centralized Federal government and an independent confederation of individual states. Slavery was important, but it represented a piece of the much larger concept of states' rights, and it was over states' rights that the Civil War would be fought.[26] In Cleburne's opinion this was clearly an effort on the part of the North to dominate Southern social and economic systems, thereby abrogating the balance of power between the two regions. He sided with the South on the issue of tariffs and free trade. He recognized the significance of the issue of slavery but abhorred the surrounding propaganda.

Cleburne was certainly influenced by the conditions around him. Arkansas was growing rapidly, and though it was not a large slaveholding state in comparison with the Deep South, it was changing politically, economically,

---

[26] Alexander Stephens, *A Constitutional View of the Late War between the States*, 2 vols. (Philadelphia: National Publishing Company, 1868) 9–12; *Boston Atlas and Bee*, 3 December 1860; *Boston Transcript*, 18 March 1861; Mary B. Chesnutt, *A Diary from Dixie* (1905; repr., New York: Random House, 1997) 72, 200; Stephen W. Sears, *Controversies & Commanders* (New York: Houghton Mifflin, 1999) 15; Ernest B. Furgurson, *Chancellorsville 1863* (New York: Alfred A. Knopf, 1992) 14–15; Bruce Catton, *Grant Moves South, 1861–1863* (1960; repr., Edison NJ: Castle Books, 2000) 15; Gary Gallagher, *Lee and His Generals in War and Memory* (Baton Rouge: Louisiana State University Press, 1998) 25; James M. McPherson, For Cause and Comrades (New York: Oxford University Press, 1997) 18–24; John B. Gordon, *Reminiscences of the Civil War* (New York: Charles Scribner's Sons, 1904) 18–24; Ulysses S. Grant, *Personal Memoirs of U. S. Grant*, 2 vols. (New York: Charles L. Webster & Co., 1885) 2:542–43; William T. Sherman, *Memoirs of Gen. W. T. Sherman*, 2 vols. (New York: Charles L. Webster & Co., 1991) 1:293; R. M. T. Hunter, "Origin of the Late War," in *Southern Historical Society Papers*, 52 vols. (Millwood NY: Kraus Reprint Co., 1977) 1:1, 11–12; Joseph Wheeler, "Slavery and States Rights" as quoted in the *Richmond Dispatch*, 31 July 1894, in *Southern Historical Society Papers*, 52 vols. (Millwood NY: Kraus Reprint Co., 1977) 22:25–31; Alexander Stephens, "Cornerstone Speech, 21 March 1861.

and culturally.[27] Cotton production was on the rise, and the farmers were tied to its fortunes. C. F. M. Noland had stated that "if cotton will only hold present prices for five years, Arkansas planters will be as rich as cream a foot thick."[28]

Many prominent Confederate leaders, such as Robert E. Lee, Stonewall Jackson, and Jefferson Davis, believed in the fundamental right of secession but fervently opposed its practice. Pat Cleburne shared this view. Unfortunately, by winter 1860 efforts at compromise were failing. While most lawmakers wanted to preserve the Union, extremists on both sides were simply unwilling to negotiate. Fire-eaters such as William Yancey of Alabama and Edmund Ruffin of Virginia were vocal advocates of secession. As the editor of the Charleston *Mercury*, Robert Barnwell Rhett was a constant source of unrest. In the North, Wendell Phillips of Massachusetts and Zachariah Chandler of Michigan were just as obstinate. William L. Garrison, founder of the newsletter *The Liberator*, was perhaps the most hated man in the South.[29]

Still, most Northerners thought first in terms of a unified nation and had no strong feelings whatsoever regarding the issue. Ulysses S. Grant actually owned a slave and his wife had owned several.[30] In 1859 William T. Sherman had stated, "I would not, if I could, abolish or modify slavery."[31] In his inaugural address on 4 March 1861 President Lincoln declared that he had no desire to abolish the practice where it existed, though it should be noted that he was strongly opposed to its extension in the Western territories.

The differing views on both the institution of slavery and the wisdom of secession provide great insight into the thought process of the times. The importance of the word "united" is often overlooked in the study of the Civil War. The Northern determination to prevent the disintegration of the Union

---

[27] James M. Woods, *Rebellion and Realignment* (Fayetteville: University of Arkansas Press, 1987) 91–97.

[28] Michael B. Dougan, *Confederate Arkansas* (Tuscaloosa: University of Alabama Press, 1976) 9.

[29] Chesnutt, *Diary*, 6; Potter, *Impending Crisis*, 47; 123; Bruce Catton, *The Coming Fury* (New York: Doubleday, 1961) 130; Margaret Leech, *Reveille in Washington* (New York: Harper & Brothers, 1941) 21–22.

[29] Catton, *Grant Moves South*, 33.

[30] Catton, *Grant Moves South*, 33.

[31] Hudson Strode, *Jefferson Davis Confederate President* (New York: Harcourt, Brace & Co., 1959) 25.

would prove to be the overriding factor in the prosecution of the war. On the other hand, the Confederacy was severely handicapped by the independence of each state. Despite a general desire to form a new nation, the Southern states lacked the resolve to bind together to achieve a common goal. The inability of the different factions to work with one another doomed the election for the Democrats. Douglas, Breckinridge, and Bell all appeared on the ballot in November, but the failure to agree upon a single candidate weakened support for each one. When the returns were counted Lincoln emerged victorious, even though he had failed to win a majority of the popular vote.

With the election of Abraham Lincoln the calm, undisturbed life of the lower South was instantly changed. The Republican Party was only six years old, but open hostility was already apparent. Radicals vented their anger in the press, while the expansion of slavery was expressly prohibited in the party platform. The president of the United States had the power to appoint his own cabinet, and it was feared that future policy would be specifically directed against the Southern states.[32] The future looked grim indeed. January 1861 saw a flurry of activity. Mississippi, Florida, Alabama, Georgia, and Louisiana followed South Carolina out of the Union and on 1 February Texas also seceded.

Pat Cleburne could not avoid the turmoil surrounding the election. He had only lived in America for eleven years, but in a letter to his half-brother Robert he showed remarkable foresight. Writing in January 1861, he stated:

> The fever of revolution is very contagious…. My own opinion is that the first blood shed on Southern soil in a collision between the Federal troops and the State authorities of any Southern state will be the signal for civil war. As to my own position, I hope to see the Union preserved by granting to the South the full measure of her constitutional rights. If this cannot be done I hope to see all the Southern states united in a new confederation and that we can effect a

---

[32] William J. Cooper, Jr., *Liberty and Slavery: Southern Policies in 1860* (New York: Alfred A. Knopf, 1983) 256–57; Fehrenbacher, *Dred* Scott, 542–43; Clement Eaton, *A History of the Southern Confederacy* (New York: Macmillan Company, 1954) 1–2; E. Merton Coulter, *The Confederate States of America* (Baton Rouge: Louisiana State University Press, 1950) 13; Eggleston, *History of the Confederate War*, 147–49; Moneyhon, *Impact of the Civil War*, 93; Bearss, *Fields of Honor*, 22.

peaceable separation. If both of these are denied us, I am with Arkansas in weal and woe.[33]

Unlike many officers who served in the Civil War, Cleburne was a naturalized citizen and held to the construction of the original constitution. He felt strongly that it represented an ideal of national unity embodied by stars and stripes. This fostered a very personal appreciation of the United States as a nation, one he was determined to protect. The break in that bond cut deeply, and the dissension was only getting worse.[34]

The South was filled with uncertainty but nervous apprehension gripped the North as well. Although the government was established, the country was not prepared for war. The army was small and posts were scattered from the East Coast to California and Oregon. It would take a great deal of time to assemble an effective fighting force and there were not even enough men to protect the capital. Upon receiving the news that South Carolina had seceded, the departments of war, navy, and the interior were thrown into confusion. On 29 December Secretary of War John B. Floyd resigned, followed on 8 January by Secretary of the Interior Jacob Thompson.

There was no provision for actual secession, but there were a few troops in place. Major Robert Anderson had arrived in South Carolina on 19 November to take command of sixty-five Union soldiers stationed at Fort Moultrie. Although the fort was not a strong one, the winter had been quiet. The political developments of 1860 threw South Carolina into turmoil. With the secession of the Palmetto State, Moultrie was surrounded and it became necessary to evacuate. Anderson made plans to move to Fort Sumter.

The construction of the fort had begun in 1829 but it had never been completed. It was evident that much work would have to be done inside the walls. Equipment of all kinds lay strewn about the grounds and very few of the field pieces were mounted in their proper position. The men worked quickly to improve the defenses as there was grave concern that the fort would be unable to withstand a sudden attack. Vulnerable points were strengthened, casemates were repaired, and heavy cannon were placed along the parapets. The

---

[33] Patrick R. Cleburne to Robert Cleburne, [?] January 1861 and 7 May 1861, Patrick R. Cleburne Collection, Special Collections, University of Arkansas. Fayetteville, Arkansas.

[34] Lonn Ella, *Foreigners in the Confederacy* (Chapel Hill: University of North Carolina Press, 1940) 53.

arduous work continued, but President Lincoln knew that the small force could not hold out indefinitely. Anderson would need to be reinforced.

The government began to organize a relief expedition and decided to use a merchant ship to carry military supplies. The steamer *Star of the West* left the New York harbor on 5 January, loaded with 200 men as well as additional arms and provisions. The position in Washington was that if the Confederate batteries opened fire, South Carolina would have attacked a commercial vessel carrying food. If the ship were allowed to reach the fort, Anderson would be relieved. On 9 January, she sailed through the Morris Island channel. The Southerners viewed the approach of the *Star* as an act of invasion and fired a shot across the bow. This had no effect and two more shots were fired, striking the hull of the ship. She sailed back out of the harbor and the ill-fated mission came to an end. The attempt at assistance had failed and tempers flared. Washington maintained that any vessel under the United States flag must be protected and that the military aggression was completely unwarranted. The country was one step closer to war.

The *Star of the West* had not accomplished its mission, but President Lincoln had still another plan. On 4 April he ordered Gustavus Fox to deliver "subsistence" to Sumter; if Fox met any opposition he was to defend himself. In addition, the voyage would bring 200 men to Anderson's assistance, thereby succeeding where the *Star* had failed. Here again, Lincoln demonstrated shrewd political instincts and a keen grasp of prevailing sentiment. On 4 April the country was not at war, but seven states had seceded. At this point it was still possible to lay the blame for the current unrest at the doorstep of the South. Few citizens could understand political intrigue, but the overt act of secession was a tangible reality that was easy to comprehend. There was not much risk in a second attempt to sustain Anderson's command.

Fox traveled to New York and began to make the necessary preparations. He secured a large steamer, the *Baltic*, to transport both men and food. It would be escorted by the *Harriet Lane*, *Pocahontas*, and *Pawnee*. All four ships were too large to pass into the harbor unassisted, so Fox enlisted the services of three special tugs, *Freeborn*, *Yankee*, and *Uncle Ben*. The operation may have been too complicated to assemble in such a short time, but it struggled from the start. The owners of *Freeborn* refused to let her participate, and horrible weather scattered the rest of the ships. The expedition was a complete failure, making a precarious situation even worse.

In the west, Arkansas began to witness an undercurrent of unrest as the national troubles deepened. The tragic chain of events finally led to the opening bombardment on April the twelfth. The opening attack created great excitement, and while there was not a unanimous cry for revolution, emotions ran high among younger men. Slavery was an economic necessity and the new administration in Washington was widely viewed as a threat to local interests. The changing course of life in Arkansas had a great impact on Pat Cleburne's outlook. Citizens could suddenly feel a sense of kinship to Mississippi, Alabama, and Georgia, and there was a need to defend it.[35]

It was against this backdrop of tumultuous events that Patrick Cleburne viewed the crisis. Like Robert E. Lee he was opposed to secession, but his devotion to his state led him to fight for Arkansas. On 6 May 1861 the formal ordinance was passed. Cleburne decided to cast his lot with the South.

---

[35] Dougan, *Confederate Arkansas,* 47–57, 63–69.

2

1861

After a decade in America, Pat Cleburne had come to love his adopted country. By and large Helena had been a peaceful little town, but by 1860 the mood of the nation had changed. Differences between North and South became more pronounced and political rhetoric intensified. It was readily apparent that Arkansas was not prepared for war. Troops must be found, armed, and clothed but there were no factories to provide this type of materiel. There was almost no military experience in the town. For Cleburne, it marked a new beginning to an old career. It was imperative to bring order to a collection of men distinguished by their enthusiasm yet hindered by their ignorance. As war clouds gathered in the summer, Cleburne helped to establish a company of 115 volunteers known as the Yell Rifles. They were named for a former governor, Archibald Yell, who had been killed in the Mexican War at the battle of Buena Vista. The Rifles were comprised of young planters and professional men who represented Helena's upper class. The Helena *Southern Shield* wrote that they were "hardy, industrious men, inured to toil and privation of frontier life—the best material out of which to make the effective, reliable soldier, if properly armed, drilled and disciplined."[1] Despite their economic advantages, these men understood that they needed a strong leader with some formal training. They admired Cleburne's experience in the 41st British Regiment of Foot and elected him captain of the company. In turn, Cleburne enlisted the services of J. H. Calvert as his drillmaster. Calvert was an Irishman and a resident of Helena, but he had also been a sergeant in the United States Army. His experience proved invaluable, and he later served as an artillery officer in Cleburne's brigade.[2]

Cleburne experienced a remarkable transformation in personality from civilian life to army officer. By nature he was very shy, particularly around women. However, when instructing raw recruits as a captain or leading battle-

---

[1] *Arkansas State Gazette* (Little Rock), 1 January 1861, 2.
[2] Howell and Elizabeth Purdue, *Pat Cleburne Confederate General* (1973; repr., Gaithersburg MD: Olde Soldier Books, 1987) 64.

hardened veterans as a major general, he was confident and assertive. Physically he was not imposing. He stood 5 feet 10 inches tall and weighed less than 150 pounds, but he had piercing gray eyes and seemed impervious to danger. His modest character, strong sense of duty, and unswerving loyalty made a lasting impression on the men in his command. Pat Cleburne would never admit to it in public, but the force of his will and the lessons of Wellington would come to drive his troops farther than they ever believed they could go. As the fall wore on and training continued, he attempted to mold 115 civilians into a well-organized company. While the men made considerable progress, life was unexciting. March and drill were necessary, but the men hungered for action. In January 1861 their wish was granted.

A telegram arrived from Little Rock stating that a steamer filled with Federal troops was on its way to the capital. The troops intended to reinforce the arsenal there, placing Governor Henry Rector in an extremely difficult position. Personally Rector was a strong advocate of states' rights, but he could hardly attack a contingent of United States soldiers. On the other hand, South Carolina and five other states had already seceded, and the governor was determined to protect the people of Arkansas. He needed help. Civic leaders in Helena offered their militia, which included the Yell Rifles. Rector's adjutant replied that the governor had "no authority to summon you to take possession of a Federal post" but added that "should the people assemble in their [own] defense, the governor will interpose his official position in their behalf."[3] Upon receiving this thinly veiled request for troops, the Yell Rifles and Phillips Guards marched off to Little Rock.

Both companies boarded a steamer at Front Street. Sixty miles to the south they entered the Arkansas River and reached Little Rock on 5 February. Much to their chagrin, their arrival was greeted with little enthusiasm. Hoping to avoid an outbreak of hostilities, Governor Rector asked them not to attempt to take possession of the arsenal. Cleburne's men marched to the capital grounds, where they joined other commands from around the state. Approximately 1,000 men[4] from a dozen militia units had made their camp in the area. The sight of armed soldiers alarmed the people of Little Rock, and they asked the governor for his assistance. Governor Rector met with James

---

[3] *Arkansas State Gazette* (Little Rock), 29 January 1861.

[4] Craig L. Symonds, *Stonewall of the West* (Lawrence: University of Kansas Press, 1997) 46.

Totten, the Federal commander, and explained that he could not control the actions of so many men. Rector advised Totten to prevent any bloodshed and evacuate. After a very short deliberation, on 8 February the Federals turned over the arsenal. Although no bullets had been fired, the Yell Rifles felt they had contributed to an important victory. Satisfied with their performance, the men returned to Helena.

On 18 February the Arkansas legislature authorized a referendum to determine whether a convention should be held to deal with the issue of secession. By a margin of almost 2 to 1, the electorate voted in favor of the proposal. It would assemble on 4 March, the day that Abraham Lincoln was to be inaugurated. By this time Texas had also seceded, but the Arkansas delegates preferred to wait until they had heard President Lincoln's address. The general tone of the speech was conciliatory, placating the Arkansas contingent for the moment. However, he included the following words:

> In your hands, my dissatisfied country men, and not in mine, is the momentous issue of civil war. The government will not assail you. You have no conflict without being the aggressors. *You* have no oath registered in heaven to destroy the Government, while *I* shall have the most solemn one to preserve, protect and defend it.
>
> We are not enemies, but friends, then continued to say that "the power confided to me will be used to hold, occupy, and possess the property and places belonging to the Government, and collect the duties and imports; but beyond what may be necessary for these objects, there will be no invasion, no use of force against or among the people anywhere."[5]

On 12 April the bombardment of Fort Sumter began. All hopes of reconciliation were gone, but danger had not yet reached the Western theatre and for the moment Cleburne's men were not materially affected. Even though South Carolina had erupted in flames, Arkansas remained uncommitted. However, there was a great deal of uncertainty among the populace. Any form of coercion would certainly force a break from the Union. On 15 April Lincoln called upon the states to field an army of 75,000 men, including 780

---

[5] Paul M. Angle and Earl S. Miers, *Tragic Years, 1860–1865,* 2 vols. (New York: Simon & Schuster, 1960) 1:46–47; emphasis original.

from Arkansas. An incensed Governor Rector replied to Secretary of War Simon Cameron: "In answer to your requisition for troops from Arkansas, I have to say that none will be furnished. The demand is only adding insult to injury. The people of this commonwealth are freemen, not slaves, and will defend to the last extremity their honor, lives and property against Northern mendacity and usurpation."[6]

The convention had recessed until 19 August but it was immediately called back into session. It appeared as though the state would join the Confederacy. Military activity intensified and Cleburne could feel a sense of urgency. His men made up one of the first companies to have been organized and as such they were well equipped. Other units were not so fortunate; many had no weapons of any kind. Despite a lack of arms, the pressure from the Federal government was too great to bear. On 6 May the ordinance of secession was passed by a vote of 69 to 1, plunging Arkansas into war.[7] The Yell Rifles formed at the steamboat landing once again, urged on by the cheers of an enthusiastic crowd. They traveled up river to Camp Rector, which was nothing more than an expanse of open ground approximately 6 miles north of Memphis on the west bank of the Mississippi River. Bands of volunteers from Arkansas and Tennessee quickly formed into regiments, each one containing ten companies. Elections were held for officers and Cleburne was a leading candidate. He did not campaign for the position but his qualities as a leader were obvious. He was chosen without opposition and on 14 May received his promotion from captain to colonel. Shortly thereafter Cleburne's Rifles, along with several other companies of Arkansas troops, were moved to Fort Randolph, 14 miles further north.

In 1861 regimental commanders were chosen by the men in the ranks, but generals were appointed. In this case Governor Rector would make the selections. The highest rank went to James Yell, who as a major general would command all forces within the state. Nicholas B. Pearce and Thomas H. Bradley became brigadiers, with Pearce commanding the western half of Arkansas. Bradley led the troops in the east, which included the Yell Rifles and Phillips Guards. Early in the war both the Confederate and Union governments had difficulties with unqualified leaders, and Bradley proved to be no exception. A sixty-five-year-old planter without any military experience

---

[6] John C. Hammock, *With Honor Untarnished* (Little Rock: Pioneer Press, 1961) 5.

[7] The lone dissenter was Isaac Murphy, who represented the Ozark region of Arkansas.

whatsoever, he arrived at Camp Rector in the third week of May and immediately claimed authority.

Most of the volunteers had no military training either and they resented the attitude of a man they had never met.[8] Less than one week later a rumor surfaced that a Federal force was advancing on Bearsfield Point, only 25 miles up river. Bradley ordered a reconnaissance of the area. Cleburne's 1st Arkansas had the most experience and was chosen to lead the expedition. The men were assembled, but Bradley's lack of training was quickly exposed. The supplies he had ordered were insufficient, there seemed to be no purpose to the routes of advance, and there was no enemy in sight. Finally, upon the withdrawal of the troops large quantities of equipment were abandoned and the location of one scouting party was still undetermined.

The 1st Arkansas had a great deal of pride and this unmitigated fiasco left them absolutely furious. Several of the captains suggested that Colonel Cleburne place Bradley under arrest and put himself in charge. Cleburne faced a terrible dilemma. He understood and respected military authority, yet he recognized incompetence and felt a strong sense of loyalty to his men. A few days later the scouts arrived back in camp only to announce that there never had been any Union troops near Bearsfield Point. This report decided the issue and a guard was stationed in front of Bradley's headquarters. The colonel revealed his true feelings in a telegram he sent to Judge Hanly, now a member of the state convention in Little Rock: "Arkansas forces returned from Bearsfield Point between two suns; a quantity of material abandoned; scouting party of picked men abandoned; no enemy nearer than Cairo; we are the laughing stock of the Tennesseans."[9]

As if to add further emphasis to his disgust, Cleburne sharply demanded "Answer." The situation was a difficult one, but it was exacerbated by a telegram from a captain in the Jefferson Guards. These men were under Cleburne's command, and Charles Carlton sent the following message to a friend in the state capital: "We have deposed Bradley," followed by "appoint Col. Cleburne and satisfy [the] regiment."[10]

The whole affair was a low point in Pat Cleburne's military career. The failure to follow established protocol was a horrendous mistake. Regardless of

---

[8] Symonds, *Stonewall of the West*, 49.

[9] Purdue and Purdue, *Pat Cleburne Confederate General*, 80–81.

[10] Symonds, *Stonewall of the West*, 50.

his affection for his men, he had not only ignored the orders of a superior but had also forbidden any communication with Little Rock unless Bradley promised to leave Camp Rector. Bradley, realizing that his authority had vanished, returned to Little Rock, but the separation of the two men did not solve the problem. Upon his charges of mutiny, a court-martial was scheduled to convene in Mound City in the middle of June. It did not take long for Bradley to see that a public inquiry would do more damage to himself than it would to Cleburne. The resolution of the matter was left to Gideon Pillow, the commander of the Provisional Army of Tennessee. Pillow decided not to prefer charges and Bradley resigned in disgrace.

With his difficulties behind him, Cleburne took the 1st Arkansas and one company of field artillery to a high bluff on the east side of the Mississippi in order to set up the advance post in the region. Thirty-eight miles north of Memphis, the site afforded an excellent view of the river and any ship that might try to pass was within easy range of Confederate cannon. The Graycoats worked through the end of the month erecting proper fortifications. They called the encampment Fort Cleburne in his honor, though the name was changed to Fort Pillow in July.

The Arkansas Military Board sent James Yell to replace Bradley; however, jurisdiction was thrown into confusion when Jefferson Davis appointed General William J. Hardee to command the area of Arkansas north of the Arkansas River and west of the White and Black Rivers. Hardee was well known in military circles; he had written a book on tactics that became the standard manual for both armies. However, as he was a stranger to Cleburne's men it was not clear how they would respond. Hardee anticipated the situation, traveling to Little Rock in order to meet with the Military Board. He was well received and all seven regiments of infantry, one cavalry regiment, and five batteries of artillery were reassigned. Governor Rector did attach some conditions: no troops could be transferred to Confederate service without their consent, each company must have the option of serving in the Confederacy or remaining in Arkansas, and Hardee would have to provide a receipt for any men who did muster into the army.

Under this new arrangement, James Yell would lose his promotion. Naturally he objected to any transfer of troops, hoping to retain them in eastern Arkansas. Cleburne held the opposite view and preferred to fight for the Confederacy. His opinion was probably impacted by his experience with Thomas Bradley. He had little regard for state militia and may well have believed that a national army had a better chance of success than local defense units. He must have had some influence, as approximately 60 percent of the men at Camp Rector went with him, including eight of the ten companies in his own regiment.[11]At the end of the reorganization he had 488 men under his command. On 23 July it became official: Pat Cleburne was a Confederate.

The association with William Hardee would become the most important one of Cleburne's Civil War career. The two men formed an immediate friendship based on mutual respect for the other's talents. A graduate of West Point in the class of 1838,[12] the forty-five-year old Hardee just looked like a soldier. He recognized Cleburne's ability and over time these Arkansas troops would become the backbone of Hardee's corps. Dr. Nash, who knew both men, wrote that "Hardee's friendship for Cleburne was not born of a military character alone, but from the high merit of a moral man."[13]

Hardee assumed command on 22 July and established new headquarters at Pittman's Ferry. Only 400 yards from the Missouri border, the location provided a good base for offensive operations to the north and offered protection for Arkansas in case of an invasion.[14]The camp served as a training ground in an attempt to make the first really serious effort to turn civilians into soldiers. This was not an easy task as the lack of discipline so apparent back in Helena had not fully disappeared. Shortly after Hardee's arrival a private on picket duty invited his commander to join him for dinner. The general understood the situation and was merely amused at the young man's mistake. Progress was slow but Cleburne worked tirelessly to transform his ragged group of volunteers into a structured regiment. At first they resented his stern approach but they grew to appreciate the effort which he put forth. They finally realized that the monotony of repetition would come to serve them well. Firm, yet compassionate, Pat Cleburne had won the hearts of his soldiers.

---

[11] Seventy-one men in the Yell Rifles transferred into Confederate service.

[12] The West Point class of 1838 also included P. G. T. Beauregard, Edward Johnson, and Irvin McDowell.

[13] Charles E. Nash, *Biographical Sketches of Gen. Pat Cleburne and Gen. T. C. Hindman, together with Humorous Anecdotes and Reminiscence of the Late Civil War* (Little Rock AR: Tunnah and Pittard, 1898) 111.

[14] Diane Neal and Thomas W. Kremm, *Lion of the South: General Thomas C. Hindman* (Macon GA: Mercer University Press, 1993) 91; Nathaniel C. Hughes, *General William J. Hardee: Old Reliable* (Baton Rouge: Louisiana State University Press, 1965) 76.

The time spent at Pittman's Ferry was marred by a deep personal tragedy. Along with Hardee, Cleburne had made his quarters in the courthouse. A lieutenant had brought in some Federal prisoners who were also housed in the building. Late at night Cleburne was awakened by a noise outside his room. He drew his pistol and rushed to the door, where he heard shouts that the prisoners were escaping. He saw a figure running down the corridor and fired into the darkness. It was the lieutenant; he fell mortally wounded. He had been walking in his sleep and had wandered into the hall. He lived only an hour more, and the memory of the incident haunted the Irishman for the rest of his life.[15]

Early in the war cooperation was difficult and the overall plan from Pittman's Ferry was somewhat disjointed. The Federals did not hold eastern Missouri with a strong force and St. Louis was protected by a contingent of only 4,000 home guards. It appeared as if there were a chance to strike a decisive blow. To underscore this point, Ulysses S. Grant stated in his *Memoirs* that the United States forces were extremely vulnerable. Many of the soldiers were ninety-day men whose enlistment had already expired. They were poorly clothed and morale was low. Grant even commented that "[a] squadron of cavalry could have ridden into the valley and captured the entire force."[16] The opportunity was there, but the Confederate strategy was loosely defined and certain to cause some confusion. From their position at New Madrid, Gideon Pillow and Jeff Thompson planned to attack the garrisons at Bird's Point, Cape Girardeau, and St. Louis.

The capture of St. Louis was of paramount importance to the fledgling nation. The arsenal held 60,000 stand of small arms, 35 pieces of artillery, and a countless supply of other equipment. Perhaps even more significant were the potential repercussions of the secession of Missouri. The loss of the arsenal would tilt public sentiment in favor of the South and neutralize Federal forces in Illinois and Iowa.[17]Despite the great benefits of such an attack, at this stage of the war the undertaking was probably too complex.

---

[15] Calhoun Benham, "Major Gen. P. R. Cleburne," *Kennesaw* (GA) *Gazette*, 1 January 1889, 2.

[16] Ulysses S. Grant, *Personal Memoirs of U. S. Grant*, 2 vols. (New York: Charles L. Webster & Co., 1885) 1:256–57.

[17] Basil Duke, *Reminiscences of General Basil W. Duke* (Garden City NJ: Doubleday, Page & Co., 1911) 5.

At the same time Sterling Price and Ben McCullough would advance on Springfield and occupy the Federals in the other half of the state. Price asked Hardee to join forces but Hardee declined, pointing out that he simply did not have enough men to be of any assistance. He did, however, agree to work with Pillow.[18] By 28 July the 5th Arkansas regiment joined Hardee. Other units were on the way, and when all of his troops arrived he would lead a force of some 5,000 men.[19]

Hardee learned that the enemy had left Ironton and Cape Girardeau and was moving south toward Greenville. Accordingly, he moved forward to meet the threat. Cleburne's 1st Arkansas led a force of 1,250 men[20] along the Black River into Missouri opposing 1,000 Federals. On 4 August Cleburne arrived at Greenville, 40 miles south of Ironton. Thomas Hindman soon joined him, but Hardee's third regiment under Colonel R. G. Shaver remained at Pittman's Ferry to guard the hospital and supplies. Hardee wanted to press his advantage and continue to Ironton but Thompson failed to cooperate. Without assistance the small force was insufficient for the operation at hand. Still, the Federals had encountered unexpected resistance and returned to their base.[21]

Hardee believed that the most effective strategy was cooperation with Pillow in an attempt to destroy the Union garrison at Ironton. Neither man had a large command, but together they would be quite formidable. Hardee could advance from Greenville while Pillow approached from New Madrid. The purpose was not only to hit the town, but also to sever the railroad between Ironton and St. Louis. This would prevent reinforcements from arriving and cut off escape routes as well. Unfortunately, Pillow was still focused on Bird's Point and Cape Girardeau. After initial success Hardee hesitated. He mistakenly believed that he was about to be attacked by Federals

---

[18] US War Department, comp., *The War of the Rebellion: A Compilation of the Official Records of the Union and Confederate Armies*, 128 vols. (Washington, DC: Government Printing Office, 1880–1901) ser. 1, vol. 3, p. 616–18.

[19] OR, ser. 1, vol. 3, p. 618.

[20] OR, ser. 1, vol. 3, p. 629; Irving A. Buck (*Cleburne and His Command* [1908; repr., Wilmington NC: Broadfoot Publishing, 1995] 83) states that there were 1,000 infantry, 250 cavalry, and 1 battalion of artillery in the party.

[21] Buck, *Cleburne and His Command,* 83; John M. Harrell, *Confederate Military History,* 12 vols., ed. Clement A. Evans (Atlanta: Confederate Publishing Company, 1899) 10:57.

on the Mississippi River. Hardee attempted to cut the railroad but his men were unable to complete the assignment. The inability of the Confederates to assist each other prevented the concentration of forces on one specific target and finally brought their operations to a close.

The campaign in eastern Missouri had stalled, but on August 10th Price and McCulloch engaged the Federals at Wilson's Creek. After a bitter contest the Union forces withdrew, but the victory near Springfield yielded William Hardee no significant benefits. During this period he saw little activity and while still at Greenville the men resumed their daily routine of march and drill. Cleburne's attention to detail was unmatched. Basil Duke, who was serving the Confederacy as a scout, recorded his observations in *Reminiscences*:

> I cannot remember that I ever saw an officer who was so industrious and persistent in his efforts properly to drill and instruct the men under his command. He took great interest in everything connected with tactics, and personally taught it all, and was occupied from morning until night superintending squad, company, and battalion drill, guard mounting, inspection, and, indeed, everything mentioned in the books or that he could conceive of. I have seen him during the hottest hours of the hottest days of August instruct squad after squad in the bayonet exercise until I wondered how any human frame could endure the fatigue that his exertions must have induced.[22]

Rumors flourished and in the second week of August it was reported that Federals were advancing from Ironton once again. Cleburne moved forward but after they had reached their position he learned that his only artillery crew had broken into the home of a woman in the vicinity. Making matters even worse, her husband was a member of the Confederate Army. No sooner had Cleburne placed all six men under arrest than a rider galloped into camp with the news that the Yankees were about to attack. The captain asked that his men be temporarily released to meet the threat. He naturally assumed that his request would be granted, but in a bold move Cleburne ordered him to the rear, responding in a loud voice that "*his* men expected to fill honorable graves

---

[22] Duke, *Reminiscences,* 68–69.

and not to rest side by side with thieves."[23] There was no attack, but Cleburne's moral courage made a lasting impression upon his men.

The Federals continued to strengthen the garrison at Ironton and on 26 August Polk ordered Hardee to return through Pittman's Ferry to Point Pleasant. The brigade broke camp on the 28 August and reached the ferry by 2 September. While Hardee had been operating in Missouri, more recruits had come into camp and the Confederates now totaled over 5,000 infantry and 800 cavalry.[24] From his position in Memphis Polk had noticed the Union activity across the Mississippi. He believed the troops were about to invade Kentucky, which until this point had maintained its neutrality. He decided to act first, ordering his forces to move on Columbus. He had hoped to prevent Brigadier General Ulysses S. Grant from taking the town, but Grant simply occupied Paducah instead and the fight for Kentucky began.

On 10 September Albert Sidney Johnston replaced Polk in overall command of the district, while the bishop retained the responsibility for the defense of the Mississippi River.[25] A 300-mile defensive line was created that spanned the entire state. Facing north, it extended from Columbus, on the Mississippi, all the way to the Cumberland Gap. Bowling Green would form the center of the line, held by 4,500 Confederates under Brigadier General Simon B. Buckner.[26] This was a very small force to secure Bowling Green, so Hardee was sent from Pittman's Ferry. It was easier and perhaps quicker for the Rebels to move by steamer up river but Hardee chose the overland route in the belief that it would harden the brigade to long and arduous marches. The Confederates would march over the Chalk Bluffs Plank Road past the north end of Crowley's Ridge in Missouri and across Cache Bottoms to Point Pleasant.

The roads were poor and contained 6 miles of trestle bridges. Hardee was not sure that it was suitable for heavy wagons and artillery so he ordered Cleburne go on ahead "as soon as practicable" in order to put the road in serviceable condition. On 17 September Cleburne moved out, taking with him the 1st Arkansas and one company of cavalry. Though the road was

---

[23] Symonds, *Stonewall of the West*, 56; emphasis original.

[24] OR, ser. 1, vol. 3, p. 690.

[25] William M. Polk, *Leonidas Polk Bishop and General*, 2 vols. (1893; repr., New York: Sprinkle Publications, 2001) appendix, 44–45.

[26] OR, ser. 1, vol. 3, 702–703; OR, ser. 1, vol. 3, p. 707.

barely passable, Cleburne reported that it was "practicable for the march of an army."[27]

Upon their arrival at Point Pleasant, Hardee's men boarded rail cars for the circuitous 175-mile trip to Bowling Green.[28] The troops arrived in mid-October only to find a city filled with Southern soldiers and homeless refugees. Although Bowling Green was the center of the Confederate line, from a military standpoint it was a very poor position. It was connected by rail to both Nashville and Columbus, which formed a salient into central Kentucky. The flanks were badly exposed, as neither city was close enough to offer any support. The right of the line was guarded by a skeleton force in the Appalachian Mountains, and the only protection on the left flank was a pair of river forts: Fort Henry on the Tennessee and Fort Donelson on the Cumberland.

With the addition of Hardee's troops Johnston reorganized the forces at Bowling Green into the Army of Central Kentucky. Generals Hardee and Buckner were the division commanders; Hardee named Cleburne, Hindman, and Shaver to lead his three brigades. Cleburne's new command was comprised of four regiments: his own 1st Arkansas, now under Colonel A. K. Patton; the 5th Arkansas; the 5th Tennessee; and the 6th Mississippi. He also added two men from Helena as aides-de-camp: his former law partner, Leonard Mangum, as well as Judge Hanly's son Sylvanus.

Cleburne led his troops forward to a position 5 miles north of Bowling Green in order to monitor any Federal movements. Although the location was a good one, he had no cavalry to reconnoiter the surrounding area. He attempted to solicit information from local citizens; however, the sympathies of Kentucky were sharply divided and most of the people in this part of the state were Unionists. Nevertheless, General Johnston continued his vigilance. Patrols were constantly on guard and each division was reviewed on a regular basis. Cleburne's brigade would not remain idle for long. In November he got his first chance at independent command.

Reports had arrived to the effect that the Federals had taken a position southeast of Bowling Green. Johnston directed Hardee to send 1,200 infantry and a half-section of artillery "under an intelligent officer" to Jamestown and

---

[27] Hughes, *Old Reliable,* 82 states that Hardee arrived in Columbus on 6 October and after a two-day rest began to move to Bowling Green.

[28] OR, ser. 1, vol. 4, p. 537.

Tompkinsville. They were to be strengthened by a squadron of Texas Rangers. It should be made clear to the officer that:

> ...if the enemy are there, and not in too great force, attack and destroy them.... Inform him in advance that he moves through wooded country.... If possible examine the roads leading to Gallatin, as it is reported that attempts will be made by the enemy to reach and cut the railway in that district. Report from time to time and return to [Bowling Green] as soon as these orders are executed or it is apparent they cannot be. Create the impression in the country that this force is only an advance guard.[29]

Cleburne was chosen to lead the mission and on the 9 November set out across very difficult terrain ideally suited to an ambush. The group reached Scottsville and still there was no enemy in sight. Their sudden appearance was quite a surprise, but the locals seemed receptive and welcomed the soldiers. Thus far the assignment had proceeded on schedule. Only one man was injured, and that occurred in a fall from a wagon. Along with two others who had become ill, Cleburne had to leave the man behind. As the Rebels continued the mood changed to one of hostility. At Jamestown a small party of infantry and cavalry was detected within a mile of Cleburne's camp. He dispatched a force of his own to monitor their movements. Despite repeated attempts to determine the location of the enemy, accurate information became increasingly difficult to obtain. On 11 November he reported back to Hardee and then began his march to Tompkinsville, arriving one day later at 5:00 P.M.

On 13 November Cleburne sent his second dispatch. Most of the men were absent and the women had been told that the Confederates would loot and burn their houses. An advance guard was sent forward to select a campsite, and although the troops put on a great show of strength there were few people left to witness the display. Rumors had circulated to the effect that a Union body in excess of 10,000 men was only a few miles away and that the Federals held the railroad south of Bowling Green. Cleburne was unconcerned, as he had heard false rumors every day and knew that the railroad was in Confederate control. He certainly was not impressed by the

---

[29] OR, ser. 1, vol. 4, p. 531.

actions of the men in Tompkinsville. The women had been abandoned and it appeared as if the men had deserted the town for small monthly wages.

The wooded country made it almost impossible to maintain proper discipline. During the march a few of the teamsters and rear guard had fallen back and stolen some poultry along the road. In this case the officers failed to prevent the crimes and by the time Cleburne learned of the incident it was too late to make restitution. The troops continued, and upon reaching the home of Colonel John Frame they discovered a large quantity of weapons and military supplies. Frame was a known Union sympathizer and the property appeared to have been used as a training ground for new recruits. Frame was also responsible for much of the slander of Confederate forces. Cleburne ordered several sheep confiscated, along with some tallow, turpentine, and sweet oil. He intended to board up the house, but before the work could be completed some of the men broke away on their own and began looting the premises.

Operating under very difficult conditions, Cleburne had not felt safe in sending information back to Hardee until 15 November. He had made his camp 7 miles west of Tompkinsville and expected to be back in Jamestown by nightfall. The past several days were recounted, beginning with the action on the thirteenth.

The Confederates had relied upon experienced guides to provide them with the best roads on their return to Bowling Green. They moved along the Columbia Road, intending to take the Burkeville and Glasgow Road home. Different routes were used in order to present a show of great strength to any of the local citizens. In addition, Cleburne believed that their return on the same path from whence they came might be misconstrued as a retreat. They planned to reach McRea's Crossroads, as they had been told in Tompkinsville that it was only 9 miles away. Just 2 miles out of town the advance guard came upon Union pickets. They quickly turned their horses, with the Texas Rangers in hot pursuit. After a 4-mile chase the Rangers encountered forty United States cavalry. The Southerners fell back and asked for reinforcements. Cleburne sent twenty of his own troopers forward and ordered sixty more to move out in front of the infantry. After the brigade had made 7 miles the light began to fade. Cleburne learned that McRea's was not 9 miles away, but 16. Enemy scouts had been seen on his flanks, so he took a strong defensive position on Skagg's Creek.

Cleburne was unable to determine the strength of the Federals in the area and had received no word from Bowling Green. He was very concerned that he might be surrounded, so he kept his trains loaded for an immediate movement. False campfires were lighted and a wide line of pickets covered the surrounding area. The Confederate cavalry had pressed the Federals so closely that they got lost in the woods near the crossroads. After a short skirmish the Yankees broke and ran. There were no reported casualties among Cleburne's troops, while two Union horsemen were killed.

The cavalry action yielded great benefits, as they had managed to capture horses, muskets, pistols, and sabres. According to Cleburne, they had dispersed the Federals so thoroughly that they had been scattered in all directions. However, the Confederates were also in disarray and it was time to consolidate their forces. Lieutenant John Cage was dispatched to instruct the Texans to fall back on the main body. Cage got lost around midnight and almost wandered into the Union lines. During his return he was mistaken for a Federal soldier and was fired upon by his own men. He was hit in the leg, his horse was shot twice, and one of the Texas Rangers suffered severe wounds to the leg and arm.

By 14 November the road to the crossroads was clear, but it seemed unwise to advance without better information. As a precaution the Confederates returned to their base outside of Tompkinsville. Along the way Cleburne tried to persuade the locals that they were in no danger, but his attempts were in vain. Still, he did what little he could. In response to any complaints that his men had taken personal property, Cleburne paid for the loss out of his own pocket; any abandoned articles were returned to the nearest house with the following note attached: "returned by southern soldiers."[30] In general, he was very sympathetic to the demands of local citizens. He accepted their word regarding the value of any items that may have been taken, but he refused to be convinced by one woman who claimed that men in his brigade had stolen her bible.[31] By this time it was apparent that the enemy was not present in any strength, so the brigade returned to Bowling Green.

The Confederates had not brought on a major engagement, but William T. Sherman overreacted to the movements and the Yankees fell back to protect Louisville and Cincinnati.[32] Pitched battle in the winter was rare during the

---

[30] Benham, "Major Gen. P. R. Cleburne," 2.

[31] *Chicago Times,* 22 October 1861, 2.

[32] Lew Wallace, "The Capture of Fort Donelson," in Robert Underwood Johnston and Clarence Clough Buel, eds., *Battles and Leaders of the Civil War,* 4 vols. (1884–1887;

Civil War and there was little activity in this particular area of Kentucky, but elsewhere the Confederate line of defense was in serious trouble. On 19 January 1862 they were defeated at the battle of Mill Springs. George Crittenden suffered 533 total casualties and the loss in supplies was staggering. He had abandoned all of his artillery, tents, blankets, and mules as well as a large portion of food.[33] The entire right flank of Johnston's command had disintegrated, leaving Cumberland Gap unprotected. Southern prestige in this area of Kentucky had suffered a terrible blow.

Johnston wanted to know exactly what had happened, but timely information was not forthcoming. Since several officers had delayed in writing their battle reports, Johnston did not have an accurate picture of the results. On 1 February Crittenden wrote a letter to headquarters requesting reinforcements. He suggested Chestnut Mound as a supply base, as it had both easy river transportation and a rail link to Nashville.[34] Johnston responded, and Cleburne was dispatched to evaluate the state of the Confederate forces and determine what provisions Crittenden might need.

The government in Richmond recognized that additional help was needed in the west. On 2 February the most popular general in the Confederacy left Virginia on his way to Bowling Green, arriving on 4 February. Pierre Gustave Toutant Beauregard was the hero of Fort Sumter and had received much of the credit for the decisive victory at the first battle of Manassas. Despite suffering from an acute bronchial infection, he received authority over the forces in the District of Columbus. His presence was not enough and the situation continued to deteriorate. On 6 February Fort Henry was taken with little opposition; ten days later Fort Donelson capitulated.

On 7 February Johnston and Beauregard decided to evacuate Bowling Green and Columbus. With the fall of Fort Henry, Grant now controlled the Tennessee River. On 11 February the troops began to fall back and Hardee designated Cleburne's brigade to protect the withdrawal. This would not be the last time they would ensure the safety of Hardee's command. In addition, he had to destroy any supplies which could not be salvaged. Soldiers too seriously wounded to walk were taken to southbound railroad cars to prevent

---

repr., Secaucus NJ: Castle Books, n.d.) 1:392; William P. Johnston, *The Life of Gen. Albert Sidney Johnston* (New York: Appleton and Company, 1879) 404.

[33] OR, ser. 1, vol. 7, p. 855.

[34] Larry J. Daniel, *Shiloh* (New York: Simon & Schuster, 1997) 40–41.

Federal capture. Three days later the brigade marched out of Bowling Green under a bombardment of enemy shells and on 16 February began to enter Nashville.

From a logistical sense, Nashville was a good choice. The T. M. Brennan cannon foundry, a percussion-cap factory, and numerous shops engaged in the manufacture of military equipment were located in or around the city. Five railroads offered transportation, the Sycamore Stamping Mill had provided 100,000 pounds of powder, and by February 1862 the Wilson and Armstrong meatpacking plant had slaughtered 30,000 hogs.[35]The city lay on the south bank of the Cumberland River and the approaches from the North were broken by a series of steep hills and ridges. Below it Nashville was protected by another range of hills, all of which created a sound defensive position. However, no sooner had the soldiers arrived than they received the news of the fall of Fort Donelson. Instead of much-needed rest, Cleburne's men boarded trains headed for Murfreesboro, 30 miles to the southeast.

Before the Confederates entered the city the war had seemed a distant event. Reports arrived from Virginia or Missouri, and even the battles in Kentucky gave little cause for concern. Whether from pride, arrogance, or simple indifference, no preparations had been made for a sudden evacuation. After the fall of Fort Donelson wild rumors began to surface. The entire garrison had been lost. Union gunboats had been sighted just above Clarksville, a railroad depot on the Memphis and Clarksville line located on the north bank of the Cumberland. Less than 30 miles away, Don Carlos Buell commanded 35,000 Yankees at Springfield. The two forces were about to unite and the city would be bombarded no later than that very afternoon. And so on. By mid-morning on 16 February, nervous agitation had turned to fear. Despite a driving rain the train stations were quickly jammed, and fine clothes turned to tattered rags.[36]

The situation was very serious, but tension was heightened by the belief that Governor Isham Harris had urged the civilians to leave Nashville with all possible speed. He was supposed to have said that "the women and children must be removed from the city within three hours, as at the expiration of that

---

[35] Robert Selph Henry, *Forrest: First with the Most* (1944; repr., Wilmington NC: Broadfoot Publishing, 1991) 63–64.

[36] John Miller McKee, "The Great Panic: Being Incidents Connected with Two Weeks of the War in Tennessee," *Annals of Tennessee* (Nashville: A. D. Haynes, 1862) 9.

time the enemy would shell the place and destroy it." He had never uttered the words, but the story was given immediate credibility.[37]

In an attempt to calm the crowd, Mayor R. B. Cheatham went across the river to Johnston's headquarters at Edgefield. He was told that there was no intention of defending Nashville but that supplies would be distributed as soon as possible. This would have been welcome news, but the presses had ceased publication and great uncertainty consumed the city. Officials from the commissary and quartermaster departments had already left, leaving the depots completely unguarded.[38]

There was a sense of betrayal and panic broke out. The troopers worked tirelessly to save the supplies and no greater effort could have been made. They took 250,000 pounds of bacon, 600 boxes of clothing, and thousands of pounds of flour to the railroad depot. Rifling machinery was dismantled and sent to Atlanta. Four hundred wagons loaded with ammunition were sent south to safety. Some 1,200 sick soldiers were taken back to Chattanooga. Unfortunately, the quantity of materiel destroyed was enormous. Over 70,000[39] pounds of pork remained at the Cumberland River wharf and 400,000 more were reportedly still at the insane asylum. Large quantities of quartermaster stores, 10,000 pairs of shoes, and 500 new tents were lost. More than 50 cannon were spiked or left behind.[40] Johnston's aide, Colonel St. John Liddell, estimated that due to negligence, poor transportation, weather, and fright half of the supplies of the Army of Tennessee were lost when Nashville was evacuated. With this retreat Johnston's logistical base no longer existed.[41] The efforts were halted on 22 February when heavy rains washed away two small bridges of the Nashville and Chattanooga Railroad. The only rail option left was to Decatur, Alabama, via the Nashville and Decatur line.

---

[37] Eric W. Sheppard, *Bedford Forrest: The Confederacy's Greatest Cavalryman* (London: n.p., 1930) 55–56.

[38] Brian Steel Wills, *A Battle from the Start: The Life of Nathan Bedford Forrest* (New York: HarperCollins, 1992) 66; Thomas L.Connelly, *Army of the Heartland: The Army of Tennessee 1861–1862* (Baton Rouge: Louisiana State University Press, 1967) 136–38; Henry, *First with the Most,* 63–64.

[39] Connelly (*Army of the Heartland,* 136) writes that there were 70,000 pounds of bacon; Daniel (*Shiloh,* 42–43) gives a number slightly higher at "some 75,000."

[40] Daniel, *Shiloh,* 42–43.

[41] Bruce Catton, *Terrible Swift Sword* (New York: Doubleday, 1963) 161.

On the surface it would seem impossible to have removed so much in so little time. Actually, the loss of these supplies was inexcusable. Johnston had been observing Union activity in the area since October. He expected Buell to move south from one of two bases: from their main base in the Nolin-Munfordville region, or from South Carrollton on the Green River. The Nolin force would approach on the Louisville-Bowling Green Pike. At the same time, Buell's other command could move on the road leading south from Greenville and Hopkinsville to the north bank of the Cumberland River opposite Fort Donelson. In January Johnston considered the Carrollton troops to be a great threat to the weak Confederate flank west of Bowling Green, but he was still unsure of the Federal plans.[42]

Despite this knowledge, supplies and equipment were left throughout Kentucky and Tennessee. At Clarksville a commandant left his post, stranding seventy-five wagons. No boats or railroad cars had been made available. Eight days of provisions were left at Bowling Green. Ten thousand bushels of wheat were still at Franklin. Twenty carloads of government stores remained at Columbia while additional supplies were left at Bell's Station, Kentucky, and Mitchellville, Tennessee.[43]

Bad weather, geography, and Union sentiment all contributed to Johnston's uncertainty, but the biggest problem was his reconnaissance. It had been poor since November, and in early February Buell disappeared again. On 8 February Governor Harris had suggested that the meat stores be moved further south, while two days later Captain Moses Wright of the state ordnance department offered similar advice for munitions. Clearly there had been ample time to prepare for an evacuation. Johnston made no such plans was a scathing indictment of his logistical ability.[44] The first state capital to fall had been surrendered without a fight.

The retreat continued to Murfreesboro. At this point Braxton Bragg decided to send an aide to evaluate matters in Tennessee. On 27 February Bragg wrote a letter to Secretary of State Judah Benjamin, noting that "confidence is lost on all hands."[45] One day later Johnston's Rebels moved south once again, this time on foot through pounding rain mixed with snow. High winds

---

[42] Connelly, *Army of the Heartland,* 109–10.

[43] Connelly, *Army of the Heartland,* 135–39.

[44] Daniel, *Shiloh,* 43.

[45] OR, ser. 1, vol. 6, p. 834–35.

prevented fires and made it very difficult to pitch tents. Johnston painted an entirely different picture when he claimed that the army was in "good spirits."

It was widely assumed that Johnston would put up a defense at Murfreesboro, but in reality he had no intention of halting the army. On 7 February, while still in Bowling Green, he had decided that if Nashville fell the Confederates would fall back to Stevenson, Alabama, in order to protect Chattanooga. However, once he reached Murfreesboro he began to consider other options. Decatur lay midway between Chattanooga and Corinth, where there was already a large Confederate force. A retreat in the direction of Stevenson would draw the column farther and farther away from Corinth. There is some evidence that later in the month Beauregard may have suggested the shift to Decatur as a base of operations. On 22 February, Colonel Jeremy Gilmer wrote his wife: "We expect to leave here [Murfreesboro] in a few days to some point south of this—maybe Decatur—maybe Chattanooga—maybe some other point."[46]

On 28 February, Johnston's army began the march to Decatur, but Cleburne and most of his brigade remained in Shelbyville with Hardee arranging the shipment of pork destined for Grenada, Mississippi.[47] The next month began with some welcome news. Cleburne was promoted to brigadier general, to date from 4 March. Once again, Hardee called on him to form the rear guard of the army. The two generals continued south, this time headed for Huntsville while the rank and file marched on to Fayetteville and Decatur in order to join the main body of Johnston's command. Huntsville was an important stop on the Memphis and Charleston Railroad; several days were spent forwarding commissary supplies as well as making arrangements for transportation of the men. Cleburne left the town on 18 March, arriving in Corinth nine days later.[48]

Thus far, simple assignments had been handled with diligence and skill. Cleburne had not yet been exposed to a major engagement. This was about to change. The Confederates were preparing to meet Ulysses S. Grant in western Tennessee, where the armies would converge around a little church called Shiloh.

---

[46] Jeremy Gilmer to wife, 22 February 1862, Jeremy F. Gilmer Letters, University of North Carolina, Southern Historical Collection, Chapel Hill NC.

[47] OR, ser. 1, vol. 10, pt. 2, p. 297.

[48] Hughes, *Old Reliable,* 96.

3

SHILOH

When Forts Henry and Donelson were originally constructed they were viewed as impregnable barriers to the state of Tennessee. Geographically, they were only 12 miles apart and very close to the Kentucky border. Together they would command the Tennessee and Cumberland Rivers, which would prevent an invasion from the north. In reality, their location had the opposite effect. Henry was subject to flooding and high ground outside the enclosure offered an ideal position for enemy artillery. Donelson was poorly supplied in both men and equipment.[1] Authorities in Richmond placed a high value on their strategic importance, yet the forts remained isolated. Aside from each other they had little support. If they fell the state would be open all the way to Nashville, and Ulysses S. Grant soon proved that their capture presented little difficulty. Without any opposition the Federals could move south at will, as the rivers provided easy transportation for troops and provisions. The Yankees took control of West Tennessee and were never driven from the state again.

Johnston continued to head south. He knew he was outnumbered and tried to create a diversion by sending 2,500 men[2] to Chattanooga under the leadership of John B. Floyd. Hopefully it would appear that he was retreating in that direction. After the transfer a few remnants from Henry and Donelson arrived and Johnston was able to leave Murfreesboro 17,000 strong. An additional 2,000 men from Braxton Bragg gave him renewed confidence.[3] The Confederates departed on 28 February and reached Decatur on 10 March.

The situation had improved, but only four days later Beauregard sent a wire to Johnston requesting that more troops be sent to Iuka to prevent a

---

[1] Robert Selph Henry, *Forrest: First with the Most* (1944; repr., Wilmington NC: Broadfoot Publishing, 1991) 40; Wiley Sword, *Shiloh: Bloody April* (New York: William Morrow & Co., 1974) 52; Thomas L. Connelly, *Army of the Heartland: The Army of Tennessee 1861–1862* (Baton Rouge: Louisiana State University Press, 1967) 78–79.

[2] Sword, *Bloody April,* 68–69.

[3] Nathaniel C. Hughes, *General William J. Hardee: Old Reliable* (Baton Rouge: Louisiana State University Press, 1965) 93.

Union attack. The Creole had acted in haste, but Johnston tried to respond. Thomas Hindman and Sterling A. M. Wood commanded Johnston's two lead brigades; unfortunately they were 52 miles away in Courtland, Alabama. Thirty-six hours elapsed before enough railroad cars could be assembled, and by the time Hindman and Wood arrived the danger had passed.[4]

Johnston's troops were gradually moving closer to other Confederates, the largest group being Bragg's 13,589 men,[5] who were already in Corinth. Though a small town of only 1,200, Corinth was a very important railroad junction. The Memphis and Charleston Railroad ran east and west and crossed the Mobile and Ohio in Corinth. On 16 March Brigadier General Daniel Ruggles reported that 30,000 Federals[6] were forming near the west bank of the Tennessee River at Pittsburg Landing. The target of the Federal movements was not the Confederate Army but the Memphis and Charleston Railroad.[7] Camped just across the state line, the Bluecoats were only 23 miles away.

Beauregard envisioned a juncture with Bragg in order to mount an invasion back into Tennessee. Their combination would turn the retreat into an offensive, raise morale, and win a stunning victory for the South. It would also leave Chattanooga open to attack, but in his opinion it was a gamble the Confederates had to take. His enthusiasm convinced Sidney Johnston, though Johnston was not without reservations. Columns would be strung out for 93 miles while both Grant and Buell were within easy striking distance. In addition, progress would be slow, as heavy rains had soaked the roads.

Food was limited, but there were still over 30,000 pounds of pork at Shelbyville. Cleburne had been sent to bring it out. In addition to his own brigade, he took two regiments of cavalry and one battalion of artillery. By 20 March the Confederate lines extended from Wood's and Hindman's brigades in Corinth to Breckinridge's men in Decatur, all the way back to Cleburne.

---

[4] Larry J. Daniel, *Shiloh* (New York: Simon & Schuster, 1997) 89.

[5] US War Department, comp., *The War of the Rebellion: A Compilation of the Official Records of the Union and Confederate Armies*, 128 vols. (Washington, DC: Government Printing Office, 1880–1901) ser. 1 vol. 10, pt. 1, p. 396.

[6] OR, ser. 1, vol. 10, pt. 1, p. 29.

[7] Daniel, *Shiloh*, 105; Sword, *Bloody April*, 15.

On 22 March Johnston arrived in Corinth, but the last of Hardee's 13,000 men did not reach the town until five days later.[8]

On 23 March Johnston held a conference with Beauregard, Polk, and Hardee. Ruefully he admitted that he no longer had the confidence of the army. The series of defeats in Tennessee had tarnished his reputation. Command was offered to Beauregard but the latter demurred, explaining that he had come west to assist Johnston, not to replace him.[9] Nevertheless, Beauregard's influence began to rise and he directed most of the future operations.

The Confederates assembled around Corinth and by the end of March numbered some 40,000 men. In orders issued on 29 March, Johnston consolidated the Confederate forces and brought different armies together under one central command. Leonidas Polk brought 9,136 troops from Columbus who became known as the First Corps. His two divisions were led by Charles Clark and Benjamin Franklin Cheatham. Braxton Bragg's Second Corps was the largest, with 13,589 men in two divisions under Jones Withers and Daniel Ruggles. William Hardee had started with over 13,000 soldiers, but shortly thereafter his Army of Central Kentucky was divided. Pat Cleburne commanded one brigade, while Thomas Hindman directed two others: his own, under the direction of R. G. Shaver, as well as that of S. A. M. Wood, comprising a total of 6,789. Hardee also sent three brigades to Burnsville, Mississippi, as a Reserve Corps under George B. Crittenden. On 31 March Crittenden was found drunk and promptly removed from command. He was replaced by the former vice-president of the United States, John C. Breckinridge of Kentucky. In addition to infantry, each division was to receive one regiment of cavalry and one six-gun battery was assigned to each brigade. Johnston stipulated that infantry brigades should total about 2,500 men and each division should have at least two brigades.[10]

---

[8] Joseph Parks, *General Leonidas Polk, C.S.A.: The Fighting Bishop* (Baton Rouge: Louisana State University Press, 1962) 218–19; Daniel, *Shiloh*, 90–91.

[9] David Urquhart to Thomas Jordan, 25 August 1880, in Alfred Roman, *Military Operations of General Beauregard*, 2 vols. (New York: Harper & Brothers, 1884) 1:274–75; James Lee McDonough, *SHILOH—In Hell Before Night* (Knoxville: University of Tennessee Press, 1977) 30; Francis A. Shoup, "How We Went to Shiloh" *Confederate Veteran* 2/5 (May1894): 137–40.

[10] OR, ser. 1, vol. 10, pt. 1, p. 396, gives a report submitted by Thomas Jordan, listing the total effective Confederate forces before the battle of Shiloh as follows: Polk: 9,136 men, Bragg 13,589, Hardee 6,789 and Breckinridge 6,439 for a total of 35,953 infantry

Cleburne retained his old regiment, the 1st Arkansas, though it was now classified as the 15th Arkansas due to a dispute with another unit. He also kept the 6th Mississippi. The remainder of his command consisted of four regiments from Tennessee: the 2nd, the 23rd, the 24th, and the 5th, which like Cleburne's 1st Arkansas received a new designation later in the war, becoming the 35th Tennessee.[11] The reorganization appeared seamless on paper, but it was not easy to implement. Many officers were unfamiliar with each other and discipline was difficult to maintain. In addition to the allocation of troops, the position of chief of staff was created and given to Braxton Bragg. This was an established position in Europe, but it was not yet authorized by the Confederate Congress and the duties were not well understood in the United States. Bragg was an able organizer and a strict disciplinarian, but given his acerbic personality this was a somewhat curious choice. The North Carolinian accepted his new assignment, but only on the condition that he would remain in charge of the Second Corps.[12]

There was some logic in the division of the army into four corps, though each was much smaller than the standard size. The normal strength of a corps was approximately 20,000 strong. Four corps would appear to give the Confederates 80,000 soldiers, roughly double their actual number. With Buell's 25,000[13] still en route from Nashville, Grant might think twice about any offensive operations. The downside to this was that a third of the entire

---

and artillery. He adds 4,382 cavalry under B.F. Gardner, for a combined total of 40,335. A second return, OR, ser. 1, vol. 10, pt. 1, p. 398, gives a report submitted by Braxton Bragg, which differs from Jordan's account. Bragg gives Polk 9,024 men, Bragg 14,868, Hardee 4,545 and Breckinridge 6,290 for a total of 34,727 infantry. Bragg gives a separate total for artillery, at 1,973 and cavalry of 2,073, for a combined total of 38,773 men.

[11] Originally there were two regiments referred to as the 5th Tennessee, one commanded by William E. Travis, the other under Cleburne, led by Benjamin J. Hill. Against the regulations of the War Department, Cleburne continued to use this numerical designation for his own regiment through the battle of Chickamauga, whereupon it came to be known as the 35th Tennessee.

[12] Shoup, "How We Went to Shiloh," 137.

[13] Don Carlos Buell, "Shiloh Reviewed," in Robert Underwood Johnston and Clarence Clough Buel, eds., *Battles and Leaders of the Civil War*, 4 vols. (1884–1887; repr., Secaucus NJ: Castle Books, n.d.) 1:538–39. Corroborating statements of troop totals are also given in OR, ser. 1, vol. 10, pt. 1, p. 112, as well as statements by Ulysses S. Grant and Lew Wallace. It should be noted that not all of Buell's troops reached the field in time to be of service.

army was with Bragg. The better plan would have been to assign five brigades to Bragg instead of six. Two of these would have gone to Ruggles, as they were his own he had brought from New Orleans. The other three brigades were from the Gulf Coast and would have been led by Withers. The remaining brigade assigned to Bragg should logically have gone to Polk. For his part, Hardee deserved two divisions of three brigades each, presumably commanded by Cleburne and Hindman. This configuration would have eliminated the Reserve Corps entirely, providing two distinct advantages. First and foremost, it would have simplified matters considerably, and second, Crittenden's ability was marginal at best. His subsequent removal for drunkenness only strengthens this argument.[14] At any rate, the army moved forward with four corps, determined to force a battle before Grant could be reinforced.

The Confederates' path to Pittsburg Landing was limited. There were only two main roads leading from Corinth into Tennessee. The Ridge Road ran north for 4 miles and then veered northeast for 10 miles to James Michie's[15] farmhouse. The Monterey Road went east from Corinth, then quickly turned north for 10 miles before reaching Monterey only 3 miles south of the farmhouse. Once the troops arrived at that point, they could take the Savannah Road due north and meet the Ridge Road at Michie's or the Purdy Road northwest from Monterey and intersect the Ridge Road 3 miles southwest of it. From Michie's the Bark Road ran due east for 3 miles where it ran into the Corinth and Pittsburg Road, often referred to simply as the Corinth Road. This went northeastward for 2 1/2 miles to Shiloh Church and then abruptly turned east to the landing.

In order to reach Grant's army the Confederates would have to negotiate very difficult terrain. Pittsburg Landing was located on the west bank of the Tennessee River, 80 feet above the water. The line of approach was cut with ravines, heavy underbrush, and dense forests. Rolling hills hampered movement, and though partially cultivated farms dotted the countryside, coordination would be difficult.[16]

---

[14] Daniel, *Shiloh*, 96–97.

[15] The house is often spelled "Mickey's," as it is pronounced that way.

[16] OR, ser. 1, vol. 10, pt. 1, p. 567; D. W. Reed, *The Battle of Shiloh and the Organizations Engaged* (Washington, DC: Government Printing Office, 1913) 8–9.

The Confederate battle plan and subsequent actions at Shiloh have become one of the most controversial topics of the entire Civil War. Johnston and Beauregard both wanted to attack the Federal left flank and both realized that they had to strike before Buell could reach Grant. Under Beauregard's plan the Southerners would quickly remove any remaining supplies from the landing, then retreat to Corinth. In his battle report dated 11 April 1862, he wrote:

> By a rapid and vigorous attack on General Grant it was expected he would be beaten back into his transports and the river, or captured, in time to enable us to profit by the victory, and remove to the rear all the stores and munitions that would fall into our hands in such an event before the arrival of General Buell's army on the scene. It was never contemplated, however, to retain the position thus gained and abandon Corinth, the strategic point of the campaign.[17]

Conceptually, Johnston had a different view. On 3 April he issued the following memorandum to all three corps commanders as well as Breckinridge:

> 1. As soon as the reserve shall have taken a position at Monterey a strong working party will be sent to repair the bridges, causeway, and road across Lick Creek, on the direct road from Monterey to Pittsburg, so that it may be used in any forward movement of the reserve.
> 2. In the approaching battle every effort should be made to turn the left flank of the enemy so as to cut off his line of retreat to the Tennessee River and throw him back on Owl Creek, where he will be forced to surrender. Every precaution must be taken to prevent unnecessary exposure of our men to the enemy's gunboats.[18]

In this scenario, the upcoming action would be more aggressive. Johnston intended to fold the Union Army back onto itself and push Grant away from the river. His ultimate goal was a battle; Beauregard thought in terms of a large raid.

---

[17] OR, ser. 1, vol. 10, pt. 1, p. 385.
[18] OR, ser. 1, vol. 10, pt. 1, p. 397.

The alignment of the Confederate troops turned out to be very significant in the final outcome. In a telegram to Jefferson Davis dated 3 April, Johnston described his intentions:

> General Buell is in motion, 30,000 strong, rapidly from Columbia by Clifton to Savannah; Mitchel behind him with 10,000. Confederate forces, 40,000, ordered forward to offer battle near Pittsburg. Division from Bethel, main body from Corinth, reserve from Burnsville converge to-morrow near Monterey. On Pittsburg, Beauregard second in command; Polk, left; Hardee, center; Bragg, right wing; Breckinridge in reserve. Hope engagement before Buell can form junction.[19]

Johnston may indeed have had this vision of the conduct of the upcoming action. However, he was easily persuaded to accept Beauregard's ideas, and given the remarkable difference between this proposal and the final formation of the army on 6 April, his convictions must have been weak. His apparent acquiescence provides a clear illustration of his willingness to relinquish command.

By this time operational decisions were left to Beauregard and the orders over the next several days reveal the degree of control he had assumed. The attack was governed by Special Orders No. 8, drafted by Beauregard and approved without alteration by Johnston.[20] It read as follows:

> I. In the impending movement the corps of this army will march, assemble, and take order of battle in the following manner, it being assumed that the enemy is in position about a mile in advance of Shiloh Church, with the right resting on Owl Creek and his left on Lick Creek.
>
> 1st. The Third Corps, under Major-General Hardee, will advance as soon as practicable on the Ridge road from Corinth to what is known as the Bark road, passing about half a mile northward of the workhouse. The head of this column will bivouac, if possible, tonight at Mickey's house, at the intersection of the road from Monterey to

---

[19] OR, ser. 1, vol. 10, pt. 2, p. 387.
[20] Roman, *Beauregard,* 1:269, 274–75.

Savannah. The cavalry, thrown well forward during the march, to reconnoiter and prevent surprise, will halt in front of the Mickey house, on the Bark road.

2nd. Major Waddell, aide-de-camp to General Beauregard, with two good guides, will report for service to Major-General Hardee.

3rd. At 3 o'clock a.m. tomorrow the Third Corps, with the left in front, will continue to advance by the Bark road until within sight of the enemy's outposts or advanced positions, when it will be deployed in line of battle, according to the nature of the ground, its left resting on Owl Creek, its right toward Lick Creek, supported on that flank by one-half of its cavalry, the left flank being supported by the other half. The interval between the extreme right of this corps and Lick Creek will be filled by a brigade or division, according to the extent of the ground, from the Second Corps.

These troops during the battle will also be under the command of Major-General Hardee. He will make the proper disposition of the artillery along the line of battle, remembering that the rifled guns are of long ranges and should be placed on any commanding position in rear of the infantry to fire mainly on the reserves and second line of the enemy, but will occasionally be directed on his batteries and heads of columns.

II. The Second Corps, under Maj. Gen. Braxton Bragg, will assemble on Monterey, and move thence as early as practicable, the right wing, with left in front, by the road from Monterey to Savannah, the head of column to reach Mickey's house, at the intersection of the Bark road, before sunset. The cavalry with this wing will take position on the road to Savannah, beyond Mickey's as far as Owl Creek, having advanced guards and pickets well to the front.

The left wing of this corps will advance at the same time, also left in front, by the road from Monterey to Purdy, the head of the column to reach by night the intersection of that road with the Bark road. This wing will continue the movement in the morning as soon as the rear of the Third Corps shall have passed the Purdy road, which it will then follow.

The Second Corps will then form the second line of battle about 1,000 yards in the rear of the first line. It will be formed, if practicable, with regiments in double columns at half distance, disposed as advantageously as the nature of the ground will admit and with a view to facility of deployment, the artillery placed as may seem best to Major-General Bragg.

III. The First Corps, under Major-General Polk, with the exception of the detached division at Bethel, will take up its line of march by the Ridge Road, hence to Pittsburg, half an hour after the rear of the Third Corps shall have passed Corinth, and will bivouac tonight in rear of that corps, and on tomorrow will follow the movements of said corps with the same interval of time as today. When its head of column shall reach the vicinity of the Mickey house it will be halted in column or massed on the line of the Bark road, according to the nature of the ground, as a reserve.

Meantime one regiment of its cavalry will be placed in observation on the road from Johnston's house to Stantonville, with advance guards and pickets thrown out well in advance toward Stantonville. Another regiment or battalion of cavalry will be posted in the same manner in the road from Monterey to Purdy, with its rear resting on or about the intersection of that road with the Bark road, having advanced guards and pickets in the direction of Purdy.

The forces at Bethel and Purdy will defend their positions, as already instructed, if attacked; otherwise they will assemble on Purdy, and thence advance with advanced guards, flankers, and all other prescribed military precautions, by the road thence to Monterey, forming a junction with the next of the First Corps at the intersection of that road and the Bark road leading from Corinth.

IV. The reserve of the forces will be concentrated by the shortest and best routes at Monterey as soon as the rear of the Second Corps shall have moved out of that place. Its commander will take up the best position whence to advance as required, either in the direction of Mickey's or of Pratt's house, on the direct road to Pittsburg, if that road is found practicable, or in the direction of the Ridge road to Hamburg, throwing all its cavalry on the latter road as far as its intersection with the one to Pittsburg, passing through Guersford, on Lick Creek. This cavalry will throw well forward advanced guards and vedettes toward Guersford and in the direction of Hamburg, and during the impending battle, when called to the field of combat, will move by the Guersford road. A regiment of the infantry reserve will be thrown forward to the intersection of the Gravel Hill road with the Ridge road to Hamburg, as a support to the cavalry. The reserve will be formed of Breckinridge's, Bowen's and Statham's brigades as now organized, the whole under command of Brigadier-General Breckinridge.

V. General Bragg will detach the Fifty-first and Fifty-second Regiments Tennessee Volunteers, Blount's Alabama, and Descha's Arkansas battalion, and Bains' battery from his corps, which, with two of Carroll's regiments now *en route* for these headquarters, will form a garrison for the post and depot of Corinth.

VI. Strong guards will be left at the railroad bridges between Iuka and Corinth, to be furnished in due proportion from the commands at Iuka, Burnsville and Corinth.

VII. Proper guards will be left at the camps of the several regiments of the forces in the field. Corps commanders will determine the strength of these guards.

VIII. Wharton's regiment of Texas cavalry will be ordered forward at once to scout on the road from Monterey to Savannah between Mickey's and its intersection with the Pittsburg-Purdy road. It will annoy and harass any force of the enemy moving by the latter way to assail Cheatham's division at Purdy.

IX. The chief engineer of the forces will take all due measures and precautions and give all requisite orders for repair of the bridges, causeways, and roads on which our troops may move in the execution of these orders.

X. The troops, individually so intelligent, and with so great interests involved in the issue, are urgently enjoined to be observant of the orders of their superiors in the hour of battle. Their officers must constantly endeavor to hold them in hand and prevent the waste of ammunition by heedless aimless firing. The fire should be slow, always at a distinct mark. It is expected that much and effective work will be done with the bayonet.

Therein lay the orders for one of the most important battles of the war. There were several flaws in the designs of both Beauregard and Johnston. Clearly the idea was to turn Grant's left, yet neither one had enough thrust on the Confederate right. When the battle opened Johnston had only four brigades on his right, with fourteen on hand.[21] With different commands lined up behind one another it was almost certain that several units would become entangled. All cohesion would be lost and the power of the assault would quickly dissipate. It required good roads in order to move inexperienced troops, but the weather had been very wet for several days. Yet perhaps a more fundamental error on Johnston's part was that he let a subordinate dictate strategy. After the bitter defeat his son, along with Bragg and Davis, claimed that Beauregard had deliberately changed the original plan, which lost the battle for the South. What their comments would have been had the Confederates won only raises more speculation. The untimely death of Johnston on 6 April forever clouds the issue.

While the Confederates were stumbling over themselves in their attempt to reach Pittsburg Landing, a telegram from Cheatham caused a great deal of excitement at headquarters. Cheatham was stationed northwest of Johnston's army near Bethel Station. Scouts reported that Grant had sent Lew Wallace's division down the Purdy Road, apparently intending to hit the Mobile and Ohio Railroad. Fearing that Don Carlos Buell was on the way, Cheatham telegraphed Polk to alert his corps commander. Polk received the message at 10:00 P.M. on 2 April, whereupon he notified Beauregard. The Creole presumed that Grant had divided his forces but also felt that this movement signaled the arrival of Buell. Sensing an opportunity, Beauregard felt it was imperative to launch an attack while the Confederates still held the advantage. He endorsed the telegram, adding "now is the time to advance upon Pittsburg Landing," and gave it to his aide, Thomas Jordan.[22] Jordan went to Johnston's headquarters at the Rose cottage. Johnston read the message and agreed in principle but wanted to confer with Bragg before reaching a decision. Jordan and Johnston crossed the street to the Curlee house where they roused Bragg from his bed. Johnston pointed out that the troops were not yet ready but withdrew his objections when Bragg sided with Beauregard.[23]

[21] McDonough, *In Hell before Night,* 106; Connelly, *Army of the Heartland,* 161.

[22] Thomas Jordan, "Notes of a Confederate Staff-Officer at Shiloh," in Robert Underwood Johnston and Clarence Clough Buel, eds., *Battles and Leaders of the Civil War,* 4 vols. (1884–1887; repr., Secaucus NJ: Castle Books, n.d.) 1:594; H. M. Dillard, "Beauregard-Johnston-Shiloh," *Confederate Veteran* 5/3 (March 1894): 99–100, Otto Eisenschiml, *The Story of Shiloh* (Chicago: Civil War Round Table, 1946) 25.

[23] Hughes, *Old Reliable,* 100; Connelly, *Army of the Heartland,* 152; Daniel, *Shiloh,* 118.

In command of Polk's Second Division, Cheatham had received orders so vague that they almost kept him out of the battle altogether. His instructions were to take a position in the area in order to defend the road from Savannah to Bolivar. In addition, two railroads must be protected: the Mobile and Ohio as well as the Mississippi Central. At least two regiments of infantry plus an artillery force of two to four guns must be stationed at Purdy. Cavalry would be divided between both towns. If he were about to be overpowered he should fall back slowly to Bethel. If he were attacked again he should fall back to Bolivar. This final movement would allow the remainder of Johnston's force to strike the enemy in the flank and rear. The route from Cheatham's position to Johnston's army was to remain clear as Cheatham "may be called upon to travel on it," but if he were not engaged he was to rejoin Polk's corps.[24] He was not told how long he should remain in that position, or what road he should take. Beauregard had wanted him back with Polk on 4 April, but he did not leave Bethel Station until the next morning.[25]

Following the conference orders were issued to be ready to move by 6:00 A.M. on 3 April. Each man would have five days rations—three in his haversack and two in the wagons, along with 100 rounds of ammunition. Their destination on the first day was Michie's, about halfway to Pittsburg Landing. They would then take a position near the Federal camp in preparation for a surprise attack on the morning of 5 April. Hardee's corps would lead the march and Cleburne would lead Hardee's corps. They were directed to move north along the Ridge Road. To the east, Bragg would lead his Second Corps to Monterey, about 11 miles from Corinth. At that point Withers' division would continue north and Ruggles would turn northwest. Polk's First Corps was to follow Hardee on the Ridge Road. He was to wait until Ruggles arrived and then allow him to pass. Breckinridge would march to Monterey behind Bragg, traveling "by the shortest and best routes."[26]

3 April. III Corps. The plans quickly began to fall apart. Cleburne ordered reveille for 6:00 A.M., but at 8:00 A.M. the men were still cooking rations. Beauregard had given Hardee verbal orders to be ready to move by noon but Bragg, in his capacity as chief of staff, told Hardee to move out "as

---

[24] OR, ser. 1, vol. 10, pt. 2, p. 367–68.

[25] Christopher Losson, *Tennessee's Forgotten Warriors: Frank Cheatham and His Confederate Division* (Knoxville: University of Tennessee Press, 1989) 45.

[26] Sword, *Bloody April*, 99.

soon as practicable."[27] Cleburne got under way just before noon, though Wood did not leave until 3:00 P.M.[28]

3 April. II Corps. Bragg's corps also got a late start due to a staff officer's error. Assistant Adjutant General George Garner sent an order to Daniel Ruggles to begin the march "early tomorrow morning, 6 a.m." The order was written before midnight on 2 April, and Garner expected Ruggles to be ready on the third. However, Ruggles did not receive the message until 2:30 the next morning.[29] To him, "tomorrow" meant the morning of 4 April. When the verbal orders were received, he was taken by surprise. Special orders No. 8 also stated that Bragg was to split his corps after he reached Monterey. He was to reach the Ridge Road before sunset on 3 April, but Bragg did not leave for Monterey until 4:30 P.M. The result was a long, slow-moving column winding its way into Tennessee. Commenting on the lack of organization, one of Bragg's soldiers noted: "I could see thousands of soldiers moving in different directions marching and countermarching.... Sometimes we marched very slow and sometimes double quick."[30] It was an ominous beginning.

3 April. I Corps. While Bragg and Hardee struggled, Leonidas Polk was having problems of his own. According to Beauregard, Charles Clark's 4,500-man division had blocked the Ridge Road back in Corinth before Hardee could get going. Hardee had even appeared in person to complain to Beauregard about the problem. William Polk, the bishop's son who was present on the scene, vigorously denied the allegations, claiming that Clark's men did not take the road until after Hardee had passed. It is most likely that Cleburne left Corinth unobstructed but Clark's wagons prevented Wood from advancing. Beauregard was incensed and blamed the entire delay on Polk.[31]

3 April. Reserve Corps. Like the rest of Johnston's army, Breckinridge had experienced several interruptions in his attempt to leave Corinth. On 3 April he was still in Burnsville awaiting the instructions contained in Special Orders No. 8.

---

[27] OR, ser. 1, vol. 10, pt. 2, p. 387.
[28] OR, ser. 1, vol. 10, pt. 1, p. 400; Shoup, "How We Went to Shiloh," 137.
[29] OR, ser, 1, vol. 10, pt. 2, p. 388.
[30] Daniel, *Shiloh,* 122–23.
[31] Roman, *Beauregard* 1:275–76; Shoup, "How We Went to Shiloh," 137; Eisenschiml, *Story of Shiloh,* 26; Jordan, "Notes," 1:596.

4 April. III Corps. Cleburne's men had made good time and were right
on schedule. However, just before dark on 3 April, a guide reported that there
was fresh water in a spring to the right of the main road. The general ordered
everyone to go into bivouac so he could investigate. He spoke to each camp,
giving encouragement to his men. The troops from Tennessee were proud to
be home again, and he urged them to fight for their "homes and firesides."[32]
The brigade got an early start on 4 April but after only a short distance[33]
Cleburne found the road blocked. Clark had followed half an hour behind
Cleburne, and when he found the road clear he continued onward during the
night, which avoided the turnoff to the spring. Clark's supply wagons now
halted the advance. The Third Corps had been ordered to lead, so the
teamsters had to clear the road. Slowly infantry and artillery moved past the
congestion, but the mistake had created yet another obstacle.

4 April. II Corps. Coordination in the Second Corps did not improve
with time. Once his troops had reached Monterey, Bragg was supposed to
send Ruggles's division northwest on the Monterey-Purdy Road; there he
would meet Polk, who was moving up the Ridge Road behind Hardee. Bragg
would send Withers's division due north toward Michie's by way of the
Monterey-Savannah Road. The condition of the Monterey-Purdy Road was
simply horrible, so Bragg decided to change the plans and sent Ruggles north
right behind Withers. Since Polk would be waiting until Ruggles had arrived,
Bragg wrote Polk the following note informing him of the change:

> My Dear General: Circumstances have (obliterated by fire) my
> Second Division from the Purdy road. Both my divisions will move
> from here, then direct from Mickey's on the Savannah road. I give you
> this information that you may not wait for my troops at the crossing of
> the Purdy and Ridge roads.
> General Breckinridge has not yet arrived from Burnsville, and I
> fear bad roads may delay him much. His command, forming the

---

[32] James A. Jones, "The Battle of Shiloh," *Confederate Veteran* 7/12 (December 1899):
556.
[33] Craig L. Symonds (*Stonewall of the West* [Lawrence: University of Kansas Press,
1997] 67) says "only a mile or two."

reserve, must necessarily control our movements to some extent. Let me hear from you by this courier at Mickey's.[34]

4 April. I Corps. On the same day Bragg tried to notify Johnston and Beauregard,[35] but unfortunately Polk reached the intersection before Bragg's courier arrived. After waiting three hours for Ruggles to appear, the First Corps went into bivouac on the night of 4 April. Polk's troops had marched only 7 miles in the entire day.

4 April. Reserve Corps. Breckinridge did not leave Burnsville until Friday, 4 April. With extraordinary effort his weary foot soldiers marched 23 miles to reach the outskirts of Monterey; however the artillery was still mired in the mud, well behind the infantry.[36]

Along with the frustration in the front of the column, the organization in the rear had essentially vanished as well. Although Cleburne was able to arrive at Michie's farmhouse in the afternoon of 4 April, Johnston's command was still widely dispersed. Hardee's corps was only 3 miles from Shiloh Church and Clark's division was within a few miles of Michie's. Bragg had Withers at the farmhouse but Ruggles was still on the road from Monterey. It was important to unite all four corps as close to Shiloh Church as possible, so around 3:30 Cleburne's men stopped to await further orders. Suddenly they were surprised by two companies of the 1st Alabama cavalry, closely pursued by Federal horsemen. The Yankees had no idea there was an enemy force in the area and they were greeted by a volley at close range. They quickly returned to their own lines and while they were repelled with ease it seemed as if any chance of surprise was gone. Johnston realized that much time had been lost and only Hardee was in place. He called a conference with Beauregard, Bragg, and Breckinridge in order to lay out plans for an assault the next morning. Polk was notified by messenger and the generals agreed that by 7:00 A.M. on 5 April the entire army was to be ready to attack.[37]

As it was the march into Tennessee had been slow, but during the night more rain drenched the troops and turned the roads into rivers of mud. Hardee's orders had been to move out at 3:00 A.M., but with such limited

[34] OR, ser. 1, vol. 10, pt. 2, p. 390.
[35] OR, ser. 1, vol. 10, pt. 2, p. 391.
[36] OR, ser. 1, vol. 10, pt. 1, p. 613–14.
[37] Sword, *Bloody April,* 103.

visibility Cleburne decided to wait until first light. The storm finally passed and just before 7:00 his brigade began to advance. In no time they were so close to the enemy that the men claimed to have heard officers barking orders in the Union camps. It was the early morning of 5 April and Cleburne had placed his left flank at the widow Howell's, near Winningham Creek.[38] Hindman brought his two brigades up on Cleburne's right, but the remainder of the army had not arrived. At this point Beauregard began to lose his nerve. He was still upset with Polk, and due to the weather much of the food had not yet reached the front. Most of the soldiers were unfamiliar with the rigors of a long campaign; some had even discarded their equipment along the route. Beauregard had expended a great deal of energy in the preparation of the offensive movement and when difficulties arose his resolve began to weaken. He felt that a withdrawal to Corinth was in order.[39] Johnston did not agree. Speaking to an aide, he said, "I would fight them if they were a million."[40] It was obvious, however, that no action would take place that morning.

The Third Corps sensed that a battle was imminent. Hardee put Cleburne's brigade on the left, Wood in the center, and Shaver on the right. By 10 o'clock in the morning the men were in position, waiting anxiously for their orders. Cleburne had great confidence in his old regiment and gave the 15th Arkansas the role of advance skirmishers. He placed the 23rd Tennessee on the extreme right. The 6th Mississippi was on their left near a marshy swamp called Shiloh Branch. The wet ground separated the Mississippians from the 5th Tennessee. The 24th Tennessee was next in line and Cleburne placed the 2nd Tennessee *en echelon* to the left of and 500 yards behind the 24th. Each flank was screened by a detachment of cavalry. Their nerves grew tighter with each passing moment. It was just past twelve o'clock[41] when Beauregard appeared in person, surrounded by members of his staff. He urged the men to "shoot low" and rode on to other camps, still clinging to any faint hope of surprise. Bragg's corps would form the second line, but the men under Ruggles had collided with Polk and were not prepared until almost

---

[38] Reed, *Organizations Engaged*, 12.

[39] Roman, *Beauregard*, 1:278; McDonough, *In Hell before Night*, 81–82.

[40] William P. Johnston, *The Life of Gen. Albert Sidney Johnston* (New York: Appleton and Company, 1879) 569.

[41] Symonds, *Stonewall of the West*, 69.

5:00 P.M. The battle must wait again. The Confederates were one day late and it would cost them dearly.

Shiloh was one of the most important battles of the Civil War, but it was fought in a very small area. Owl Creek to the north and Lick Creek to the south flow in an easterly direction until they empty into the Tennesee River. In front of the Union lines they were only 3 miles apart. Three dozen small farms were sprinkled throughout the area, but there was little room to maneuver on a battlefield only 9 square miles in size.[42] Hardee's corps had wanted their chance; now it came. The first contact occurred in S. A. M. Wood's sector. At 4:55 A.M. Federals under James Powell encountered pickets from Aaron Hardcastle's 3rd Mississippi battalion.[43] At dawn on 6 April, Cleburne's skirmishers moved forward through the dim light.[44]

Facing south astride the Pittsburgh-Corinth Road were two Federal infantry divisions. William T. Sherman's men held the right in front of Cleburne while Benjamin Prentiss blocked Hindman's path. John A. McClernand's First Division took a position behind them in support. Just after 5:00 A.M. both of Hindman's brigades discovered patrols in Fraley Field on Cleburne's right. Wood and Shaver struck hard and sent the Yankees reeling. Prentiss sent two Missouri regiments under Powell and David Moore to halt the onrushing tide but they were quickly overwhelmed. Wood drove Powell back to Seay Field, where he was reinforced by Moore. They were unable to stop the Confederates' momentum and Prentiss had to send in additional troops from Everett Peabody's brigade. The action would have been far more decisive had the Confederates attacked at sunrise. Nevertheless, by 8:00 A.M. Prentiss had been driven from the field and fell back to reform.[45] One hour later he was forced to retreat again and Peabody was hit in the head by a minie ball, killing him instantly.[46] When Prentiss withdrew he uncovered Sherman's flank; throughout the day the Confederates would continue to roll up the Union left, forcing them to retreat.

---

[42] John Fiske, *The Mississippi Valley in the Civil War* (New York: Houghton Mifflin Company, 1900) 73.

[43] Roman, *Beauregard*, 1:527, appendix to chap. 20, "Reports of -- Ferguson," 9 April 1862 and N. Augustin, 10 April 1862; Edwin C. Bearss, *Fields of Honor* (Washington, DC: National Geographic, 2006) 73.

[44] Jones, "The Battle of Shiloh," 556; Hardee, *Old Reliable*, 567.

[45] Reed, *Organizations Engaged*, 13; Connelly, *Army of the Heartland*, 163.

[46] Reed, *Organizations Engaged*, 13–14.

While Hindman was moving smoothly in the early morning hours, the wet ground along Shiloh Branch momentarily halted Cleburne's brigade. Running through a deep ravine, Shiloh Branch was a very small tributary of Owl Creek and did not even appear on many maps. The rains had swollen the little stream, creating a wide marsh some 40 acres in size. Cleburne decided he would move straight ahead, but his horse had other ideas. The animal balked at the obstruction and threw the general into the swamp. He emerged unscathed but it became apparent that Shiloh Branch was going to be a problem. The water divided his troops, with the 23rd Tennessee and the 6th Mississippi veering to the right. The 5th, 24th, and 2nd Tennessee, along with the 15th Arkansas, were pushed to the left, creating a gap a quarter-mile wide in the middle of his line.[47] Cleburne understood how important it was to maintain contact with Wood, so he began the fight behind the 23rd Tennessee. The topography had created a serious weakness in his alignment, but excitement overcame patience and the advance continued. With the quarry in sight Cleburne had no intention of waiting. He moved through wooded country without any opposition until the enemy first appeared, some 400 yards off of his left flank. Captain John Trigg was ordered to bring forward a howitzer and "wake them up."[48]

Sherman's division was not at all prepared for a sudden assault. Campfires were burning as men prepared bacon and coffee. Colonel Jesse J. Appler of the 53rd Ohio looked down the slope over Rea Field to the south. The woods looked calm enough, but something was not quite right. He had been agitated since daybreak when he heard the sporadic firing of skirmishers in the distance. He was standing with his adjutant Ephraim Dawes when a sixteen-man picket detachment raced back into camp. Confederates were advancing in force and they were not far away. Appler's worry increased and he decided to send another man out to confirm the report. He quickly changed his mind when a wounded soldier struggled back up the hill, crying out, "Get into line; the Rebels are coming!" It was just after 6:00 A.M. and the camp erupted in chaos. Officers shouted and men scrambled, trying to get into position while Appler sent warnings to other commands.[49]

---

[47] Sword, *Bloody April*, 177.

[48] Report of Patrick R. Cleburne, 24 May 1862, OR, ser. 1, vol. 10, pt. 1, p. 580.

[49] McDonough, *In Hell before Night*, 91–92; Sword, *Bloody April*, 171–72.

They began to deploy just in front of their camp. Dawes led the troops forward and looked to his right. The sun was up and it gleamed off of the barrels of muskets moving toward the Union flank. He turned around and ran to find his colonel. Appler grasped the danger and immediately ordered a retreat. Cooks were still preparing breakfast. A volley rang out from the woods, though it did little damage. The Yankees were able to reach the crest of a hill behind the camp, where they lay down among the brush. Sherman had taken possession of high ground about 200 yards north of the ravine. For additional protection they had constructed strong works using felled trees and large bales of hay.[50] It was a formidable defense held by three regiments of Jesse Hildebrand's Buckeyes. He had placed Appler's 53rd Ohio on the Federal left, the 57th in the center, and the 77th on his right, southeast of the church.

The commotion had caused a great deal of alarm throughout Sherman's division. The closest unit to Appler was Battery E, First Illinois Light Artillery, led by Captain Allen Waterhouse. It was not yet 7:00 A.M. when six guns were unlimbered. Waterhouse had four 3 1/2-inch (3.67) and two 4 1/2-inch (3.80) James rifled cannon, and he knew how to use them. Two of the 3 1/2-inch James went south about 150 yards across a small stream; the other four pieces stayed on the hill overlooking Rea Field.[51] The position of these guns would be a telling factor in the hours to come.

Just after 7 o'clock Sherman arrived. He looked to his left across Rea Field and could see the enemy about half a mile away.[52] As he continued his gaze the 15th Arkansas approached on his right. They had been concealed by dense woods and suddenly broke into the open. His troops tried to warn him just as a volley rang out. His orderly was killed instantly, but the general escaped with only a minor wound to his right hand. He turned his horse and galloped to safety, instructing Appler to hold on until reinforcements could arrive. Confederate lines extended as far as the eye could see. Directly in front of them was the distinctive blue flag with the white center.[53] It was Cleburne.

---

[50] Report of Patrick R. Cleburne, 24 May 1862, OR, ser. 1, vol. 10, pt 1, p. 581.

[51] Sword, *Bloody April*, 173.

[52] William T. Sherman, *Memoirs of Gen. W. T. Sherman*, 2 vols. (New York: Charles L. Webster & Co., 1991) 1:264; Sword, *Bloody April*, 174.

[53] The flags varied in size, but each flag was blue with a white moon in the center and a white border. Every regiment that captured a battery was permitted to display crossed cannons in the center of the flag.

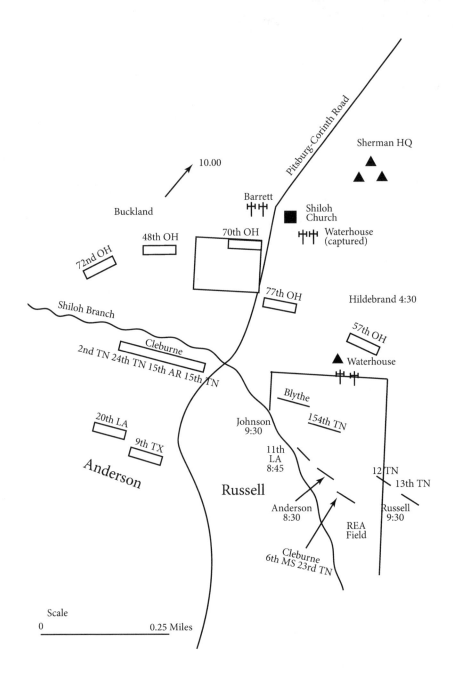

Pitsburg-Corinth Road

10.00

Sherman HQ

Buckland

Barrett

Shiloh Church

48th OH

70th OH

Waterhouse (captured)

72nd OH

Shiloh Branch

77th OH

Hildebrand 4:30

57th OH

Cleburne

2nd TN 24th TN 15th AR 15th TN

Waterhouse

Blythe

20th LA

154th TN

Johnson 9:30

9th TX

Anderson

11th LA 8:45

Russell

12 TN

13th TN

Anderson 8:30

Russell 9:30

REA Field

Cleburne 6th MS 23rd TN

Scale

0   0.25 Miles

The Rebels had taken Sherman completely by surprise, but the assault was not as powerful as it appeared. Two-thirds of Cleburne's command had been diverted from the point of attack and Bragg had not arrived. One thousand men would fight alone.[1] In front of the Southerners were 600 well-protected infantry with six field pieces in support.[2] Trigg's Arkansas battery opened up but the fire was ineffective. Heavy undergrowth limited visibility so the gunners were shifted to another position. The Confederates in this part of the field would have no artillery for the remainder of the day.

At this point in his career Pat Cleburne was still relatively inexperienced. He ordered a frontal assault and his men scrambled up the hill, their path partially blocked by abandoned tents. The 6th Mississippi was led by a physician turned colonel, J. J. Thornton. The regiment faced artillery in their front as well as obliquely to their left. About 150 yards north of Shiloh Branch, Thornton ordered his men to lie down, then charge. After a short gain they repeated the process. The Confederates pushed the infantry back past their camps but the cannon replied with deadly effect. No fewer than seven color-bearers were shot down in the assault. Thornton grabbed the flag himself, but the regiment was forced to pull back and he was severely wounded in the thigh.[3]

Cleburne had not yet earned his sobriquet as the "Stonewall of the West." He rashly ordered another charge, which was a horrible mistake. James rifles were firing downhill at a distance of less than 500 yards. Shell and canister blew gaping holes in the attackers. Blasts of musketry thinned the ranks even further. On Thornton's right was the 23rd Tennessee under Lieutenant-Colonel James F. Neill. His men fought valiantly but were badly damaged. They had brought 570 men to Shiloh, and on 26 April would count only 337 effectives. The 23rd Tennessee suffered tremendous casualties, but the 6th Mississippi took even more. In less than half an hour they lost 300 of the 425 men they took into battle, or 70.5 percent. Colonel Thornton and Major Robert Lowry lay among the wounded. The entire war saw only three other Confederate regiments record more casualties in a single

---

[1] Daniel, *Shiloh,* 159; Sword, *Bloody April,* 177.

[2] Sword, *Bloody April,* 178.

[3] T. B. Cox, "Sixth Mississippi Regiment at Shiloh," *Confederate Veteran* 18/11 (November 1910): 509.

battle.[4] When the smoke cleared, only sixty men answered the roll call. Their senior officer was Captain W. A. Harper.[5]

Sam Watkins, a private in the 1st Tennessee regiment, was stricken by the horror that suddenly confronted him. Like many young Confederates, the reality of war etched a picture in his mind he would never forget. He gave a graphic depiction of his experience:

> I had heard and read of battlefields, seen pictures of battlefields, of horses and men, of cannon and wagons, all jumbled together, while the ground was strewn with dead and dying and wounded, but I must confess that I never realized the "pomp and circumstance" of the thing called glorious war until I saw this. Men were lying in every conceivable position; the dead lying with their eyes wide open, the wounded begging piteously for help, and some waving their hats and shouting to us to go forward....It all seemed to me a dream; I seemed to be in a sort of haze, when siz, siz, siz, the minnie balls from the Yankees line began to whistle around our ears, and I thought of the Irishman when he said, Sure enough, those fellows are shooting bullets![6]

The battle on Cleburne's right was going poorly, but the troops on the left side of Shiloh Branch were faring no better. At 8 o'clock 1,500 men advanced against Ralph Buckland's Ohio brigade, 2,200 strong. Three regiments, the 70th, 48th, and 72nd, lined up just west of the Corinth-Pittsburg Road; the 72nd overlapped the Confederate left by half a brigade. They had pushed their right flank toward a ravine, then turned their line

---

[4] Francis T. Miller, ed., *The Photographic History of the Civil War*, 10 vols. (New York: Review of Reviews Co., 1911) 10:158; Thomas A. Wigginton, *Tennesseans in the Civil War*, 2 vols. (Knoxville: Civil War Centennial Comission, University of Tennessee Press, 1964) 1:223. Hood's 1st Texas at Sharpsburg had 226 men present, 45 killed and 141 wounded, for a loss of 82.3 percent. Ewell's 21st Georgia at the first battle of Manassas went into battle with 242 men, losing 38 killed and 146 wounded, for a loss of 76.0 percent. Third was Harry Heth's 26th North Carolina at Gettysburg. Heth had 820 men present, with 86 killed and 502 wounded, for a loss of 70.9 percent.

[5] Report of Patrick R. Cleburne, 24 May 1862, OR, ser. 1, vol. 10, pt 1, p. 581.

[6] Samuel R. Watkins, *Co. Aytch* (Dayton OH: Morningside, 1982) 34.

back toward Cleburne, creating a very difficult formation to attack.[7] In addition, the Confederates had to cross the marshes of Shiloh Branch under an enfilading fire from the 70th Ohio, posted on a ridge that commanded the field. Cleburne could not have selected a worse position but he was determined to forge ahead. The Confederates exploded from the woods and unleashed a tremendous volley. The Northerners recoiled but held the line. William Bate boldly moved his Tennesseans up in support, but to no avail. The 72nd was waiting, lying under the cover of tall grass. The Rebels came under a murderous fire and could go no further. They pulled back to the creek, leaving 13 officers and nearly 100 men killed or wounded. Colonel Bate was taken off the field when his left leg was shattered by a minie ball; Major W. R. Doak fell mortally wounded.[8] Like the 6th Mississippi, the 2nd Tennessee was without a leader.

On Bate's right, the 24th had been ravaged. Lieutenant-Colonel Thomas H. Peebles was a dynamic, forceful leader who weighed some 240 pounds. With a booming voice he urged his men forward. His horse was killed, his clothes were shredded, and the regimental battle flag had twenty-seven holes, yet somehow Peebles survived unharmed. The 24th fought well despite heavy casualties. They lost over 200 men killed or wounded, but Cleburne wrote that Peebles "showed that he possessed all the qualifications of a commander in the field."

Each of Cleburne's regiments had suffered severely, and the 15th Arkansas was no exception. Major J. T. Harris moved forward without regard for his own safety, firing upon the enemy with his revolver. He was instantly killed in the futile charge, and by 8:30 the attack had stalled.[9]

Next to the swamp the 5th Tennessee under Benjamin Hill was trying to make some progress against the 70th Ohio. He had been separated from Thornton's Mississippians by the soggy marsh and a deep ravine full of green briers and grapevines.[10] Again the Union held the high ground and artillery raked the Southern lines. Captain Samuel Barrett had posted his guns just west of Shiloh Church with a clear shot on Hill's regiment. No more vivid image of the struggle could be offered than Hill's own report,

[7] Report of Patrick R. Cleburne, 24 May 1862, OR, ser. 1, vol. 10, pt. 1, p. 581.
[8] Report of Patrick R. Cleburne, 24 May 1862, OR, ser. 1, vol. 10, pt. 1, p. 581.
[9] Report of Patrick R. Cleburne, 24 May 1862, OR, ser. 1, vol. 10, pt. 1, p. 581.
[10] Report of Benjamin J. Hill, 15 April 1862, OR, ser. 1, vol. 10, pt. 1, p. 587–89.

written on 22 April. In it, he gave the following description of a private in
Company D: "John Roberts, a very young soldier, behaved with the greatest
coolness and bravery throughout the whole action. He was frequently in
advance of his company, was knocked down twice by spent balls, and had
his gun shattered to pieces. He was but fifteen years old, but displayed the
coolness and courage of a veteran."[11]

Hill was determined to take Barrett's guns, but each time the
Confederates tried to advance they were stopped in their tracks. Thus far, the
armies had fought to a standstill. There was little Cleburne could do without
the reinforcements from Bragg's corps, so he returned to the right. He
organized what was left of his shattered command, pulling together some
200 men. The action had been constant, with the Confederates desperately
searching for a crack in Sherman's lines. His men were devoted to him, but
after the action that morning his reappearance may well have brought mixed
emotions.[12]

The carnage had been horrific, but it was not without its benefits. The
Federals had dominated the morning but Appler's nerves were frayed.
Somewhat predictably, Cleburne ordered a third charge. This time it
worked. Though he was in no particular danger Appler panicked and cried
out, "Retreat, and save yourselves!"[13] By 8:00 A.M. his troops were in full
flight, leaving only the 57th and 77th Ohio in line east of the Pittsburg-
Corinth Road.[14]

With shrinking numbers Cleburne was unable to take advantage of
Appler's mistake, and he began to struggle. Fortunately, help was on the
way. Just as the 53rd collapsed, Confederate reinforcements began to appear.
At 8:30 Patton Anderson was on the field; he sent two regiments towards
Cleburne's right, forming on the left of the 6th Mississippi. In addition, he
ordered the 20th Louisiana and 9th Texas to support Cleburne's left wing.
Robert Russell arrived at 8:45 and also went to the right, next to Anderson.
At the north end of the Rea property the Confederates were getting ready to
turn Sherman's left flank. Less than an hour later Bushrod Johnson's

---

[11] Report of Benjamin J. Hill, 15 April 1862, OR, ser. 1, vol. 10, pt. 1, p. 587–89.
[12] Daniel, *Shiloh*, 165; Sword, *Bloody April*, 183.
[13] Sword, *Bloody April*, 178–79.
[14] Sword, *Bloody April*, 189.

Tennesseans moved into the northwest corner of Rea Field and formed on
Russell.[15] The pressure was mounting.

The troops were new but the results were unchanged. Like Cleburne,
they were unable to negotiate the mire in Shiloh Branch. Poor
communication resulted in uncoordinated assaults, all of which were turned
away with heavy loss.[16] The 57th and 77th Ohio had been forced to give up
their original positions, but they regrouped and made a stand around 8:45.
They blasted Russell's 11th Louisiana with canister, tearing huge holes in
the lines. A few brave survivors from Cleburne's 6th Mississippi tried to
support the Tigers, but they were of little help. The initial attacks were halted
and the men broke to the rear. The Rebels were thrown into further
confusion when the second lines saw their own troops streaming back toward
them.[17]

Bushrod Johnson met a similar fate. The Tennesseans split apart, with
two regiments moving straight ahead toward Barrett's guns while the other
two turned to the right to attack Waterhouse. North of Rea Field the forward
thrust had temporarily lost its momentum but at 9:30 the advance resumed.
Bragg ordered Johnson—supported by Anderson, Russell, and perhaps 350
of Cleburne's men—to continue the attack. When Appler left his position he
exposed the artillery under Waterhouse. Despite determined resistance, three
of his guns were easily captured and the other three were disabled.[18]

As Hildebrand fell back he continued to uncover Buckland's left.
Historian Larry Daniel notes that Buckland's regiments "toppled like
dominoes."[19] By 10:00 the Confederates had passed Shiloh Church and
both Hildebrand and Buckland had been driven back across the Purdy
Road.[20] Part of McClernand's division was forced to retreat as well. As
Prentiss was no longer a factor, A. P. Stewart, Wood, and Shaver wheeled to
their left to hit Sherman's flank one more time. They received courageous,
though quite limited, assistance from the other units, which had already
suffered so severely. Cleburne was virtually destroyed and Johnson had lost

---

[15] Reed, *Organizations Engaged,* 14; Daniel, *Shiloh,* 165.
[16] Sword, *Bloody April,* 191.
[17] Daniel, *Shiloh,* 191–92.
[18] Sherman, *Memoirs,* 1:295; T. W. Connelly, *History of the 70th Ohio Regiment*
(West Union OH: Adams County Historical Society, 1978) 21.
[19] Daniel, *Shiloh,* 169–70.
[20] T. W. Connelly, *70th Ohio,* 21.

62 percent of his men.[21] By this point the Confederates had become wildly scattered. Two of Anderson's regiments remained near the 6th Mississippi; the other two still supported the left side of Cleburne's brigade. Russell's 11th Louisiana was between Anderson and Johnson, but the 12th and 13th Tennessee were actually east of Cleburne's 23rd. It was a horrible mess.

The Confederate lines had little organization left, but the Federal situation was even worse. As the Pittsburg-Corinth Road ran north across the Purdy-Hamburg Road it turned sharply to the east. Hildebrand had been blown apart and Buckland was still west of the intersection. McClernand intended to act in support, so he had established his headquarters about half a mile north of Review Field. The Federals were now engaged along their entire front. Still further east, Braxton Bragg continued to pour men onto the field in another attempt on Sherman's flank. Almost 8,000 men were sent into the fray as Stewart moved forward on Russell's right. By 11 o'clock the Yankees were on the run again.[22] Different commands converged at the same time and the crossroads became jammed with men, horses, and equipment. It looked as if they would be swept from the field, but once again poor coordination robbed the Confederates of a decisive victory.

To the right of Shiloh Branch Cleburne's troops lost any semblance of organization. Between the campsite obstructions and their own wounded men it was impossible to manage an attack. Both regiments broke apart and fled back down the hill. About 100 yards to the rear, half of the 23rd Tennessee was able to reform, where they were joined by fragments of the 6th Mississippi. They fought with the 8th Arkansas of Wood's brigade until just after noon,[23] when they joined A. P. Stewart and charged into Duncan Field. Casualties were light but Cleburne lost a few men to capture by the 7th Illinois. He understood all too well the sacrifice that had been made on the right. At 12:30 the 6th and 23rd were sent to the rear. With their departure Cleburne was a brigadier general without any troops, so he headed left once again. On the way he ran into Hardee, who ordered him to assemble any stragglers he could find. He met with very limited success and

---

[21] Daniel, *Shiloh*, 191–94.
[22] Daniel, *Shiloh*, 181–83.
[23] Reed, *Organizations Engaged*, 14–16.

at 2:00 P.M. Cleburne returned to the front.[24] He found the 2nd Tennessee utterly exhausted. The Volunteers had taken terrible losses and had no food, so he sent them from the field as well. The 2nd fell back to regroup and Cleburne did not see them for the remainder of the fight. He was unaware that Beauregard had transferred the regiment to the center of Hardee's corps.

While Cleburne was busy with McClernand, disaster struck the Confederacy. Winfield Statham led the Third Brigade of the Reserve Corps. The afternoon found the Rebels in Sarah Bell Field just west of the Hamburg-Savannah Road. Albert Sidney Johnston was riding in front of the troops when he was wounded four times. A minie ball cut the sole of his left boot in half and a spent bullet hit the outside of his right thigh. A small bit of a shell lodged just above his right hip, but these wounds were not particularly serious. The last one proved to be fatal. Johnston was hit behind his right knee and an artery was severed. The stream of blood was hidden by his boot and his staff did not grasp the danger. Unfortunately, Johnston had dispatched his personal physician earlier in the day to care for other wounded soldiers, many of them Federals. A tourniquet would probably have saved his life, but he did not receive the necessary attention. At 2:30 Johnston was dead and Beauregard took over.

The 5th and 24th Tennessee, along with the 15th Arkansas, had taken cover under the brow of a steep hill. They had moved forward to join the Confederates under Preston Pond and Robert Trabue in an attack on the position held by Colonel C. C. Marsh. Originally Marsh had deployed four Illinois regiments on the Pittsburg-Corinth Road, with their left anchored on Woolf Field and their right in the northwest corner of Review Field. Marsh had been forced backward by Hardee and Stewart but made a stand around noon. They fought the Confederates until 2:30, when Cleburne finally located his troops.[25]

Upon reaching the ground, Cleburne ordered an immediate assault. There was a short delay due to a Confederate battery that was firing over their line of advance but he stopped the barrage and sent out skirmishers. What was left of the 23rd came up to join him, still under James Neill. Cleburne turned to the east and crossed Tilghman Creek in a frantic attempt to turn

---

[24] Report of Patrick R. Cleburne, 24 May 1862, OR, ser. 1, vol. 10, pt. 1 p. 582; Reed, *Organizations Engaged,* 71.

[25] Reed, *Organizations Engaged,* 46–47.

McClernand's left flank. The 5th, 23rd, and 24th were soon engaged and drove the enemy back half a mile. The afternoon wore on and Cleburne could smell a victory. McClernand was on the run, but ammunition was running low. The wagons could not reach the field due to the difficult terrain, so a strong party was sent to the rear to replenish their supply. Time was of the essence and the men were still over a mile away. As soon as they returned the advance resumed. The chase continued until they came under the fire of gunboats on the Tennessee. The shells did little damage to the Confederates but fell instead among their own wounded, causing only additional suffering. Pat Cleburne was both horrified and enraged. In his battle report he wrote that "history records few instances of more reckless humanity than this."[26]

To the north, the Federal Army had been forced back toward the river but was able to reform. The troops established a defense along an old wagon road that connected the Pittsburg-Corinth Road with the Savannah-Hamburg Road. Approximately two-thirds of a mile in length, it ran across the northeast corner of Duncan Field. Years of erosion had created a trench up to 3 feet in depth and the Yankees took cover behind this line. The depression was commonly referred to as the "Sunken Road," but after the bloody fighting of 6 April the area behind the ground became known as the "Hornet's Nest." Braxton Bragg found stubborn resistance from Prentiss, Stephen Hurlbut, and W. H. L. Wallace. Most of Cleburne's command continued to go after McClernand, but some of the men from the 23rd Tennessee and 6th Mississippi joined Bragg. Wave after wave of Confederates were thrown into the assault but the attacks were uncoordinated. Although 10,000 men were engaged at some point,[27] they were unable to move in concert and their advantage in numbers was negated. Around 5:30 P.M. the Yankees finally collapsed. They surrendered 2,200 men but their courage was rewarded. As darkness fell Buell began to arrive, and at 8:00 P.M. a steady downpour fell over the battlefield. The effort at the Hornet's Nest had given the army just enough time to regroup and staved off almost certain defeat.[28]

---

[26] Report of Patrick R. Cleburne, 24 May 1862, OR, ser. 1, vol. 10, pt. 1, p. 583.

[27] Daniel, *Shiloh*, 214.

[28] T. W. Connelly, *70th Ohio*, 23–24.

Beauregard knew that Buell's reinforcements were on the way, but he remained confident that the Confederates could finish the battle in the morning. The pursuit was ordered to stop. The wisdom of this order is open to debate, as the Federals had been decisively beaten, their backs were at the river, and Buell had not arrived. Therefore, he should have attacked. However, there could be another conclusion. Although the enemy had retreated all day long, it was not quite driven from the field. Grant had been able to make a final stand. The Confederates were worn out, hungry, and disorganized. In consideration of these factors, withdrawal was the wiser course of action. Regardless of the reader's personal opinion, the fact remains that Beauregard was several miles from Cleburne when the order was issued, and it is highly unlikely that he fully understood the situation of either army. It is interesting to note that his original purpose, well before the Confederates even reached the battle, was to strike Grant before Buell could arrive. Despite the difficult circumstances within his army, he now abandoned his own strategy.

It was just after dark when Cleburne received the news that Johnston had been killed. He was only 400 yards from Pittsburg Landing.[29] He knew how close he had come and was filled with disappointment. Cleburne turned back to the Confederate lines and pitched his tents in an abandoned camp near the Bark Road. He wanted to reunite his diminished brigade, but like the other Confederate officers he was unable to find his own men. Major Francis A. Shoup of the Arkansas artillery searched through the night and finally came upon the dejected Irishman at 11:00 P.M., sitting on a stump drinking some coffee from a bucket.[30]

By Monday morning Buell was in position. The Union could now bring some 40,000 soldiers onto the field, the Confederates only half that number.[31] At daybreak William Nelson, Alexander McCook, and Thomas Crittenden advanced on the left, intent on recapturing their old camp sites. On the right wing Hurlbut, Sherman, McClernand, and Lew Wallace moved on Shiloh Church. Aided by heavy brush, the Confederates were

---

[29] Irving A. Buck, *Cleburne and His Command* (1908; repr., Wilmington NC: Broadfoot Publishing, 1995) 94.

[30] Shoup, "How We Went to Shiloh," 139.

[31] Jasper Kelsey, "The Battle of Shiloh," *Confederate Veteran* 25/2 (February 1917) 73; Eisenschiml, *The Story of Shiloh*, 49.

able to hold their ground around the church for about three hours, but by 1:00 P.M. it was apparent that the battle had turned in the North's favor.[32]

On the second day Cleburne fought as part of Breckinridge's corps. His brigade was so broken up that of the 2,700 men he had taken to Shiloh, he could find only 800.[33] Just after daylight he received orders to advance along the Bark Road. He collected the few troops he had left and formed between Breckinridge, on his right, and S. A. M. Wood's brigade. Union forces were seen marching through the woods on his left, pressing toward his rear. Buell had arrived. Cleburne was able to advance about a mile, where he told his men to lie down and form a line of battle. The guns of the Washington Battery[34] opened up and drove the enemy from their cover. At this point Cleburne received an order from Breckinridge to attack. It was obvious that any attempt would be futile, yielding only additional loss of life. He tried to point out that he was hopelessly outnumbered, but the order had come down through Bragg and must be obeyed.

The Southern artillery seized a momentary advantage, but the Federals replied with rifled cannon and quickly gained the upper hand. The duel occurred over Cleburne's intended line of advance, which gave the men a much-needed rest. They moved into a valley to open a clear line of fire for the artillery and were safe for the moment, although several men were killed by falling tree limbs. The Rebels were overmatched, so the guns fell silent and the infantry charged. Once again the terrain favored the North. Heavy undergrowth obscured the Confederates' vision yet offered no protection against a hail of lead. Cleburne could not see anything in front of him, but his men were dropping everywhere. Captain Ed Cowley, the acting major of the 15th Arkansas, was shot in the head; Lieutenant-Colonel Neill of the 23rd Tennessee was struck in the chest.

---

[32] T. W. Connelly, *70th Ohio*, 24–25.

[33] Report of Patrick R. Cleburne, 24 May 1862, OR, ser. 1, vol. 10, pt. 1, p. 583, Confederate losses in killed, wounded and missing from the battle of Shiloh. This figure would indicate a loss of roughly 1,900 men. After stragglers, missing, and slightly wounded men had returned, his casualties were revised. Several sources list his total losses at 1,013. OR, ser. 1, vol. 10, pt. 1, p. 395, gives a slightly higher number and, in a report prepared by Thomas Jordan, he gives casualties as 188 killed, 790 wounded and 65 missing, for a total of 1,043.

[34] The battery was part of the famous Washington Artillery of New Orleans; it had a company of 156 soldiers.

The brigade was routed; there was no choice but to retreat. By this time Cleburne's command consisted of little more than the 15th Arkansas. They fell back behind a ridge as the enemy continued to follow. Suddenly Cleburne ordered a counterattack. Completely stunned, the Federals were forced to regroup. It was during this charge that Lieutenant-Colonel A. K. Patton of the 15th was killed. The pursuit went on until all of the ammunition was gone, and when the action was over only fifty-eight men returned to the lines.[35]

The Confederates were heavily pressed along their entire front and within an hour they had been driven south of the Purdy-Hamburg Road.[36] The Butternuts fell back throughout the afternoon and at 5:00 P.M. were finally forced to withdraw.[37] Cleburne's troops were spread out all over the field, but he did what he could to organize small bands of men. The Yankees were in no condition to press their advantage. Cleburne remained where he was, burning any supplies that could not be saved and giving aid to wounded soldiers.

The second day at Shiloh resulted in ultimate victory for the Union, but the battle had been costly to both sides. Casualties for the Federals were 1,754 men killed, 8,408 wounded, and 2,885 captured or missing, for a total of 13,047. The Confederates lost 1,728 men killed, 8,012 wounded, and 959 captured or missing, for a total of 10,699.[38]

Cyrus Boyd of the 15th Iowa attempted to put his impressions of the battle into words as he walked among the Confederate dead: "Where the retreat commenced on Monday afternoon are hundreds and thousands of wounded rebels. They had fallen in heaps and the woods had taken fire and burned all the clothing off them and the naked and blackened corpses are still lying there unburied. On a hillside near a deep hollow our men were hauling them down and throwing them into the deep gulley. *One hundred and eighty* had been thrown in when I was there."[39]

---

[35] Report of Patrick R. Cleburne, 24 May 1862, OR, ser. 1, vol. 10, pt. 1, p. 584.

[36] Daniel, *Shiloh,* 289.

[37] T. W. Connelly, *70th, Ohio,* 24.

[38] OR, ser. 1, vol. 10, pt. 1, p. 100–108 and OR, ser. 1, vol. 10, pt. 2, p. 395–99.

[39] Cyrus F. Boyd, *The Civil War Diary of Cyrus F. Boyd* (1953; repr., Iowa City: State Historical Society of Iowa, 1976) 9 April 1862; emphasis original.

On orders from Hardee Cleburne began the slow retreat on the road to Corinth. The skies opened and a violent storm erupted, breaking the darkness with streaks of lightning. Captain Isaac Avery rode at Cleburne's side, but neither man could stay awake. Their heads would drop, then suddenly rise again. At. 9:00 P.M. they stopped to feed their horses before haulting at a creek. As Hardee's troops approached Monterey, the column was thrown into confusion. Southern cavalry galloped along the lines, screaming that Federal troops had broken through the rear guard. Panic broke out among the teamsters and they quickly unhitched the mule teams. Food and supplies were discarded as the men dissolved, but there was no cause for alarm. The Yankees were simply too worn out to pursue.[40]

While Grant was not a problem, the march did not go smoothly. The dirt roads had turned into deep mud and many of the troops wandered into the woods. It was very difficult for the officers to maintain cohesion as the battered army slowly made its way into Mississippi, but by 8 April most of the troops and wagons had arrived.[41]

The battle of Shiloh was Pat Cleburne's first major engagement, and though he acted with courage, he showed neither vision nor wisdom. He continually hurled his troops forward in senseless frontal assaults, losing just over 1,000 of the 2,700 men he had taken into battle.[42] The 23rd Tennessee and the 6th Mississippi were completely destroyed. Whether he would have achieved ultimate success had he been allowed to continue his attack, or whether he sacrificed too much in the morning to be able to close the battle in the afternoon, are questions that will remain unanswered. There is a great deal of validity in both statements. Cleburne apppeared to have a clear understanding of the overall strategy, and the early action on 6 April provides a good illustration of the admiration he held among his troops. However, Cleburne's initial grasp of the conditions around him was nonexistent. He did not appreciate the impact Shiloh Branch would have on his own brigade, and as a result his disjointed attacks lacked the power of a

---

[40] Isaac W. Avery, " Patrick R. Cleburne," *Kennesaw* (GA) *Gazette*, 15 May 1887, 3; John Kent Folmar, *"From that Terrible Field": Letters of James M. Williams* (Tuscaloosa: University of Alabama Press, 1981) Williams to wife, 10 April 1862 54.

[41] Hughes, *Old Reliable*, 113.

[42] Wiley Sword, "The Other Stonewall," *Civil War Times Illustrated* 36/7 (February 1998): 36–45.

concentrated thrust. On the left side of the swamp he made a serious tactical error in attacking a position in which he was outflanked on one side and enfiladed on the other. There can be no doubt that his men gave a good account of themselves, but Pat Cleburne's performance at Shiloh was marked by mistakes he would never repeat.

For the South the loss at Shiloh was devastating. It was a battle they could not afford to lose. With a victory the balance of power in the Western theatre would have been restored and the Mississippi Valley protected. With possession of Tennessee there would be another chance to establish a foothold in Kentucky. In hindsight, it is quite possible that a resounding triumph in April would have extinguished the fortunes of Ulysses S. Grant and William T. Sherman, relegating each one to brief mention in a protracted conflict. There will be some conjecture that the battle was lost when Sidney Johnston died, and this debate will never end. It could also be argued that Beauregard's order to halt allowed Buell to arrive in time to save Grant.

Beauregard's supporters would point out that the Confederates had suffered heavy casualties and were thoroughly disorganized.[43] The power of the advance had outdistanced the supply wagons. Many of the troops had had limited experience with large-scale warfare, and it was simply too much to expect from exhausted men. Those with an opposite view contend that when the day was done the Federals had been pushed across the field and their backs were at the river. Furthermore, Beauregard was too far away from the battlefield to accurately assess the situation. His actions were premature and deprived the Confederates of a chance to eliminate Grant's army as an effective fighting force.[44] Objectively, the attempt to defeat Grant on 6 April should probably have been made, despite the uncertainty of its outcome. The stakes were too high and the benefits too great to give Grant one more chance.

In any case, the failure of the Confederate high command is undeniable. Organization was poor from the outset, the movement from Corinth was uncoordinated, and most importantly Beauregard's battle plan was abysmal. The attack designed in parallel lines ensured confusion. It

---

[43] Daniel, *Shiloh,* 316.
[44] Sword, *Bloody April,* 382; Bruce Catton, *Grant Moves South 1861–1863* (1960; repr., Edison NJ: Castle Books, 2000) 244.

should have been made with three corps abreast of each other to ensure greater striking power at the point of attack. This was the formation Johnston suggested in his telegram of 3 April. Would it have worked?

When the battle was over, no ground had changed hands and both sides were disappointed. Davis blamed Beauregard for his failure to pursue the enemy and Lincoln faulted Grant for a similar mistake on 7 April. The importance of the battle of Shiloh simply cannot be underestimated, as the Confederates came very close to destroying Grant's entire army. It was perhaps the greatest of missed opportunities.[45]

---

[45] Catton, *Grant Moves South*, 247; Buck, *Cleburne and His Command*, 100.

4

KENTUCKY

After the bitter defeat at Shiloh, Pat Cleburne brought his men back to Corinth and settled just south of the town at a site known as Camp Hill. Food was scarce, much of the equipment was gone, and the soldiers in the ranks believed that a great victory had slipped away. Morale was horrible.[1] The revitalization of the army was a formidable task, but Cleburne worked diligently to supply his troops. Regimental officers were brought to his headquarters to receive instruction in tactics. He labored continuously to provide adequate food and water, and each day he sent an ordnance officer into Corinth to procure additional rifle cartridges.[2] Still, there was much more to be done. The disastrous frontal assaults of 6 April had taken their toll, making it necessary to reorganize the brigade. The 23rd Tennessee was replaced by the 48th Tennessee, led by Colonel George Nixon. As the 15th Arkansas was practically nonexistent, it was merged with the 13th Arkansas. A. K. Patton had been killed, so Lucius Polk assumed command of the consolidated regiment. The 2nd, 5th (35th), and 24th Tennessee comprised the remainder of the infantry, though the latter was transferred to Frank Cheatham's division on 8 July. In addition, Cleburne received the artillery battery of Captain J. H. Calvert.

Cleburne had made several mistakes at Shiloh, but he did learn a valuable lesson. Prior to the Civil War officers in both armies had been trained in Napoleonic tactics, in which both sides faced each other on relatively open ground. Upon reaching the battlefield the action was confined to a very small area and casualties were heavy. Dense undergrowth around Pittsburg Landing had shown that large bodies of troops could be severely hampered by difficult terrain. This led to a desire for smaller units, which Cleburne believed could be very effective under capable leadership. To this end he

---

[1] Craig L. Symonds, *Stonewall of the West* (Lawrence: University of Kansas Press, 1997) 80.

[2] Howell and Elizabeth Purdue, *Pat Cleburne Confederate General* (1973; repr., Gaithersburg MD: Olde Soldier Books, 1987) 120.

began to organize companies of sharpshooters to serve in an advance capacity. His intent was to attack the enemy artillery before his own infantry became engaged. This would decrease Confederate casualties and provide an immediate advantage in the early stages of an assault. Contests were held to find the most skilled marksmen in each regiment. Not only did this produce the intended result, but the competition raised morale throughout the entire brigade.[3]

Although great progress had been made, the Confederates were still extremely vulnerable to a sudden attack. After the battle of Shiloh, Henry Halleck replaced Grant, arriving at Pittsburg Landing on 11 April. He led 125,000 men, while Beauregard had only 30,000 at his disposal. Despite this numerical superiority, Halleck gave the Southerners time to regroup. He was deliberate by nature, but the Army of Tennessee managed to crawl south at the lethargic rate of 1 mile per day.[4] The delay allowed Earl Van Dorn to bring reinforcements from the Trans-Mississippi. He arrived on 1 May with 20,000 Rebels, raising the army to a total effective force of 49,212.[5] Still, the Confederates remained severely outnumbered and Cleburne grew concerned that the Federals were trying to move around their flank. It appeared that their objective was a high ridge east of town, running southward some 3 miles in length.

General Beauregard decided to attack. He ordered Hardee to advance by the Farmington Road while Van Dorn attempted to find the Union right. On 3 May Cleburne left early in the afternoon and placed his men in line three-quarters of a mile beyond Farmington on the east side of Seven Mile Creek. Sharp skirmishing ensued and the Confederates fell back. Trees were cut down to obstruct the road and the bridge over the creek was destroyed. The Federal troops were able to cross, but only after a two-hour delay. Artillery shells went

[3] Symonds, *Stonewall of the West*, 81.

[4] Clifford Dowdey, *The Land They Fought For: The Story of the South as the Confederacy, 1832–1865* (Garden City NJ: Doubleday, Inc., 1955) 154; A. P. Stewart, "The Army of Tennessee," *Military Annals of Tennessee*, ed. John B. Lindsley (Nashville: J. M. Lindsey and Co., 1886) 75.

[5] Irving A. Buck, *Cleburne and His Command* (1908; repr., Wilmington NC: Broadfoot Publishing, 1995) 101; US War Department, comp., *The War of the Rebellion: A Compilation of the Official Records of the Union and Confederate Armies*, 128 vols. (Washington, DC: Government Printing Office, 1880–1901) ser. 1, vol. 10, pt. 2, p. 489–91 lists a total force present for duty of 21,895, according to the return of 4 May 1862.

back and forth for another hour, though casualties were light. Late in the afternoon, Cleburne retreated again to the safety of the Confederate lines.[6]

With Van Dorn's arrival they would move in tandem and continue to press their advantage. Unfortunately, Van Dorn was nowhere to be found, as he had lost his way in the dark. The confusion soon became irrelevant. Beauregard believed that the force in his front was merely one brigade and as such he was not alarmed. Since a full-scale attack was highly unlikely, such a large contingent of troops was not required to protect the area. To Cleburne's dismay, Beauregard ordered Hardee to withdraw.[7]

For the next three weeks, Halleck continued to move at a snail's pace. He advanced until his troops were only a few hundred yards from the Confederate entrenchments. Beauregard ordered another reconnaissance and at 11:00 A.M. on 28 May Cleburne took his four Tennessee regiments out the Farmington Road, again with Van Dorn in support. The 15th Arkansas and Calvert's battery had been detached to Tuscumbia Creek and were not involved. His orders were to prevent the Federals from extending their picket line around the Confederate flank.

Cleburne's command totaled some 800 men, and he divided his troops. He gave the 2nd and 48th Tennessee to Sidney Stanton, with instructions to advance on the right. Cleburne accompanied Benjamin Hill of the 5th Tennessee. Along with R. D. Allison's 24th, Hill's regiment made up the left wing of the formation. Upon reaching the ground they went into line of battle around an old cotton gin. In Cleburne's front was the Shelton house and though it was apparently occupied, he was uncertain of the Federal strength. Seeking more information, he sent a messenger to Van Dorn in order to get more information. Van Dorn had found an excellent location on the Memphis and Charleston Railroad that provided a clear view of the surrounding area. Cleburne was informed that the artillery had already shelled the house, and it was now empty.

Cleburne saw that the enemy was outflanked and dispatched a courier to find Stanton. Cleburne wanted to know exactly where he was in order to coordinate a simultaneous attack. Stanton had taken a position on the right of the Farmington Road and could see the Federals in his front as well as to his left. It looked to him as though they occupied the house and he believed that

---

[6] OR, ser. 1, vol. 10, pt. 1, p. 713–17; OR, ser. 1, vol. 10, pt. 2, p. 488.

[7] OR, ser. 1, vol. 10, pt. 2, p. 488.

he would need support. Accordingly, he asked Cleburne to come up on his left and unite both wings of the army. Cleburne arrived and examined the ground. He concluded that it was not favorable for an advance of his own, though he did move Hill forward as far as possible. Having explained the situation, he expected Stanton to arrive at any moment but the colonel had yet to move. Instead of coming forward he had waited for his commander to join him. His men were lying down beside the road, but when Cleburne sent further instructions to advance Stanton said he would comply. The brigade was certainly not acting in concert. While the right wing was mired in inertia, Hill had taken a few picked men to reconnoiter the area in his front. They approached the building, which did appear to be vacant. However, as they drew closer Union guns erupted. The Federals had taken cover in a ravine behind some plum bushes and suddenly burst into view. Hill's regiment charged forward, with most of the fire coming from their right. They fought alone, but the 5th Tennessee still managed to drive the Federals backward until a fresh battery opened up. Hill was momentarily stunned by the explosion of a shell and the Rebels were compelled to withdraw.

Up to this point Cleburne had focused on the action in front of him, and he was very upset over Stanton's absence. He knew that the 5th Tennessee was engaged, but thick undergrowth limited visibility. He sent an aide along his lines to ensure proper alignment within the left half of his brigade. Some fifteen minutes had elapsed before he realized that Allison had not reached the field either. Cleburne turned his horse and rode to the rear. He found Allison dismounted and out of uniform with no desire to attack. Cleburne was seething and demanded to know why the advance had not been made in a timely manner. Allison weakly replied that a creek had blocked his path and the forest was too dense to allow any coordinated movement. Cleburne finally got the troops to move forward, but his best efforts produced only negligible results. The 24th fired one round, then most of the regiment fled the field.[8]

Cleburne was furious at Stanton and Allison for their failure to obey his orders. He rallied Stanton's regiments and prepared to lead another charge when Hardee called off the action. The brigade was pulled back 50 yards and pickets were thrown out. He was very disappointed with the entire affair. Under different circumstances many of these men had fought well at Shiloh, and he had no patience with this lack of leadership. Allison was soon removed,

---

[8] Report of Patrick R. Cleburne, 23 June 1862, OR, ser. 1, vol. 52, p. 35.

replaced by Major Hugh Bratton. In his report of the battle, Cleburne noted that Bratton was one of the few men of the 24th who had held their ground. The Confederates lost "between eighty and ninety" men in the brief contest, with most of the casualties coming from Hill's 5th Tennessee.[9]

There is no question that the performance of his subordinates was lacking, but Cleburne was not without blame. He had failed to ensure Stanton's cooperation before the left wing advanced. He was in command of four regiments, yet he had controlled only a portion of the battlefield. These factors combined to result in an ineffective, piecemeal attack. If nothing else, the minor engagement demonstrated that the brigade still needed a lot of work.

The Confederates had not been defeated on the field of battle, but there were still several weaknesses in their position. Halleck was closing in, clean water was in short supply, and Beauregard knew that he would not be able to withstand a siege. Corinth itself was a filthy town and sickness had increased. Ambrose Bierce, an aide on William Hazen's staff, described it as "the capital of a swamp."[10] Beauregard decided to move to a more desirable location. Due to the fact that the Confederates were completely outnumbered, several ruses were used to make their escape. Trains were sent back and forth and when they halted the soldiers were instructed to cheer loudly, as if to welcome incoming reinforcements. Wooden logs disguised as artillery were strategically placed along the lines, and phony deserters filled with rumors of fresh troops were sent into Union lines. During the night of 29 May the Confederates left their campfires burning and began their 30-mile march southwest to Baldwin. The Federals were completely surprised the next morning to discover that the enemy had vanished.[11] The degree of success in Beauregard's operation was reflected in a telegram sent from John Pope to Henry Halleck on 30 May: "The enemy are reinforcing heavily on my front and left. The cars are running constantly, and the cheering is immense every time they unload in front of me. I have no doubt, from all appearances, that I shall be attacked in heavy force at daylight."[12]

---

[9] Report of Patrick R. Cleburne, 23 June 1862, OR, ser. 1, vol. 52, p. 36.

[10] Ambrose Bierce, *Ambrose Bierce's Civil War* (1956; repr., Washington, DC: Regnery, Gateway 1988) 12.

[11] Alfred Roman, *Military Operations of General Beauregard,* 2 vols. (New York: Harper & Brothers, 1884) 1:390; Judith Lee Hallock, ed., *The Civil War Letters of Joshua K. Callaway* (Athens: University of Georgia Press, 1997) 21.

[12] OR, ser. 1, vol. 10, pt. 2, p. 225, Pope to Hallock, 30 May 1862.

They marched 7 miles to Tuscumbia Creek and arrived the next day. The 15th Arkansas, Calvert's battery, and four companies of cavalry held the bridge over the turnpike while the rest of the army marched across. When everyone was safe they set it on fire. The Confederates spent the next week in Baldwin regaining their strength. They made camp in anticipation of an assault, but it became obvious that the Federals had no such intentions. On 7 June Beauregard led his men south to Tupelo, where they arrived two days later.[13] The armies had spent the month of May in almost constant contact but the time in Tupelo was very quiet, providing the soldiers some much-needed rest. Conditions improved as more attention was paid to camp hygiene. Hardee put the time to good use. He maintained strict discipline and drilled his men for several hours each day. The work was unpleasant, but it would soon pay large dividends.

On 20 June Beauregard was replaced by Braxton Bragg. His health had never completely recovered, and he was suffering from a severe attack of laryngitis.[14] Bragg was an able administrator, but several problems greeted him. Desertions persisted and the food was poor. It was very difficult to transport supplies over single-track railroads, and the stockpiles of fresh meat were quickly disappearing. Any offensive movement required the Confederates to leave the proximity of the railroads and utilize wagons for transportation. There were too few in number and many of those were in need of repair. It was simply impossible to live off the land. The country between Tupelo and the Tennessee River was, in Bragg's own words, "entirely destitute of any supplies." The losses at Shiloh, where so many officers had been killed, had dealt a devastating blow to organizational structure. Making matters even worse, the elective feature of the conscript law led to the elevation of popular individuals with little military experience. Bragg vented his frustration at the promotion of unqualified general officers:

> Of all the major-generals, indeed, in this army now present, since the transfer of Van Dorn, Breckinridge and Hindman, but one (Hardee) can now be regarded as a suitable commander of that grade. Among the junior brigadiers we have some excellent material, but it is

---

[13] Grady McWhiney, *Braxton Bragg and Confederate Defeat*, 2 vols. (Tuscaloosa: University of Alabama Press, 1982) 1:258; Roman, *Beauregard*, 1:389–91.

[14] For the physician's report and complete diagnosis, see Roman, *Beauregard*, 1:403.

comparatively useless, being overshadowed. Could the Department by any wholesome exercise of power or policy relieve this army from a part of this dead-weight it would surely give confidence to the troops and add much to our efficiency.[15]

Finally, many of the Confederates including Cleburne had doubts as to Bragg's ability to command. Cleburne may well have harbored some resentment over Bragg's 7 April order to charge during the second day at Shiloh. At this point, Jefferson Davis faced a difficult decision. Despite the immediate threat Halleck posed, the security of eastern Tennessee simply could not be ignored. Union control of the region would have grave consequences. Railroad connections in Chattanooga served the war effort in Virginia as well as Tennessee, and the supply line to Robert E. Lee would be severed if it were to fall. Confederate arsenals in Atlanta, Macon, Augusta, and Columbus were within easy striking distance of a Federal thrust into Georgia. Bragg had accumulated supplies for 60,000 infantry and 6,000 cavalry in Dalton, just 23 miles to the south. Finally, there were significant deposits of copper, coal, and saltpeter in Georgia and Tennessee. The gravity of the situation was not lost on Richmond. On 21 July the Army of the Mississippi was moved to Chattanooga.[16]

Bragg began the evacuation that day, but Cleburne brought up the rear guard and did not depart until 26 July. His men boarded railroad cars bound for Chattanooga and headed south to Meridian, then on to Mobile. They detrained and marched through the city until they reached the Pearl River. Steamers ferried the troops across the water, where they boarded yet another train for a trip to Montgomery. They changed one more time and headed to Atlanta, then Chattanooga, arriving on 1 August.

The Department of East Tennessee was commanded by Edmund Kirby Smith. He had fought well at the first battle of Manassas and received his promotion on 11 October. Smith was a capable general, but he overestimated his own ability. He could lead but had difficulty cooperating with others. He viewed himself as a superb commander on the threshold of greatness, hampered by this present assignment that offered little excitement. While the

---

[15] OR, ser. 1, vol. 17, pt. 2, p. 628.
[16] Thomas L. Connelly, *Army of the Heartland: The Army of Tennessee, 1861–1862* (Baton Rouge: Louisiana State University Press, 1967) 190–91.

army was stationed in Tennessee, Kirby Smith considered more ambitious plans. He began to offer ideas for another campaign into Kentucky. There were numerous reasons to return. Within Bragg's own army many of the soldiers favored the move. It was assumed, perhaps too optimistically, that new recruits would flock to the Southern cause in large numbers.

Congressional leaders supported the idea as well. Like Missouri and Maryland, Kentucky was a border state. The Ohio River ran along the northern boundary for 500 miles before it emptied into the Mississippi. Possession by the South would offer access to both rivers and neutralize Union forces in Ohio, Indiana, and Illinois. The upper half of the Mississippi would be denied to southbound river traffic and a vital artery would be closed. However, the benefits of a Confederate Kentucky were not limited to the water. Railroad connections emanating from the Bluegrass State were extensive. The Louisville and Nashville line ran directly into the capital of Tennessee. Once in Nashville, connections on the Memphis and Charleston Railroad reached into Alabama at Decatur and Stevenson. From Columbus, the Mobile and Ohio ran through Jackson, Tennessee, and then on to Corinth for a junction with the Memphis and Charleston before continuing to Mobile. Finally, the Memphis, Clarksville, and Louisville road left Kentucky from Bowling Green and reached the Mississippi River at Memphis.

Northern occupation would open Tennessee to invasion, and Abraham Lincoln could not bear the thought of losing the state in which he was born. He emphasized the importance of retaining Kentucky in the following words: "I think to lose Kentucky is nearly the same as to lose the whole game. Kentucky gone, we cannot hold Missouri, nor, as I think, Maryland."[17]

Geographically, Bragg had few options. With the evacuation of Corinth, its railroad connection had been lost and the construction of new lines to Meridian and Selma had not been completed. The area north of Tupelo was very barren and the creeks were dry. It had become necessary to move into a more moderate climate. From a political standpoint, a move to the east would clearly illustrate the strategy that had been adopted by the South. They would simply establish a defensive position and await an opportunity for a counterattack.[18]

---

[17] David E. Roth, "The General's Tour: The Battle of Perryville," *Blue and Gray* 1/2 (October/November 1983): 23.

[18] Connelly, *Army of the Heartland*, 198.

Smith appreciated the advantages of a northern invasion but he also felt that the time was right to begin the advance. The mountainous terrain around Chattanooga made communication and transportation extremely difficult along a thinly held front 180 miles long. This part of Tennessee was strongly Unionist and many of his troops were twelve-month men who were merely waiting to go home. They had been soundly defeated earlier in the year at Mill Springs. Smith envisioned a magnificent victory to reverse their fortunes. Any delay would allow the Federals time to assemble a large force between the Confederate armies and the Ohio River. If the South moved quickly, the state might be taken. Jefferson Davis agreed.

After continued persuasion, Bragg decided to cooperate. Smith had only a small force of 9,000 men in Knoxville, which was clearly insufficient for any offensive operations. In order to strengthen it Bragg dispatched two brigades, one under Cleburne and the other under Colonel Preston Smith. They were formed into a division to be commanded by Cleburne. Kirby Smith would move north into Kentucky via Barboursville, near the Cumberland Gap. It was a small town 29 miles north of the pass, but it had been a supply depot for the Union Army. Smith's plan was to hold the Federals in the Cumberland Gap with one division under Carter Stevenson. Thomas Churchill and Pat Cleburne would march northeast up Powell's Valley through Rogers' Gap and into Barboursville. The fourth division, led by Henry Heth, would cross the Cumberland Mountains at Big Creek Gap and follow the roads into the town. Once they were united the Confederates would move in the direction of Lexington. Approximately 100 miles to the west, Bragg would advance from Chattanooga to Louisville.

Cleburne's command boarded trains and arrived in Knoxville on 6 August. In addition to infantry and artillery, the Confederates had 900 cavalry under John Scott. Five days later Cleburne was ordered to move his brigade forward to the Clinton Road and occupy the position just vacated by Thomas Churchill's division. At dawn on 14 August they began their march toward Cumberland Gap. The hills were so steep that the infantry pulled the wagons over the rocky slopes by hand. Nevertheless, spirits were high as the army was advancing.[19] Two days later the Confederates embarked on an arduous march. They crossed at Rogers' Gap and arrived at Barboursville on 18 August,

---

[19] Symonds, *Stonewall of the West*, 87; Purdue and Purdue, *Pat Cleburne Confederate General*, 134.

having covered 60 miles in fifty hours. Three hundred ardent Unionists were stunned at the capture of "some fifty prisoners, a train of near fifty wagons, and a few stores."[20]

In addition to large quantities of bacon, coffee, corn, and beef, they found every type of military equipment. Tents, coats, axes, saws, and arms were there for the taking, all of which were in short supply.[21] They had not received any aid from the local citizens, the commissary was essentially empty, and the men were living on a diet of apples, green corn, and biscuits.[22] For the famished Confederates, the prize was a gold mine.

Progress was not as rapid for Heth. He had been forced to move over badly broken ground on his way through Big Creek Gap, and his heavy artillery proved to be a serious encumbrance. Mules were ineffective, so the men had to resort to ropes to bring the cannon forward. Teams of twenty to thirty men were detailed to complete the work, but the division did not arrive in Barboursville until 22 August.[23]

John Scott's cavalry skirmished throughout the week with Federal troopers, but Smith preferred to withhold his infantry until Heth had arrived and each division was ready. During the morning of 27 August Cleburne led the march out of Barboursville. Late in the afternoon a halt was ordered and the troops went into bivouac, having made 15 miles that day. With an early start in the morning they were able to reach the Rockcastle River by noon. Churchill took a position by the river, with Cleburne a bit further ahead. Kirby Smith received a message from Scott that there were Federals in the area advancing in force, so at 3:00 A.M. on 29 August, Cleburne was ordered to move forward to support the cavalry.

His brigade formed the vanguard of the Confederate advance. They marched along the Richmond Road to a point where the road leaves a gap in the hills, about 5 miles from the foot of Big Hill. It was 625 feet high and divided the rocky, barren ground in the southern portions of the state from

---

[20] OR, ser. 1, vol. 16, pt. 2, p. 777.

[21] Kenneth Noe, *Perryville: This Grand Havoc of Battle* (Lexington: University Press of Kentucky, 2001) 37.

[22] "Diary of J. G. Law," in *Southern Historical Society Papers*, 52 vols. (Millwood NY: Kraus Reprint Co., 1977) 12:391–94.

[23] Paul F. Hammond, "General Kirby Smith's Campaign in Kentucky in 1862," in *Southern Historical Society Papers*, 52 vols. (Millwood NY: Kraus Reprint Co., 1977) 9:247–49.

the lower, rolling topography to the north.[24] A stream ran around the base of the hill and the men were told to fill their canteens. It promised to be a strenuous march and some of the men did not have enough water for half a day. From the other side of Big Hill the Richmond Road ran northwest for 8 miles to the village of Kingston, then after another 8-mile journey it entered Richmond itself.

The Confederates made their camp that night on the north side of the mountain. The contrast between northern portions of Kentucky and the ground they had just covered was a striking one. The broken road became a macadamized turnpike that required very little effort. Captain Frank Ryan of the Arkansas First Mounted Rifles recorded his observations:

> Then the beautiful and luxuriant blue-grass meadows which extended on each side as far as the eye could reach, with here and there a fine grove of large forest trees, with no undergrowth, and occasionally we would pass one of those old ante-bellum Kentucky houses, a fine two-story mansion set back from the turnpike probably half a mile, with an avenue leading up from the pike, bordered on both sides with majestic forest trees, whose branches overlapped, obscuring the rays of the midday sun. In one of the meadows could be seen a herd of fine Jersey cattle; feeding just a little way off was a flock of Southdown sheep, whose broad backs indicated that they were full ready for market. Everything indicated peace and plenty, and it seemed almost a crime to invade such ideal happiness with war's rude alarums.[25]

They reached the outskirts of Richmond on 29 August, and thus far they had met with little opposition. Around 5:00 P.M. Confederate cavalry encountered some Federals and were driven back. Although Cleburne received word from Scott that the enemy was not advancing, he remained uneasy. He alerted his officers to form a line of battle, although this was not completed until after dark. The battery under Captain James Douglas was thrown forward and placed on high ground to the left of the road, supported by two companies of sharpshooters from the 48th Tennessee. Almost immediately

---

[24] Frank T. Ryan, "The Kentucky Campaign and the Battle of Richmond," *Confederate Veteran* 26/4 (April 1918): 158–59.

[25] Ryan, "The Kentucky Campaign," 159.

part of Scott's cavalry came galloping back down the road accompanied by stragglers, wounded men, and baggage wagons, all fleeing in disarray. Federal troopers under Leonidas Metcalfe were close behind. The Tennesseans waited until the Yankees were within twenty-five paces and then unleashed a tremendous volley that stopped the horsemen in their tracks. They dismounted to regroup but quickly resumed their advance. The night was pitch dark and Cleburne could barely see his own troops. The Federals had no better visibility but continued to fire at Cleburne's campfires, some 300 yards behind his lines. He sent the sharpshooters forward and their fire caused the enemy to retreat. Cleburne reported only one man wounded but the Federals lost 30 prisoners, 100 stand of arms, and several horses. Although his brigade had won a momentary victory, the danger was not over. Cleburne's men slept on their weapons, in line, and without supper.[26]

Smith's command had marched 100 miles through barren country. In a 29 August letter to his wife, he described the hardships his men had endured: "I am with my advance in the bluegrass region.... We have marched over 100 miles through a mountain region over almost impassable roads, through a country destitute of supplies of all kinds—ragged bare foot almost starved marching day and night, exhausted from want of water. I have never seen such suffering.... Such fortitude, patriotism and self control has never been surpassed by any army that ever existed."[27]

It would be impossible for the men to live off the land, and forage was scarce as well. Retreat was not an option, so the army would have to continue.[28] On the night of 29 August, Kirby Smith gave orders to Cleburne to move out at first light. The morning was clear and bright and Cleburne was on the march by daybreak. Confederate cavalry soon located the enemy at Mount Zion Church near the village of Rogersville. The 6,500 Yankees in their front were under the command of Mahlon Manson, a career politician.[29]

[26] Report of Patrick R. Cleburne, 1 September 1862, OR, ser. 1, vol. 16, pt. 1, p. 944.

[27] Edmund Kirby Smith to wife, 29 August 1862, quoted in Joseph H. Parks, *General Edmund Kirby Smith, C.S.A.* (Baton Rouge: Louisiana State University Press, 1954) 212.

[28] Hammond, "Smith's Campaign," 249; Joseph H. Parks, *General Edmund Kirby Smith, C.S.A.* (Baton Rouge: Louisiana State University Press, 1954) 212; Basil Duke, *Reminiscences of General Basil W. Duke* (Garden City NJ: Doubleday, Page & Co., 1911) 315–16.

[29] OR, ser. 1, vol. 16, pt. 1, p. 910–16. According to Manson, the Union troops did not exceed 6,500, and of these there were never more than 3,500 engaged at one time.

Cleburne led the advance with Churchill close behind. The Federals had taken a position covering both sides of the Richmond Turnpike. At 7:00 A.M. Cleburne placed Hill on the right of the pike behind the crest of a low rise that ran parallel to and 500 yards in front of the Union lines. The 2nd Tennessee held the left of his brigade with the 48th Tennessee on their right, followed by Polk's 13th and 15th Arkansas. The 5th Tennessee took a position in support behind the 48th, and the front line, located on higher ground in the center of the formation, was completed by an artillery battery under James Douglas. Preston Smith's men formed a second line one-quarter of a mile behind Hill. While these dispositions were made with ease, the Confederates did receive some annoying fire from a small howitzer that had been captured from Scott the day before.

Cleburne sent out the Buckner Guards, a company of cavalry under Scott's command. He wanted to know both the strength and position of the Federals in his front. Half a mile north of Kingston they discovered the lead Federals, 500 to 600 yards in front of the main line. He could see one regiment to the right of the road, with another extending all the way to the woods on the other side of it.

A small group of Federal horsemen appeared on the pike and Cleburne ordered Douglas to open his artillery. The troopers scattered under the bombardment and revealed a Union battery. Cleburne sent one company of skirmishers across the turnpike to extend his left, which secured the flank for the remainder of the day. Shortly before 9:00 A.M. he sent a courier back to Preston Smith, instructing him to send another battery to the front. J. M. Martin promptly arrived and he was placed on a hill near the Confederate right. The guns began to fire, but before a full-scale attack could get under way Cleburne received a message from Kirby Smith not to bring on an engagement before Churchill arrived. The artillery fire slackened and a duel ensued for about two hours. Casualties were light, with the Confederates losing two men killed and eight wounded.[30] The waste of ammunition with no apparent purpose left Manson frustrated. Eager to attack, he decided on a flanking movement that would encircle Cleburne's right.

From the very beginning Kirby Smith had realized that his force was too small to attempt a frontal assault, so he ordered Churchill to turn the Union right. The Federals acted in mirror image and tried to outflank Cleburne.

---

[30] OR, ser. 1, vol. 16, pt. 1, p. 950.

Manson moved his troops forward and drove the skirmishers back, but Cleburne responded. He transferred the 154th Tennessee from Preston Smith's brigade and brought it up to stabilize the line. The action was intense for another two hours, and when Smith needed reinforcements Cleburne brought up the consolidated 13th and 15th under Lucius Polk. Cleburne was certain that Churchill would arrive on the left at any moment, so he ordered Smith to send up his remaining three regiments and extend the right even further. It was imperative to hold his own flank, but if he overlapped the enemy and the opportunity to attack arose, he was given the authorization to do so.[31]

Cleburne realized that with the Federals massing to attack his right they had weakened their center. He decided to wait until he heard the sounds of Smith's artillery and then bring Benjamin Hill's 5th Tennessee up to strike the middle of the Union formation.[32] Cleburne rode to the right in order to observe Smith's attack and found the Confederates moving in good order. Since the Union attempt had been stopped, Cleburne headed back to Hill. He had just begun to return when he saw Polk being carried from the field with a serious wound to the head. Polk tried to speak and when Cleburne began to reply he was struck in the mouth by a minie ball. It entered his mouth and passed through the left cheek, taking out five lower teeth. While the bullet did no significant damage to the rest of his mouth, he was unable to speak. He sent aides to Hill and Preston Smith informing them of his condition, and Smith received temporary command of the division. Cleburne was taken from the field, but he remained just long enough to witness Hill's successful attack.[33]

The Federals were overwhelmed. Brigadier General Charles Cruft wrote that "it was...impossible, with the troops composing our lines, to stand against the impetuosity of [the enemy] charge." Most of the Confederate

---

[31] OR, ser. 1, vol. 16, pt. 1, p. 947. The regiments referred to are the 12th, 13th, and 47th Tennessee.

[32] Report of Patrick R. Cleburne, 1 September 1862, OR, ser. 1, vol. 16, pt. 1, p. 946.

[33] William J. Hardee, "Biographical Sketch of Major-General Patrick R. Cleburne," in *Southern Historical Society Papers*, 52 vols. (Millwood NY: Kraus Reprint Co., 1977) 31:153.

casualties fell upon the 2nd and 48th Tennessee, which lost 140 and 128 men, respectively.[34]

Churchill's initial thrust forced Manson to fall back 2 miles, where the Federals regrouped at White's Farm. Despite the success, Kirby Smith was not satisfied and once again ordered Churchill to turn the Federal right. Holding one brigade in reserve, he would pin down the flank while Preston Smith advanced in support. The Confederates moved forward at 1:00 P.M., but before Smith could arrive the Federals made a furious counterattack. The Butternuts held their ground and the charge was handily repulsed. Although they were unsupported, T. H. McCray's brigade surged through a cornfield and poured a concentrated fire into the enemy flank.[35] The Confederates quickly overran the position at White's Farm and continued to advance through the empty camps. There they learned that William "Bull" Nelson had arrived with reinforcements, increasing the Federal total to 10,000 men. Nelson superseded Manson and the third phase of the battle for Richmond was fought under his direction.

As Churchill advanced on the left side of the turnpike, Benjamin Hill advanced over open ground. They received artillery fire but the shells did little damage and the lines remained intact. Hill detailed companies of sharpshooters to each side in order to pick off enemy gunners and horses. Churchill had been able to turn the flank and the Federals began to give way. The 48th Tennessee charged forward and captured 165 prisoners, all armed with new Springfield rifles. At 3:00 P.M. a halt was ordered and the lines were restored. Skirmishers were thrown forward 400 yards, driving the Federal marksmen from the field. The Confederates continued to approach Richmond, but the Yankees had taken cover in a cornfield behind haystacks and rail fences. They had changed to grape and canister, but Southern casualties were light.

Despite a numerical advantage at White's Farm, the Federals were forced back again. They retreated after a fight of only thirty minutes and occupied a ridge on the south side of Richmond. Their right was secured by dense woods on the west side of the Lexington Road; their left was anchored behind a stone wall in the Richmond cemetery. At 5:00 P.M. the Rebels attacked again and for

---

[34] Robert M. Frierson, "Gen. E. Kirby Smith's Campaign in Kentucky," *Confederate Veteran* 1/9 (September 1893): 295.

[35] Report of Thomas Churchill, 8 September 1862, OR, ser. 1, vol. 16, pt. 1, 940.

the third time Churchill went after the Union right. Preston Smith supported the advance in perfect order and the Confederates moved through another field, but once beyond it a gentle slope rose up to the cemetery. Hill's regiment cleared a rise in the ground when the Federals unleashed a blast at close range that inflicted heavy casualties, particularly among the 2nd and 48th Tennessee.[36] The fight was hard but brief, and within fifteen minutes the Federals were forced to abandon the town.[37]

Once again, the 2nd and 48th took the majority of the losses. In total, the brigade had 27 men killed and 194 wounded in the final assault, for 221 casualties.[38] The Confederates had fought all day long with no water, continuing to press their advantage at a furious pace. The enemy had been routed, but the men had no energy left to give. With fading light the pursuit was limited to only a mile before the Rebels fell back to their camps. The Federals saw 206 men killed and 844 wounded, but also lost 4,144 soldiers to capture. In addition, Nelson had been wounded in the thigh and Manson was taken prisoner. Against Union casualties of 5,194, Kirby Smith had 78 killed, 372 wounded, and 1 missing, for a total of 451.[39]

While the Southern loss had been comparatively small, Colonel Edward Fitzgerald of the 154th Tennessee and Lieutenant-Colonel John A. Butler of the 2nd Tennessee lost their lives while leading their regiments into action. As George Nixon guided his Tennesseans up the slope to the cemetery he was hit in the left breast by grapeshot, smashing his watch. His life was saved by the

---

[36] OR, ser. 1, vol. 16, pt. 1, p. 949–51.

[37] Hammond, "Smith's Campaign," 253; Joseph Wheeler, "Bragg's Invasion of Kentucky," in Robert Underwood Johnston and Clarence Clough Buel, eds., *Battles and Leaders of the Civil War,* 4 vols. (1884–1887; repr., Secaucus NJ: Castle Books, n.d.) 3:5 says the fight lasted "fifteen minutes"; Smith's battle report, OR, ser. 1, vol. 16, pt. 1, p. 934 also says fifteen minutes.

[38] Report of Benjamin J. Hill, 15 September 1862, OR, ser. 1, vol. 16, pt. 1, p. 949–51. Hill breaks down the losses as follows: 13th Arkansas: 3 killed, 19 wounded, total casualties 22; 15th Arkansas: 2 killed, 15 wounded, total casualties 17; 2nd Tennessee: 15 killed, 94 wounded, total casualties 109; 5th Tennessee: 2 killed, 12 wounded, total casualties 14; and 48th Tennessee: 5 killed, 54 wounded, total casualties 59,. for a combined loss of 221 men.

[39] Don Carlos Seitz, *Braxton Bragg General of the Confederacy* (New York: The State Company, 1924) 168.

bible he kept in his pocket.[40] Finally, Benjamin Hill had been wounded three times and both Lucius Polk and Pat Cleburne were forced to leave the field.

After being wounded at Richmond, Cleburne was taken to a local farmhouse for convalescence. While not life-threatening, the injury had caused considerable swelling and bleeding. He felt it would be wise to record his thoughts when the events were fresh in his mind, so he spent a great deal of his time composing battle reports. Thus far the campaign through Kentucky had been a difficult one. After the battle was over Kirby Smith gave his men some much-needed rest and replenished their supplies of food and ammunition. Much of their clothing was badly torn but some of the infantry had captured new pants and coats, ironically made of blue wool.[41]

During his recovery some of Cleburne's troops were sent to Frankfort to protect the state capital. The remainder were distributed throughout Georgetown, Paris, Cynthiana, Williamsburg, and Crittenden, all under Heth. Further west, Braxton Bragg was moving forward with relative ease. He arrived in Glasgow on 14 September and two days later captured the village of Munfordville. While this did force Buell to evacuate Bowling Green, neither place had the importance of Louisville, Bragg's original target. After decisive victories at Munfordville and Richmond he turned cautious, and the race through Kentucky for possession of Louisville turned into a static occupation of small towns with little military value.

From Glasgow Bragg ordered the return of the brigades he had loaned to Kirby Smith. Pat Cleburne and Preston Smith were sent to Shelbyville, approximately 28 miles east of Louisville. Cleburne's condition had substantially improved and on 25 September he rejoined his command. Physically he was sound, but a visual transformation had taken place. He had been unable to shave, and a short beard covered the scar on his cheek. He was told to hold the town but if pressed was to fall back to Frankfort. Other troops were dispatched to Shepardsville, Mount Washington, and Taylorsville. By dispersing his forces Bragg had squandered the advantages gained at Richmond. A stagnant foe gave Don Carlos Buell badly needed time to regroup and he seized the opportunity. The initiative was his.

---

[40] Frierson, "Gen. E. Kirby Smith's Campaign," 295.

[41] Current research has failed to uncover the name of the farmer who cared for Cleburne.

The position in Shelbyville was a tenuous one. Bragg's decision to defend several points at once weakened the strength of each one, and Cleburne's brigade numbered barely 1,000 men. The Yankees had the availability of the rail network to the north, whereas Cleburne was limited to the roads in his vicinity. Supplies had run low again and the men were forced to live off the land. Finally, the entire brigade had not been paid for over nine months.[42] On 29 September pickets reported railroad traffic just north of Shelbyville. Cleburne concluded that the Federals were massing for an attack, and on 2 October he sent a note to Polk. As of 10:00 P.M. the previous night, the Federals had been only 5 miles away. Cleburne could not be specific but did state that the enemy was "moving in force" and that one of the divisions was led by Lovell Rousseau.[43] He explained that in accordance with his earlier instructions he was falling back to Frankfort.

Cleburne was under pressure, but Polk was having trouble as well. Two Federal forces had started out from Louisville. On 2 October Polk learned that in addition to the one advancing on Frankfort, another strong force was moving on Bardstown. Polk decided to fall back to Harrodsburg in the general direction of Bryantsville and Camp Dick Robinson, two Confederate supply bases.

At this point Bragg made a serious mistake. He believed that the Army of Ohio was moving east from Louisville in order to get between Smith in Frankfort and Polk at Bardstown. On 2 October at 1:00 P.M. he ordered Polk to march via Bloomfield to Frankfort. This movement would allow Polk to strike the Federals in their right flank, somewhere between Taylorsville and Lawrenceburg. At the same time, Bragg told Polk that Smith would attack the Federals in their front. Polk did not receive the order until the next day, and at 3:00 P.M. he responded:

> General: I am in receipt of your note of the 2nd, 1 p.m., directing me to move with all my available force via Bloomfield and Frankfort to strike the enemy on the flank and rear. The last twenty-four hours have developed a condition of things on my front and left flank, which I shadowed forth in my last note to you, which make compliance with this order not only eminently inexpedient but

---

[42] Symonds, *Stonewall of the West*, 93.
[43] Leonidas Polk to Bragg, 2 October 1862, OR, ser. 1, vol. 16 pt. 2, p. 898.

impractical. I have called a council of wing and division-commanders to whom I have submitted the matter, and find that they unanimously indorse [sic] my views. I shall, therefore, pursue a different course, assured that when the facts are submitted to you, you will justify my decision. I move on the route indicated by you toward Camp Breckinridge. The head of my column moves this afternoon. I will keep you advised. I send this by a relay of couriers I have established at intervals of ten miles from here to Lexington via Danville.[44]

Once again the location and movement of the Army of Ohio had eluded Braxton Bragg. The Federals were not marching east but rather south. Their right flank was actually west of the road to Bardstown, their left toward the Shelbyville Pike. The proper instructions would have sent Polk against the Union front, while Smith hit their left. This alignment would have placed Cleburne in the middle of a flank attack, which could have had serious consequences for the Union. Whether Polk's objections were genuine or not is immaterial, but the message did reach Bragg in time for him to cancel Smith's offensive.[45]

On 4 October Kirby Smith moved his army in the direction of Harrodsburg as well. South of the capital the Confederates were starting to come together. Cleburne received orders to unite with Polk; this brought him back under Hardee as a brigadier in the division led by Simon Bolivar Buckner. Cleburne went by way of Lawrenceburg and Salvisa and reached Harrodsburg on 5 October. There the division formerly under Cleburne was divided: Preston Smith was sent to Frank Cheatham and Cleburne received command of his old brigade.[46]

Two nights later Polk ordered Cleburne's brigade, along with Patton Anderson's division and a detachment of cavalry, back to Perryville to support Hardee. He was not particularly concerned with the Federal force in Hardee's front, writing to Bragg, "I cannot think it large."[47]

---

[44] C. C. Gilbert, "Bragg's Invasion of Kentucky," *Southern Bivouac* (November 1885): 340.

[45] Gilbert, "Bragg's Invasion of Kentucky," 340; Kenneth A. Hafendorfer, *Perryville* (Louisville KY: KH Press, 1991) 98.

[46] Purdue and Purdue, *Pat Cleburne Confederate General,* 145.

[47] OR, ser. 1, vol. 16, pt. 1, p. 1095.

The principal target of Buell's advance was still somewhat uncertain. Bragg had managed to concentrate Polk's troops around Harrodsburg and Hardee was only 9 miles to the southwest in Perryville, but Kirby Smith was still badly dispersed. Some of his men were 12 miles southeast of Frankfort at Versailles and the remainder was strung out between Versailles and Harrodsburg. For his part, Bragg believed that most of the action would take place in Smith's front.[48] On 7 October Bragg still thought the big battle would be at Versailles. He dispatched his largest division, 11,000 men, under Carter Stevenson.[49]

Bragg had seemingly discovered the Federal intent, though as the day wore on he became more confused. He had always believed that Polk and Hardee faced only minor opposition, but during the day he received two alarming messages. The first came from Joe Wheeler, commander of the Confederate cavalry. It was sent to Hardee, then forwarded to Polk, and then on to Bragg. The second, sent at 3:20 P.M., came from Hardee himself. Both reports indicated that a sizeable force was approaching Perryville, and the attack would apparently occur in Hardee's sector. Unfortunately, the language was somewhat ambiguous. Hardee explained that Wheeler had already engaged Federal cavalry: "There is a sharp cannonade in front between Wheeler's force & the enemy. He is advancing this evening to gain position. Tomorrow may expect a fight, if the enemy does not attack us, you ought to unless pressed in another direction send forward all the reinforcements necessary, take command in person, and wipe him out. I desire earnestly that you will do this."[50]

The message was one of urgency, yet it contained no specifics. Hardee did not elaborate on the size of the columns in front of him or their precise location. Bragg directed Polk and Hardee to deal quickly with the Union troops at Perryville, then march north to oppose what Bragg assumed was the larger body. Although Bragg believed that Versailles was the target, he was concerned about Hardee's position. At 5:40 P.M. he wrote the following note to Polk: "You had better move with Cheatham's Division to his support, and

---

[48] Luke W. Finley, "The Battle of Perryville," in *Southern Historical Society Papers*, 52 vols. (Millwood NY: Kraus Reprint Co., 1977) 30:238–50.

[49] Connelly, *Army of the Heartland*, 254, 257.

[50] William J. Hardee to Braxton Bragg, 7 October 1862, Braxton Bragg Papers, Western Reserve Historical Society, Cleveland OH, from microfilm edition at University of West Florida, Pensacola FL.

give the enemy battle immediately; rout him, and then move to our support at Versailles."[51]

The countryside around Perryville was marked by rolling hills and small farmhouses. Chaplin's Fork of the Salt River flowed north through the town. West of Chaplin's Fork was Doctor's Creek, a smaller stream that emptied into Chaplin's Fork northwest of Perryville. It was only a little tributary, but it would prove to be very important. The creek ran in a northeasterly direction but about 1 mile from Perryville it turned due north for half a mile. The east bank was a gentle slope, but across the water a high ridge rose 80 feet above the creek bed. In the center of the ridge was a gap, broken only by the Mackville Turnpike. General Hardee noted that the key point in the battle was the intersection of the pike and the creek, roughly 1 1/2 miles west of Perryville.[52]

Cleburne received orders from Polk to have his men move out at 4:00 A.M. on 7 October with two days' cooked rations in their haversacks. The brigade reached Perryville that night and the next day a courier arrived at Cleburne's headquarters with orders to form up "in line of battle east of the Harrodsburg and Perryville road." Cleburne was to cross a small creek and "support the brigade of Brigadier General [Bushrod] Johnson" in its attack.[53]

The general direction of Hardee's line was north to south with the left near the town, west of Chaplin's Fork. The right extended down the stream. Bragg advanced this line around noon, with Buckner's division holding the center. Frank Cheatham was on his right, Patton Anderson's division to his left. Buckner led three brigades and placed them one behind the other. Bushrod Johnson's men formed the first line followed by Cleburne, with St. John Liddell in the rear. Cleburne's brigade was posted on high ground overlooking the creek bottom.[54] The Federal forces held a dominant position along the crest of a ridge, refusing their left in order to prevent a flanking movement from Cheatham. Cleburne placed the middle of his brigade behind a stone fence at the apex of this angle.

---

[51] OR, ser. 1, vol. 16, pt. 1, p. 1096.

[52] Report of William J. Hardee, 1 December 1862, OR, ser. 1, vol. 16, pt. 1, p. 1119.

[53] Report of Patrick R. Cleburne, October 1862, OR, ser. 1, vol. 52, pt. 1, p. 51.

[54] Kenneth Hafendorfer, ed., "The Kentucky Campaign Revisited: Major-General Simon B. Buckner's Unpublished After-Action Report on the Battle of Perryville," *Civil War Regiments: A Journal of the American Civil War* 4/3 (1995): 57.

Across the road in Cleburne's front was the property of Henry Bottom. Bottom owned 800 acres of land, which was roughly this entire section of the battlefield. He was a wealthy farmer, cabinet maker, and local justice of the peace. Despite his prominence in the community, his house was relatively modest. It stood on the south side of the Mackville Turnpike just west of the intersection of the road and the creek, with a barn farther up the pike. Sentiments were sharply divided in Kentucky, and Bottom was an ardent secessionist as well as a slave owner. This area would be the center of Cleburne's attack.

Three quarters of a mile west of the ridge and south of the road was a two-story white home that provided an excellent view of the surrounding land. It belonged to John Russell, also a prosperous farmer but a strong Union man. The house overlooked a valley with woods to the left and front and open ground to the right. In subsequent battle reports the dwelling would come to be known simply as the "white house."

Bushrod Johnson advanced shortly after 2:00 P.M., with Cleburne in support and Liddell in reserve. Cleburne moved his troops along the Mackville Pike northwest of town and arrived above the nearly dry creek around 2:30. Opposing him was William Lytle's brigade of Rousseau's division. Lytle had five regiments at his disposal—the 42nd and 88th Indiana, 3rd and 10th Ohio, and 15th Kentucky—as well as the First Battery of the Michigan Light Artillery under Captain Cyrus O. Loomis. Loomis commanded long-range Parrott guns and placed them in the front and to the left of John Russell's house.

The 42nd was given the role of skirmishers and they went forward down the hill. The fall of 1862 had seen a severe drought and water was in short supply. There were still a few scattered pools in the parched creek bed, so they stacked their arms and attempted to fill their canteens.[55]Although Lytle did not anticipate an immediate attack, he sent a section of artillery in support. Lytle's other regiments lined up along the pike as well. The 10th Ohio was behind the Hoosiers, also north of the pike with the 3rd Ohio across the road in front of the 15th Kentucky. The very green troops of the 88th Indiana fell in on the right of the 15th.

---

[55] David E. Roth, "The General's Tour: The Battle of Perryville," *Blue and Gray* 1/2 (October/November 1983): 21–39.

Buckner looked down the slope from his informal headquarters at the home of John Dye. The undulating ground ran down 150 yards to the property of R. F. Chatham, just north of the creek. The contour of the land could be problematic all by itself, but it got worse. Beyond the house a split rail fence ran north and south, bisecting Chatham's field. When they reached the creek the ground rose sharply and the west side of its bed was over 5 feet high in some places.[56] Once across the top his men would encounter a series of stone and rail fences. He surveyed the approaches and characterized the situation: "This was the key point on that part of the field…. It was a strong position, the enemy being well covered by a natural parapet caused by an accident of the ground and several stone fences. A battery of artillery occupied its right, and its front was protected by the fire of another of his batteries towards his right, which swept partially the ground in front of his position."[57]

In light of the terrain Buckner modified Bushrod Johnson's orders to attack. Instead of attacking due west, Johnson was ordered to shift his lines obliquely 20 degrees to his left. This would give the Confederates the advantage of the ground and offer some degree of protection from Federal artillery. Unfortunately not every regiment received the order, and as he advanced Johnson came under heavy fire. The two factors combined produced a great deal of confusion. On the far right of Johnson's brigade the 37th Tennessee continued to move straight ahead, but the 44th Tennessee executed the shift correctly, creating a huge gap between them. The 25th Tennessee was next in line but their troops broke apart as they crossed the fences in their front. Finally, the 5th Confederate was so disorganized that even though they held Johnson's left flank they moved to their right, actually arriving on the right of the 25th.[58]

Despite the problems on the Confederate side, the Federals were in trouble. The 42nd Indiana had drifted south and taken a forward position by the creek with no immediate support. Not only was Johnson moving quickly in their front, but the Louisiana brigade under Daniel Adams was approaching rapidly from the southeast. The 42nd was caught in an advance from Adams on their right and the 37th Tennessee on their left. Two Confederate batteries opened up from the south side of the turnpike and what

---

[56] Noe, *Perryville,* 173–74.

[57] Noe, *Perryville,* 219.

[58] Noe, *Perryville,* 219.

Lytle hoped would be an orderly retreat turned into a rout. Lytle moved them back up the hill as quickly as possible and placed them across the pike behind the 10th Ohio, where they were able to reform along some rail fences. Johnson continued to pursue and soon both regiments had opened fire on the Rebels.[59]

The stubborn resistance and strong defensive position brought Johnson's advance to a halt. Cleburne had maintained a supporting distance throughout the day, but at 4:00 P.M. he received orders to go to Johnson's aid. They came under fire as soon as they descended the slope, as Confederate artillery bombarded the Yankees and a shell exploded in Henry Bottom's barn. Stacked with hay, the barn burst into flames and thick smoke filled the air. Nevertheless, the attack continued. Cleburne was hit in the ankle and thrown to the ground. His horse was killed but he continued to lead the charge on foot. Captain W. E. Yeatman described his commander in a post-war address to Confederate veterans: "only a man such as Cleburne...could inspire me to go up against such odds, and win—and he did."[60]

When they finally reached the bottom of the creek bed, the contour of the land gave Cleburne's troops some measure of protection and the bullets began to pass harmlessly over their heads. Cleburne advanced in two lines with his Arkansans on the right side of the first line and the 2nd Tennessee on their left. The 48th and 5th Tennessee made up the second line. The Federals had settled on high ground but the 3rd Ohio began to run low on ammunition. They fell back again, leaving only the 15th Kentucky in Johnson's front. Roughly one-third of the regiment had been killed or wounded. The pressure increased as Adams sent John Austin's sharpshooters forward to enfilade the Federal right. Austin's attack succeeded, but in a limited fashion. Adams recognized that reinforcements from his brigade would place Lytle in the mouth of a trap, just waiting for the Confederates to snap it shut.

As Johnson continued to advance, Cleburne moved the 15th Arkansas to a hill on his right, perpendicular to both Johnson and to Lytle. They deployed behind a stone wall that lined the Mackville Turnpike, giving them a clear shot at the Federals without risking any meaningful response. Buckner then placed a section of the Washington Artillery on the Union right, leaving

---

[59] Noe, *Perryville*, 224–26.

[60] W. E. Yeatman, excerpt from address to Confederate veterans, Knoxville, Tennessee, quoted in the *Knoxville Sentinel*, n.d., in scrapbook, United Daughters of the Confederacy, Helena, Arkansas.

Lytle in a murderous crossfire.

Cleburne reached the creek bed and at 5:00 P.M. halted in order to confer with Johnson. The initial attack had ground to a halt at Bottom's house and Johnson was almost out of cartridges. He asked if it would be possible for Cleburne to take the lead while he replenished his supplies. The offer was readily accepted and the attack on Lytle's right flank continued. The 15th Kentucky held the ground to the south of the turnpike, with the 3rd Ohio in support. Along with Adams's brigade on his left, Cleburne surged forward.

The combination forced the Yankees to retreat again. Their movement allowed Cleburne to bring his Arkansans back to their original position on the right of his line. Lytle collected both regiments along with fragments of the 10th Ohio and 88th Indiana in an attempt to form in a ravine on the north side of the turnpike; however, when the Federals withdrew they surrendered their line of vision. They could no longer fire directly upon the Confederates but were forced to wait until they came into view above them. Cleburne sensed an opportunity. He sent forward flag bearers and skirmishers and placed his infantry ten paces behind them, just below the top of the ridge. When everything was ready he sent the men forward.

As they advanced up the hill they received fire not from the Federals in their front but from their own artillery behind them. In the distance the new pants made it look as though they were Union infantry. Cleburne ordered his brigade to fall back and immediately dispatched a courier with orders to stop the shelling. Once the problem was resolved the attack resumed. As soon as the flag bearers came into view the Federals fired one salvo and inflicted heavy casualties. However, the infantry was still concealed and they burst over the hill before the Yankees could reload their weapons. They halted and emptied their muskets at less than 100 yards. The line collapsed and the Rebel muskets continued to play upon them as they fled. Lytle tried to rally about 100 men, but they were quickly routed as well.[61]

Thus far the battle had been a one-sided affair, but on the Union left the 10th Ohio made a brief stand. From that location to the burning barn the casualties bore witness to the slaughter. The victory in this area of the field was

---

[61] W. E. Preston, "Memories of the War," *Confederate Reminiscences and Letters, 1861–1865,* 22 vols. (Atlanta: Georgia Division of the United Daughters of the Confederacy, 1995) 14:143–45; report of Patrick R. Cleburne, October 1862, OR, ser. 1, vol. 52, pt. 1, p. 52.

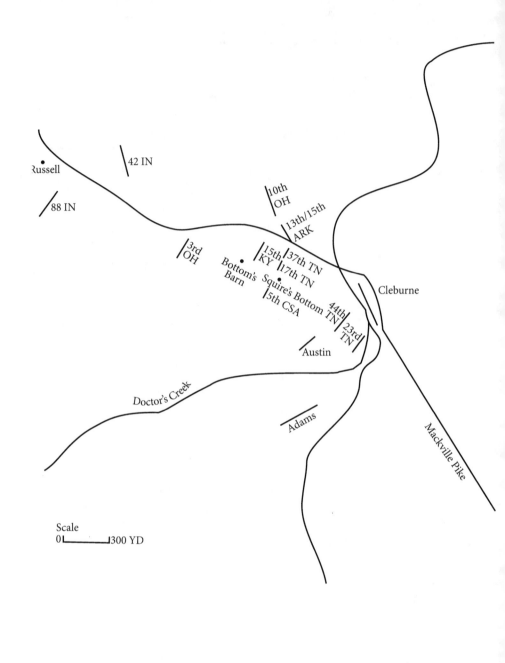

Russell

42 IN

88 IN

10th
OH

13th/15th
ARK

3rd
OH

37th TN

15th
KY

17th TN

Bottom's
Barn

Squire's Bottom TN

5th CSA

44th
TN

23rd
TN

Cleburne

Austin

Doctor's Creek

Adams

Mackville Pike

Scale
0 ⌐————⌐ 300 YD

so complete that a sharpshooter in the 14th Louisiana battalion wrote: "The dead lay in two straight lines as they had fallen.... I could have walked on their bodies without touching the ground several hundred yards. Scarcely a man could be seen out of his place in line."[62]

As Lytle fell back once more he was wounded in the head and captured by Austin's sharpshooters. He was certain he would die, but instead he was taken to the rear and treated by Confederate surgeons. He survived the action at Perryville only to delay his fate until the battle of Chickamauga.

Randall Gibson's 13th Louisiana advanced to the ridge south of the road to the spot where the 15th Kentucky had been. Only the reformed 42nd Indiana and the inexperienced 88th Indiana stood between Cleburne and the Russell house. These clearly were not Lovell Rousseau's best troops, but he had to make a decision. The 88th was the fresher of the two, and they deployed in front of Cleburne roughly 100 yards from the house. The 42nd changed front and deployed perpendicular to George Humphrey's 88th, facing Gibson. There they lay down behind some fences and awaited the attack.

In contrast to the rest of Cleburne and Adams, the 13th Louisiana presented quite a spectacle. They were a curious mixture of men, Aregno Zouaves, Irish, Dutch, Spaniards, and Mexicans. Bright reds, blues, and gold hardly resembled the tattered "butternut" clothing of their fellow Southerners. One soldier from the 42nd described the scene in the *Daily Evansville Journal*:

> They advanced in heavy lines toward our position. Their appearance, as regiment after regiment, and mass after mass, came forth from beneath the woods, and advanced down the slopes of the hills, was imposing in the extreme. Distance concealed the rags composing their uniforms; the bright sunbeams glancing from their bayonets flashed the lightning over the field, and the blue flag with the single star waved all along their lines, as proudly as though it were not the emblem of treason, slavery and death.... However one might hate these traitors, he could not help admire this conspicuous and daring valor.[63]

---

[62] Noe, *Perryville*, 269.

[63] Noe, *Perryville*, 270; Larry J. Daniel, *Shiloh* (New York: Simon & Schuster, 1997) 93.

James Jones's 42nd took heavy casualties but in a desperate move countercharged and momentarily stopped Gibson. As the 13th fell back Cleburne advanced, but this movement temporarily exposed his left. He selected twenty sharpshooters equipped with Kerr rifles and sent them under Charles Carlton of the 15th Arkansas to secure his flank. With this accomplished he turned his attention back to the 42nd and tore into the Hoosiers. In addition to their other obstacles, the Federals saw their ammunition disappearing; they quickly retreated, taking more casualties as they ran.

Once they had reached the house, parts of all five regiments formed on Loomis's battery. Sensing disaster, Alexander McCook galloped onto the field and attempted to reorganize Lytle's broken command. He could see Cleburne and Adams rolling up his lines, so he ordered Loomis to wait until the Confederates were closer. Satisfied for the moment, he headed back to the Union left. Shortly thereafter Rousseau arrived and ordered Loomis to open fire but Loomis refused, abiding by McCook's earlier instructions. Rousseau replied that Cleburne was close enough and repeated the order.

Loomis fired a blast at point-blank range. Different units became separated, making it necessary for Cleburne to halt and reform his lines. The left was now on the Mackville Road and perpendicular to it.[64] When each side established their position an artillery exchange broke out. The Confederates advanced to the right side of the road, where they placed their guns on high ground, while the Union artillery replied from the Russell house.[65]

Cleburne was hit again, this time in the body, but he refused to leave the field. As he pressed the attack across the pike the Federals continued to retreat until they found support in a second line near the white house. Cleburne advanced through a cornfield to within 75 yards of the enemy, but he had outdistanced both flanks and came under enfilading fire. By this point his brigade had been reduced to no more than 800 men. Though his men were almost out of cartridges, they were able to hold their position until darkness covered the field and Liddell could move forward to fill the gap between Cleburne and Cheatham.

---

[64] Report of Patrick R. Cleburne, October 1862, OR, ser. 1, vol. 52, pt 1, p. 52; Buck, *Cleburne and His Command,* 114.

[65] Noe, *Perryville,* 276.

The Federals had completely abandoned this section of the field. Lytle's brigade had suffered severely, though the 88th Indiana escaped relatively intact. Perhaps their inexperience made Lytle reluctant to use them on his front line, but they lost only twenty-two men. Combined, the Federals suffered 193 men killed, 606 wounded, and 23 missing, for a total of 822.[66] Cleburne collected his wounded and 375 stand of small arms before he fell back along the Harrodsburg Road.[67] Around midnight Buckner's division returned to their original position beyond Chaplin's Fork.

Braxton Bragg had always thought that the threat to Perryville was posed by the weaker of the Union armies, but by that evening it was clear that Perryville was the principal target, not Frankfort or Versailles. The Confederates had followed their victory at Richmond with stunning success at Perryville. On the right side of the field Cheatham had driven the enemy back over a mile, and the South controlled Buckner's left as well. The Rebels were confident that they would renew the attack in the morning, but during the night more Federal troops arrived on the Confederate left.

Bragg was now facing 61,000 men with Don Carlos Buell in command. Deciding that it would not be wise to give battle in the face of such overwhelming odds, he issued orders that night for an immediate retreat and the Confederates withdrew into Perryville. Bragg wanted to fall back and concentrate at Harrodsburg. At dawn they began to head east.[68]

The Graycoats reached the town around noon. They soon began their retreat to the supply bases at Bryantsville and Camp Dick Robinson, near the confluence of the Kentucky and Dick Rivers 18 miles east of Perryville. There, on 11 October, Bragg united his command with Kirby Smith. The armies had finally come together but the lack of provisions, their inferior numbers, and the onset of winter led Bragg to advocate a withdrawal from Kentucky altogether. He had little choice. There was no longer any hope of reinforcements, as Sterling Price and Earl Van Dorn had just suffered defeat at the battle of Corinth. Breckinridge was still in Mississippi and rumor had it that additional Union forces were moving south from Cincinnati. The stores were not as plentiful as Bragg had been led to believe, and he would be able to

---

[66] OR, ser. 1, vol. 16, pt. 1, p. 1033.

[67] Report of Patrick R. Cleburne, October, OR, ser. 1, vol. 52, pt. 1, p. 52.

[68] Wheeler, "Bragg's Invasion," 17.

supply his men for only four more days.[69] Finally, there was simply no enthusiasm for the Southern cause. High hopes for large numbers of new recruits evaporated into reality.

The Rebels marched back through country with strong Union ties. Women and children hurled rocks and insults, and the troops were confronted with an occasional ambush as well. The weather was bitter and rations were poor. The men were forced to subsist on little more than biscuits and onions. The Federals attempted to capture the retreating columns but the Confederate cavalry was able to obstruct the roads, making the pursuit ineffective. The Rebels separated into two columns, one under Polk, the other under Smith. On 13 October they left bound for Knoxville via the Cumberland Gap. The long procession was slowed by thousands of wagons that contained 20,000 stand of arms. Bragg had ordered the weapons in anticipation of the volunteers he assumed would join his army, but he had overestimated the Kentuckians' enthusiasm for military service. All of this equipment, as well as the materiel captured during the battle, needed to be transported. The trains were barely making 5 miles per day, severely delaying the remainder of the army. The incline was so severe around Big Hill that it seemed as though everything would have to be abandoned. On 15 October Smith notified Bragg of the predicament, stating, "I have little hope of saving any of the trains, and fear much of the artillery will be lost."[70] Accordingly, orders were issued to have the wagons destroyed. Cleburne was not on duty as he was still recuperating from his wounds. He understood the value of the supplies and requested the authority to do anything possible to save them. Taking 1,500 men from Heth's division, Cleburne put them to work to salvage the provisions. Hardee described the bold display as follows:

> The enemy was pressing the rear, our trains were immovable, and nothing seemed left but to destroy them, to prevent them from falling into the hands of the enemy; orders had actually been given for their destruction, when Cleburne, who was disabled and off duty on account of his wound, came up. He asked and was given unlimited authority in the premises. He at once stationed guards on the roads;

---

[69] Thomas Claiborne, "The Battle of Perryville," *Confederate Veteran* 16/5 (May 1908): 227.

[70] OR, ser. 1, vol. 16, pt. 2, p. 949.

arrested every straggler and passing officer and soldier, collected a large force, organized fatigue parties, and literally lifted the trains over the hills. The trains thus preserved contained munitions and subsistence of the utmost value and necessity to the Confederates. It is by no means certain that even that the army could have made its subsequent long march through a sterile and wasted country without them.[71]

Despite the one-sided results of the battle, the opposing forces at the outset had favored the Union. Buell stated that he had 61,000 men in total, some 40,000 of which actually took part in the battle. He had lost 4,281 men, plus 15 pieces of artillery. According to Leonidas Polk, the Confederate force did not exceed 15,000, and it had suffered 3,396 total casualties.[72]

For the Army of Tennessee, there were remarkable similarities between the results in Kentucky and those at Shiloh. Initial success had turned to defeat, and many of the officers laid the blame squarely at the feet of Braxton Bragg. Pat Cleburne agreed. Once again he had led his brigade with great energy, and his courage set an example to the men in the ranks. However, his performance in Kentucky revealed more than steady competence. It may be said that this was the campaign in which Cleburne emerged to become one of the finest generals in the Confederacy and certainly the best infantry commander in the Western theatre. At Richmond he had handled his men with skill. Reinforcements had been brought up when needed and correctly placed. Whenever Manson had made a mistake, Cleburne had capitalized. At Perryville the brigade had dominated the field in its sector, and the decision to conceal the infantry until the Federals had fired upon the flag bearers dealt the enemy a punishing blow. However, while the Southerners had defeated the enemy, they had not destroyed him. When the action was concluded Union forces held the field.

The first frost of the season appeared on 18 October, freezing an already dejected army. Long, winding columns entered the gap the next day, and on

---

[71] Hardee, "Biographical Sketch." 154.

[72] Don Carlos Buell, "East Tennessee and the Campaign of Perryville," in Robert Underwood Johnston and Clarence Clough Buel, eds., *Battles and Leaders of the Civil War,* 4 vols. (1884–1887; repr., Secaucus NJ: Castle Books, n.d.) 3:30.

24 October the Confederates began to arrive in Knoxville. Two days later, as Cleburne entered the city, snow fell on the mountains.[73]

---

[73] OR, ser. 1, vol. 16, pt. 1, p. 1093.

5

STONES RIVER

The loss of Kentucky had serious repercussions for the Confederacy. From the very beginning, Jefferson Davis had elected to adopt a policy of diffusion in which every section of the South must be defended. His adamant refusal to concentrate Southern forces behind shorter, more defensible lines was politically popular but militarily unwise. Lee, Jackson, Longstreet, and Beauregard recognized the inherent flaws in Davis's misguided intentions, but perhaps Joseph Johnston summarized their frustration most succinctly in a letter to his brother Beverly. He complained that "by attempting to defend all valuable points at once he exposes his troops to being beaten everywhere."[1] The policy was not at all consistent with the actions of each state, which had its own interests at heart. Governors were reluctant to send troops outside their own borders, which made any attempt at a coordinated defense very difficult to implement. The boundaries of the new nation were stretched far too thin even before the war had started, and Federal control of additional territory only exacerbated an already deteriorating situation.

Despite Bragg's attempts to paint it otherwise, the overall results of the campaign were disappointing. Additional recruits had not materialized and Kentucky had fallen into Union hands. Decisive victories had been won at Richmond and Perryville, yet the Confederates were in retreat. Miserable weather turned the roads to mud as a downcast army slowly made its way to Nashville. Fortunately, Don Carlos Buell did not seize the opportunity in front of him. His lack of enterprise did not sit well with Abraham Lincoln, and on 30 October he was replaced by William Rosecrans.

The Army of Tennessee was never known for cooperation, and problems soon began to surface. Bragg undoubtedly realized that Confederacy's goals of holding Kentucky, obtaining new recruits, and general military successes had not been fulfilled. On 31 October he went to Richmond, ostensibly to win presidential approval for a foray into Middle Tennessee. Quite likely he

---

[1] Johnston to Beverly Johnston, 7 May 1863, in Gilbert Govan and James Livingwood, *Joseph E. Johnston: A Different Valor* (1956; repr., New York: Smithmark, 1995) 196.

attempted to convince Davis that but for the failures of his subordinates, victory would have been won. Davis approved of Bragg's conduct during the campaign but did not agree that the other generals were at fault. In order to clarify matters, he decided to confer with his old friend Leonidas Polk, who had attended West Point with Davis. On 3 November Davis summoned Polk to the capital. For his part, the bishop went seeking Bragg's removal. More importantly, he sought to deflect any personal blame for the reversal in Confederate fortunes. He suggested that Bragg be replaced by Joseph Johnston, who had commanded the Army of Northern Virginia until he was wounded at Fair Oaks. To underscore his position, Polk stated that both Smith and Hardee agreed with him. Kirby Smith also went to Richmond to meet with Davis. By this point Davis knew what to expect. Not surprisingly, Smith also called for a change in commanders. In the face of an intolerable situation, Davis chose the worse possible course of action. He neither relieved Bragg nor transferred Smith or Polk. The president's inactivity laid the groundwork for disaster at Stones River.[2]

Bragg had returned to the army on 2 November but his problems remained. The weather had varied in the extremes. A recent drought had devastated the crops and early winter left 6 inches of snow on the ground. As usual, the Confederates were destitute of every sort of clothing. Blankets, food, and other supplies were also lacking. Sickness was rampant as pneumonia, typhoid, scurvy, and dysentery ravaged the ranks. As a result, returns taken one day later list only 30,800 men present for duty. Faced with these conditions, a move into Tennessee made sense. The destination of Murfreesboro did not.[3]

Bragg's believed that the Murfreesboro area was the nearest source of food and would protect the vital railroad links from Chattanooga. Though this was true, Murfreesboro was not his only option. A position further south at the foot of the Cumberland Mountains could have accomplished identical results. While this may have abandoned some territory, it would have thwarted Federal designs on more important targets. The Duck and Elk River valleys provided an abundant supply of food, and the Duck River was ideal for

---

[2] Peter Cozzens, *No Better Place to Die* (Urbana: University of Illinois Press, 1990) 8–11.

[3] Thomas L. Connelly, *Army of the Heartland: The Army of Tennessee 1861–1862* (Baton Rouge: Louisiana State University Press, 1967) 16–17.

defense as it meandered through numerous defiles and heavy timber. Bragg's ignorance of the topography would soon prove costly.

Realistically, the selection of Murfreesboro as the base of operations eliminated any chance of success. The town was simply too isolated to defend and could be easily bypassed on either flank. To the west, the Columbia Pike was in good condition and the Nashville and Decatur Railroad entered Columbia 15 miles below Murfreesboro. A small country road ran through Nolensville, Triune, and Eagleville on its way to Shelbyville, 25 miles distant. To the northeast, another pike linked Lebanon and McMinnville, circumventing a Confederate force in the central part of the state.

Without any significant activity the troops went into winter quarters at the end of November. Bragg took the opportunity to reorganize his command and the Army of Mississippi combined with Smith's Army of Kentucky, formally earning the name "Army of Tennessee," which it would retain for the duration of the war. Three corps of infantry were created, led by Polk, Hardee, and Smith. Polk had three divisions at his disposal, under Frank Cheatham, Jones Withers, and John C. Breckinridge. At the time of the reorganization Hardee commanded two divisions, one under Patton Anderson and the other under Simon B. Buckner, but in early December Buckner was transferred to garrison duty in Mobile. His replacement was Patrick Cleburne. A man of rare ability, Cleburne held another distinction: he was one of the few Confederate generals in the Western theatre who was not repeatedly excoriated in Bragg's all-too-frequent eruptions. Buckner had been popular, but Cleburne's hard work and attention to detail won over his men. Kirby Smith's divisions were led by Carter Stevenson and John McCown. Like Smith, neither man had any desire to serve under Braxton Bragg; this spelled more trouble ahead.

Bragg's current difficulties were by no means limited to the infantry. Overall direction of the cavalry was given to a personal friend, twenty-five-year-old Georgian Joe Wheeler. This created another problem. Nathan Bedford Forrest had more experience and far more talent, yet he was passed over in favor of a loyal lieutenant. Despite Wheeler's prior lack of success and marginal qualifications, Forrest was sent into Middle Tennessee and Bragg's most valuable cavalry officer was no longer available. Decisions such as this exposed a tendency to reward subservience over ability. It was a shortcoming Bragg was never able to overcome.

Thoroughly frustrated by the situation he faced, Bragg tried to explain his predicament in a 3 November letter to Samuel Cooper. There was no ordnance depot for the repair of arms or materiel, and under present conditions there was not a suitable location to establish one. The commissary depots were in Kirby Smith's department, and while he did not anticipate any problems with his counterpart, he did express concern over the relationships he might have with other members of Smith's command. From a purely numerical standpoint, 30,000 men were not enough to conduct the operations Richmond had envisioned. These were all valid points, but perhaps foremost in Bragg's mind were the current enrollment statistics. His own numbers were shrinking, as an arduous campaign had seen casualties in battle, an increase in disease, and a failure to enlist new recruits. On the other hand, the Union Army continued to grow. Bragg correctly believed that time was working to the Federals' advantage.[4]

In order to personally evaluate the state of affairs, President Davis embarked on an inspection of the army, arriving in Murfreesboro on 12 December. That evening he dined with the senior officers and inquired as to the army's true condition. The generals painted a positive picture, claiming that the men were ready to fight and that Rosecrans had adopted a purely defensive strategy. Obviously Bragg was disappointed, as his prior complaints appeared wildly exaggerated. This gave Davis a newfound optimism, though one that was completely unwarranted.

Later in the month Jefferson Davis made another disastrous decision. Federal forces had begun their campaign against Vicksburg, and Davis had no intention of relinquishing one square inch of Mississippi. The city must be reinforced, so on 16 December Carter Stevenson and 7,500 men boarded southbound trains. Without Stevenson there was little purpose in retaining Smith, so McCown's division went to Hardee and Smith headed back to East Tennessee. Several days earlier Breckinridge had been transferred to Hardee as well, allowing Patton Anderson's division to be divided. This created a two-corps army more evenly balanced between Polk and Hardee. The new arrangement appeared to simplify the organizational structure, but it also removed a large portion of Bragg's infantry that would be sorely missed.

---

[4] US War Department, comp., *The War of the Rebellion: A Compilation of the Official Records of the Union and Confederate Armies*, 128 vols. (Washington, DC: Government Printing Office, 1880–1901) ser. 1, vol. 20, pt. 1, p. 386–87.

The winter was quiet in Murfreesboro, but while Cleburne had not taken part in the festive atmosphere the other officers enjoyed, the month was not without personal reward. On 20 December he received a promotion to major general. Bragg and Buckner both gave favorable endorsements, but Hardee offered the strongest recommendation. In a letter written to Samuel Cooper on 28 October, he praised the Irishman in the following terms:

> Gen Cleburne has been a Brigadier under my command for about a year, & has given unmistakable proofs of military talent of a high order. He unites the rare qualities of a strict disciplinarian, a brave and skillful leader, and a popular commander.
>
> General Cleburne has distinguished himself in every engagement in this campaign. At Shiloh, his Brigade was among the first to go into action, the last to come out, and suffered more severely than any other Brigade in the Army of the Mississippi.
>
> When the army reached Chattanooga, Cleburne's & Preston Smith's Brigades were detached for duty with Maj Gen Kirby Smith; and as shown in the official report of that officer to Gen. Bragg, these two brigades, under command of Gen Cleburne, completely routed the enemy in the first action at Richmond, before the remainder of the column could be deployed into line. Gen Cleburne was wounded in this engagement. At Perryville, his Brigade pierced the Center of the Federal forces, and was the first to break their lines. Here he was again wounded.
>
> [I feel] assured that the services of this gallant officer will meet with the recognition they merit, and [am] convinced that the interest of the service would be advanced by his promotion....[5]

The promotion displayed Hardee's confidence in his young lieutenant, and Cleburne's responsibilities grew dramatically. Instead of commanding four regiments, he now led four brigades. Bushrod Johnson, S. A. M. Wood, St. John Liddell, and Lucius Polk became his brigadiers. The additional duties required a much larger support system, which grew to twelve members. Calhoun Benham assumed the position of chief of staff and Irving A. Buck

---

[5] Howell and Elizabeth Purdue, *Pat Cleburne Confederate General* (1973; repr., Gaithersburg MD: Olde Soldier Books, 1987) 163.

became assistant adjutant-general. Leonard Mangum and Sylvanus Hanly remained aides-de-camp.[6]

William Rosecrans was a cautious general, but he no longer had the luxury of remaining in Nashville. Rations were plentiful and by Christmas the army had enough food to last until February. He could hardly claim he was outnumbered, as Union intelligence had already reported the departure of Forrest and Stevenson. Washington had come to the conclusion that Bragg's army had settled down for the winter. Rosecrans had a stationary opponent, and it was time for him to strike.

The Ohioan was reluctant, but current events controlled his actions. Ambrose Burnside had suffered a devastating defeat at Fredericksburg and William T. Sherman was stuck in the waters around Chickasaw Bayou. The Republicans needed a victory somewhere, and it fell upon Rosecrans to deliver one. In the early morning hours of 26 December he consulted with his subordinates and revealed his plan of attack. The army would move at first light on three separate objectives. The direct route to Murfreesboro was given to Thomas Crittenden. In the center, Alexander McCook would march along the Nolensville Pike to Triune, 28 miles away. Rosecrans mistakenly thought that most of Hardee's corps was located in that particular area. George Thomas would march in supporting distance of McCook's right on two roads: the Franklin and Wilson's turnpikes. At the intersection of Wilson's Pike and the Old Liberty Pike he would turn east toward Nolensville. This would allow him to pass around Hardee's left and hit the Confederates in the flank. This probably would have worked quite well had Hardee actually been where Rosecrans expected him to be.

Bragg saw no more urgency to attack than Rosecrans, but he reacted in the opposite manner. Feeling that Union inactivity allowed him the opportunity to rest, Bragg dispersed his forces over a front 50 miles wide. Hardee's corps was not in Triune as the Federals had believed but instead was further south in Eagleville. Cleburne's division and one brigade under Dan Adams held the town. Leonidas Polk was in Murfreesboro, along with the three brigades of Breckinridge's division. John McCown was at Readyville and smaller units were sprinkled throughout the region. Still, with the harsh

---

[6] For an excellent discussion of the entire staff see William P. Buck in Mauriel P. Joslyn, ed., *A Meteor Shining Brightly* (Macon GA: Mercer University Press, 2000) 58–74.

winter weather Bragg was unconcerned. The Union army would never begin serious movements in December.

On 26 December the brigades under Johnson, Liddell, and Polk were with Cleburne in College Grove near Eagleville, 20 miles southwest of Murfreesboro. Wood was stationed 4 miles to the north in Triune acting as an advance guard. During the morning Cleburne received the first of several worrisome reports. Fifteen miles to the west a Confederate garrison at Franklin had been overrun and another Union column was advancing from the north. If successful, the Federals could slice the Confederate line in two and drive a wedge between Hardee and Polk. The Rebels were already outnumbered and it would be a simple matter to defeat them in detail.

Wheeler's cavalry had provided scant information and Bragg's grasp of conditions around him was weak, but Rosecrans had over 54,000 men at his disposal and a movement this large was impossible to conceal.[7] Hardee directed Cleburne to be ready to evacuate the area at a moment's notice and provided instructions regarding which roads to take in order to reach Murfreesboro. Early the next morning Cleburne received additional orders from Hardee to shift 1 mile north of his present position. It was during this movement that Hardee finally recalled Cleburne and three of his brigades, uniting his command with the remainder of Bragg's troops. Wood was to remain in Triune and cooperate with John Wharton's horsemen in an attempt to impede the Federal advance.

Cleburne had his men on the move before dawn. The division crept along the Salem Turnpike, but wet conditions hindered their march and a heavy fog limited visibility. The weather did nothing for the Confederates' temperament, in fact it was a blessing. At times the Federals could not see more than 50 yards in front of them.[8] The Graycoats needed time to unify their forces, and the thick screen gave Wood and Wharton time to reform their lines and cover their retreat.

---

[7] OR, ser. 1, vol. 20, pt. 1, p. 200–201, 207. This total is derived from Union figures, which show 43,400 effectives in the returns taken on 31 December 1862. Revised figures covering the period of 26 December 1862 to 5 January 1863 lists total casualties of 13,249.

[8] Report of Alexander D. McCook, 8 January 1863, OR, ser. 1, vol. 20, pt. 1, p. 253–58.

Wood had taken his small brigade to a position 1 1/2 miles north of Triune along the Nolensville Turnpike. The group was comprised of the 45th Mississippi, the 16th and 33rd Alabama, and two companies of sharpshooters, totaling some 950 men. As Wood fell back along the pike he placed the 45th Mississippi in the first line of defense. Four companies deployed on the right of the road as skirmishers with three companies and one section of artillery on the left. At 9:00 A.M. enemy forces appeared. They made three attempts to place a battery 500 yards in front of the Confederate lines but were unable to hold a position.

The Federals continued to bring up fresh reinforcements and pressure mounted. If the skies cleared, Wood's brigade would be quickly overwhelmed. He pulled the Mississippians and the battery back across Nelson's Creek to a second line held by the 16th Alabama. At the same time he sent a detail of twenty picked men to destroy the bridge. Captain J. W. Green accomplished the task and did not retreat until his men came under heavy bombardment. The Federals finally took possession of the high ground near Triune, but without the bridge the artillery would have to remain where it was. For McCook this was not a serious problem; with much greater firepower he was out of range of the Confederate guns. Wood brought his artillery back to the front, where he observed cavalry trying to outflank his left. He gave the order to fire and the batteries broke up the party.

At 1:00 P.M. the fog lifted and gave way to a chilling rain. McCook's corps tried to continue, skirmishing with Wharton's cavalry along the way. Battery B of the First Ohio Artillery shelled the Rebel columns with great effect, but the weather was still on the Southern side. The rain soon turned to sleet and the pursuit ground to a halt.

The storm broke just before 4:00 P.M. and the attack resumed. Putnam Darden brought up one field piece to cover the escape, and with Wharton's assistance the Confederates withdrew in good order. The troopers fired one volley, turned their horses, and sped down the Eagleville Pike to rejoin the infantry 3 miles north of the town. It was growing dim and the roads began to form ice, so McCook decided to pitch his tents for the night. Wood reported a loss of six men, while the Federals suffered sixty-five casualties. He gradually made his way east and on 29 December found Cleburne.[9]

---

[9] Cozzens, *No Better Place to Die,* 57.

Cleburne was forced to stop as well. He made his camp on the Salem Turnpike only 1 mile from the river. The division had been saved, but not by any efforts of Joe Wheeler or Braxton Bragg. Bragg was still somewhat unsure of the Federal intent, but he had committed himself to the defense of Murfreesboro. At 9:00 P.M. on 27 December, he gave his general officers the following instructions:

1st. The line of battle will be in front of Murfreesborough; half of the army, left wing, in front of Stone's River; right wing in rear of river.

2d. Polk's Corps will form left wing; Hardee's Corps, right wing.

3d. Wither's Division will form first line in Polk's Corps, Cheatham's the second line. Breckinridge's Division forms first line Hardee's Corps; Cleburne's Division, second line, Hardee's Corps.

4th. McCown's Division to form reserve, opposite center, on high ground, in rear of Cheatham's present quarters.

5th. Jackson's brigade reserve, to the right flank, to report to Lieutenant-General Hardee.

6th. Two lines to be formed from 800 to 1000 yards apart, according to the ground.

7th. Chiefs of artillery to pay special attention to posting of batteries, and supervise their work, seeing they do not causelessly waste their ammunition.

8th. Cavalry to fall back gradually before enemy, reporting by couriers every hour. When near our lines, Wheeler will move to the right and Wharton to the left, to cover and protect our flanks and report movements of enemy; Pegram to fall to the rear, and report to commanding general as a reserve.

9th. Tonight, if the enemy has gained his position to our front ready for action, Wheeler and Wharton, with their whole commands, will make a night march to the right and left, turn the enemy's flank, gain his rear and vigorously assail his trains and rear guard, blocking the roads and impeding his movements every way, holding themselves ready to assail his retreating forces.

10th. All quartermasters, commissaries and ordnance officers will remain at their proper posts, discharging their appropriate duties.

Supplies and baggage should be ready, packed for a move forward or backward as the results of the day may require, and the trains should be in position, out of danger, teamsters all present, and quartermasters in charge.

11th. Should we be compelled to retire, Polk's Corps will move on Shelbyville, and Hardee's on the Manchester Pike, trains in front, cavalry in rear.[10]

The countryside around Murfreesboro made it extremely difficult to conduct military maneuvers. There were a few small farms in the area and the ground was broken by several roads that ran east and west. A turnpike ran through Triune to Franklin; the line roughly 1 mile south of this road marked one boundary of the battlefield. One and one half miles north of the road and parallel to it ran the Wilkinson Turnpike. Still further north and also parallel was a smaller dirt road. Stones River, which ran in a northerly direction before emptying into the Cumberland, cut the Confederate Army in half. Bragg felt compelled to protect both sides of the river, owing both to poor intelligence from Wheeler and to his own ignorance of the surrounding terrain. As a result, he had no information as to the direction of the Federal attack. They could advance along the Lebanon Turnpike from the north, the Nashville Turnpike from the northwest, or either the Franklin or Wilkinson road from the west. Had Bragg chosen a more defensible location from which to give battle, Rosecrans's options would certainly have been more limited.

Bragg's choice to occupy Murfreesboro placed the Confederates at a serious disadvantage, but his dispositions made matters even worse. As Hardee pointed out, "The open fields beyond the town are fringed with dense cedar brakes, offering shelter for approaching infantry, and are almost impervious to artillery. The country on every side is entirely open, and was accessible to the enemy."[11]

Any army at Stones River was extremely vulnerable, regardless of the weather. In dry conditions none of the fords was more than ankle deep, while sudden rain quickly flooded the low banks. Bragg had placed his army in such a manner that this would separate the two wings of the army.

---

[10] OR, ser. 1, vol. 20, pt. 1, p. 672–73.

[11] Report of William J. Hardee, 11 March 1863, OR, ser. 1, vol. 20, pt. 1, p. 772.

On the morning of 28 December the Confederates began to deploy. Breckinridge took a position between the river and the Lebanon Turnpike, 1 1/2 miles northwest of town. Roger Hanson and his Orphan Brigade held the left flank of the division and lined up on the river. J. B. Palmer, William Preston, Dan Adams, and John Jackson completed the first line of the right wing. Cleburne's division formed the second line, 800 yards in the rear. Facing north, his left rested on the water with his right near the pike. Lost in indecision, Bragg almost surrendered his most obvious advantage. Only 600 yards in front of Breckinridge stood a rise in the ground known as Wayne's Hill. Enemy artillery posted on the crest could enfilade Polk's right flank on the west side of the river. The Confederates had been in Murfreesboro for more than a month, yet Bragg had failed to account for this critical strategic position. On the next day the Federals tried to take possession of the hill, but that evening they were thoroughly repulsed by Hanson's troops.[12]

As late as the next day Bragg thought that Rosecrans would attack at dawn on 30 December, and by midnight the Confederate lines were basically complete. Initially, Bragg believed that the Federals would strike along the Nashville and Lebanon Pike. He continued to hold to this line of reasoning until the morning of 30 December when Wharton reported Alexander McCook's presence near Overall's Creek. Bragg became alarmed that his left flank would be turned, so he sent McCown's division across the river to form on Polk's corps. The expected attack failed to materialize as Rosecrans was busy arranging his own lines. Still, Bragg continued to hear skirmishing to the south, so he ordered Hardee to take Cleburne's division and support McCown. This movement left Breckinridge to protect the east side of the river by himself. Cleburne departed, but Hardee told him to wait at the ford until he could examine the ground and properly place the division.[13]

The Confederates planned to turn McCook's right with coordinated attacks by McCown, Cleburne, and Polk, moving in succession. This would push the Federals back into Stones River. By placing Wharton's cavalry along the Nashville Turnpike, the Federals would be cut off from their supply base in Nashville. Bragg never understood the complexity of his orders. He wanted to advance simultaneously and maintain uniform spacing while moving through heavy undergrowth, large outcroppings of limestone boulders, cleared

---

[12] Report of William J. Hardee, 11 March 1863, OR, ser. 1, vol. 20, pt. 1, p. 771–75.

[13] Report of Patrick R. Cleburne, 31 January 1863, OR, ser. 1, vol. 20, pt. 1, p. 844.

farms, and rail fences.[14] The Federal intent was the same but far more realistic. In mirror image Rosecrans decided to place the weight of his army on his own left. A strong demonstration by McCook would cause Bragg to weaken his right in response to the threat. The Federals could then easily overpower Breckinridge and the battle would be won.[15]

On the night of 30 December Hardee placed McCown in position. His division faced northwest, with James Rains on the left flank, M. D. Ector on his right, and Evander McNair in reserve. After further deliberation Hardee adjusted his dispositions and ordered McNair to advance until he formed part of the first line. This alignment would allow McNair to connect his right with the left flank of Polk's corps, held by Colonel John Q. Loomis. At this point Hardee sent a staff officer to Cleburne with instructions to come forward.

Cleburne was ready before daylight and aligned his division in a parallel formation 500 yards behind McCown. Lucius Polk took Calvert's battery to Cleburne's right. In the center, Bushrod Johnson's brigade was accompanied by the guns under Putnam Darden. St. John Liddell's infantry and Shannon's artillery formed the left side of the division. S. A. M. Wood was placed in reserve behind Polk, but on 30 December his artillery had been detached and given to Breckinridge.

On the morning of 31 December, Hardee had 10,045 infantry and roughly 2,000 cavalry. He ordered Wharton to encircle the Union right. They left at daybreak and reached the Wilkinson Turnpike, 2 1/2 miles beyond enemy lines. Wharton attacked and captured 1,500 prisoners. The brief engagement pushed the Federals back 2 miles until they passed Overall's Creek. Rosecrans surrendered several hundred wagons and 400 additional prisoners, but his loss was insignificant. Far more importantly, the Southern cavalry had been diverted from the critical point of attack.[16]

On Hardee's left, McCown's division opened the action a few minutes after 6:00 A.M. They could see the Yankees' lines less than half a mile ahead. As the Confederates advanced they held their fire. At 200 yards the Union

---

[14] Grady McWhiney, *Attack and Die* (Tuscaloosa: University of Alabama Press, 1982) 84.

[15] W. D. Pickett, "Reminiscences of Murfreesboro," *Confederate Veteran* 16/9 (September 1908): 449–54; A. P. Stewart, "The Army of Tennessee," *Military Annals of Tennessee*, ed. John B. Lindsley (Nashville: J. M. Lindsey and Co., 1886) 67–78.

[16] Report of William J. Hardee, 11 March 1863, OR, ser. 1, vol. 20, pt. 1, p. 771.

lines exploded and the Rebels charged, only to receive another round at close range. Huge gaps appeared in the lines, but these were quickly filled. The wave of gray swept through the cannon and one battery was captured before the Federals retreated to a second position. They tried to rally around another artillery emplacement but there was no time to form. At this point McCown's division began to split apart. Rains and Ector continued to the west; they drove their enemy over 2 miles before they realized that their right flank was suddenly uncovered. McNair had veered to his right and joined Liddell.

To the north, McCook faced Hardee with two divisions. Richard Johnson held the west side of the line. He placed August Willich on the right, Edward Kirk on the left, and Philemon Baldwin's brigade in reserve. Jefferson C. Davis formed his division on Kirk's left, with Sidney Post, William Carlin, and William Woodruff completing the formation. Willich's right flank was three-quarters of a mile beyond the river with its line extending south of the Triune Road and north almost to the Wilkinson Turnpike.

The first day's action occurred in an area only 3 miles wide, bounded on the east by Stones River and on the west by Overall's Creek. Cleburne advanced in a damp, misty morning and struck shortly after McCown.[17] The Yankees, still preparing breakfast, were completely surprised by an attack so intense that the artillery could be heard 40 miles away. The charge bent back Johnson and casualties were heavy. In Kirk's brigade "500 men were killed or wounded in a few minutes," and Willich lost almost as many. As they fell back Post's right became exposed. Davis ordered him to change front, but as Post shifted he uncovered Carlin and Woodruff. Carlin melted away, but Woodruff was able to make a brief stand until he was pressured on both sides and had to retreat as well.[18]

As the Federals fell back from this position, Willich was hit and taken prisoner. At roughly the same time Kirk was also wounded, adding to the confusion. Richard Johnson had no choice but to bring Baldwin forward. He arrived in a timely manner, but his right was outflanked and he was forced

---

[17] Pickett, "Reminiscences," 451; report of Richard W. Johnson, 8 January 1863, OR, ser. 1, vol. 20, pt. 1, p. 296 places the time of impact at 6:22 A.M.

[18] G. C. Kniffin, "The Battle of Stone's River," in Robert Underwood Johnston and Clarence Clough Buel, eds., *Battles and Leaders of the Civil War,* 4 vols. (1884–1887; repr., Secaucus NJ: Castle Books, n.d.) 3:613–19; report of Jefferson C. Davis, January 1863, OR, ser. 1, vol. 20, pt. 1, p. 264; Mary Jones Polk Branch, *Memoirs of a Southern Woman "Within the Lines"* (Chicago: Joseph G. Branch Publishing Co., 1911) 33.

back to regroup. In his own opinion, had he remained in position his entire command would have been surrounded.[19]

The Confederates continued to push forward. At 7:00 A.M. Loomis began to advance, but he was soon disabled and the brigade made little progress against the Federal center. As the attack developed, Cleburne's right side began to crack. Loomis had not advanced as quickly as Lucius Polk, so Hardee sent Wood forward to reconnect their brigades. When Wood reached his destination, he created a single line with no support. They drove the Federals through the cedars between the Triune Road and the Wilkinson Pike, but their success opened McCown's flank. McNair halted and Liddell continued forward to seal the line, whereupon they resumed their attack.

McCown and Cleburne crushed the Federal right and as they advanced Hardee ordered them to pivot to their own right, with McCown in the lead. They were to form on Loomis while Wharton harassed their rear. Cleburne executed this movement with great skill but McCown was still having trouble. He faced more opposition and continued to move toward Overall's Creek when Cleburne wheeled and turned northeast. Another opening appeared, this time between McNair's right and Liddell's left.

The enemy in front of Wood and Polk was concealed in a wooded area. Johnson and Liddell advanced over open ground that revealed well-posted artillery. This half of Cleburne's brigade saw the first serious action. They were joined by McNair, and though the fight was bloody it lasted only twenty-five minutes before the Federals fell back, momentarily ending that phase. The 2nd Arkansas seized two rifled cannon and the 8th Arkansas captured two colors, but it was during this movement that the Confederates took their heaviest losses. Colonels Moses White of the 37th Tennessee and J. M. Hughs of the 25th Tennessee were wounded, along with one of the finest colonels in Cleburne's command, A. S. Marks of Johnson's 17th Tennessee. In total, nine field officers were either killed or wounded.

Union artillery did considerable damage but after a stubborn fight the 17th charged forward and captured the entire battery, in the process killing eight men and several horses. The Volunteers chased the Federals into the woods, where they came upon a second line. The Federals were quickly broken and fell back toward the Wilkinson Pike. They tried to make a stand but were

---

[19] Report of R. W. Johnson, 8 January 1863, OR, ser. 1, vol. 20, pt. 1, p. 296; report of Philemon P. Baldwin, 8 January 1863, OR, ser. 1, vol. 20, pt. 1, p. 336–38.

forced back upon a third line, strongly supported by artillery. Most of Johnson's brigade had gone to the rear to replenish their ammunition and the Federals temporarily checked the pursuit. On Cleburne's left, St. John Liddell had been joined by the 17th Tennessee and they had considerable success. Polk and Wood, however, had been forced to contend with natural obstructions and encountered much stiffer resistance.[20]

The entire division pursued with great speed but little organization, halting only when the Federals reformed along the south side of the Wilkinson Turnpike. Predictably, Bushrod Johnson and Lucius Polk continued to bunch together. They were constantly fighting the terrain and Cleburne had to straighten their lines more than once. Johnson fell back to replenish his ammunition, but the remainder of the division continued to press forward.

The casualties were severe but the Confederates took the field. The results of their sacrifice were substantial. Cleburne's men had captured almost 1,000 prisoners, a train of ammunition wagons, 2 wagons loaded with medical supplies, and 2 hospitals. Union general Joshua Sill lost his life near one of these hospitals.[21]

Cleburne had been able to turn their lines toward the river, but in so doing he had outdistanced his support. Without protection, his right flank received an enfilading fire. Darden and Calvert quickly responded, but the infantry was in shambles. Wood had run low on ammunition and was forced to leave the field while Polk was ordered to change front and attack the battery. In spite of the confusion, Polk's attack combined with the artillery bombardment drove the Federals backwards. They abandoned their position and the 5th Confederate and 1st Arkansas were given credit for the capture of four field pieces. By this time Wood had returned and came up on Polk's left. Johnson moved forward in support, but as he reached his position the firing stopped. This enabled them to change front again and resume their northward advance. In order to maintain alignment, Cleburne moved Johnson to the right of Polk, with Wood still on Polk's left.[22]

The Federals continued their retreat. They made another stand on the north side of the Wilkinson Pike and took cover behind heavy boulders. Polk

[20] Report of Bushrod R. Johnson, 15 January 1863, OR, ser. 1, vol. 20, pt. 1, p. 875–76.

[21] Report of Patrick R. Cleburne, 31 January 1863, OR, ser. 1, vol. 20, pt. 1, p. 846.

[22] Report of P. R. Cleburne, 31 January 1863, OR, ser. 1, vol. 20, pt. 1, p. 846.

took most of his losses in this fighting, but he did receive some assistance. A. J. Vaughan's brigade had started the day behind Loomis, but as the battle progressed he had gradually shifted to his left until he was fighting with Cleburne. His arrival was timely. Wood ran out of ammunition again and Cleburne sent him to the rear in order to protect the trains. His command was the smallest to begin with, and by this time it had been reduced to no more than 500 men. Vaughan stepped forward to join the attack. The Union right had been badly beaten by Hardee's troops, but the center of Rosecrans's line held firm. For a second time, Cleburne's men were exposed to a raking fire from their flank.

The units on Cleburne's right were moving as planned, but Liddell was not. He had advanced for roughly 1 mile before forming on McNair's right. No more than 75 yards away, Federal infantry occupied a rise in the ground. The 6th Indiana and 1st Ohio had taken cover behind some rail fences and placed artillery 150 yards behind their front lines. After a thirty-minute fight they were driven off the crest. The Confederates charged and captured the battery before Ector and Rains arrived. The Yankees fell back 400 yards and formed a new line with the 5th Kentucky. As the Butternuts pushed forward they kept moving in the direction of Overall's Creek. There the Federals made another stand, but McCown was able to bring his artillery forward. He delivered an enfilading fire into the Union right, driving them from their position.[23]

Although Liddell was making some progress, the occupation of Overall's Creek was of little importance. Cleburne knew that he needed to reunite his infantry. It had become necessary to shift Johnson to his left and Liddell to his right and reconnect their lines. Once that was accomplished, the Confederates continued their advance. Liddell and Polk held the flanks while Johnson and Vaughan formed between them and somewhat to the rear. Liddell had not moved 100 yards before he came upon Federals posted in a neck of woods with open ground on either side. He kept his brigade moving, but the advance was contested to within 25 yards of the Union line before the Yankees finally gave way. Colonels John H. Kelly of the 8th Arkansas and S. G. Smith of the 6th and 7th Arkansas (consolidated) fell wounded in the action.[24]

---

[23] Alexander F. Stevenson, *The Battle of Stone's River* (Boston: James R. Osgood and Company, 1884) 42–43.

[24] Report of St. John R. Liddell, 10 January 1863, OR, ser. 1, vol. 20, pt. 1, p. 859.

Hardee had repeatedly emphasized the importance of constant pursuit to prevent the Federals from reforming as they fell back. Cleburne urged his men on. They advanced for one-quarter of a mile, where they encountered a fresh line backed by more artillery. The Rebels were suddenly at a serious disadvantage, as Liddell's battery was the only one on the field. Polk's guns had been stopped in the thick cedars and Hardee had transferred Johnson's artillery to the rear as a reserve.[25]

The weight of the charge had a telling effect. The Yankees tried to hold their position but the Confederates continued to surge forward. Johnson's brigade finally pierced the defenses and was able to capture a battery of Parrott guns. There was no choice but to retreat to the Nashville Turnpike. It was 3 o'clock and Cleburne's division was physically spent. They had pressed the Federals throughout the day and driven them back toward the river; the pursuit had been constant. As was so often the case throughout the war, there were no more troops to pour into the fight. Ammunition was running low and due to the terrain the supply wagons had not been able to follow the infantry. The more success Cleburne achieved, the more precarious his situation became. He paused to assess matters, but by the time he was able to organize his command for one final assault, Union reinforcements had arrived and partial fortifications had been constructed.

Without any support, Cleburne was vulnerable. Liddell had not come under direct attack and was able to withdraw relatively unharmed, but Polk, Vaughan, and Johnson were driven backwards in considerable disorder. Artillery posted on the railroad tracks inflicted tremendous casualties in Polk's brigade. From his position somewhat to the rear of Polk, Vaughan's right was uncovered and he was forced to leave the field altogether. Cleburne fell back some 400 yards from his foremost position and regrouped. He placed Liddell on the left, Johnson in the center, and Polk on the right and awaited the impending assault.

It did not come. This turn of events forced Cleburne to make a decision. By 3 o'clock he had taken 3 miles of ground and beaten the Federals at every point. In addition to numerous prisoners, his division had taken arms, horses, artillery, and supplies. Should he protect it and consolidate his gains, or gamble everything in one final thrust that would be spectacular if successful but disastrous otherwise? He conferred with Hardee, who instructed him to

---

[25] Report of Patrick R. Cleburne, 31 January 1863, OR, ser. 1, vol. 20, pt. 1, p. 848.

remain in place. Cleburne threw out his pickets and went into camp for the night. Hardee reported that his wing had taken 23 field pieces and over 4,000 captives, yet he was somewhat dismayed. He knew that the victory was not complete. The decision to send the cavalry in pursuit of the Federal wagon trains had robbed the infantry of mounted strikers when a sudden attack may well have shattered their lines, ended the battle on 31 December, and left the region in Southern hands. He believed that had the Confederates been able to support Cleburne in a timely manner, when the Federals fell back to their final position they would have been destroyed.[26]

No finer performance could have been expected than the one Cleburne gave on 31 December. The Federals in his sector had been bent back in a 90-degree angle to the main line and soundly defeated at every encounter until he finally outdistanced his support. But Cleburne had paid a steep price for success. In addition to two wounded staff officers, Liddell lost 607 men, Johnson 606, Wood 504, and Polk 347. Of the 6,045 men he had taken into battle, Cleburne had lost 2,066.[27] The returns taken on 17 January paint a vivid picture of the carnage at Stones River. Liddell had only 1,709 men present for duty, Johnson 1,922, Wood 1,150, and Polk 1,343.[28]

The Confederates anticipated that the Federals would renew their attack on New Year's Day, but all was quiet. Cleburne sent Liddell forward to make a cautious reconnaissance, then added Wood and Johnson to protect his right. They were not to bring on a battle but only to determine the location of the enemy. Liddell, however, did make contact and discovered that the Federals were flanking his left. He pulled his brigade out of danger but they were attacked. Before Wood could withdraw he had lost almost 100 men.

The next day Hardee rode to over to Polk and the two men conferred alone. They crossed to the north side of the river, where they were met by

---

[26] Bruce Catton, *Never Call Retreat* (Garden City NY: Doubleday, 1965) 45; Pickett, "Reminiscences," 451.

[27] Irving A. Buck, *Cleburne and His Command* (1908; repr., Wilmington NC: Broadfoot Publishing, 1995) 122 gives the following information on Confederate casualties: Staff: none killed, 2 wounded, none captured or missing, total casualties = 2. Liddell: 86 killed, 503 wounded, 18 captured or missing, total casualties = 607. Johnson: 61 killed, 488 wounded, 57 captured or missing, total casualties = 606. Wood: 52 killed, 339 wounded, 113 captured or missing, total casualties = 504. Polk: 30 killed, 298 wounded, 19 captured or missing, total casualties = 347.

[28] OR, ser. 1, vol. 20, pt. 1, p. 780.

Breckinridge. Bragg had already decided to turn the Union left, though none of the generals agreed with the orders. Enemy artillery was strongly posted on high ground on the west side of the river. It was an ideal position, and the Confederates would take fire in front and flank. Polk and Hardee received orders from staff members to return to their own corps; they took no part in the final battle at Stones River. A pointless affair, the entire contest lasted less than one hour. Bragg's adherence to a plan that was doomed to failure cost Breckinridge over 1,500 men, roughly 30 percent of his division.

The Union lost 8,778 men at Stones River, the Southerners 10,266,[29] but the numbers do not reveal the whole picture. The Confederates would technically remain in the state, but for all intents and purposes Tennessee was gone. The story was one all too familiar for the Army of Tennessee. A decision beyond their control had deprived the rank and file of yet another victory. The Federal right had been virtually destroyed, and Carter Stevenson had been sent to Mississippi. What would have happened had Stevenson been present? In the words of Bruce Catton, the Confederates "almost certainly would have won decisively if Stevenson's missing division had been there to help."[30] Around midnight they turned around again and headed for Tullahoma.

[29] OR, ser. 1, vol. 20, pt. 1, p. 200–201, 674–75.
[30] Catton, Never Call Retreat, 45.

6

TULLAHOMA

The Tullahoma campaign actually amounted to little more than a series of Confederate retreats. There were several reasons for Braxton Bragg's lack of initiative, but in a cold rain the Army of Tennessee left Murfreesboro and headed south. Initially the idea was to take up a new line behind the Elk River, but there was no real direction. The central problem was that Bragg had never formulated a plan of defense for Murfreesboro itself, and now he had no idea where to turn.[1]

The Confederates assembled on 5 and 6 January at Tullahoma, 18 miles southeast of Murfreesboro on the Duck River. They began to dig entrenchments on the north and west sides of town; felled trees were added to create an abatis. Fortunately the Federals did not pursue, even though William Rosecrans had 63,000 men against fewer than 47,000 Confederates.[2] Although he possessed superior numbers, he did not believe that he had a sufficient force to accomplish the task at hand. The hesitation gave Bragg renewed confidence and the army returned to the Duck. He placed Leonidas Polk on the left at Shelbyville, with William Hardee on the right at Tullahoma. Save for a few minor adjustments in the latter part of April, both corps remained in these positions until June.[3]

A great deal of unrest gripped the army, and Braxton Bragg was determined to rid himself of any opposition. He began with John McCown. Bragg held that McCown's failure to attack promptly and execute the

---

[1] Thomas L. Connelly, *Autumn of Glory: The Army of Tennessee 1862–1865* (Baton Rouge: Louisiana State University Press, 1971) 68.

[2] Kniffin lists the effective strength of each army as follows: Union: 40,746 infantry, 6,806 cavalry, 3,065 artillery, 12,575 in a reserve corps, for a total effective strength of 63,192 men. Confederate: 30,449 infantry, 13,962 cavalry, 2,254 artillery, for a total effective strength of 46,665 (G. C. Kniffin, "Maneuvering Bragg out of Tennessee," in Robert Underwood Johnston and Clarence Clough Buel, eds., *Battles and Leaders of the Civil War,* 4 vols. [1884–1887; repr., Secaucus NJ: Castle Books, n.d.] 3:635–37).

[3] Nathaniel C. Hughes, *General William J. Hardee: Old Reliable* (Baton Rouge: Louisiana State University Press, 1965) 147.

wheeling maneuver against the Union right led to the defeat at Stones River. Hardee's report, completed on 28 February, also censured McCown for his poor performance. McCown had openly criticized Bragg, and some of those comments undoubtedly made it back to headquarters. Bragg offered the charge, somewhat technical in nature, that McCown had defied regulations by ordering men and officers to Charleston "and such other points" on 3 February. A court-martial convened on 16 March at Shelbyville. Among others, Cleburne presided to determine McCown's fate and McCown was removed from rank for six months.

During the winter new recruits came in. Although drill and discipline increased, morale continued to fall. Earlier in the year Joseph Johnston had been dispatched to Tullahoma to assess conditions within Bragg's army, and he had come back with a favorable report. However, the situation had deteriorated to the point where the internal unrest could no longer be ignored. On 9 March, Davis ordered Johnston to return and assume permanent command. Upon his arrival on 19 March, he learned that Mrs. Bragg had become quite ill. Johnston assumed control of the army, but he failed to act decisively. Instead of sending Bragg back to Richmond, he allowed the North Carolinian to remain in Tullahoma.[4]

Confederate plans were predicated on the belief that Rosecrans could be held at Tullahoma long enough for Polk to attack him. This line of reasoning was false, but Bragg remained oblivious to his own mistakes. First of all, the position was extremely vulnerable to a flanking maneuver. The Union Army had established a base in Murfreesboro, and Rosecrans could pass Bragg's right flank by either of two roads that led from McMinnville through the Cumberland Mountains, where they emerged near Jasper. It was a small town, but Union control of it would cut off Bragg's route of escape. The turnpike from Murfreesboro to Manchester was another option. It went through Hoover's Gap before it crossed the Duck River. Once there, Rosecrans had several options from which he could block a retreat and trap the Army of Tennessee along the water. To the southwest, Rosecrans could move on Decherd, only 12 miles below Bragg's headquarters. Decherd lay on the turnpike to Chattanooga, as well as the Nashville and Chattanooga Railroad. Finally, the Federals could attack Tullahoma with a frontal assault.

---

[4] Gabor S. Boritt, *Jefferson Davis's Generals* (New York: Oxford University Press, 1999) 78.

In any event, the loss of Tullahoma would entail the loss of Middle Tennessee.[5]

Hardee understood the weaknesses in Bragg's position. If Cleburne's division at Liberty Gap was defeated, his corps would be split in half. As he also pointed out to Bragg, the force that held Hoover's Gap was too small to withstand a strong attack. The army was too widely scattered, so Hardee recommended a more logical concentration. On 26 January he wrote the following correspondence: "It will be seen by the map I send you that this position offers few, if any advantages for defense. It can be turned, not only by the direct road leading from Manchester to Decherd and Winchester, but, from the nature of the country, our flanks can be turned at this point. I see no advantages in this position which can compensate for superiority of numbers."[6]

Nearly three months later, writing from Tullahoma, Joseph Johnston warned Samuel Cooper:

> The position of our troops is disadvantageous, because for subsistence it is compelled to take ground west of the direct route from Murfreesborough to Chattanooga. It can, therefore, be turned by our right.... Should we be compelled to abandon Middle Tennessee, it will be difficult to feed this army; the cavalry (amounting to nearly 15,000) could not be kept together in East Tennessee or Georgia; it would be necessary to divide it into several bodies.... Such a movement would be attended with great risk, however, as we could prepare no supplies for our troops before their passage of the river, that district being occupied by the enemy.[7]

William Preston Johnston shared their concerns and on 15 April wrote to Jefferson Davis. Attempting to select a more secure location, he evaluated the position in these terms:

---

[5] Connelly, *Autumn of Glory,* 112–13.

[6] US War Department, comp., *The War of the Rebellion: A Compilation of the Official Records of the Union and Confederate Armies,* 128 vols. (Washington, DC: Government Printing Office, 1880–1901) ser. 1, vol. 23, pt. 2, p. 617–18.

[7] OR, ser. 1, vol. 23, pt. 2, p. 741.

Tullahoma is regarded as the central point, but the greater part of the army is to the left of it. It is not the intention of or expectation of Generals Johnston and Bragg to await attack there, unless made in front, and this they do not expect....

General Bragg seems to have been governed in his selection of Tullahoma as his chief point of defense by the convergence there of several roads. General Hardee preferred Decherd, as stronger and less easily turned, but Tullahoma having been determined on, under orders from General Bragg, marked out the line of fortifications. I examined these fortifications, which are a line of slight redoubts extending in a semicircle from the Fayetteville to the Manchester road. Our advantage of ground is not very obvious, although the engineer in charge assured me it does exist, and the earthworks are low redoubts, not flanked by rifle-pits, except for some 20 yards or so.... The works are either too strong or too weak. Much labor has been wasted on them.[8]

The difference between Bragg's thought process and that of his subordinates speaks volumes of his strategic ability. He paid no heed to wiser counsel and Tullahoma was fortified. Compounding the problem of Bragg's geographical position was the state of affairs within the Confederate commissary. During the spring of 1863 agents had stripped the area's food supply, sending hogs, corn, and beeves to Atlanta for shipment to the Army of Northern Virginia. In one two-week period Bragg fell 400,000 rations short. Both Bragg and Johnston complained, but their repeated warnings failed to bring about the necessary reforms.

The dialogue between the officers in the field and the authorities in Richmond reveal the difference between bureaucratic intent and operational reality. On 15 March, Major A. D. Banks, assistant adjutant-general in Atlanta, sent the following correspondence to Joseph Johnston:

Major Cummings today informs me that the agents sent by him last week into Middle Tennessee and Northern Alabama report a most encouraging prospect. They are much embarrassed for transportation to collect the supplies at depots on the railroad, the country having

---

[8] OR, ser. 1, vol. 23, pt. 1, p. 757–61.

been stripped completely of every description of wagons and carts. Would it not be well to call General Bragg's attention to this matter, and get him to order his chief quartermaster to furnish a certain amount of transportation to be employed for this purpose?[9]

Both men were acutely aware of the problem. Braxton Bragg and Joseph Johnston had already "given their attention to this matter," taking great pains to make Richmond understand their plight. Meat was being hauled from distant points, some as far away as Kentucky—a process that placed an insurmountable burden on the wagons. These factors served to pin Bragg in his current position; they made him feel the need to stay tied to his food supply, poor though it was. Bragg placed the left flank at Columbia and Spring Hill, held by the cavalry under Earl Van Dorn. Leonidas Polk remained at Shelbyville. Hardee held the right center, and a small detachment of Joe Wheeler's horsemen guarded the right flank. These dispositions created a thin line 70 miles in length, protected by roughly 38,000 troops.

It did not take long for the Federals to expose the errors in this deployment. On 10 March a large force drove Van Dorn out of Columbia and the left flank collapsed. On 21 April several Federal columns attacked along a front from Shelbyville to McMinnville. One force struck the Confederates at Guy's Gap while a second defeated Bate at Hoover's Gap before falling back. A third column flanked Hoover's Gap and destroyed the line between McMinnville and Manchester. Further north, yet another force moved on the Nashville-Knoxville Turnpike at Liberty.[10]

Hoover's Gap was formed by a range of hills 11 miles south of Murfreesboro. The gap ran 4 miles long between 1,100-foot ridges that divided the Duck and Stones rivers. It was so narrow that two wagons could barely pass through it side by side. The ridges offered excellent positions for artillery, yet it remained almost undefended. William Bate's brigade, the nearest infantry on the Manchester Road, was 4 miles away at Beech Grove. Rosecrans would be able to attack before Bate could react.[11]

In April rumors began to surface. A Federal movement was imminent but specific details were lacking. One report had the Yankees marching

---

[9] OR, ser. 1, vol. 23, pt. 2, p. 695–96.

[10] Connelly, *Autumn of Glory,* 116.

[11] Report of William B. Bate, 15 July 1863, OR, ser. 1, vol. 23, pt. 1, p. 611.

toward the railroad that connected Manchester and McMinnville. Another story suggested that Rosecrans would move through Hoover's Gap and emerge at Beech Grove. Bragg was undecided, but he ordered Hardee to shift his corps to Wartrace. The Confederates were ordered to prevent the Federals from breaking through the gap and thereby securing the railroad.[12]

Cleburne's division crossed the Duck River on 23 April, forming the van in the retreat. Hardee's corps formed the right wing of the army. On 30 April Cleburne established his headquarters at Wartrace, 15 miles north of Tullahoma on the Nashville and Chattanooga Railroad. He occupied a small wooden building 1 mile north of the center of town, about 50 yards west of the tracks. While there, Bushrod Johnson's brigade was removed from his command and replaced by a similar force of Thomas Churchill's Texans.[13]

Rosecrans knew there were large bodies of Southern troops at Shelbyville and Wartrace, and he knew Wartrace had been well fortified. He planned to move around Hardee's right and force a crossing of the Elk River. From there he would attempt to sever Bragg's supply line from Chattanooga.[14] It was vital to protect the rail connections in Eastern Tennessee, but Braxton Bragg was not the only focus of Richmond's attention. Davis understood the need to defend Vicksburg, but he divided the Confederates in the hope of saving both Chattanooga and Vicksburg. He made a very ill-advised decision and lost them both. On 23 May John C. Breckinridge received orders to take 6,000 men to Mississippi. This force was too small to do any good there, but it weakened the garrison at Tullahoma considerably. Texas, Louisiana, and Arkansas were permanently lost, and Middle Tennessee was abandoned.

On 31 May the Confederate authorities adopted the new "National Flag." Orders were issued at Wartrace for the conversion but Cleburne's men strongly protested. Desiring to keep their independence, each regiment retained the old blue-and-white banner; the stitching around the border displayed the battles in which they had participated. Though a great distinction, this also marked the division for Union guns.[15]

---

[12] Hughes, *Old Reliable,* 154–55.

[13] Howell and Elizabeth Purdue, *Pat Cleburne Confederate General* (1973; repr., Gaithersburg MD: Olde Soldier Books, 1987) 184; Irving A. Buck, *Cleburne and His Command* (1908; repr., Wilmington NC: Broadfoot Publishing, 1995) 125.

[14] Hughes, *Old Reliable,* 156.

[15] Purdue and Purdue, *Pat Cleburne Confederate General,* 188.

Pat Cleburne was noted for his attention to detail. He labored continuously to give his men every advantage when going into battle. He placed a great deal of emphasis on proper care of the rifle and bayonet. The man with the cleanest gun among those assigned to daily guard duty was excused from one round of service.[16] Cleburne began to make improvements in the corps of sharpshooters he had first organized at Corinth. He formed the best marksmen from each regiment into squads under the command of a lieutenant. They were trained in the use of the Whitworth rifle, a British make with a telescopic sight. With a range of up to 2,000 yards, the rifle was the most accurate long-range weapon for infantry use. The Whitworth was very expensive; a rifle and 1,000 rounds of ammunition cost the government $1,000. Cleburne had five of these prized weapons, which armed the first detachment of Whitworth sharpshooters in the Army of Tennessee. His initiative at this early stage was rewarded later in the war. Prior to the Atlanta campaign, the ordnance department procured a shipment from England through the blockade. Cleburne received twenty Whitworth and ten Kerr rifles, more than any other division.[17] Calhoun Benham gave instruction on every part of the rifle and in the morning reviewed its technical aspects. Each afternoon the men studied topography. They practiced over difficult terrain, learning just how to march, stop, and properly estimate distance without the use of a range finder.[18]

On 2 June Bragg was still unsure of Federal intentions. Indications were that William Rosecrans might either move his own men south or send troops to reinforce Ulysses S. Grant in Mississippi. Polk and Hardee were ordered to make a two-day reconnaissance on the Wartrace, Shelbyville, and Manchester roads in the direction of Mufreesboro. Cleburne's division marched over a narrow road through Hoover's Gap and continued until they were 4 miles from Murfreesboro. They drove in Federal pickets, then fell back to Wartrace.

On 6 June reports arrived stating that Rosecrans was not reinforcing Grant, but rather gathering his forces in front of Bragg. Four thousand troops had joined Rosecrans from Kentucky, so Hardee was pulled back to Wartrace while Polk took a position behind fortifications in Shelbyville.[19]

---

[16] Purdue and Purdue, *Pat Cleburne Confederate General,* 186.

[17] Anonymous, "Attention—Whitworth Rifles." *Confederate Veteran* 1 (1893): 117.

[18] Buck, *Cleburne and His Command,* 128.

[19] Connelly, *Autumn of Glory,* 121–22.

Bragg had spent much of the year struggling with dissension in the infantry, but as the month progressed he began to experience problems with his cavalry as well. He had instructed Joe Wheeler to guard Hoover's Gap, as well as points to the east of it, but during the last week of June Wheeler neglected his orders. On the 22 June he pulled most of his men out of the gap in the direction of Shelbyville, where there had been reports of strong Union activity. The only cavalry left guarding the pass was the 1st Kentucky regiment, which was far too small to secure the area.[20]

The Federals began to move on 23 June, and their plan was well conceived. Rosecrans decided to divide forces. To the west of Shelbyville lay cultivated land, an easy march for a large body of men. The area east of the town was crossed by rocky, winding roads and the countryside was badly broken. It seemed logical to move the army over stable ground and attack the Confederate left. Rosecrans had other ideas. He sent one body to Shelbyville, which was nothing more than a feint. This would attract Bragg's attention and hold Polk in place. Liberty Gap was to be occupied, but no significant action would occur there either. The main body would march through Hoover's Gap, while one corps would move around the east side of the mountain. From Hoover's Gap the Yankees would march southeast to Manchester, where Rosecrans would reunite his army.[21]

On 24 June Cleburne was still at Wartrace. He stationed St. John Liddell's brigade at Bell Buckle, 5 miles to the north. A range of hills that parted the headwaters of the Duck and Stones rivers separated the Confederates and the Federals. There were several gaps in the hills. Railroad Gap and Liberty Gap approached Liddell's position and he was ordered to picket both places. Railroad Gap was 4 miles from Bell Buckle, Liberty Gap only 3 miles distant. Two other gaps, Dismal and Hoover's, were to Liddell's right.[22]

In Cleburne's front, most of the Union activity was aimed at Liberty Gap. Liddell described the ground as " a narrow defile about 300 yards in length, cutting the range of hills 2 miles east of New Fosterville. About 4 miles farther to the east the turnpike from Murfreesborough [sic] to Manchester passes through Hoover's Gap, which is an open gorge (or more

---

[20] Connelly, *Autumn of Glory,* 126.
[21] Purdue and Purdue, *Pat Cleburne Confederate General,* 193.
[22] Report of Patrick R. Cleburne, 3 August 1863, OR, ser. 1, vol. 23, pt. 1, p. 586.

properly the narrow valley of a small stream running northwestwardly into Stone's River) between ranges of hills that skirt it on both sides for 4 miles nearly to the Garrison Fork of Duck River, where it begins."[23]

Lucius Featherston of the 5th Arkansas held the left side of Liberty Gap, with another regiment under John Josey on his right. At 1:00 P.M. he reported that his cavalry pickets had been driven in and the enemy was rapidly approaching. Liddell wanted to see for himself. When he arrived he found that although Josey was still fighting, Featherston had repulsed the enemy. The Confederates fought alone, and when the Yankees regrouped both regiments were compelled to fall back. Deep mud had detained part of Liddell's command, but by 5 o'clock the rest of brigade had reached the field. One section of artillery was placed in a valley on the Confederate right, the other on a hill off the left flank. The guns covered the gap and delayed the Federal advance, but skirmishers returned and drove the Confederates back for half a mile. It was raining heavily, so Liddell decided not to renew the contest. He withdrew through the hills and made camp near Bell Buckle; though he had been driven from the center of the gorge, Liddell was still in possession of two densely wooded hills at the south end of it.

On the morning of 25 June the Federals had not changed their position, so Liddell left the 8th Arkansas under John Kelly to cover the approaches to Bell Buckle by way of the railroad cut. He placed Daniel Govan's 2nd Arkansas on a hill southwest of the town on a precipitous rise above Wartrace Creek. They deployed in a line almost perpendicular to the Union left. Featherston and Josey placed their regiments on high ground on the other side of the stream. The elevation ran to 100 feet, covered with thick undergrowth. Liddell posted his battery left of the stream 1 mile to the rear, which commanded the gap, and held the 6th and 7th Arkansas (consolidated) in a reserve position.

The Federals continued to pour fresh troops into the gap, but there was only minor skirmishing until 4:00 P.M. Cavalry reports indicated that some of the wagons were retreating back through the gap, so Liddell ordered Featherston to cautiously throw out his skirmishers. He gradually developed the enemy, and the intensity grew until the armies were hotly engaged. Liddell had anticipated his numerical disadvantage and ordered Josey

---

[23] Report of St. John R. Liddell, 1 August 1863, OR, ser. 1, vol. 23, pt. 1, p. 588.

forward. This drove the Federals back, but the Confederate advance caused them to return in much greater strength.

Liddell brought Govan forward toward Wartrace Creek and hit the Federal left. He pushed the line back upon itself into a cornfield, and the 6th and 7th Arkansas came up in support. While this put heavy pressure on the Union flank, it also left the Confederates without any reserves. The action was furious and Govan began to run low on ammunition. Under the best of circumstances this would have stalled the attack, but the wet ground compounded the problem. The trains were too far to the rear to resupply the infantry; as a result the 2nd Arkansas was ineffective. Liddell estimated that he was outnumbered 6 to 1. With all of the reserves on the front line, the Confederates were unable to hold their ground. The Federals attacked Liddell's left but without success, and both sides returned to their original positions.

Despite efforts to reclaim the pass, the stubborn resistance convinced Cleburne that a force of division size held the ground. He withdrew his right and established his artillery on a hill 400 yards to the rear. Cleburne ordered three regiments of Wood's brigade to come forward, along with a section of Semple's battery, leaving one of Wood's regiments along with one of Liddell's at New Fosterville.

The Confederates fought all day on 26 June, but no progress was made. In the morning both regiments rejoined the army at Liberty Gap and were replaced by Texans who belonged to Churchill. Cleburne's remaining two regiments were drawn to Liberty Gap and held in reserve. In the engagements at Liberty Gap Cleburne's division had lost only twelve men, most of whom had come from Govan's 2nd Arkansas.[24]

While Cleburne fought the Federals to a stalemate, the action on the right had not fared as well. In the late morning 24 June the Yankees had moved through a drizzling rain and taken the ground with very little effort. Bate was horribly out of position, 4 miles away at a Masonic picnic. In essence the fight was over before it began, but he continued to storm the lines in a series of foolish frontal assaults. His lack of judgment cost him 25

[24] OR, ser. 1, vol. 23, pt. 1, p. 587. Cleburne states that he lost 121 men (OR, ser. 1, vol. 23, pt. 1. p. 591). Liddell 591 gives his total casualties at 120. Casualties in Govan's 2nd Arkansas are reported at fifty-eight men.

percent of his brigade.[25] This defeat threatened to cut off Cleburne from Wartrace. During the night he received orders to retreat to Tullahoma using Schoefner's Bridge. The troops left at daylight and the movement was accomplished with minimal loss. It rained constantly on the men, who were already exhausted. By now they had no dry clothes or tents, nor were they able to build any fires.[26]

Braxton Bragg had completely misjudged his adversary. He spent three days reacting to Union movements, always one step behind Rosecrans. Initially he was convinced that a fight would take place at Shelbyville. This appeared to be the case on 24 June as Federal cavalry attacked the Confederates northwest of the town. By the next day the threat had abated, and it became clear that any battle would occur elsewhere. Bragg shifted his focus to Liberty Gap, but once again he was too late. He called Polk to his headquarters and gave orders to strike east through Guy's Gap, hitting the Federals in the flank. Before the bishop could mobilize, Bragg received a report from A. P. Stewart. The Confederates had been swept from the Manchester front by a massive force that appeared to be as large as Hardee's entire corps. The Manchester Road was open and the Federals were heading through Fairfield, only 5 miles east of Wartrace. Bragg realized that Cleburne could be surrounded at the south end of Liberty Gap while Polk was stranded on the north side of the Duck River at Shelbyville. At 11 o'clock Bragg ordered both corps to fall back across the Duck River and into the fortifications at Tullahoma.[27]

After dark Liddell learned that Hoover's Gap had been lost. At daylight the next morning he retreated to Wartrace, but the short journey was a misera-ble one. The division plodded through rain and 300 men lost their shoes along the way. Polk's wagons clogged the road and, he showed no inclination to give way to a subordinate who was moving in much better order. This simple lack of common sense caused Cleburne to halt several times during the march.[28]

---

[25] Connelly, *Autumn of Glory*, 126–27.

[26] Report of Patrick R. Cleburne, 3 August 1863, OR, ser. 1, vol. 23, pt. 1, p. 587.

[27] Connelly, *Autumn of Glory*, 128.

[28] Mark K. Christ, *Getting Used to Being Shot at: The Spence Family Civil War Letters* (Fayetteville: University of Arkansas Press, 2002) 57.

Bragg was thoroughly bewildered. He knew that Rosecrans was on his heels and he had the army in retreat, but beyond that there was little thought of a defense. By 29 June the Confederates, back in Tullahoma, were truly in dire straits. Constant pressure threatened to cut Bragg off from Chattanooga. The swollen Elk River had swamped many of the crossings. Poor cavalry intelligence left Bragg's line of communications at Chattanooga not only vulnerable, but almost unguarded as well.

Indecision ruled the day. Early in the morning Bragg learned that the Federals were moving along the Manchester Pike, headed for Tullahoma. At 9:00 A.M. Polk and Bragg conferred. Even though the Federals were moving around his rear, Bragg still wanted to hold his ground and fight at Tullahoma. Polk, concerned that the army would be cut off from its base of supplies, advised evacuation. Polk sought out Hardee to solicit his opinion. At 3:00 P.M. the two men went to Bragg, but as they were debating the proper course of action a telegram arrived from Decherd. Federal strength was not as strong as originally feared. This report shed new light on the matter and the generals decided to await more definite information. In a pouring rain the troops began to construct breastworks.

By the next morning Bragg learned that both of his flanks were in danger. He determined to retreat again and abandon Tullahoma. The army received some protection from the cavalry and the Rebels crossed the Elk River, but by noon the town was in Union hands. Knee-deep mud forced a slow pace. It took almost twenty-four hours to cover a distance of 8 miles, and the infantry was not across until the first of July. The cavalry arrived by nightfall and the bridges were burned. The new line of defense had Hardee on the Confederate right at Bethpage Bridge, while Polk held the left flank at Allisonia Bridge.[29]

After all this, the army was still not safe. Neither end was secure and the march continued. The only factor working in Bragg's favor was the weather. The river was falling, but it was still too high to permit easy passage for the Federals. By the first of July Polk and Hardee felt convinced that they could no longer trust Bragg's judgment; he was unable to focus on one destination, and he vacillated between giving battle on the Elk River and retreating to Cowan.

---

[29] Connelly, *Autumn of Glory*, 128–32.

Very early on 2 July, Bragg decided to continue, aimlessly drifting south-ward. Shortly after 1:00 A.M. orders were issued for Polk and Hardee to move back to Cowan at the base of the Cumberland Mountains; however, it did not appear as though Bragg ever intended to make a stand there. Almost as soon as Polk and Hardee arrived, Bragg issued orders to depart for Chattanooga.

On the morning of 3 July, Cleburne's division began to climb the hills in the direction of Brakefield Point. By this time the Confederates had outdistanced their pursuers, and Cleburne was no longer acting as a rear guard. The group passed through Sewanee and bivouacked on a plateau, where Cleburne remained for a few days before crossing the Tennessee River at Shell Mound. In the eyes of the Army of Tennessee, Braxton Bragg had led them through a year of futility. The road from Murfreesboro to Chattanooga had barely seen a battle. In fact, casualties had been so light that with new recruits coming in along the way Polk's corps was actually stronger at this point than it had been at the beginning of the campaign. Hardee had seen the majority of the losses, and most of those had occurred at Liberty and Hoover's gaps. In total Hardee lost some 1,700 men, whereas the Federals suffered only 570 casualties.[30] Both strategically and tactically, Rosecrans had bested the Rebels—or more precisely Braxton Bragg.

The Duck River line was surrendered, and with it went much of the morale. Lack of leadership, confidence, organization, planning, reconnaissance, or information as well as poor cavalry support all contributed to the debacle, and without any actual plan of operations, no strong defensive line was ever drawn. Middle Tennessee was simply given away. Lee had been defeated at Gettysburg and on 4 July Vicksburg had fallen. Tennessee was lost and Bragg's army was stationed only miles from the Georgia line. The Union war effort in the West could now be concentrated against the Army of Tennessee.[31]

On 6 July, Hardee had left for Chattanooga. He placed Cleburne in temporary command of both of his divisions. Rutted roads forced a march of 12 difficult miles. The 15th Arkansas rode by train to Chickamauga Station to guard the depot where the Western and Atlantic connected to Atlanta. By

---

[30] OR, ser. 1, vol. 23, pt. 1, p. 419–24 Union losses were tabulated as follows: XIV Corps, 206; XX Corps, 274; XXI Corps, 1; Cavalry, 89; total casualties, 570.

[31] Hughes, *Old Reliable*, 156–58.

10 July the rest of Hardee's corps arrived at Tyner's Station, a small village 9 miles east of Chattanooga on the railroad to Rossville. They camped around the town, with A. P. Stewart nearby and Leonidas Polk closer to Chattanooga. At least for the moment, their march was over.

In the middle of the summer the army was reorganized. With the loss of Vicksburg, Hardee was transferred to Jackson as part of Joseph Johnston's department. Thomas Churchill was also sent west, and James Deshler took command of his Texas brigade. The Confederates had been in Chattanooga before, having used it as a base of movements for the Kentucky campaign as well as the march to Murfreesboro. Now conditions had changed. New reports revealed that Grant was coming from Mississippi, and Burnside was headed south from Knoxville. Against this onslaught Bragg could field but 29,000 men.[32]

---

[32] Connelly, *Autumn of Glory,* 137.

7

CHICKAMAUGA

William Hardee received his orders on 15 July. It was decided to bring someone in from outside of Bragg's influence, and Daniel Harvey Hill was sent from Virginia. For Cleburne the departure of Hardee was quite a change, but Deshler was new as well. As a reorganization of this magnitude could have serious repercussions for the health of the army, it was important to maintain continuity during the transition. Hardee decided to place Cleburne in charge of the corps until Hill arrived; he continued to serve in this capacity whenever Hill was absent.

While the transfer of Hardee was unwise, the choice of his replacement was worse. From the outset, the relationship between Hill and Bragg was a stormy one. They had not seen each other since 1845, when Hill and George Thomas were lieutenants in Bragg's artillery battalion. Hill's new commander had changed considerably. Before him now was a mere shell of a man: "He was silent and reserved and seemed gloomy and despondent. He had grown prematurely old since I saw him last, and showed much nervousness. His many retreats, too, had alienated the rank and file from him, or at least taken away that enthusiasm which soldiers feel for a successful general and which make them obey his orders without question, and thus wins for him other successes."[1]

Both men were quick-tempered, irritable, and apt to blame others for their mistakes. Given Bragg's failure-littered career and Hill's naturally disagreeable nature, the operations in the West were certain to fall apart.[2]

The ground in this part of North Georgia was extremely rugged. It made movement difficult and presented an excellent opportunity for an offensive

---

[1] Daniel Harvey Hill, "Chickamauga—The Great Battle of the West," in Robert Underwood Johnston and Clarence Clough Buel, eds., *Battles and Leaders of the Civil War*, 4 vols. (1884–1887; repr., Secaucus NJ: Castle Books, n.d.) 3:639.

[2] Peter Cozzens, *This Terrible Sound* (Urbana: University of Illinois Press, 1992) 27–28; Thomas L.Connelly, *Autumn of Glory: The Army of Tennessee 1862–1865* (Baton Rouge: Louisiana State University Press, 1971) 155.

should the enemy become separated. In a series of post-war articles written for the *Kennesaw Gazette*, Calhoun Benham described the surrounding terrain:

> The Tennessee River may be regarded as the northern boundary of the general scene of these operations, beginning at Chattanooga on its left bank, and following to Bridgeport, about twenty-eight miles below, in a direction a little west of south. From a point on the left bank, about a mile below the center of Chattanooga, makes off in a direction a little west of south the celebrated Lookout Mountain. It is an isolated ridge upwards of thirty miles long, about 1,800 feet high above the waters of the river, with a plateau on the top of an irregular width. From its base to within 100 feet of the plateau-top of the mountain, its sides steep, yet sloping, are covered with huge masses of rock, fallen from above, and are barely practicable of ascent for infantry. The remaining distance to the edge of the plateau above are sheer cliffs…only a few rude and difficult roads ascending to the top. From the easterly side of the mountain, at a point about thirty miles from Chattanooga, a large spur breaks off, and, bending sharply around to the north, runs some ten or twelve miles in an almost unbroken ridge, parallel with Lookout. This last ridge is known as Pigeon Mountain. The valley between Lookout Mountain and Pigeon Mountain is a cul-de-sac, a blind alley, with sides impracticable even for infantry, except at a few points, about six miles wide, and chiefly cultivated farms and here and there clumps of forest trees. It is known as McLemore's Cove. This valley is for the most part level, perfectly practicable for field evolutions, though perhaps somewhat embarrassed by the west branch of Chickamauga Creek [river it is called] and by Chattanooga Creek, which drains it.[3]

Tyner's Station was only a small depot on the Knoxville Railroad. Cleburne established his headquarters in the home of J. S. Tyner, a captain in the Confederate Army. Logically the Federals would cross the Tennessee River above Chattanooga, since the terrain was much more favorable in that area and

---

[3] Calhoun Benham, "Major Gen. P. R. Cleburne," *Kennesaw* (GA) *Gazette,* 15 March 1889, 2; L. G. Bennett, and William Haigh, *History of the 36th Illinois Volunteers* (Aurora IL: Knickerbocker & Hodder, 1876) 446–47.

would facilitate a junction with Burnside's troops moving south from Knoxville. The Confederates began to build fortifications. Cleburne supervised the construction of four large, round forts, each one some 12 feet high and 200-300 feet in diameter.[4]

Rosecrans made several demonstrations to the north in the hope that Bragg would believe his intent was in fact to isolate Buckner. Bragg reacted to the movements by assigning Cleburne the task of protecting the fords. Cleburne dispersed his command between Blythe's, Thatcher's and Gardenshire ferries as well as at Harrison's Landing. In addition, he placed several companies in a line from the mouth of Chickamauga Creek to the Hiwassee River. Each location was strengthened by rifle pits and artillery, but the Union activity was merely a feint. The main thrust would come further south. The ruse worked and Bragg based his dispositions on a false assumption. On 21 August the Federals appeared on the right bank of the river at Bridgeport, 24 miles southwest of Chattanooga. Suddenly the Confederates were out of position.

Despite all his precautions, Bragg knew that he needed reinforcements. Initially he tried to go through the proper channels. Without any Federal presence in Mississippi, he felt confident that many of the troops there could be reassigned. Richmond hesitated, leaving the decision to Johnston. Johnston agreed in part and on 23 August released Walker's Reserve Corps, followed by Breckinridge's division two days later.

With the arrival of these men the army would grow by 9,000,[5] and while this was certainly welcome news Bragg knew he needed troops from Virginia. Lee was against the idea; however, James Longstreet sought an independent command and began to lay the groundwork for a transfer. He considered himself far superior to Robert E. Lee as a military man. On 2 September he penned a note to Lee, who was then in Richmond discussing the very subject with Jefferson Davis.

On 22 August the Federals had shelled Harrison's Landing, and as the week wore on the men began to sense an attack. On 29 August, Irving Buck wrote the following to his sister:

---

[4] Howell and Elizabeth Purdue, *Pat Cleburne Confederate General* (1973; repr., Gaithersburg MD: Olde Soldier Books, 1987) 203–204; Irving A. Buck, *Cleburne and His Command* (1908; repr., Wilmington NC: Broadfoot Publishing, 1995) 134.

[5] Cozzens, *This Terrible Sound,* 37–38.

... a battle was considered as imminent—it has not transpired although the enemy is still in our front & shells our position every day or two—but so far has succeeded in killing only one man, a sharpshooter assigned to these Hdqrs.... Genl Cleburne was watching the fight with one of their batteries yesterday, when they threw a shell which fell about three feet in front of him but fortunately did not explode.... Am afraid his intrepidity will cause his death yet. A battle may be fought very soon.[6]

H. W. Kinsey, a captain of the 15th Arkansas Company C, echoed these sentiments from his position at Chickamauga Station: "We are expecting a fight here soon. Rosey [Rosecrans] is pegging away at Chattanooga from the opposite bank of the river & I can hear the booming of his cannon while I write."[7]

It soon became clear that the Confederates could not possibly hold Knoxville. Bragg transferred A. P. Stewart's division to Buckner and assigned Breckinridge to Harvey Hill. On 26 August, Buckner received orders to evacuate and was pulled back to the Hiwassee. Four days later Bragg learned that two Federal columns had crossed the river southwest of Chattanooga. When Thomas established his headquarters at Trenton, the Confederate rear was in danger.[8]

The Union Army continued to advance, and by 4 September large bodies of troops were in Will's Valley, west of Lookout Mountain. Bragg sent cavalry to watch their movements and considered mounting an attack. He wrote a note to Hill, instructing him to consult Cleburne on the feasibility of such a movement. At 10:00 P.M. the next day, Cleburne responded:

General: I have just received the private letter of General Bragg, dated 10 a.m., September 4. I am of the opinion that we should crush the corps opposite us if we can. I do not know, however, what force you have. I have a fraction over 5,000 men. I do not know how we could cross our artillery. This is a necessary calculation, as the enemy

---

[6] Purdue and Purdue, *Pat Cleburne Confederate General*, 206.

[7] Purdue and Purdue, *Pat Cleburne Confederate General*, 207.

[8] William M. Polk, *Leonidas Polk Bishop and General*, 2 vols. (1893; repr., New York: Sprinkle Publications, 2001) 168.

have had time to fortify, and doubtless have done so at the foot of the mountain.

I have ordered the trains to start as early as possible in the morning. The men had little, if any, sleep last night; they should have some tonight. I selected camp at Ooltewah as directed by you. My inspectors are all absent now for that purpose. If the camps at Ooltewah are taken up, I will occupy Stewart's old camps.

Colonels Smith and Nixon will probably not reach this point before the middle of the day tomorrow.

I will let you know early in the morning where my headquarters will be.[9]

This tepid response caused Bragg to abandon any offensive plans he may have entertained. On 5 September, Lee reluctantly agreed to release two divisions under Longstreet to the Army of Tennessee; their journey would be a difficult one. Without Southern control of Knoxville, they would be forced to take a much more circuitous route through the Carolinas and Georgia—a 775-mile journey over a horribly dilapidated rail system. John B. Hood commanded some of the finest troops in Virginia and Lafayette McLaws had a steady, if not spectacular, division in his own right. At the time McLaws was in Atlanta, so Joseph Kershaw temporarily led his troops. On 9 September, along with a twenty-six-gun artillery battalion under Porter Alexander, the trains began to leave Richmond.

Early on 6 September, Cleburne consolidated his division and marched from Harrison's Landing through Tyner's Station until he reached Chattanooga. At dusk on the following day, he led the Confederates down the LaFayette Road, a central artery that ran north and south all the way through the battlefield at Chickamauga. Five miles from Chattanooga they filed through Rossville Gap and halted for the night at Lee and Gordon's Mill. Cleburne had been given the task of securing the right flank of the army, but his ability to do so was somewhat diminished. St. John Liddell had been transferred temporarily to Walker's Reserve Corps, leaving Cleburne with only three brigades to hold the passes in Pigeon Mountain. Deshler held the

---

[9] US War Department, comp., *The War of the Rebellion: A Compilation of the Official Records of the Union and Confederate Armies*, 128 vols. (Washington, DC: Government Printing Office, 1880–1901) ser. 1, vol. 30, pt. 4, p. 601.

north end of the line at Catlett's Gap with S. A. M. Wood in the center at Dug Gap. Further south, Lucius Polk's brigade watched Bluebird Gap.[10]

The Rebels continued, marching 14 miles to LaFayette. Hill's corps concentrated around the town while the remainder of the army made camp around the mill.[11] In the early morning, Will Martin's cavalry reported the presence of Federal forces at Stevens and Cooper's gaps, with the opinion that the enemy was so badly separated that nothing could save them from a prompt attack. Martin added that James Negley's advance had pushed into McLemore's Cove, a densely wooded tract of land between Pigeon and Lookout mountains. The troopers withdrew and fortified the areas in front of Wood and Polk. Several warnings went back to headquarters throughout the day, but they seemed to have little effect.

Martin sent the 3rd Alabama Cavalry back into the cove to watch the Federals and, on the afternoon of 9 September, sent Bragg a final message. A Union force believed to be between 4,000 and 8,000 men was isolated at Davis's Cross Roads. It was nothing more than a small intersection northwest of Dug Gap, but it lay only 10 miles from Lee and Gordon's Mill. This finally caught Bragg's attention, as it offered the chance to destroy a comparatively helpless target. However, as was his custom, he failed to act. While he halted the army between Chattanooga and LaFayette, he took no further action.[12]

Thomas Crittenden took possession of Chattanooga without opposition, but Rosecrans failed to unite his army. Instead of bringing his troops together, he continued to divide his forces. He believed that Bragg was trying to escape. The Federals began a hasty pursuit of a foe that had no intentions of flight. Crittenden was dispatched to Ringgold while Thomas marched to McLemore's Cove. McCook was in Alpine, too far away to offer any assistance. As the Federals continued to enter the cove, Cleburne sent Wood to the top of Pigeon Mountain to hold the gaps. He placed obstructions in the gorges while Polk and Deshler remained at LaFayette.[13]

During the night, Bragg divulged his plans. Hindman would take his division through Worthen's Gap into the northern rim of the cove, where he

---

[10] Buck, *Cleburne and His Command,* 135–37.

[11] Purdue and Purdue, *Pat Cleburne Confederate General,* 209.

[12] Polk, *Leonidas Polk,* 171.

[13] Hill, "Chickamauga," 641.

would turn south until he reached Davis's Cross Roads. Cleburne would
cross the ridge at Dug Gap and connect their forces. Hindman would assume
command of both divisions and attack the Federals, then believed to be at the
base of Lookout Mountain near Stevens's Gap. Hill received a copy of the
orders, but their vague language caused several problems. Bragg's generals
were suddenly given the latitude to use their own initiative, but having been
persistently criticized by Bragg during the repeated retreats, they were reluctant
to act decisively. Second, the orders to Hindman did not indicate whether he
was to communicate with Hill prior to reaching the crossroads, nor did they
give instructions on how to deal with any of the Federals still at Cooper's Gap.
Furthermore, Hill was not told when to start his movement. He was either to
put his forces under Cleburne or take charge of them himself, then "unite"
with Hindman in the morning. Bragg added that "if unforeseen
circumstances" prevented his movement, he was to notify Hindman.[14]

Shortly after daylight on 10 September, Hill received a directive from
Bragg's chief of staff dated 9 September, 11:45 P.M.:

> I inclose [sic] orders given General Hindman [commanding a
> division]. General Bragg directs that you send or take, as your
> judgment dictates, Cleburne's division to reunite with Hindman at
> <u>Davis'</u> Cross-Roads tomorrow morning. Hindman starts at 12 o'clock
> tonight, and has 13 miles to make. The commander of the columns
> thus united will move upon the enemy at the foot of Stevens' Gap, said
> to be 4,000 or 5,000. If unforeseen circumstances should prevent
> your movement, notify Hindman. A cavalry force should accompany
> your column. Hindman has none. Open communications with
> Hindman by your cavalry in advance of the junction. He marches on
> the road from Dr. Anderson's to Davis' Cross-Roads.[15]

Hill could only offer excuses as to why he was unable to comply. He
stated that the directive had been received at a very late hour and Cleburne had
been sick in bed all day. Two of Cleburne's regiments that had been detailed
to guard the crossings near Harrison's Landing had yet to rejoin the division,
the gaps were still obstructed, and it would consume a great deal of time to

---

[14] Connelly, *Autumn of Glory*, 175–77.
[15] Report of Daniel H. Hill, n.d., OR, ser. 1, vol. 30, pt. 2, p. 137–38.

reopen them. Hill's lack of initiative was deplorable. Cleburne was not sick at all, but regardless of his health, the absence of one general should not have cancelled the entire operation. Hill made no attempts to ascertain the location of Cleburne's troops or to find out how long it would take to open the gaps. He acted on the defensive when he should have looked to attack.

During the early hours of 11 September, Polk and Deshler marched from LaFayette to Dug Gap, followed by Walker's corps. The Federals made a stand on the opposite side of the creek, but Semple's battery drove them from their position. Wood began to remove the obstructions, and within three hours the passes were clear. Bragg clearly wanted action, and at 4:20 A.M. Hindman received his instructions: " Headquarters are here [in LaFayette] and the following is the information: Crittenden's corps is advancing on us from Chattanooga. A large force from the south has advanced within 7 miles of this. Polk is left at Anderson's to cover your rear. General Bragg orders you to attack and force your way through the enemy to this point at the earliest hour that you can see him in the morning. Cleburne will attack in front the moment your guns are heard."[16]

Cleburne and Walker proceeded to Dug Gap, where they waited for the sound of Hindman's guns. At daylight Wood's brigade deployed on the edge of the cove at Jay's Mill. Deshler followed at 8 o'clock; he planned to move on the Federal flank and rear as soon as the action opened. Hill and Bragg joined Cleburne but the attack did not materialize. Couriers were sent along the top of Pigeon Mountain all the way to Catlett's Gap, but they were unable to report anything more than a body of troops lined up across Davis's Cross Roads. Finally at noon, still having heard no sounds of battle, an exasperated Braxton Bragg ordered Cleburne and Walker to go ahead. In order to stimulate his reluctant lieutenant, he sent the following message to Hindman: "If you find the enemy in such force as to make an attack imprudent, fall back at once on LaFayette by Catlett's Gap, from which obstructions have now been removed. Send your determination at once and act as promptly."[17]

Soon thereafter Bragg received a second dispatch, now estimating the troops in the cove to be some 12,000 men. Combined, the Confederates still held a numerical advantage of 4 to 1, but Hindman hesitated. To obtain more specific information, he sent an aide on a very circuitous route around the east

---

[16] Report of Thomas C. Hindman, 25 October 1863, OR, ser. 1, vol. 30, pt. 2, p. 294.

[17] Cozzens, *This Terrible Sound,* 72.

end of Pigeon Mountain. The ride took several hours to complete and it was 4 o'clock before Hindman received a reply. Captain Taylor Beatty arrived as daylight began to fade. The instructions read, "The attack which was ordered at daybreak must be made at once, or it will be too late."

It was already too late. Although sharpshooters from Wood's brigade drove back the skirmishers, the Federals were withdrawing through Stevens's Gap. Cleburne found Hindman at Davis's Cross Roads as darkness fell, but by then Negley was gone. Negley's capture or defeat at this point would have dealt Rosecrans a serious blow. With his troops so badly dispersed, he had already lost any advantage of position and could have been beaten in detail.

Negley had moved past a small cluster of cabins known as Bailey's Cross Roads and simply ventured too far into the cove. As he wrote following Chickamauga, the mistake was not lost on him:

> ...it would be impossible to hold this or any other position south of Bailey's Cross-Roads and fight a battle without involving the certain destruction of the trains, which, from the contour of these ridges and uneven nature of the ground, we would be obliged to park in close proximity to our position.... Buckner's corps was deployed and moving steadily on our left, within short range.... The firing increased and indicated an immediate general engagement along our entire front, and would have terminated in an assault from the enemy in a few moments, which would unquestionably have been disastrous to us, considering the overwhelming force of the enemy and our very unfavorable position.[18]

Here again, a lack of communication among the Confederates ruined the day. Hindman did not trust Bragg's evaluation of conditions on the field. He feared that the opposing force was too large to attack and that additional reinforcements were close at hand. He also worried that his movement might be observed by Federal outposts on Lookout Mountain, which would then notify Crittenden and give Negley ample time to withdraw. Hindman

---

[18] Report of James S. Negley, 17 September 1863, OR, ser. 1, vol. 30, pt. 1, p. 327–28; Bennett and Haigh, *36th Illinois,* 452.

rationalized his vacillation by regarding the order as discretionary, not peremptory.[19]

After the debacle at Dug Gap, Bragg grew confused. By 3:00 A.M. on 12 September, Bragg had received a cavalry report confirming that the Federals were still far apart and the Bluecoats were indeed divided. Ten miles separated Crittenden from Thomas's left flank, while McCook faced 30 miles of mountainous terrain if he hoped to reunite his army. Bragg left Cleburne to guard the gaps, but he still worried that McCook would move on his flank. The Confederates were moved back to LaFayette, where they awaited an attack. This allowed Crittenden to withdraw to Lee and Gordon's Mill and extricate himself from a hazardous position. By nightfall of 12 September, he had established communications with Thomas and the Yankees had escaped again.[20]

Bragg believed that he still had an opportunity to move against Crittenden, and Leonidas Polk's corps was the closest force at hand. The Confederates were to attack at dawn at Rock Spring Church, 6 miles southeast of the mill at the intersection of the State and Pea Vine Church roads. During the day of 13 September, Bragg issued four separate directives but Polk did not advance. Like Hindman, Polk thought that his target was well supported. After missing a second chance, Bragg ordered Polk to return to LaFayette, leaving Cleburne's lone division to hold Pigeon Mountain against Thomas's whole corps.

By this point, any hope of effective cooperation was gone. Bragg felt that all of his subordinates had failed him, and he could no longer rely on them to execute his orders. However, the distrust was mutual. No one had any confidence in Bragg as a leader or in the success of his battle plans. The fundamental problem was that no one knew where the Federals were. On 13 September, while Bragg was with Polk at Rock Spring Church, he received a note from Hill stating that McCook was within a few miles of LaFayette. Buckner's corps was shifted to block the attack, but the Federals did not appear. On the same day Martin reported that McCook was not advancing at all but was in fact retreating in the direction of Alpine. Two days later

---

[19] Purdue and Purdue, *Pat Cleburne Confederate General,* 214–15; Buck, *Cleburne and his Command,* 140–41.

[20] Polk, *Leonidas Polk,* 171–72.

Wheeler's cavalry claimed that he had left Alpine, headed for "unknown parts."[21]

In a diary entry dated 13 September, George Brent wrote that the reports of Rosecrans's location came "as thick as leaves...from all quarters and directions."[22] In an article written for *Century* magazine, Hill described the commanding general: "The truth is, General Bragg was bewildered by 'the popping out of the rats from so many holes,' the wide dispersion of the Federal forces, and their confrontal of him at so many point, perplexed him, of congratulation that such grand opportunities were offered for crushing them one by one."[23]

At 8:00 A.M. Hill learned that cavalry pickets had been driven in along the Alpine Road the prior evening. It was imperative to secure the road, so he ordered Breckinridge to replace them with a detail of infantry. When Hill arrived he found that the assault had come against Adams's brigade but had been turned away with heavy loss. Still, the size of the demonstration made it seem as if the Federals were advancing in force, so Hill brought Lucius Polk down from his position at Pigeon Mountain. McCook observed what he believed was a contingent of fresh reinforcements and decided to pull back rather than risk a battle under conditions he could not control.[24]

As of 14 September Rosecrans had still failed to correct his mistakes. McCook remained at Alpine, with Thomas at McLemore's Cove and Crittenden around Lee & Gordon's Mill. Rosecrans finally realized his predicament and ordered McCook to move north. He was to join Thomas with all possible speed, and the Ohioan could not have given a greater effort. His men marched day and night and by 17 September McCook had brought the two armies together at Stevens's Gap. For the moment, the danger had passed.[25]

Now Thomas and McCook, on the west side of Pigeon Mountain, and the Confederates on the east of it all marched north toward Lee and Gordon's Mill. Bragg wanted to deploy his forces with his right at Reed's Bridge and

---

[21] Connelly, *Autumn of Glory*, 189–90.

[22] George Brent, diary, 13 September 1863, Braxton Bragg Papers, Western Reserve Historical Society, Cleveland OH, from microfilm edition at University of West Florida, Pensacola FL.

[23] Hill, "Chickamauga." 644.

[24] Report of Daniel H. Hill, n.d., OR, ser. 1, vol. 30, pt. 2, p. 139–41.

[25] Buck, *Cleburne and His Command*, 142.

his left at McLemore's Cove. At dawn on 18 September Cleburne's division marched to Dr. Anderson's property, 4 miles south of the mill where he formed a line of battle on the Confederate left. Breckinridge was sent to guard the crossing at Glass's Mill.

By nightfall Rosecrans had placed his command in a line 11 miles long running from Lee & Gordon's Mill to Stevens's Gap. He was concerned that Bragg would try to hit his left in order to take possession of the Dry Valley and Rossville roads. Rosecrans had correctly divined his opponent's intentions, as Bragg understood that an attack in that sector would force the Federals back up Chickamauga Creek and turn them away from Chattanooga.[26]

Bragg had wanted to begin his attack at 6:00 A.M. on 18 September, and he had drafted orders sending Walker across the Chickamauga at either Alexander's Bridge or Byram's Ford. On his left, Buckner would cross at Thedford's Ford while Polk would cooperate by drawing Crittenden's attention at Lee & Gordon's Mill. Once again Bragg's orders lacked specifics. They were clear on where to cross but provided no details to govern Confederate movements after they had forded the creek. Regardless, from a military standpoint the routes of advance offered few benefits. Even if the initial movement were uncontested, there was not enough distance between the Confederates and Crittenden's left flank. The northernmost crossing—that at Alexander's Bridge—was only 3 miles behind Lee & Gordon's Mill. The plans had to be revised, and another day was lost.

This careless mistake allowed Rosecrans the critical time necessary to extend his left. He brought Thomas forward in a desperate nightlong march. The head of the column reached Union headquarters at the Widow Glenn's house at dawn. With Thomas now on the left, Crittenden in the center, and McCook on the right, the new line ran roughly parallel to the LaFayette Road.[27]

The Federals had an entire corps facing Forrest, which gave George Thomas an opening. He lashed out with two brigades from John Brannan's division, under John Croxton and Ferdinand Van Derveer. The impact caused Forrest to ask Walker for reinforcements, but the Georgian responded

---

[26] Russell K. Brown, *To the Manner Born: The Life of General William H. T. Walker* (Athens: University of Georgia Press, 1994) 168.

[27] Buck, *Cleburne and His Command,* 143.

with only Claudius Wilson's infantry, and on Wilson's right, the troopers under H. B. Davidson.

This small contingent fell far short of the number of men Forrest sought, so Polk agreed to add George Dibrell's brigade of Tennessee cavalry. He formed on Davidson and when he did so the line extended beyond Croxton's left. Dibrell shifted further to his right in an attempt to turn the corner, but he ran straight into Van Derveer. Brisk skirmishing ensued with Forrest riding back and forth, urging his men to hold their ground, as more of Walker's infantry were on the way. Matthew Ector arrived on the scene at 9:30 and Forrest quickly put him in place. Wilson had Croxton under control, so Ector was sent to Dibrell's assistance. Van Derveer met him with a storm of lead, and by 10:30 the Confederates had been turned away with heavy loss.

By this point Croxton was running low on ammunition, but just before his supply was exhausted he was reinforced by John King's Regulars. He fell back through King's men, who then hit Wilson in the right flank. Although he had seen early success, Forrest worried that he might outdistance his support. Wilson now had Federals on his right while Benjamin Scribner's brigade attacked his left, and John Starkweather had come up in reserve. This caught Wilson in a trap, shattering his command. He lost about 50 percent of his men. By 11:00 A.M. Scribner had gathered his forces on the edge of Winfrey Field.[28]

The battle was moving north and Thomas continued to struggle. Rosecrans sent him three divisions, led by Johnson, Palmer, and Reynolds. While Rosecrans was rushing to send more troops to his left, Bragg had heard the firing from Jay's Mill. He ordered Walker to release Liddell, then he moved Cheatham to his right to support the Reserve Corps.

Liddell formed in two lines on the south side of Winfrey Field. Daniel Govan's brigade held the left with Edward Walthall's Mississippians on his right. Just after 11 o'clock the Confederates passed the Winfrey house, 500 yards south of Scribner's brigade. Half an hour later Govan moved through dense woods and across the Brotherton Road with Walthall right behind him.

The Federals were brimming with confidence. They had just destroyed Wilson and the field was theirs, but they had no idea there were Confederates

---

[28] Report of Claudius C. Wilson, 1 October 1863, OR, ser. 1, vol. 30, pt. 2, p. 248–49; report of Absalom Baird, 25 September 1863, OR, ser. 1, vol. 30, pt. 1, p. 275; report of John C. Starkweather, 23 September 1863, OR, ser. 1, vol. 30, pt. 1, p. 299–300.

on their right. When the Rebels hit the flank they threw the Yankees into complete disorder. Scribner lost almost half the brigade, 400 of whom surrendered. Stunned by the suddenness of the attack, they were unable to hold their ground and fell back on Starkweather's Midwesterners. The Confederates continued to press the attack and forced both of them back to Baird's third brigade, which was King's. Along with troops under Van Derveer and John Connell, the Federals were finally able to form a line. After a fight of half an hour against parts of five brigades, the exhausted Confederates were forced to fall back. Federal reinforcements continued to arrive and, for the moment, William Rosecrans led the race for control of the LaFayette Road.[29]

Around 3:00 P.M. Harvey Hill went to confer with Bragg at Thedford's Ford. He was instructed to move Cleburne's division from Dr. Anderson's and occupy the far right of the Confederate line. The orders directed Cleburne to report to Leonidas Polk, and 5,000 men plunged through chest-deep water at Dalton's Ford. Cleburne crossed an open field on the property of the Hunt family and arrived at 6 o'clock. Initially, Polk placed him in line behind Cheatham and Liddell. He deployed roughly 300 yards to their rear, with his right on Jay's Mill and his left extending southward for approximately 1 mile. Lucius Polk held the right flank of the division, supported by Calvert's battery. Wood's infantry and Semple's artillery were in the center, with Deshler's Texas brigade and Douglas's guns on the left. The clearing in front of Wood was the only break in an otherwise wooded area. Along with Cheatham, Cleburne would move forward to attack, with Liddell and Walker in support.

The Union position in front of Cleburne was a strong one, as he would be forced to attack higher ground, and the Yankees had been able to throw up light breastworks. He faced three brigades of Richard Johnson's division: Joseph Dodge on his left, August Willich in the center, and Philemon Baldwin on the right. To Baldwin's left and rear, Thomas had brought up Starkweather and Scribner from Baird's division.

Night had fallen but Leonidas Polk decided to attack. Not only were the orders ill advised, but they were unnecessary as well. Thomas recognized that his position was untenable, and he had already determined to withdraw all five brigades to a new line half a mile behind the first one. This was all the

[29] Cozzens, *This Terrible Sound,* 140–45.

distance Polk could realistically have expected to gain in the first place, and any casualties on the Confederate side would be a needless waste of life.[30]

S. A. M. Wood's men were the first Confederates to make contact. From left to right, Wood commanded the 33rd, 16th, and 45th Alabama infantry regiments, followed by the 32nd and 45th Mississippi (consolidated). He sent the 15th Mississippi sharpshooters forward as skirmishers, but their Union counterparts were armed with Henry repeating rifles. Wood was clearly outmatched. The Rebels attempted to advance, but little progress was made in a somewhat tentative and uncoordinated assault. Colonel E. B. Breedlove's 45th Alabama moved forward in the face of artillery fire from the 5th Indiana battery. To his left, John McGaughey's 16th started in good order, then stopped only halfway across the field. Sam Adams halted the 33rd Alabama for ten minutes while he waited for McGaughey to continue. Mark Lowrey's Mississippians began to lag and soon trailed the Alabama troops by 75 yards. They were hopelessly out of position, and when they opened fire they hit Breedlove in the right flank. It was a decidedly inauspicious beginning.

When Lowrey crossed Winfrey Field he ran into Baldwin's 1st Ohio regiment, which made up the right side of the front line. Both sides were extremely nervous and the Buckeyes opened fire. Most of the shots went high and revealed their position. Lowrey's men climbed over a rail fence and continued through the clearing, but the 5th Kentucky joined the attack.

With help from John Jackson's brigade, the 33rd and 16th struck Willich, driving him from the field. With their support gone, the right flank of the 1st Ohio was suddenly exposed. Adams led his men in pursuit, but again McGaughey abandoned his attack for no apparent reason. His right had taken thirty prisoners and his left was pounding the enemy before him, yet he called retreat. On this night discipline was lacking, and the regiment did not give a good account of itself. Most of the men tried to reform and come back to the front, but companies E and G left the field and never did return.

Philemon Baldwin was with his old regiment, the 6th Indiana, in the right rear of his brigade. Fragments of the 1st Ohio suddenly appeared, pouring back through his lines. He tried to rally the men in the dark but he was fighting a losing battle. Richard Johnson had already given him the orders to retreat; however, the pressure was too great to withstand and his brigade was rapidly melting away. At this point Baldwin made a gallant but tragic

---

[30] Cozzens, *This Terrible Sound,* 264–66.

decision. He grabbed the colors and screamed, "Follow me!" As he turned his horse to the front for just an instant, at 7:00 P.M., a bullet brought him to the ground.

The Hoosiers held just long enough to receive another charge, this time from Sam Adams. Fighting was hand to hand, and although the Rebels had the initiative the 33rd was in trouble. Jackson's brigade had come up behind him and was now shooting into his rear while Deshler drifted into his left flank. Adams began to worry that McGaughey might do the same on his right so he called a halt. The momentary pause gave the Federals enough time to retire into the woods, where they regrouped 200 yards away.

Adams rode back to Winfrey Field, where Wood gave him instructions to fall back. The Union line was in shambles. With Baldwin gone, the brigade command went to William Berry, senior colonel of the 5th Kentucky. After the first wave of gray, as he tried to hold his ground, a brief lull in the action occurred. His Yankees looked out into the night, hoping to identify the dark shadows in their front, when just at that moment the field exploded. Breedlove and Lowrey lunged forward in a second attack so sudden that despite the cover of darkness thirty-two men surrendered to the Mississippians.

Berry's regiment received something of a reprieve as many of the Confederates held their fire, thinking that they were shooting into their own ranks. Unfortunately, the blessing was short-lived. John Starkweather's 79th Pennsylvania moved up in support but charged into their own Kentuckians by mistake. With great difficulty the Yankees were finally able to withdraw, but Berry estimated a loss of 7 officers and 100 men in only thirty minutes of stupidity. Harvey Hill arrived, instructing Wood to hold his ground and await further orders from Cleburne. For all of their sacrifice, the Confederate center had gained only 300 yards.

On Cleburne's right Lucius Polk had greater success, though he received a great deal of assistance from Union mistakes. The Yankees' nerves were taut, the Confederates were in their front, and there was little more light than the flash of muskets. For some reason Starkweather decided to return to the very same position his brigade had lost only seven hours earlier; it was still covered with his own dead and dying.

Needless to say, the grizzly sight did not inspire confidence among the rank and file. They were carrying their wounded from the field when they heard gunfire break out on their right. When Baldwin dissolved, Johnson knew that his division was in trouble. He wanted both brigades to wheel to their right and hit the Confederates in the flank, but this was just too much to expect. The Federals only managed to become entangled with each other. They began firing in every direction just as Polk charged and the Yankees were driven back over the hill for good. At a loss of sixty men, most of whom were only slightly wounded, Polk had taken the ground in his front, gathered fifty prisoners, and captured three pieces of artillery. His advance had far outdistanced Wood, so he wisely stopped the pursuit.

The action on Cleburne's left was disorganized at best. While Wood and Polk had moved to the northwest, Deshler headed west. As he continued he created a gap 500 yards wide. Jackson brought up his brigade to fill the space, but he thought he was holding a supporting position and did not realize he was under attack. It was only after his lead elements began taking casualties that he became aware of the conditions in his front. He rushed forward, but Willich countered with the 15th Ohio and 89th Illinois. Both regiments were forced back 300 yards under the weight of the charge, but they were able to make a stand and Jackson could not go any further. The attack was so disjointed that his aide-de-camp and inspector-general rode into the Union lines and were captured.

Deshler's performance was woeful. He stopped almost 200 yards before reaching the enemy and his skirmishers were taken prisoner. No one fired on them but many of his men fell back to the safety of Preston Smith's brigade, which held the ground on Jackson's left. With a great deal of effort they were sent back to the front, but the line held for only a moment before it began to waver. Thoroughly confused, Deshler moved even further to his left and uncovered two of the regiments behind him. Smith looked ahead, barely able to distinguish what looked like a line. In light of the past few moments he thought he had run across more of Deshler's stragglers. He attempted to hit one man with the flat of his sword, but the Yankee dodged the blow and aimed his rifle. Preston Smith toppled from his saddle.[31]

On the left of his line Deshler finally saw some progress. In brief hand-to-hand fighting he drove in Dodge's right regiment, the 77th Pennsylvania. Although most of the men were able to escape, the Bluecoats lost their colonel, 7 line officers, and 73 men to capture. The battle shifted to the 79th Illinois, but when they sought to evade the Texans, they headed right into Alfred

[31] Report of Samuel Adams, 8 October 1863, OR, ser. 1, vol. 30, pt. 2, p. 161.

Vaughan's Tennessee brigade and surrendered ninety-one men. The Confederates clearly held the upper hand, but they were in no condition to take advantage of their success. In the darkness there was no telling where a bullet might land. By 10:00 P.M. the battle was halted and the Federals had been driven back over a mile. Cleburne's loss was small, occurring principally in Wood's brigade. The next day he discovered that they had captured three pieces of artillery, several caissons, 300 prisoners, and 2 stand of colors.[32]

The night was bitterly cold, and the wounded suffered severely under the first frost of the season. Captain W. P. Herron of the 72nd Indiana spent the night frozen in a pool of his own blood and had to be chopped free in the morning. The still was broken by cries of agony. Cleburne could hear the work of axes in preparation for the fight that was sure to come.[33]

Strategically, the intent was to cut off Rosecrans from his base at Chattanooga. The key point at Chickamauga was the LaFayette Road. Without its possession, the Federals would be trapped. If they could hold it the army would remain in tact, regardless of the outcome of the battle.

When the Confederates had extended their lines to the north, their right flank passed beyond the Federals for some distance. The road to Chattanooga was free from obstructions and completely unguarded. This was precisely the situation Cleburne wanted, but despite the opportunity in front of him Bragg held to his original plan of attack, which was to move from right to left in successive fashion. Hill recognized the possibility of turning the Federal left and overrunning their earthworks, so early in the night he directed Breckinridge to move from Lee and Gordon's Mill and report to Polk. The Kentuckian crossed at Alexander's Bridge around 10 o'clock and went into bivouac. Polk ordered him to form on Cleburne's right, which was accomplished shortly after daylight. With Ben Helm on his left, Marcellus Stovall in the center, and Dan Adams on the right, Breckinridge was parallel to the LaFayette Road and 400 yards east of it.[34] The alignment on 20 September had Breckinridge on the far right covering Reed's Bridge Road with Forrest guarding his flank. Cleburne formed in one line on Breckinridge's left, with Cheatham in two lines next to Cleburne and Walker in reserve.

---

[32] Report of Patrick R. Cleburne, 18 October 1863, OR, ser. 1, vol. 30, pt. 2, p. 154.

[33] James M. McCaffrey, *This Band of Heroes* (Austin TX: Eakin Press, 1985) 73.

[34] Connelly, *Autumn of Glory,* 215.

Breckinridge would begin the attack, and he was ordered to move at 9:30 A.M. Initially Adams had little trouble. He worked his way past the 42nd and 88th Indiana on the east side of the McDonald property and across the LaFayette Road. To his left Stovall pierced a gap between the 42nd and the 104th Illinois. Their lines came together at the road, where they met with Breckinridge and regrouped.[35] Once they turned south, one avenue of escape for the Union was effectively shut down and the Confederates controlled that portion of the field. Both brigades chased the Yankees into open ground on the Kelly property, where they fell upon reinforcements and were able put up some resistance. The Federals opened fire, and without any support both Adams and Stovall were shredded. Adams was badly wounded as a minie ball shattered his left humerus. With only 897 men, Stovall commanded the smallest brigade in the Army of Tennessee. After a difficult pursuit, they were simply unable to withstand the concentrated firepower in their front. By 11:15 the attack was over.[36]

Helm formed his line along the crest of a ridge and both armies paused. With the Rebel yell they surged forward with tremendous force, but Helm had attacked before Cleburne moved. The Federals were able to train their sights on a single target and the Confederates suffered the consequences. Three separate charges were made, lasting almost an hour. The effort was valiant, but it had no hope of success. In the third attempt to break the lines, Helm took a bullet in his right side that knocked him from his horse, mortally wounded. Abraham Lincoln's brother-in-law would die the very next day.[37]

The right wing was struggling, but reinforcements were on the way. The loss of Knoxville prevented the artillery from reaching the field, but Hood's division had begun to arrive on 18 September. Longstreet reached Catoosa Station early in the afternoon the next day and appeared at Bragg's headquarters around 11:00 P.M. His troops came in throughout the night and he received his orders for the morning's attack. It was at this late hour that Bragg decided to reorganize the army. It would be split into two wings, a very risky maneuver in the middle of a battle, but to make matters worse he decided to divide his forces in the middle of the night. Leonidas Polk would command the right side, with Hill and Walker's corps plus Cheatham's

---

[35] Connelly, *Autumn of Glory*, 221–22.
[36] Cozzens, *This Terrible Sound*, 325–26.
[37] Cozzens, *This Terrible Sound*, 321.

division, totaling five divisions. This amounted to 18,794 infantry and artillery, along with 3,500 cavalry under Forrest. Longstreet was given Buckner and Hood's corps plus Hindman's division, or six divisions. He had 22,849 infantry and artillery with Wheeler's 4,000 horsemen. Kershaw's troops were en route, but they did not arrive until the morning of 20 September.

About midnight Hill learned that he had been placed under Polk's wing. He received a message that Bragg wanted to see him at Alexander's Bridge, 3 miles distant. Hill was worn out and waited until 3:00 A.M. before he left. In the dark he was unable to find the courier who could escort him to Bragg's tent. He returned to his lines and reached the field just before dawn.[38]

Longstreet was completely unfamiliar with the area and had no idea of the location of Polk's left flank. He sent A. P. Stewart half a mile to the right and brought Hood's division forward to a position on the front line. However, instead of resting his flank on Cleburne's left, Stewart overlapped the Irishman by one-fourth of a mile, blocking Cheatham, Deshler, and part of Wood. Stewart adjusted his alignment and bent back his right; though this alignment was a great deal of help to Longstreet, it left the right wing far too thin. It would have been better to let Stewart remain in a straight line and move Cheatham over to strengthen Polk.[39]

The heaviest Union concentration was in the Brotherton woods. Longstreet decided to mass his wing 300 yards east of the cabin in the forest, completely hidden from view. He placed Bushrod Johnson in the lead with two brigades in his front and one in reserve. Hood's division would follow, and his troops were aligned in identical fashion. Orders were sent to Kershaw to bring his men forward as soon as they reached the field in a position behind Hood. No more than 600 yards to the south, Hindman and Preston's divisions would form on the east side of the LaFayette Road.[40]

Around 5:00 A.M. Leonidas Polk learned that during the night his courier had not been able to find Hill. One hour later he dictated the orders and gave them to his inspector-general, Captain Frank Wheless. Hill claimed that he first received the instructions at 7:25, but this is most likely in error.

---

[38] Cozzens, *This Terrible Sound,* 303.

[39] H. J. Eckenrode and Bryan Conrad, *James Longstreet Lee's War Horse* (1936; repr., Chapel Hill: University of North Carolina Press, 1986) 230.

[40] Cozzens, *This Terrible Sound,* 316, 366.

The distance from Polk to Hill was only 1 1/2 miles; it would hardly have taken Wheless over an hour to ride that distance. When he arrived he found Hill, Cleburne, and Breckinridge sitting by a fire 200 yards behind Cleburne's lines.[41]

Polk sent Cleburne a message, explaining that he had been unable to find Hill during the night but to attack as soon as possible. He sent the identical order to Breckinridge and instructed him to move forward on Cleburne's right. Bragg rode up at 8 o'clock; it was at this time that Hill stated he first learned he was supposed to have moved at daylight. Preparations had been nonexistent. The field had not been reconnoitered and the Confederates were not in lines of battle. Cleburne's men were still distributing rations. The orders said to attack "as soon as you are in position," not "at daylight," which almost guaranteed a delay. Cheatham's right was perpendicular to Cleburne, not parallel to it as it should have been. Finally, there was no cavalry support on Hill's flanks.[42]

It was almost 10 o'clock when Hill's courier gave Cleburne his orders.[43] Wood received the information in a timely manner, but Lucius Polk was not as fortunate. Polk and Lowrey had gone only a short distance when they came under heavy fire. They held their position but were forced to lie down for ninety minutes.[44]

With the loss of Helm's brigade Polk tried to close the gap in their lines, but he failed to notify anyone else. Before he was able to shift he got tangled up with the Confederate center. In their front were three brigades under William Hazen, Charles Cruft, and William Berry. At 4,000 strong they faced 1,100 Butternuts. Against these odds the casualties were staggering. Polk lost 350 men, most of whom went down in the first assault. One company in the 2nd Tennessee saw thirty-three men fall of the forty-four they had carried into battle. Fighting behind strong entrenchments, Union losses were negligible. Hazen had thirteen men wounded, while not one enlisted man was killed in Cruft's command. Berry reported similar results.[45]

---

[41] Connelly, *Autumn of Glory*, 216; Cozzens (*This Terrible Sound*, 305–307) states that Wheless arrived "a few minutes after 6:00 a.m."

[42] Hill, "Chickamauga," 140.

[43] Cleburne lists the time at 10:00 A.M. in his battle report, but based on the accounts and movements of his subordinates, the correct time appears to be closer to 9:30.

[44] Report of Patrick R. Cleburne, 18 October 1863, OR, ser. 1, pt. 2, p. 154.

[45] Cozzens, *This Terrible Sound*, 339–46.

When Polk left his side, Lowrey had no support. He tried to maintain contact but began to lose control of his own regiment. He abandoned the effort and turned toward the Poe house. They found a low ridge, but the gentle rise provided little cover and five different batteries pounded the Mississippians. At this point the breastworks turned abruptly to the west, with the angle held by John Turchin and the guns of the 21st Indiana. When the Rebels reached the crest they emerged in front of six 12-pounder Napoleons, fully loaded with grapeshot. The muzzles roared and in short time Lowrey lost over one-fourth of his command, including one of his most highly regarded subordinates, Major F. C. Karr of the 32nd Mississippi. The fire was so thick near the regimental colors that nineteen men filled one grave.[46]

R. M. Collins described the advance as his 15th Texas dismounted cavalry approached the works in from of Turchin and Hazen: "As we reached the crest of the hill in our front, we struck the same sawyer that had knocked Wood's brigade out at the first round. The rain of lead that the Federals poured into our line was simply terrific. Our loss in officers and men for the first few minutes was alarming in the extreme.... We were ordered to lie flat down and hold it."[47]

Breedlove advanced on Lowrey's left, but he was much more fortunate. Due to the contour of the breastworks, his 45th Alabama was 400 yards away from the artillery; as a result he was not subjected to the bombardment on his right. He had lost sight of the 16th and 33rd, as both regiments had veered away. Cleburne's original formation was quickly torn apart. Inconceivably, Wood had managed to lead his brigade around Deshler and now held Cleburne's left, with Deshler in the center. Wood's troops drifted for almost half a mile until they reached a point 500 hundred yards from the Union lines. They had moved so far that they went through Bate's division and stopped on Brown's right. Finally they halted to take cover in a narrow ravine that split the ridge in front of the earthworks.

The 16th Alabama lost 124 of the 285 men they had taken into battle, the 33rd left 149 men on the field, and Wood was at a loss as to his next move. When Cleburne arrived Wood explained his situation. He had run into Bate while Deshler was blocked behind Clayton's men. He maintained

---

[46] Report of Mark P. Lowrey, 28 September 1863, OR, ser. 1, vol. 30, pt. 2, p. 169–71.

[47] R. M. Collins, *Chapters from the Unwritten History of the War between the States* (St. Louis: Nixon-Jones Printing Co., 1882) 158.

that Polk had pushed him to his left, but Cleburne seemed to have felt that Wood was to blame for the confusion. In his battle report he gave generous praise to Polk and Deshler, without any mention of his third brigade. Shortly after the battle of Chickamauga, Wood resigned from the army and Mark Lowrey received command of the Alabamians.

Polk and Wood had met with disaster, but Deshler had no better luck and now stood in the middle of the division. He advanced past Jackson, whereupon he ran into A. J. Vaughan's brigade. He worked his way through this mess only to find his way blocked by A. P. Stewart. He finally decided to halt and await further orders.

Cleburne saw the gap created by Wood's surprising withdrawal and ordered Deshler to shift to his right to connect with Polk. Unfortunately, Polk's left had been beaten back and they were unable to effect the junction. Cleburne sent orders to Polk instructing him to fall back on Wood and told Deshler to remain in position as long as he could. Deshler went along his lines to relay the orders to his regimental commanders. The 10th Texas was almost out of ammunition, and Colonel Roger Mills sent a courier to find out how they could resupply. Shortly before noon Deshler was returning with the answer. When he was only 40 yards away, a cannon shell ripped through his chest. Mills assumed command and, despite the sudden change in leaders, at 2:00 the Texans still held the ground. Unfortunately, they had nothing to show for their courage other than a long list of casualties. Cleburne recognized the futility of the assault, so a few skirmishers were left in place and the Texas Brigade slowly withdrew.[48]

Wood's attack disintegrated almost before it began. Breedlove tried to move forward, but he was pinned down by Turchin's brigade. McGaughey came under a murderous flanking fire, also from Turchin. The 16th was able to reach a point 150 yards from the fortifications, but McGaughey was killed and the command of the brigade devolved to Captain Frederick Ashford. He ordered them to take cover under anything they could find and try to hold their ground.

The 33rd Alabama charged across the road and reached the Poe house. Adams, along with some seventy men, reached the small dwelling, which was now in flames. Along with a few Tennesseans from Brown's division they charged the works, only 75 yards away. They broke through a rail fence and

---

[48] Report of Patrick R. Cleburne, 18 October 1863, OR, ser. 1, pt. 2, p. 155.

almost reached the lines, but without support they were turned away. Adams had no choice but to fall back across Poe Field and into the woods, where he rejoined the division 800 yards to the rear. By 11:30 the last of the Confederates had been driven out of Poe Field.

William Rosecrans believed he was well prepared. He had ten divisions of infantry at his disposal, generally facing east across the LaFayette Road. From his left to right, he began with the divisions of Baird, Johnson, Palmer, and Reynolds. He extended his lines with the troops under Brannan, Negley, Sheridan, and Davis and left Thomas Wood and Horatio Van Cleve in reserve. They had constructed lengthy fortifications, and the breastworks would tell a powerful story in the casualties at Chickamauga.

George Thomas was very disturbed about the safety of his left flank and continued to call for reinforcements. At 2:00 A.M. his troops had not even reached the McDonald property, on the south side of Reed's Bridge Road. He knew that a strong attack would have no trouble in turning his line, and he asked Rosecrans to send him Negley's division. The Ohioan replied that the reinforcements would be sent at once, but the cries for help were far from over. Thomas now wanted Brannan as well.

He was under the false impression that Brannan was stationed in the role of a mobile reserve, ready to come forward should the need arise, but instead the division had taken a position on the front line next to Reynolds. It was quiet in this sector, so Reynolds told Brannan to shift his division to the north as the problems there were much more serious. He was unaware that Thomas Wood had come forward to replace Negley and assumed that with Brannan's departure his right would be uncovered. Brannan, however, was hesitant to abandon his position. According to Colonel John Connell of the 17th Ohio, he issued the orders to move only to rescind them moments later. When Reynolds noticed that Brannan had yet to leave he seemed reassured, but as there was little activity in his front, he paid no more attention to his right.[49]

Rosecrans heard the volume of the attack on his left and began to worry. Like Thomas, his fear was that the Confederates would overrun his flank and sever the escape routes to Chattanooga. He wrote a series of orders that became his undoing. At 10:10 A.M. he directed McCook to send as many men as possible to Thomas. Twenty minutes later he repeated his instructions, this time with particular attention to Phil Sheridan's division. At the same time, he

---

[49] Cozzens, *This Terrible Sound*, 359–60.

directed Crittenden to shift two of Van Cleve's brigades to the left. These three dispatches merely weakened the Union right, but the final one lost the battle.

Rosecrans did not have a clear picture of his own alignment, and Thomas was still quite nervous. He dispatched an aide with yet another request for help. Rosecrans replied that if Brannan went to Thomas, Wood must replace him. He added that Thomas must hold his position; the entire army was shifting toward him. Turning to Major Frank Bond, his senior aide-de-camp, he dictated the words that decided everything: "The general commanding directs that you close up on Reynolds as fast as possible, and support him."[50]

Rosecrans was too tired to function. He neglected to read the note, as everything was predicated on the assumption that Brannan was no longer on Reynolds's right. He handed the paper to an aide, directing him to tell Wood to "close to the *left* and support him." The language used made it impossible to execute, and the entire matter should have been clarified before any action was taken.

There has been a great deal of blame attached to both Wood and Rosecrans for the disaster at Chickamauga, principally from one side or the other. John Turchin was a brigadier in Reynolds's division, and as such he was somewhat removed from their accusations. He offered the following analysis, far more objective in its tone than many other accounts:

> The way things stood at the time, the order contradicted itself. The first part of it meant for General Wood to move his division to the left in the line and join Reynolds, and the second meant to move it out of the line and place it in the rear of Reynolds. According to the phraseology accepted in military language the order had no sense; one part of it was contradicting the other part. Why then not to ascertain the meaning of it from the person who wrote the order before moving? The idea of implicitly obeying orders by such officers as commanders of divisions, without reasoning about them, is absurd.[51]

Wood received the order at 11:00, and were it not for an unusual set of circumstances, it would have been completely disregarded. Rosecrans had delivered to Wood two stern rebukes in the presence of other officers, the

[50] Cozzens, *This Terrible Sound,* 361.
[51] John B. Turchin, *Chickamauga* (Chicago: Fergus Printing Co., 1888) 113–14.

principal offense being the failure to obey orders. Inside, Wood was seething with anger and embarrassment. At that point Brannan was still in place, Reynolds was secure, and there was actual skirmish fire in his own front. Nevertheless, determined to obey his commander, he ordered Buell, Harker and Barnes to pull out of line.[52]

While the Federals were sinking in technicalities, James Longstreet was preparing for his attack. He had amassed a force of nearly 11,000 men in a forest less than 70 acres in size. Eight brigades were placed in five lines, creating a front only 500 yards wide, or roughly the same size as the Brotherton field.[53] At 11 o'clock the Rebels were ready to advance, and the results were overwhelming. There were pockets of resistance, but the lines disintegrated under the weight of Longstreet's assault. They were completely routed and fled north without any organization whatsoever.

Longstreet was summoned to Bragg's headquarters at 2:30 P.M., and their conversation revealed much of the story at Chickamauga. All had gone well on the left wing. With the exception of Thomas, the Federals had been driven from the field; sixty pieces of artillery as well as many prisoners had been taken. The Union Army was on the run. Rosecrans, McCook, and Crittenden had left their posts in a rapid flight to Rossville. Longstreet asked for reinforcements from Polk in order to pursue the enemy down the Dry Valley Road, but Bragg could only reply that there were no troops to be had. Polk's command was spent, and Longstreet should remain where he was.

Unfortunately for the Confederates, this was not actually the case. There were, in fact, additional forces at hand. In Cheatham's division, only Jackson had been engaged and Liddell still had some fresh units, but Bragg was unaware of the conditions around him. McLaws was expected to arrive with Alexander's artillery. Bragg had even gone so far as to violate one of his own maxims, uttered shortly after Shiloh: "to never, on a battlefield, lose a moment's time...but to press on with every available man."[54] The failure to understand his own battle may well have squandered another opportunity for the South.

---

[52] Cozzens, *This Terrible Sound*, 363.

[53] Grady McWhiney, *Attack and Die* (Tuscaloosa: University of Alabama Press, 1982) 89.

[54] OR, ser. 1, vol. 10, pt. 1, p. 470.

George Thomas was clinging to Snodgrass Hill, the last hope for a battered army, and although the focus of the battle had shifted to the south, Cleburne's day was far from over. His lines were reformed and at 3:30 he received the orders to advance. Jackson had opened the action on Deshler's left, but in the early part of the afternoon his brigade was moved to Cleburne's right and took the lead in the attack. As this action took place in the northern sector of his division, neither Wood nor Mills played any role in the battle. Polk moved some 400 yards to join Jackson, and though Wood did form on Polk's left in support, there was little more than skirmish fire in his front.[55]

Polk had been soundly defeated during the morning, but at 4:00 P.M. Cleburne ordered him forward on Jackson's left. He took heavy fire and the Confederates halted. Cleburne brought up his artillery and they fired double charges of canister into the Union flank, only 200 yards away. The line collapsed and at 4:30 the Confederates charged again. Polk lost another 200 men, but the Federals had been dealt a crushing blow.[56]

Cleburne lost 1,749 of the 5,115 men he had taken into battle, or 34 percent of his command. He had been forced into a night attack against his better judgment and spent both days attacking breastworks. On the right wing Helm, Deshler, and Preston Smith had lost their lives. In total the Confederates lost 2,389 killed, 13,412 wounded, and 200 captured or missing, for a total of 17,804. Fighting on the defensive, Union losses were fewer. They lost 1,656 men killed, 9,749 wounded, and 4,774 captured or missing, for a total of 16,179.[57] They did, however, lose the services of William Lytle, who fell while leading a charge in Sheridan's division. Mere numbers do not tell the whole story. In addition to losing fewer men, a large part of the Northern losses were either captured or missing, whereas the Confederates saw a higher percentage of men actually killed or wounded, unable to be readily exchanged. The Confederacy could ill afford to trade casualties at this rate.

The effects of the battle of Chickamauga were devastating to the Southern Cause. Harvey Hill offered the following assessment:

---

[55] Report of S. A. M. Wood, 9 October 1863, OR, ser. 1, vol. 30, pt. 2, p. 162; report of E. B. Breedlove, 6 October 1863, OR, ser. 1, vol. 30, pt. 2, p. 167–69; report of Lucius E. Polk, 10 October 1863, OR, ser, 1, vol. 30, pt. 2, p. 176 78.

[56] Report of Lucius Polk, 10 October 1863, OR, ser. 1, vol. 30, pt. 2, p. 176–78.

[57] List of casualties at the Battle of Chickamauga, *Battles and Leaders*, 3:673–76.

It seems to me that the *elan* of the Southern soldier was never seen after Chickamauga—that brilliant dash which had distinguished him was gone forever. He was too intelligent not to know that the cutting in two of Georgia meant death to all his hopes. He knew that Longstreet's absence was imperiling Lee's safety, and that what had to be done must be done quickly. The delay in striking was exasperating to him; the failure to strike after the success was crushing to all his longings for an independent South. He fought stoutly to the last, but, after Chickamauga, with the sullenness of despair and without the enthusiasm of hope. That "barren victory" sealed the fate of the Southern Confederacy.[58]

The credit for success at Chickamauga largely went to James Longstreet, and his performance was excellent. However, the armies fought two separate battles. The right wing's persistent attacks on Thomas caused Rosecrans to shift more troops to the north, and had the Confederates managed the battle more effectively, the already resounding defeat might have been even greater. Adams and Stovall had overrun the Federals in their front only to be destroyed for lack of support. The road to Chattanooga should have been closed but was not. Cheatham had been largely idle, and Hill's entire corps failed to advance on time. Finally, Bragg's complete bewilderment allowed Thomas to remain long enough to cover the Federal escape.

From any perspective, the battle at Chickamauga was a victory for the South, provided that the examination of events ends on 20 September. Controversy emerges when the issue of pursuit is addressed. Braxton Bragg failed to consolidate his gains and totally vanquish his enemy in the very early stages of their retreat. That being said, could Bragg have realistically put together an attempt to eliminate Rosecrans before he had time to organize an effective defense?

Opinions differed on both sides of this debate. To Brigadier-General John Beatty, the Federals had no chance of survival: "At this hour of the night [between 11 and 12 o'clock], the army is simply a mob. There appears to be neither organization nor discipline. The various commands are mixed up in

---

[58] Hill, "Chickamauga," 662; Philip D. Stephenson, "Reminiscences," in *Southern Historical Society Papers*, 52 vols. (Millwood NY: Kraus Reprint Co., 1977) 12:35.

what seems to be inextricable confusion. Were a division of the enemy to pounce down upon us between this and morning I fear the Army of the Cumberland would be blotted out."[59]

Braxton Bragg never really understood the battle at Chickamauga, and he failed to grasp the fact that the Confederates had won a great victory. Despite the reality that Rosecrans, McCook, and Crittenden had actually left the field, Bragg decided to wait and lay siege to Chattanooga. His vacillation allowed the Federals precious time to regroup, which ultimately resulted in the late-November struggle for Chattanooga. The absence of any tangible result in favor of the Confederacy led to the battle's designation as the "barren victory" of the war.

Although the investment of Chattanooga would be a lengthy process with no guarantee of success, the essential question was not what the coming months would bring, but what could be done in the next two days. At the very outset, the ability to withstand an assault was limited. The longer the Confederates waited, the more time the Federals would have to regroup. Now was the time to strike.

As Bragg opted to remain on the field, there can be no definitive answer to this dilemma. He tended to his wounded and gathered the abandoned supplies that littered the ground. The opportunity in front of him was enormous. He certainly was not the best-informed Confederate at Chickamauga—Bragg's field commanders had a clearer picture of the situation—and he had Rosencrans at a serious disadvantage, yet he balked at the chance to eliminate him. With the set of circumstances before him, it was a risk worth taking.

---

[59] John Beatty, *The Citizen Soldier* (Cincinnati: Wilstach, Baldwin, 1879) 345.

8

MISSIONARY RIDGE

On the night of 21 September, Cleburne's division began to move north. They reached the outskirts of Chattanooga at noon the next day. Rosecrans sent a wire to Washington with news of the disastrous defeat, but President Lincoln realized that the Federals still held both Chattanooga and Knoxville. As long as they remained in Union hands, Bragg's options would be limited.

The Federals were a beaten army, but they possessed the means to recover if subsistence could be guaranteed. In order to disrupt the flow of provisions it was imperative to take and hold Lookout Mountain. The mountain commanded the railroad from Bridgeport, which was the nearest and most practicable line of supply. Southern control would force the Federals to use the long wagon roads in the Cumberland Mountains.[1] Perhaps with this in mind, but more probably due to simple indecision, Bragg decided to lay siege to the city. He deployed his troops along a front that ran from the north end of Missionary Ridge, down the valley, and then across to the western slope of Lookout Mountain.

After the battle at Chickamauga some changes took place in Cleburne's division. Liddell's brigade was returned to Cleburne, but after he was reassigned to the Trans-Mississippi it was led by Daniel Govan. J. A. Smith of the 5th Confederate received command of the Texans, who had belonged to Deshler. Still lingering under the cloud of Cleburne's harsh rebuke for his performance in September, Wood resigned and was succeeded by Mark Lowrey. Finally, Hiram Granbury's 7th Texas was transferred from John Gregg's brigade and given to Smith. Despite a lack of tents, blankets, shoes, and clothing, the troops were basically stationary for two months, situated on the crest and eastern slopes of the ridge 3 miles from the north end of the line.[2]

---

[1] Irving A. Buck, *Cleburne and His Command* (1908; repr., Wilmington NC: Broadfoot Publishing, 1995) 158.

[2] Howell and Elizabeth Purdue, *Pat Cleburne Confederate General* (1973; repr., Gaithersburg MD: Olde Soldier Books, 1987) 237.

Missionary Ridge rises to 600 feet in elevation and runs from
McFarland's Gap at Rossville in a northeasterly direction for 6 miles until it
meets the Chickamauga River. At first glance it appears as though it is one
mountain, but actually it contains several broken hills, cut by wagon roads
that lead eastward from Chattanooga. The gaps allow the passage of two
railroads, the Western and Atlantic to the north and further south the
Chattanooga and Cleveland. The most significant point on the ridge occurs at
Tunnel Hill, roughly 250 yards north of the pass for the Cleveland line. This
area was very good for defense if used properly, and it was here that Cleburne
would make his stand.[3] South of this point the ridge becomes continuous and
extends down to Rossville Gap. The ground along the western base is
relatively flat save for a few thinly wooded knobs. The Federals had made their
camps on this level plain.

They had barely escaped from a horrible debacle and were quite fortunate
to be in Chattanooga at all. Initially Bragg's plan of investment seemed to be
working. The Federals' biggest problem was food. Some of the men were
placed on half-rations from the moment they entered the city, and by the
middle of October the entire Army of the Cumberland was starving. Despite
the best efforts of some creative quartermasters, each soldier was given only
four crackers per day, each a small 3-inch square about three times the
thickness of a normal soda cracker. There appeared to be little hope of survival;
defeat or capture was certain.[4] Abraham Lincoln realized that new leadership
was needed for the army to survive. In a telegram dated 16 October, Henry
Halleck issued a set of orders that sent George Thomas to replace Rosecrans
and gave Grant overall control of the forces in Chattanooga. Grant arrived on
23 October, and more troops were on the way. Joe Hooker had been sent from
Virginia and Sherman was bringing the Army of the Tennessee from
Memphis.

In his capacity as an engineer for the Union, William F. "Baldy" Smith
had other ideas. He devised a plan that would use the natural features of the
Tennessee River to the Federals' advantage. Just west of Chattanooga the
Tennessee runs south, then turns sharply north again, creating a neck of land
known as Moccasin Point. If some way could be found to cross this ground
without bringing on a general engagement, the Federals would remain out of

---

[3] James M. McCaffrey, *This Band of Heroes* (Austin TX: Eakin Press, 1985) 157.
[4] Peter Cozzens, *Shipwreck of Their Hopes* (Urbana: University of Illinois Press, 1994) 8

range of the Confederate guns posted on Lookout Mountain. Smith's target was Brown's Ferry, the possession of which just might open a supply route for an overland relief effort.

Smith decided to use both water and land forces to accomplish his mission. He selected troops from William Hazen's brigade to negotiate the river, with John Turchin in support. Fifty pontoon boats were procured and some 1,400 men began a hazardous journey. They not only faced potential discovery by Confederates on the opposite shore, but also would have to navigate the treacherous waters of the Tennessee River. The changing current formed dangerous pockets of water, known as "sucks," that could shatter the little expedition. By 3:00 A.M. on 27 October the men were on board. Under the cover of darkness the boats began to move slowly westward. Although they were observed by a few pickets, there was no real opposition. The Yankees were able to reach Brown's Ferry with a loss of only thirty-five men.

Baldy Smith's part in the drama was over, but the task was not complete. Joe Hooker was moving up the valley and the surrounding area would have to be secured before any wagons could arrive. Hooker's Easterners had not moved with the same efficiency as Hazen's command, but by 28 October the area was in Union control. The siege had been broken and a "cracker line" was now open. Grant was saved and the struggle for Chattanooga continued.

Bragg's response to all of this was strange. Instead of seeking to strengthen his position, he decided to rid himself of Longstreet's constant criticism. On 4 November Longstreet was sent to Knoxville with 15,000 men. His departure would have grave consequences. To make matters worse, Longstreet was extremely dissatisfied with the number of men he had been given, and he began to lobby for reinforcements.

Longstreet persisted in his demands, and on 22 November Bragg decided to send Cleburne to Knoxville as well. At midnight he was ordered to go to Chickamauga Station, where he would take command of his and Bushrod Johnson's divisions and head into East Tennessee. Not only did this weaken Bragg's army even further, but it removed his best division from the right wing, where Sherman was collecting his forces.

The Rebels broke camp at dawn and Johnson boarded first. Grant observed the movements, which he perceived as withdrawal. It seemed imperative to prevent any of Bragg's forces from reaching Longstreet, so he began to examine the ground in front of him. Several positions had been fortified to some degree; the strongest of these was a low rise called Orchard Knob.

Grant decided to form his men on display as if they were on parade, then attack the overmatched Graycoats before they could react. The plan worked to perfection. The Federals had covered 800 yards before the Confederates opened fire. They were overwhelmed before they could reload, with the 24th and 28th Alabama taking heavy losses. Combined, they lost roughly 175 men as well as the colors of the 28th.

All but one of Cleburne's brigades was on the train when around noon a message arrived from Bragg. The Confederates were under attack and Cleburne was to return immediately with every available man. He left Lucius Polk in charge of the division, and when he arrived back at the tunnel he found Major D. H. Poole waiting for him. Poole was ready to escort him over the ground Hardee was expected to defend, but daylight was slipping away.[5]

During the morning of 24 November, Cleburne was in reserve. He watched the battle unfold on Lookout Mountain. The heavy cloud cover had allowed Hooker to move forward undetected, and he crushed the Confederates with the weight of superior numbers. Union morale soared as Captain John Wilson unfurled the colors of the 8th Kentucky. The victory forced Bragg to evacuate, and those troops began to fall back to Missionary Ridge Bragg was left atop the heights with both ends of his line exposed. The Federals now had Hooker on Bragg's left, Sherman on his right, and Thomas in the center.

On the same day Sherman crossed the Tennessee River and established his headquarters among a series of hills, one named for J. A. Lightburn on his left, another for Jesse Alexander on his right. Late in the morning Cleburne was informed of the movement. He was directed to send one brigade and a battery to the bridge of the East Tennessee and Georgia Railroad to guard that point. He selected Polk's brigade, which was accompanied by the Alabama battery under Richard Goldthwaite. Just after 2:00 P.M. Cleburne received additional orders to move all of his remaining forces to the right and take possession of the higher ground near the mouth of the South Chickamauga.

Lowrey's brigade was on the south side of the tunnel and Cleburne intended to put Govan on his left. This deployment would allow Smith to connect Cleburne's left with States Rights Gist's division and prevent the

---

[5] James Walker, "The Battle for Chattanooga," *Civil War Times Illustrated* 10/5 (August 1971): 35.

capture of the route by which the Confederates might need to retreat. However, the threat on the right caused him to shift Govan from the main ridge to a spur at the rear of it. This rocky projection extended out just north of the tunnel and covered a valley in front of Sherman. The Arkansans would now face north, and although Hardee approved of the dispositions he moved two of Lowrey's regiments along with some artillery to the Confederate right. The flank was now secure, but this left the area between Smith and Gist with only two regiments to hold it.

Smith's Confederates went into position shortly after 3:00 P.M. They formed on the main ridge; with the two left regiments facing the detached ridge, the right one refused to protect the flank. In their front were the 4th Minnesota, 30th Ohio, and 6th Iowa, which screened the advance of John Smith, Morgan Smith, and Ewing's divisions, respectively. Unfortunately, the Federals had already secured a lodgment before Cleburne could arrive. No sooner had skirmishers been thrown forward than they came in contact with the Ohioans. The ground being badly broken, when the Texans went down the northern slope and approached the rise they took fire from three directions. The Rebels were driven back through the gully and up the hill, where they formed on four Napoleons under Lieutenant H. Shannon. After dark the fighting in front of Smith began to fade and Cleburne assumed that Bragg would withdraw.[6] Longstreet had been detached to Knoxville while Hooker and Sherman had arrived in Chattanooga. Lookout Mountain had just been lost, Bragg's left was in danger, and the Confederates were seriously outnumbered. In light of the situation, Cleburne left his artillery and ordnance on the other side of the Chickamauga.

It was here that Sherman's weakness in reconnaissance revealed itself. He did not have an accurate set of maps, but his preparations were careless. He had ample time to examine the area or question local citizens as to the nature of the terrain, but he failed to do so and the advantage in numbers began to disappear. From his headquarters, Smith's troops were the only Confederates in sight and he was unsure of their strength. He decided to hold his position and ordered his men to dig in for the night.

There are two drastically differing views regarding his performance that evening. In his own defense, Sherman wrote: " From studying all the maps, I

---

[6] Stanley Horn, *The Army of Tennessee* (Norman: University of Oklahoma Press, 1952) 298–99.

had inferred that Missionary Ridge was a continuous hill, but we found ourselves on two high points, with a deep depression between us and the one immediately over the tunnel, which was my chief objective point. The ground we had gained, however, was so important that I could leave nothing to chance, and ordered it to be fortified during the night."[7]

Henry Boynton, a lieutenant-colonel under George Thomas, had a far less complimentary view. As the first official historian of the Chickamauga and Chattanooga National Military Park, he offered the following analysis:

> The astonishing error, an error which caused utter failure to the whole movement against Bragg's right, and which ever since has been covered thick in official reports and misleading histories, was the first day's occupation of a range of detached hills north of Missionary Ridge, and completely separated from it. Since the plan of battle turned on occupying the north end of the ridge, it was certainly one of the most remarkable oversights of the war that this position was not thoroughly identified....[8]

Baldy Smith was also highly critical: "Finding this unexpected break in the hills, Sherman, though he had met no resistance, and was expected by Grant to seize the ridge from the tunnel to the Chickamauga, determined to halt for the night and fortify his position. This was the blunder of the battle."[9]

Cleburne anticipated an attack, and without any orders his anxiety began to grow. At 9:00 P.M. he delivered the following instructions to Irving Buck: "Go at once to General Hardee and ask what has been decided upon, and say that if we are to make a stand it is necessary that I should know, in order to get my artillery and ammunition trains in their proper place without delay."[10]

Hardee was in the middle of a conference at Bragg's headquarters, and opinions were divided as to the proper course of action. Hardee felt that it was wiser to minimize their losses and fall back across Chickamauga Creek, but Breckinridge countered that Missionary Ridge was a strong position and it was

---

[7] William T. Sherman, *Memoirs of Gen. W. T. Sherman*, 2 vols. (New York: Charles L. Webster & Co., 1991) 1:403.

[8] Cozzens, *Shipwreck of Their Hopes*, 154–55.

[9] Cozzens, *Shipwreck of Their Hopes*, 155.

[10] Buck, *Cleburne and His Command*, 166.

not possible to evacuate the mountain without detection. The Kentuckian's logic was faulty, but his energy persuaded Bragg to remain in place. Hardee replied to Buck, "Tell Cleburne we are to fight; that his division will undoubtedly be heavily attacked, and they must do their very best." The position at Tunnel Hill was indeed a perilous one, as the line was so thin that men stood less than elbow to elbow and in single rank. A powerful assault would be overwhelming, but Hardee felt that the difficulty of the terrain would make up for the weakness in numbers. Regardless, he was sure that Sherman would concentrate his efforts on Cleburne's right.[11] It was close to midnight when Cleburne received Hardee's orders, and he made his dispositions as rapidly as possible. In addition to the rocky, uneven footing, the task was made more difficult by a lunar eclipse that left the night exceptionally dark.

Hardee reached Cleburne's division around 2:00 A.M. He ordered Smith to abandon his original fortifications and take a new position with his left some 150 yards north of the tunnel along the crest of the main ridge. The 6th, 10th, and 15th Texas (consolidated) held this line under Roger Mills. The right of the regiment extended all the way to the ground under the peak of Tunnel Hill. Above them Cleburne placed Shannon's Mississippians, and the lieutenant turned his guns to the north. Smith then resumed his defense with two Texas regiments, the 7th under Granbury and the 17th, 18th, 24th, and 25th (consolidated) under W. A. Taylor. This point was the weakest, as it contained a salient in the center, but Cleburne bent Smith's right back to within 200 yards of Govan's left. In this way each brigade was able to come to the assistance of the other. This completed the formation, which now ran from Tunnel Hill on the left over to Chickamauga Creek.[12]

Sherman's failure to act decisively was a welcome relief to the Confederates, as it had given John Brown just enough time to make an all-night march from Lookout Mountain to Missionary Ridge. Hardee and Stevenson debated on where to place the Tennesseans but settled on a location on the ridge between Smith's left and the railroad tunnel. Brown divided his forces, with the 3rd Tennessee next to Smith and the 45th Tennessee on their left. In addition, he sent skirmishers down the mountain to the base of the ridge. They went into line several hundred yards west of the ridge with their left thrown forward to deliver an enfilading fire on any approaching force.

---

[11] Horn, *Army of Tennessee,* 299.
[12] Buck, *Cleburne and His Command,* 168.

Cleburne continued with artillery batteries under Key and Goldthwaite between the 39th Tennessee and Alfred Cumming's 39th Georgia, which had reached the ground around 9:30 that morning. At the same time Joseph Lewis's Orphan Brigade of Kentuckians arrived from the Confederate center and fell into a reserve role, some 200 yards behind Smith.

Sherman rode the length of his lines and by 5:00 A.M. had determined to attack from the north and northwest. He had nine brigades at his disposal but decided to begin with only two, those of John Corse and John Loomis. Corse would lead, attempting to move through a narrow valley between Alexander's Hill and Tunnel Hill. On his right, Loomis would approach the Confederates through the open fields that lay between the railroads. The remainder of Sherman's forces were dispersed throughout the area and given vague instructions to act in supporting roles.

At sunrise Sherman gave Ewing his orders to advance, but they seemed to lack conviction and resulted in a weak exchange from Ewing to Corse. Corse was to dislodge the skirmishers and then get rid of the infantry along a low rise north of Tunnel Hill. Only after both of these missions were accomplished was he allowed to go after Smith. Just before daylight on 25 November, picket fire broke out. By 11:00 A.M. the armies were fully engaged. Smith tried to erect fortifications to protect his batteries, but Union artillery shelled his work details and he abandoned the effort.

Corse had only 920 men and Ewing may have felt that he lacked the firepower to accomplish even this limited assignment. Perhaps fearing a sudden repulse, Ewing urged Loomis to proceed with caution. Loomis was to keep his left flank along the slope of the ridge and continue until he reached the front of an open tract of land half a mile west of Tunnel Hill. He would then wheel to his left, form a line of battle, and drive in any skirmishers he might find. The orders were very confusing. Ewing wanted him to move south and actually defeat the Confederates in his front, yet not bring on any general engagement.

With a command this size, Corse arranged his troops in such a manner that they were only two lines of skirmishers, backed by the rest of the brigade and pulled together in double columns. Five companies of the 40th Illinois led the advance under Hiram Hall, totaling 130 rifles. They were followed by the 46th Ohio, 103rd Illinois, and 6th Iowa, but it was 8 o'clock before Hall began to move down Alexander's Hill. Less than 100 yards away were the lead elements of the Texans, partially hidden among the trees.

One regiment of Joseph Lightburn's brigade was sent to Corse's left in support: the 30th Ohio under Theodore Jones. This small contingent amounted to only 170 men, so Lightburn added 30 soldiers from the 4th West Virginia. This was pointless; even with the addition Corse numbered barely 1,100 bayonets against 1,300 Texans. Halfway down the slope of Lightburn's Hill, Jones came upon Samuel Foster's 24th Texas and the fighting became tree to tree. The Confederates gradually gave ground, but they did inflict some casualties and bought Cleburne precious time.

The Yankees moved up the ridge and swept over the earthworks Foster had just abandoned. Jones got to within 250 yards of the crest of Tunnel Hill, where he saw the four 12-pounder Napoleons looming above him. They were an enticing target to be sure, and Shannon had yet to fire a shot. Perhaps the battery was not as fearsome as it looked. In front of the guns was Hiram Granbury's 7th Texas, crouching behind another row of fortifications. The works were not particularly strong, but between the two armies was a long, narrow ravine that ran east to west.[13] A direct assault would not be easy.

It would take a vigorous attack to dislodge the Rebels, and Ewing's lieutenants were not working together. Jones was furious, as the assistance he had expected from Corse had not arrived. He sent word to Lightburn, but it was almost an hour before the 37th Ohio formed on Jones's left. At the same time Hall arrived with his 40th Illinois and hit a small number of Confederate skirmishers. He also saw the Napoleons and charged forward on the right of the 30th Ohio. They burst over the logs, but the second line failed to advance. Without any support, the effort had little impact and more than thirty men fell in the early action. Only after this first attack had stalled did Corse finally make his first appearance at Tunnel Hill.

He placed the 46th Ohio in his first line with the 103rd Illinois and 6th Iowa to the rear. Originally he had favored an assault, but upon reflection he concluded that his small force would not have the weight to carry the works. He began to have some doubts, and asked Jones to go back to headquarters for further instructions. He found Sherman at 10 o'clock, and the Ohioan was very impatient. Sherman's continual failure to pause and calmly assess current conditions had resulted in a stream of mistakes, but he was in no frame of mind to wait. Sherman ordered Jones to return: "Go back and make that charge immediately; time is everything. If you want more men I will give you

---

[13] Cozzens, *Shipwreck of Their Hopes,* 205–209.

all you want; if you want artillery, I will give you that."[14] Of course, this begs the question as to why Sherman did not use more men and artillery.

At 10:30 Corse's infantry began to move and batteries opened from Lightburn's Hill. He stood with Hall's Illinoisans, and at the sound of the bugles they stormed the empty breastworks and charged through the ravine before ascending the slope of the hill. Shannon waited until the Federals had almost reached the top and then opened fire, tearing huge holes in the Union lines. Cleburne unleashed a counterattack with the right side of Mills's consolidated regiment combined with the left of the 7th Texas. The shock drove the Federals 80 yards back down the slope, but the 46th Ohio was able to form in the hollow and put up a spirited resistance. Both Smith and Mills were wounded and the brigade fell to Granbury.

The 46th had been rudely treated, but neither the 103rd Illinois nor the 6th Iowa had gotten into the action. At 11:30 Corse moved them forward. Both regiments had witnessed the battle in their front and their desire to attack was somewhat muted. They tried to fight from behind trees but the Yankees dropped like leaves, many within a few feet of the works. Their losses included Corse, who went down with a wound to the knee from a spent bullet.

The Federals were in the middle of a mismanaged disaster, but the heavy casualties were not restricted to the Northern side. Shannon was struck by a shell fragment that broke his collarbone and punctured a lung. The first lieutenant had been killed, so Shannon struggled back to the guns, blood streaming from his chest. He was unable to continue, the second lieutenant was hit, all of the sergeants were gone, and the command of the battery ended in the lap of a corporal, F. M. Williams. The losses were so high that Granbury was forced to pull men out of line to service the guns.

Clearly the Texans needed help. Cleburne moved Douglas's battery to a position near Granbury's right so that he could deliver an enfilading fire into Corse's left flank. He then extended the line to the east with the 9th and 2nd Kentucky regiments and placed them in position to attack the 30th Ohio. The decisive repulse was enough to convince Sherman that this approach simply was not going to work. By noon Corse's brigade was essentially destroyed and the action on that part of the field was over.

---

[14] Theodore Jones to E. A. Carman, 2 January 1908, 30th Ohio file, Chickamauga and Chattanooga National Military Park.

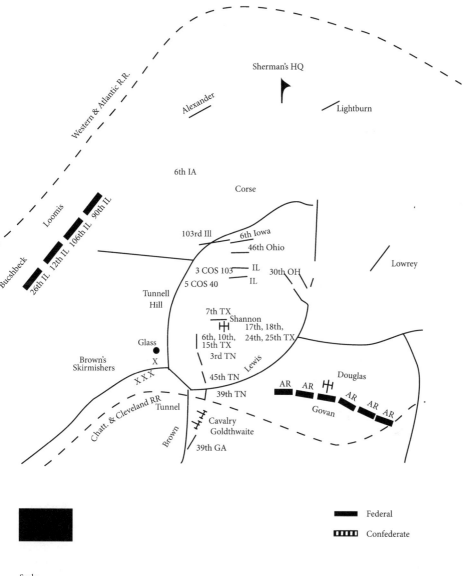

Western & Atlantic R.R.

Sherman's HQ

Alexander

Lightburn

6th IA

Corse

Loomis

90th IL

106th IL

12th IL

26th IL

Bucshbeck

103rd Ill

6th Iowa

46th Ohio

Lowrey

3 COS 103 — IL

5 COS 40 — IL

30th OH

Tunnell
Hill

7th TX

Shannon

17th, 18th,
24th, 25th TX

6th, 10th,
15th TX

Glass

X

3rd TN

Brown's
Skirmishers

Lewis

45th TN

Douglas

AR   AR

AR

XXX

39th TN

Govan

AR   AR

Chatt. & Cleveland RR

Tunnel

Cavalry
Goldthwaite

Brown

39th GA

Federal

Confederate

Scale

0   0.4 Miles

Loomis was desperately trying to obey Ewing's orders to the letter, with particular emphasis on the necessity to avoid bringing on a battle. His men sat down to breakfast and it was 8:00 A.M. before they moved. One mile to the southeast Tunnel Hill was visible, but so was the activity upon it as reinforcements were in plain sight, moving to Granbury's aid.[15]

The Federals formed just west of Alexander's Hill, with the 90th Illinois on the left, followed by the 100th Indiana, 12th Indiana, and 26th Illinois. In addition to one section of artillery Loomis had Adolphus Buschbeck's brigade in reserve. He marched half a mile and turned left where the Western and Atlantic crossed an old dirt lane. After only a few hundred feet Loomis emerged from the woods and saw that his men would have to cross half a mile of wet fields under the eyes of Confederate cannon before they even reached the tunnel. In their path were three ditches and three fences, and aside from a few isolated tree stumps there was no other protection whatsoever.

Blocking the entrance to the tunnel were the farmhouse and outbuildings of the Glass family, and south of the dwelling Brown's Tennesseans were already in place. An attack was not an inviting prospect, so the Federals waited for half an hour. At 10:30 an aide from Ewing's staff handed Loomis a set of orders. They informed him that Corse was about to advance and he was to cooperate. He wanted to obey, but a large hill separated their brigades and Loomis had no idea in what direction Corse had moved. Nevertheless he proceeded, although somewhat in the dark. He believed that the Federals were heading toward the tunnel in concert, but he took a line too far to the south and created a gap of 400 yards.

When the Yankees stepped into the field they were quickly shredded, as the batteries on the hill raked their lines with deadly precision. While the Federal side displayed no lack of courage, much of their failure resulted from poor communication on Sherman's part. His lack of supervision during the attack eliminated any chance of success. As a result, the Army of Tennessee was still in check, and the advance Grant had wanted to begin at dawn had gotten absolutely nowhere.

At noon, during a brief lull in the action, Cleburne worked feverishly to adjust his lines. He moved Colonel E. Warfield's 2nd, 15th, and 24th Arkansas (consolidated) to the support of the guns above the tunnel. For all intents and purposes Shannon's battery had been destroyed, so Cleburne

---

[15] Cozzens, *Shipwreck of Their Hopes,* 212–16.

removed two of his pieces from the hill and replaced them with four light cannon under Thomas Key. Hardee arrived to assist in the deployment, instructing Cumming to take two of his Georgia regiments down the slope and take possession of the Glass property. The 39th and 56th were dispatched immediately and formed on Brown's men at the bottom of the ridge.

Cleburne had Hardee at his side, but Loomis was still fumbling without direction. Through Ewing, Sherman gave him general instructions to advance toward the base of Tunnel Hill. The Federals suffered under a withering fire and sought the nearest protection they could find. Unfortunately, this was the railroad embankment to the south, which moved them several hundred yards further away from Corse. On Loomis's left the 90th Illinois was vainly trying to keep in contact, but the distance was simply too great. By this time the regiment had lost so many men that it made up a front only two companies in width.

With Cumming at the farm and his losses mounting, Loomis sent for Buschbeck. At 12:30 he asked the German to get rid of Cumming and secure his left. Buschbeck sent in the 73rd Pennsylvania under Joseph Taft, with the 27th Pennsylvania some 200 yards behind. They came out of the woods at the double-quick and as the Confederates shifted their artillery they sprinted for the farm. Cumming had placed skirmishers in front of the buildings behind rudimentary breastworks; at 50 yards they unleashed one volley and fell back to the safety of the house. A pointless exchange developed with no particular harm to either side, but Taft felt that it might be possible to turn the Georgians' right. He sent the remainder of the 27th to his left and his plan succeeded. With the Graycoats running low on ammunition, Cumming was forced to pull back to the ridge. His losses were slight, but in their haste to escape his men had failed to burn the buildings.

Four companies from his 39th Georgia pleaded with Cumming to allow them to go back and rectify the mistake. Cumming relented, and they completed their mission just before the Yankees arrived. The Pennsylvanians surged through billowing smoke past the farm, where Taft called a halt to reorganize. The 73rd formed in good order, but the 27th kept going up the hillside.

Without Corse to worry about, Key was able to train all six guns on one brigade and canister ripped through the ranks with gruesome results. The Yankees kept coming, and 30 yards from the top they paused to rest. They soon regrouped and opened an incredibly accurate fire that forced Key to pull back. Granbury's men could not reply without exposing themselves, so they began to hurl rocks at the enemy. It was a primitive mode of warfare; however, as the distance was negligible and they were throwing downhill, it achieved the desired result.

Once again Federal troops were shifted intermittently, ineffectively, and without cohesion. Loomis was convinced that he was about to receive a punishing counterattack, made possible by the large numbers of Confederate reinforcements massing in his front. In reality it was only the 39th Georgia, who had replenished their ammunition and returned to Brown's assistance on the top of the ridge. He finally brought Karl Matthies's brigade up in support of Taft's remnants. After a great deal of confusion Matthies moved forward around 1:00 P.M. He broke through the woods, still half a mile from Tunnel Hill. He deployed the 10th Iowa on the left, followed by the 93rd Illinois, the 26th Missouri, and the 5th Iowa. To his right were the outbuildings of the farm. Matthies took heavy fire, but he settled in behind a fence along the wagon road at the base of Tunnel Hill.

Matthies soon realized that, like Taft, he had drifted too far to his left to protect Loomis's flank. The Pennsylvanians had run out of ammunition and Taft was pinned to the ground, unable to advance or retreat. Matthies tried to close the gap, but as he was shifting his troops he was struck in the head. The wound was not serious, and though he was only momentarily stunned, he turned over his command to Colonel Benjamin Dean with directions to bring up Green Raum's brigade and press the attack. The Federals continued to search for an opening, but they found that Cleburne was one step ahead of them. He had moved Warfield's Arkansans to a position just in front of Granbury's breastworks, where they lay waiting for the Federals to advance. When they rushed forward the Rebels charged and Key opened fire. Heavy casualties, lack of coordination, and nearly impassable terrain led the Northerners to exhaustion only 60 feet from the Confederate lines.

At 2:00 P.M. John Smith and Ewing left Sherman's headquarters and found Raum, who had been observing the action for some time. It was clear to him that Matthies needed assistance, but he had no permission to advance. Raum formed in two lines, with the 80th Ohio and 17th Iowa followed by the 10th Missouri and 56th Illinois. The first line was given to Clark Wever while Raum remained in the rear. At 2:30 they went forward, and since the Confederates were busy with Matthies his men were able to run 200 yards without any response at all. When the artillery opened, their aim was high and

Raum charged at the double-quick. Just after 3 o'clock they reached a fence, only 75 yards in front of the works. The 80th Ohio moved to the left in good order and lay down with the Iowans on their right. By this point Matthies's attack had spent itself, as the 93rd Illinois had been virtually obliterated. Fragments of their regimental flag lay strewn about the ground. They caved in, and moments later the 26th Missouri followed.

Even though Matthies had been destroyed, Sherman still had fresh troops available. Cleburne did not have this luxury. The Federals rose and moved forward in unison. Warfield was in trouble, as he suddenly had pressure from both his right and front. The situation did not look good, but unlike Sherman, Hardee was managing the battle with great attention to detail. He used interior lines to his advantage, and when he saw Raum move he had Stevenson send Cumming's 39th Georgia to Cleburne's support once again. About half of Brown's brigade had left the ridge when they took the Glass farm and Cumming filled the void on Granbury's left. Stevenson also saw the problem and sent the 34th Georgia as well.

Cumming pulled his last two regiments out of line and marched them to the rear of Tunnel Hill. As Raum moved into the valley he reported to Cleburne. He was told to take the 36th and 56th Georgia to the top of the hill and deploy as close to the breastworks as possible. Cleburne now had more troops in hand than the small expanse of ground would allow. The 7th Texas had been fighting for the better part of five hours, but they held on with a fierce determination. In the words of one soldier, they "declined to be relieved."[16]

George Maney reported with his Tennessee brigade from States Rights Gist's division at the same time that Cumming arrived. Cleburne placed him behind Granbury, adding, "when I send for reinforcements, send me the best regiment you have."[17] Maney waited only ten minutes. Just as Wever surged past Dean's troops he sent in the 1st and 27th Tennessee (consolidated) under Colonel Hume Feild. They charged up the back of the ridge and into

---

[16] Nathaniel C. Hughes, *General William J. Hardee: Old Reliable* (Baton Rouge: Louisiana State University Press, 1965) 175.

[17] Report of Patrick R. Cleburne, n.d., US War Department, comp., *The War of the Rebellion: A Compilation of the Official Records of the Union and Confederate Armies*, 128 vols. (Washington, DC: Government Printing Office, 1880–1901) ser. 1, vol. 31, pt. 2, p. 751; Hughes, *Old Reliable*, 174–75.

the fray but ran right into a blast of musketry. Cleburne yelled to go over the breastworks and fall in on Warfield's right. The men jumped the barricades and lay down less than 100 feet from the Yankees.

The Rebels appeared just in time for Warfield, but he was still fighting a losing battle. In desperation he went to look for Cleburne. Pointing out that the men were only wasting ammunition, he proposed a charge down the mountain. The suggestion was readily approved, and since Cumming was in the closest position, the 56th lined up 10 yards ahead of the 36th and waited for Cleburne's order. The officers were given last-minute instructions. They were to hold their fire until the Federals gave way, then drive them from their position at the point of the bayonet.

The opening in the Confederate lines was not nearly as wide as Cumming had expected. The 56th met with some confusion, and before he could reform Dean unleashed a volley that momentarily checked the Georgians. Cumming regrouped, and when he charged through the gap Warfield and Feild were on his heels. They filled in on his right, no more than 60 feet from the 10th Iowa and what little remained of the 93rd Illinois. Cleburne had already gone to his left, where he found the 6th, 10th, and 15th Texas. He told them to hit the flank as soon as Cumming made contact. At 4:00 P.M. the Rebels burst over the logs and struck with devastating effect. Dean's command was exhausted as it was, and the 1st and 27th Tennessee swarmed over the Iowans. The men were packed together so closely that Feild hit a man on the head with a rock, and one Confederate tore off part of the regimental flag with his bare hands.[18]

The outcome was never in doubt. Large numbers of Federals dropped their weapons and just surrendered. Cumming delivered a punishing blow, but the results were decided by the Texans on Dean's right. Green Raum had witnessed the disaster. After the battle he wrote: "This front attack could, and no doubt would, have been resisted; but the movement upon the right flank was pushed with such energy and determination that there was no time to make a change of front to meet it. Our right flank was practically in the air."[19]

The helpless victims were the men of the 5th Iowa. An unusual curvature of the ground produced a hill in their front that concealed the Rebels from view until they were almost on top of them. Granbury appeared out of

---

[18] Cozzens, *Shipwreck of Their Hopes*, 233–36.
[19] Cozzens, *Shipwreck of Their Hopes*, 236.

nowhere and pounded the defenders into submission. The 5th had gone into action with 227 men and lost 106, 82 of whom were captured. When they collapsed, the 27th Pennsylvania was exposed and the men were easily driven from the hillside at the expense of their colors. The 93rd Illinois lost ninety-three men as well as their flag. Further south, the 73rd Pennsylvania had seen casualties of roughly 50 percent. The only unit to survive in reasonable condition was the 26th Missouri, which had held a supporting position behind the 93rd.

As the Yankees dashed for safety, the panic was contagious. Every man rushed from the hill, but the men were able to form a stout line at its base behind the 10th Missouri and 56th Illinois. They unleashed a volley at 30 yards and the charge abruptly came to a halt. The action quickly shifted from a frenzied chase to a more even exchange of rifle fire before the Confederates slowly made their way back up the incline with their captives in tow. The Federals had no energy left. The hill was covered not only with prisoners, but with Union wounded as well. Adding to the misery of a total failure, Green Raum received a thigh wound. As his left boot began to fill with blood, he sat down against a tree and sent for Colonel Francis Deimling of the 10th Missouri. Explaining that Wever was also wounded, he transferred the brigade.

Despite their success, neither Cleburne nor Cumming was satisfied. They wanted to press their advantage. The Georgians regrouped for a fifteen-minute rest. Cleburne brought up Maney's 15th Tennessee and added it to his first attack force. At 5 o'clock they rushed down the slope again, but this time with little resistance. The Federals had seized the opportunity and made their escape.

While the rest of Missionary Ridge was melting away, Cleburne could not have given a stronger account of himself. He certainly had some help, as Sherman's effort was dismal. He had John Smith, Morgan Smith, and Hugh Ewing on hand as well as Jefferson Davis in close support; by 2:00 P.M. Carl Schurz had brought up still another division and Howard had loaned Sherman Buschbeck's brigade. Yet Sherman failed to use his advantage. The ground was not properly examined, and given the position and numbers he failed to consider the use of either calculated maneuver or a simultaneous, overwhelming attack. Even with the talent Cleburne possessed, it would have been impossible to fend off such an onslaught.[20] As it was, the Confederates

---

[20] Cozzens, *Shipwreck of Their Hopes,* 239–41.

lost only 42 men killed, 178 wounded, and 2 missing. The Federals had been soundly beaten, and Sherman failed to mention any Union casualties in his battle report. Ewing, however, was not so bashful; he gave their total losses as 891.[21]

As the sun began to set, Hardee felt pleased with Cleburne's performance. However, he had no time to reflect on the stand at Tunnel Hill. He soon learned that the left and center of the ridge had been broken. He immediately ordered Cleburne to take command of his own, Walker's, and Stevenson's divisions and form a line across the ridge to delay the flank attack that was sure to come. Vehicles were taken across the Chickamauga if possible, and Polk's brigade was dispatched to the Shallow Ford Bridge with instructions to hold it at all costs. Govan was sent to cover the road that approached Polk's position.[22] Soon after dark Hardee gave the word to withdraw and assigned Granbury to cover the rear. By 9:00 P.M. almost everything was across the creek, save for a few isolated stragglers.

The rank and file of the Army of Tennessee had lost all respect for Braxton Bragg. The series of retreats from seemingly dominant positions had eroded any confidence they might have had in his leadership, and his lack of preparation had cost them dearly as they fled the crest of Missionary Ridge. Sam Watkins observed the general's haggard appearance: "I felt sorry for General Bragg. The army was routed, and Bragg looked so scared. Poor fellow, he looked so hacked and whipped and mortified and chagrined at defeat, and all along the line, when Bragg would pass, the soldiers would raise the yell, 'Here is your mules; Bully for Bragg, he's h--l on retreat.'"[23]

---

[21] Report of Hugh Ewing, 28 November 1863, OR, ser. 1, vol. 31, pt. 2, p. 632; and Report of Patrick R. Cleburne, OR, ser. 1, vol. 31, pt. 2, p. 752. According to Ewing's figures, the losses in his division were as follows: Loomis: 37 killed, 342 wounded, 18 missing, for a total of 397; Corse: 35 killed, 186 wounded, 3 missing, for a total of 224; Cockerill: 3 wounded; Artillery: 3 wounded, Pioneers: 1 wounded, for a total of 72 killed, 535 wounded, 21 missing, for a total of 628. To this he adds the losses in Buschbeck's brigade, which belonged to Steinwehr's division in Howard's XI Army Corps. At Tunnel Hill, Buschbeck lost 37 killed, 145 wounded, 81 missing, for a total of 263, bringing the combined total casualties to 891.

[22] Buck, *Cleburne and His Command*, 171.

[23] Samuel R. Watkins, *Co. Aytch* (Dayton OH: Morningside, 1982) 105; Philip D. Stephenson, "Reminiscences," in *Southern Historical Society Papers*, 52 vols. (Millwood NY: Kraus Reprint Co., 1977) 12:36.

Pent-up frustration consumed the troops. Once again the failures of their commander had led them to defeat. Drained in battle and desperate for food, they streamed down the mountain, clinging to the faint hope that they could regroup. They would surely form a new line, draw rations, and prepare for the inevitable pursuit. However, the weary, hungry soldiers found only another enemy, one they had never imagined. Their food, so dear to an army with such limited means of subsistence, was disappearing before their very eyes.

Great piles of corn in sacks, and bacon, and crackers, and molasses, and sugar, and coffee, and rice, and potatoes, and onions, and peas, and flour by the hundreds of barrels, all now to be given to the flames, while for months the Rebel soldiers had been stinted and starved for want of these same provisions. It was enough to make the bravest and most patriotic soul that ever fired a gun in defense of any cause on earth, think of rebelling against those authorities as they then were. Every private soldier knew these stores were there, and for the want of them we lost our cause.[24]

In 1867 postwar comments by Willam Hardee assessed the struggle on Missionary Ridge and reveal again the talent displayed by the Irishman:

Cleburne's position on the right was most insecure from its liability to be turned. He maintained it with his accustomed ability, and upon the repulse of the last assault, directed in person a counter-charge which effected the capture of a large number of prisoners and several stands of colors. The assailants gave up the contest and withdrew from our front. But while the cheers of victory raised on the right were extending down the line, the left of the army had been carried by assault and the day was lost.... If the right in stead of the left had been carried it would have given the enemy possession of the only line of retreat, and no organized body of the Confederate army could have escaped.[25]

---

[24] Watkins, *Co. Aytch,* 107; Stephenson, "Reminiscences," 35.
[25] Buck, *Cleburne and His Command,* 172–73.

9

RINGGOLD GAP

The Army of Tennessee had dissolved before the three-sided assault, and its very existence was in danger. With the three divisions heading south, combatant R. M. Collins described their emotions:

> About 11 o'clock the order was passed down the line in a whisper, from post to post, for us to move out by the left flank, and to be careful as to making any sort of noise, not to allow saber or gun to strike with canteens, and not to tread on any sticks that might break and make a noise. We were old soldiers enough by this time to know what all this meant. We knew that the day had been lost, and in less time than it requires to pen one of these lines, such thoughts passed through our minds in rapid succession; if we can't hold such a line against these blasted Federals, where is the line or position between here and the coast of Georgia that we can hold?… We moved out as quietly as if there had been but one man only. Up, over the mountain and down through a deep gorge, wrapped in deep darkness inside and outside. Not a word being uttered.[1]

When Bragg left the station on 26 November, heavy rains had turned the roads to mud. He decided to burn the bridges over Chickamauga Creek and then retreat through Tunnel Hill to Dalton. Once there, he would give the soldiers a chance to recuperate. The poor conditions forced the long column to wind its way south along a single road. As Cleburne made up the rear guard, the slow pace placed his men in great jeopardy. Most worrisome was the possibility of a strong flank attack from Hooker at Graysville, only 3 1/2 miles from the station. Departing from Rossville, the Federals had passed Bragg's left only one day earlier and could cross the West Chickamauga at Red House Ford, which would place them squarely across Cleburne's line of

---

[1] R. M. Collins, *Chapters from the Unwritten History of the War between the States* (St. Louis: Nixon-Jones Printing Co., 1882) 188–89.

retreat. Fortunately for the Rebels, the rains offered protection as well as resistance. The banks of the Chickamauga had risen, and the swollen creek delayed the Union crossing. Cleburne reached Graysville late in the afternoon and for the moment his division was safe.[2]

The Federals had begun their pursuit that morning. Hooker headed toward the town using the old Federal Road. It predated the Civil War and meandered across West Chickamauga Creek just north of the state line. Although they were able to keep Hooker at a distance, the Confederates were still within sight of Chickamauga Station. Cleburne knew he would not be able to face the enemy on open ground; he numbered only 4,157 men while Hooker had five divisions at his disposal. Combined, he led over 18,000 Yankees.[3] Never at a loss for confidence, Hooker was emboldened by his low estimation of Braxton Bragg. He had taken Lookout Mountain on 24 November and participated in the rout on Missionary Ridge the next day. Union sympathizers had painted a picture of panic. Hooker wrote: "Bragg's army have no heart in the cause. Their officers appear to distrust the fidelity of the enlisted men, and they have no discipline like that in Lee's army, they will retire as soon as a forward movement is made by our troops."[4]

He was soon to discover that a battle against Braxton Bragg was not the same as a battle against Patrick Cleburne. When Hooker arrived at the creek he found that the bridges had been burned. A small footbridge was hastily constructed, but it was only large enough to accommodate the infantry; the ambulances and artillery were forced to remain where they were until the following morning. Once the Federals had crossed, Hooker divided his forces. Charles Cruft, John Geary, and Peter Osterhaus headed toward Ringgold, while John Palmer took two divisions to Graysville. They would unite on the morning of 28 November and attack the railroad at Ringgold.

Two miles further down the road Hooker's column halted again at Pea Vine Creek, where they found another bridge destroyed. "Fighting Joe's"

---

[2] Irving A. Buck, *Cleburne and His Command* (1908; repr., Wilmington NC: Broadfoot Publishing, 1995) 174–75; Mauriel P. Joslyn, ed., *A Meteor Shining Brightly* (Macon GA: Mercer University Press, 2000) 76.

[3] Report of Patrick R. Cleburne, 9 December 1863, OR, ser. 1, vol. 31, pt. 2, p. 753–58.

[4] US War Department, comp., *The War of the Rebellion: A Compilation of the Official Records of the Union and Confederate Armies,* 128 vols. (Washington, DC: Government Printing Office, 1880–1901) ser. 1, vol. 31, pt. 2, p. 339–45.

frustration grew, but shortly after dark he received encouraging news. Palmer reported that a Rebel column was moving along the LaFayette-Graysville Road. The Southerners appeared to have no more than 3,000 infantry and a single battery of artillery. Hooker immediately issued the orders to attack, and around 8:00 P.M. the Federals forded the creek. The campfires were still burning, so they cautiously ascended Summit Hill to examine the situation. Upon reaching the top they discovered that the Confederates had disappeared. Thoroughly disgusted, Hooker went into bivouac on the top of the hill.[5]

Bragg held out little hope. Cleburne's predicament was a hopeless one, but the division must be sacrificed to protect the remainder of the army. He knew that the loss of the positions on Lookout Mountain and Missionary Ridge had dealt a serious blow to Southern morale. He also understood that many of the men he now entrusted with the safety of the army were those who had favored his removal following the battle of Chickamauga. The only Confederates left largely intact were Cleburne's, and he would be asked to save his comrades from certain destruction.[6]

When Cleburne had gone only a few miles, he was approached by a young man who claimed to have orders from Hardee instructing Cleburne to continue on his present route. Cleburne had heard no firing in his front, and there was no indication that the column ahead of his had been attacked. He was aware of the possibility of a ruse and asked for written verification, but the man had none. It was thought that the young man might be a spy, but it was discovered that he was in fact a volunteer from Hardee's staff. The man had joined the army only a few days earlier and was unfamiliar with military protocol. Cleburne sent Irving Buck to Hardee and quickly learned that the aide had made a mistake. Around midnight an officer from Bragg came with verbal orders to select a pass in the hills and hold it at all hazards until ordered to withdraw.[7]

Cleburne followed a southerly route toward Ringgold along what today is US Highway 41. The road continued past several farms until it reached a toll bridge. In addition to the covered bridge, there were two fords by which an army could cross the water. At 10:00 P.M. the men reached their destination, just opposite the town. Cleburne received orders to move out at 4:00 A.M. on

---

[5] William H. H. Clark, *History in Catoosa County* (Ringgold GA: n.p., 1994) 219–21.

[6] Joslyn, *Meteor Shining Brightly*, 76.

[7] Buck, *Cleburne and His Command*, 175.

27 November, but a bitter wind cut through the freezing cold. The river was 30 yards wide and quite deep, and its banks rose abruptly.[8] Thin sheets of ice bobbed along in a swift current. Cleburne believed he would lose more men to pneumonia than he would to Hooker. He decided to make his camp where he was but to start his movement one hour earlier. The extra time spent marching in the morning would allow his men to warm up after plunging into the waist-deep water.[9]

Daylight on 27 November found Hooker still in pursuit of the wagon trains. Osterhaus was in the lead, followed by Geary and Cruft. Along the way they saw evidence of a desperate flight as abandoned caissons, wagons, tents, and arms littered the roadside. Osterhaus reported that a good ford lay ahead, as well as a trestle bridge on the west side of town that had not been burned.

Two hundred men from the 9th Kentucky cavalry were under the command of Warren Grigsby, and with infantry support from the 33rd Alabama they were assigned to guard the creek. As soon as the Federals appeared they were to fire at long range and then retreat through the town. This would create the impression that the Federals were facing nothing more than a cavalry detachment. The men were barely in place when the Yankees attacked and drove the 9th backward. The troopers were unaware that Cleburne held the gap, but they could see Bragg's long wagon train in the distance. Benjamin Seaton, a private in Granbury's 10th Texas regiment, observed that they came "as tho they was driving hogs before them." The horsemen delivered a volley and quickly turned around. The Federals forded the water, then turned to their right toward the bridge. The Kentuckians reformed, fired another round, and fell back again.

The Federal cavalry took the bait, charging straight toward the trap that was just waiting to snap shut. As Grigsby passed safely into the Confederate defenses, Cleburne deployed the men as dismounted cavalry and sent them into position on the right flank of the second line. He then moved the 33rd Alabama along with Lowrey's other regiments into the center of his formation. This apparent weakness strengthened Hooker's conviction that he was chasing

---

[8] W. W. Gibson, "Reminiscences of Ringgold Gap," *Confederate Veteran* 12/11 (November 1904): 526–27; Collins, *Unwritten History*, 189.
[9] Report of John W. Geary, 15 December 1863, OR, ser. 1, vol. 31, pt. 2, p. 401–402.

a beaten foe. It would be a simple matter to destroy Bragg's army without the need for additional reinforcements.[10]

Cleburne knew Hooker had tremendous numerical superiority and he knew Cleburne had no support. A successful defense would be extremely difficult, but the order must be obeyed. In case there might be any question of his actions in the future, Cleburne requested that Bragg put the order in writing. At 3:00 A.M. on 27 November, Cleburne received confirmation of the earlier instructions: "General: The General [Bragg] desires that you will take strong position in the gorge of the mountain and attempt to check pursuit of enemy. He must be punished until our trains and the rear of our troops get well advanced. The reports from the rear are meager and the General is not thoroughly advised of the state of things there. Will you be good enough to report fully?"[11]

While staff officers put the troops in motion, Cleburne rode ahead to reconnoiter the ground. Here he put a lesson from Shiloh to good use. His failure to fully understand the position and strength of the enemy in that battle had led to a series of costly frontal assaults. He would not repeat the mistake. His grasp of the terrain was the deciding factor in the defense of Ringgold Gap. Once again he relied on Irving Buck, sending him to obtain further instructions from the commanding general. After a 3-mile journey Buck arrived at Catoosa Station, where Bragg had made his temporary headquarters in a large freight room. Braxton Bragg was gruff and aloof by nature, but there was desperation in his voice. He came forward, grasped Buck's hand, and said, "Tell General Cleburne to hold his position at all hazards, and keep back the enemy, until the artillery and transportation of the army is secure, the salvation of which depends upon him."[12]

In 1863 Ringgold Gap was roughly 1,000 feet wide and 4,000 feet long, leaving little room for a defending force to maneuver. On the south side, Taylor's Ridge rose abruptly to 400 feet, 1 mile east of Ringgold. A break in the hills allowed only the passage of the Western and Atlantic Railroad, the Atlanta Wagon Road, and the east branch of Chickamauga Creek. Within in few hundred yards of the eastern, or rear, mouth of the gap, the winding

---

[10] OR, ser. 1, vol. 31, pt. 2, p. 339–45.

[11] Report of Patrick R. Cleburne, 9 December 1863, OR, ser. 1, vol. 31, pt. 2, p. 753–58.

[12] Buck, *Cleburne and His Command*, 177.

stream was bridged three times by the wagon road. The topography made it a hazardous position to occupy in the face of a turning movement, and troops must be deployed very quickly. Here Cleburne placed the 16th Alabama of Mark Lowrey's brigade. Three companies of Govan's 6th and 7th Arkansas (consolidated) were positioned in their front. Together they would protect the left flank.

White Oak Mountain, on the right, or north, of the gap, is a more gentle rise. As Cleburne rode along the ridge he found most of the cover too light, but at the base of the mountain a heavily wooded section ran some 300–400 yards long. From this vantage point he could see the tracks of the Western and Atlantic as they passed along the wagon road through the narrow cut in the mountains. The creek meandered through the gap and the water had not receded. He realized that his position between both mountains could spell the death of his command. If the enemy were to turn either flank, there would be no escape. He decided to conceal his troops among the trees and wait for Hooker to approach.

The defenses on the north side of the gap began with several consolidated regiments of Arkansas troops, also under Govan. The 5th and 13th placed their left flank on the tracks and their right on the hill. Parallel to the first line and some 50 yards to the rear were the 8th and 19th Arkansas. They were supported by the remainder of the 6th and 7th, while the 2nd, 15th, and 24th regiments completed the formation. Skirmishers were thrown out in their front.

On Govan's right he placed Hiram Granbury's Texans. The 6th, 10th, and 15th Texas under John Kennard held the left, while the 17th, 18th, 24th, and 25th led by William Taylor anchored the right. In order to guard Taylor's flank, Granbury refused the 7th Texas and deployed two companies in a location where the ground fell down into to a steep hollow, due east of Ringgold. Commanded by C. E. Talley, they went into line at a right angle to Taylor's troops. In total, Granbury had only 1,226 men.[13]

The 1st Arkansas, 3rd and 5th Confederate (consolidated), and 2nd Tennessee regiments comprised Lucius Polk's brigade. These were held in reserve behind the crest of the ridge. Lowrey placed the 45th and 33rd Alabama on Granbury's right, with their left flank on the 7th Texas. He

---

[13] Report of Patrick R. Cleburne, 9 December 1863, OR, ser. 1, vol. 31, pt. 2, p. 753–58.

extended the line along White Oak Mountain with the 32nd and 45th Mississippi (consolidated) surrounding the 1st Arkansas. On the right of the 32nd were the men of the 3rd and 5th Confederate. Cleburne had no more than thirty minutes to arrange his lines.

In the deployment of his artillery it was imperative to avoid the mistake Bragg had made on the summit of Missionary Ridge, where poor placement had resulted in steep angles that prevented the effective use of the guns in the center and left. Cleburne's reconnaissance had discovered a small ravine that concealed the men, and the cannon were camouflaged behind screens of brush. He placed a two-gun section of 12-pounder Napoleons in the mouth of the gap facing Ringgold, commanded by Richard Goldthwaite. He could not have selected a better location. The left piece was loaded with solid shot, the right with canister, and all of the horses were sent to the rear. The general stood nearby, out of sight behind a tree.

Private W. E. Preston was a member of Company B, 33rd Alabama, and one of the last to arrive in the gap. He wrote: "We double-quicked through Ringgold and into Ringgold Gap. The cavalry was on the heels of the rear ones of Co. B.... Inside the gap, we passed two pieces of our artillery in position and unlimbered.... Several of our men carrying our blue and white flag were lying down across the Ringgold end of the gap, and on the sides of the hills, we not observing them in the bushes until we had got among them as we passed on to the rear."[14]

Private Philip Stephenson of the 13th Arkansas described his feelings as he lay hidden, watching the enemy as it approached the advance skirmish line. Step by step the men came in perfect order. "Gen. Cleburne and an aide or so were hidden behind us, Cleburne behind a tree, standing with field glasses, watching. We were not to fire until he said so.... On they came! Down the railroad track carelessly, not out of line of battle, but in marching column, no skirmishers thrown out, no sign of seeing us or suspecting our presence! As I lay in the gully, I took a look at [Cleburne] now and then. I was looking at him when he gave the order to fire."[15]

Hooker sent forward Peter Osterhaus's division of 3,375 men[16] from Iowa and Missouri. Led by Charles Woods and James Williamson, two

---

[14] Joslyn, *Meteor Shining Brightly*, 85.

[15] Joslyn, *Meteor Shining Brightly*, 86.

[16] This figure comes from the returns taken on the morning of 24 November.

brigades moved forward behind an advance guard of 170 mounted infantry. The first troops to enter Ringgold belonged to Woods, and shortly after 8 o'clock the 17th, 29th, and 31st Missouri regiments attacked the left side of Granbury's brigade. The 17th and 31st moved toward the gap with the 29th somewhat to the rear. They made contact with Confederate skirmishers and the 29th moved forward in support. The 3rd Missouri formed on the left of the 17th and the 12th Missouri continued the line.

Woods's lone remaining regiment, the 13th Illinois, held his far right. As they moved along the railroad tracks they came into view of Confederate artillery. Goldthwaite opened his guns at 150 yards, observing that "after the first discharge the field was covered in smoke. When it lifted the field was empty. The enemy did not advance in so much force again." The blast had sent the Yankees running for cover by the railroad embankment.[17]

The 13th was ordered to charge, but without any visibility they fired aimlessly, providing easy marks. Their lines were cut to pieces, the color guard was killed, and his blood spattered over the regimental flag. They hid among the buildings at the Jobe farm, but in three hours they lost Lieutenant Colonel Frederick Partridge to a shredded hand, Major Douglas Bushnell to a head wound, and Captain Walter Blanchard to a badly broken knee. Blanchard would die just a week later.[18]

At this range, Confederate artillery decimated the closely packed ranks. The visual effect was very moving. Captain William Gibson of the 6th Arkansas wrote: "Every man hit the ground and, from the way their hats, caps, guns, and accoutrements went flying in the air, I had not a doubt that the entire line was annihilated, and exclaimed, 'By Jove, boys, it killed them all.' Old Pat smiled at my boyish incredulity while saying good naturedly, 'If you don't lie down, young man, you are liable to find that there are enough left for you to get the top of your head shot off.'"[19]

The Federals tried to regroup but still fired wildly in a disorganized fashion. They were now exposed not only to the fire from Goldthwaite's

---

[17] Report of Richard W. Goldthwaite, 7 December 1863, OR, ser. 1, vol. 31, pt. 2, p. 758–60.

[18] Peter Cozzens, *Shipwreck of Their Hopes* (Urbana: University of Illinois Press, 1994) 376–77.

[19] Clark, *Catoosa County,* 231.

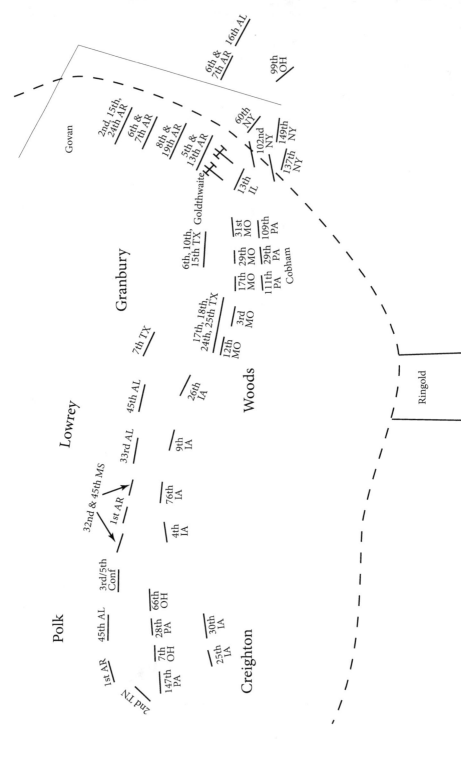

16th AL

6th &
7th AR

99th
OH

Govan

2nd, 15th,
24th AR

6th &
7th AR

8th &
19th AR

5th &
13th AR

60th
NY

102nd
NY

149th
NY

137th
NY

13th
IL

6th, 10th, Goldthwaite
15th TX

31st
MO

109th
PA

29th
MO

29th
PA

Granbury

17th
MO

11th
PA

Cobham

17th, 18th,
24th, 25th TX

3rd
MO

7th TX

12th
MO

45th AL

26th
IA

Woods

Lowrey

33rd AL

9th
IA

32nd & 45th MS

1st AR

76th
IA

Ringold

4th
IA

Polk

3rd/5th
Conf

66th
OH

45th AL

28th
PA

30th
IA

7th
OH

1st AR

147th
PA

25th
IA

Creighton

2nd TN

0   1000 FT

battery, but also to the musketry on Taylor's Ridge. Forced to retreat, they were no longer a factor in the battle's outcome. Osterhaus realized that if he could only outflank Cleburne, the day would be won. He attempted to move the battle northward, but Taylor sent word to Granbury and two companies were shifted from the left to the right as reinforcements. Along with three companies of his own, Taylor exploded down the hill in a vicious counterattack. The Rebels routed the 29th and captured their colors, along with almost 100 prisoners. The shock was infectious, and it forced the 17th and 31st to withdraw.[20]

The Federals had made no progress anywhere, but Osterhaus was undeterred. Talley now became the Union focus. Osterhaus believed he could press his advantage, so he brought up more troops. By now he was certain that the Confederates must be on the verge of collapse and the force of numbers would surely result in a hard-won victory. Cleburne saw the danger and reacted swiftly. He sent word to Lucius Polk, who was riding up the back of the ridge. Polk was already aware of the movement, as he had come upon an exhausted straggler who told him that Yankees were attacking the Confederate right. These troops belonged to James Williamson's brigade, with the 76th Ohio in the lead. They worked their way around the confusion and began to ascend the hill. The Buckeyes were supported by three Iowa regiments, the 4th on their left, the 9th and 26th on their right. They began moving forward at 9 o'clock, and for a time they were hidden by large outcroppings of sharp boulders. However, due to the difficulty of the terrain they took the least obstructed route to the top. This proved to be their undoing. As soon as they came into view, Taylor sent word to Granbury.

Unfortunately for the North, as Williamson shifted so did Talley. He wanted to connect his right flank with Lowrey, but he quickly realized that the distance was too great. Talley stopped and formed his lines at an angle to the Federals. From this new position the Texans delivered a destructive fire into their right flank.

Williamson and 1,118 Yankees were madly scaling the west side of the ridge, while Polk and 200 Confederates climbed the east side. Like Polk, Mark Lowrey was in back of the crest and when he heard the gunfire he rode toward it. Assuming the worst, he had the presence of mind to bring his infantry with him. He told Polk that help was on the way and double-quicked 1,330

---

[20] Clark, *Catoosa County,* 231.

men over the rugged ground. With no time to spare, he threw them into line as fast as they arrived. The first to appear were the 32nd and 45th Mississippi, along with the 15th Mississippi sharpshooters. It was a race to the top, and the Rebels won by twenty paces. By the time the Federals neared the summit they found double lines of Confederates. They all came together in a ferocious collision. The 1st Arkansas delivered a volley at point-blank range and fighting was hand to hand. When they ran out of ammunition the Confederates used rocks and clubbed muskets, and the Ohioans were finally forced to fall back. Along with their regimental colors, they lost 40 percent of their men.[21]

Polk and Lowrey had held by the slimmest of margins. The Confederates continued to extend their lines, far beyond the Union left. The 3rd and 5th Confederate, along with the 2nd Tennessee, shattered the flank. The 76th took fire from both sides as well as in their front and fell back down the ravine. They became badly entangled with the 4th Iowa and the hasty retreat exposed both regiments. They were hopelessly pinned, yet the distance between the lines remained less than 100 yards. The 1st Arkansas charged down the hill and captured the flag of the 76th, but the national banner was saved by the death of eight color bearers and two officers, all lost in a matter of minutes.[22] The regiment had been decimated. Two hundred and fifty men entered the fray; sixty-four lay dead or wounded.[23]

The courage of the Federal soldiers was without question, but the wisdom of their general officers was suspect. Time and again they were ordered to charge, only to be thrown back in a bloody repulse. Williamson assessed the sacrifice: "they stood manfully for a minute or two, then they gave way and came down like an avalanche, carrying everything before them, and to some extent propagating panic among my regiments."[24]

By the time Williamson could get his right two regiments going, the 1st Arkansas had made their way back up the hill and the Federals were facing eight regiments of Confederates in a strong position along the ridge. Hooker,

---

[21] Report of Patrick R. Cleburne, 9 December 1863, OR, ser. 1, vol. 31, pt. 2, p. 756.

[22] Mark K. Christ, *Getting Used to Being Shot at: The Spence Family Civil War Letters* (Fayetteville: University of Arkansas Press, 2002) 64–65; report of Charles P. Woods, 28 November 1863, OR, ser. 1, vol. 31, pt. 2, p. 606–609.

[23] Cozzens, *Shipwreck of Their Hopes,* 380; Joslyn, *Meteor Shining Brightly,* 88.

[24] Report of James A. Williamson, 28 November 1863, OR, ser. 1, vol. 31, pt. 2, p. 616–17.

however, had not earned the title "Fighting Joe" from inherent hesitation. The field was covered in Union blood, but Osterhaus had no intention of calling a halt to the slaughter. He had been soundly defeated across the entire front, but he knew that Cleburne had no reserves while Williamson still had some relatively fresh Iowans. The 9th and 26th pressed Lowrey's left but were stalled by 9:00 A.M. Thus far, Cleburne had parried every thrust.

Williamson failed to learn from the mistake Osterhaus had continued to make. Determined to turn the Confederate right, he brought up the 30th and 25th Iowa. They formed to the left of the 4th Iowa but were suddenly passed by four regiments from John Geary's division. From left to right these were the 147th Pennsylvania, 7th Ohio, 28th Pennsylvania, and 66th Ohio, with the 147th slightly to the left of and about 100 yards behind the 7th, all under William Creighton. Lucius Polk had watched the Yankees as they moved to his right. He shifted the 2nd Tennessee, 1st Arkansas, and Lowrey's 45th Alabama along the ridge.[25]

The pressure was too great for the Federals to withstand. Again, Polk and Lowrey utilized the contours of the slopes to their advantage. In order to maintain alignment, Creighton's men were forced to expose their flanks to treacherous fire. They tried to hold their ground but had no better luck than the first wave. After half an hour and another bloody repulse, Hooker was forced to concede that an attack on this position was pointless.

Their path was badly broken, but the Federals advanced as if they were on parade. As they began to move upward the rocks funneled them together. The irregular terrain allowed the Confederates to deliver an enfilading fire and the 2nd Tennessee swept down upon them in a furious counterattack. All four brigades were routed, but the 7th Ohio suffered the most. Of thirteen officers who had ascended White Oak Mountain, twelve were lost. Captain Ernst Krieger returned to the foot of the mountain to discover that he was the only one left.[26] Company C lost fourteen of twenty men. Lieutenant Colonel Orrin Crane was killed early in the action. Creighton mourned the loss of his old friend, but only for a moment. As the men fled back down the hill he was mortally wounded.

Shortly before 10:00 A.M. the Federals made their first serious move against Cleburne's left. Three Pennsylvania regiments under George Cobham

[25] Cozzens, *Shipwreck of Their Hopes*, 380–81.
[26] Clark, *Catoosa County*, 234–36; Joslyn, *Meteor Shining Brightly*, 89.

advanced on the left side of the railroad tracks. Cobham ordered the 111th, 29th, and 109th to lie down and await reinforcements, but lacking sufficient cover the 111th lay unprotected by the depot.

The rest of Geary's division was comprised of David Ireland's New Yorkers. Joe Hooker was not impressed with the conduct of his army on White Oak Mountain, so he turned his attention back to Taylor's Ridge. Just before 10 o'clock he turned to Geary and asked, "Have you any regiments that will not run?" Geary responded with confidence that these men would not abandon the field. Hooker ordered him to send his troops into the gap and hold it until the artillery arrived. The only Confederates on Taylor's Ridge were the 16th Alabama and three companies of the 6th and 7th Arkansas. Hooker was sure they would pose little trouble.

The railroad cut separated Cobham's right from Ireland's left, and around 10:40 Cobham's flank began to give way. As they fled to the rear Ireland came up along the line previously taken by the 13th Illinois.[27] The New Yorkers entered at the double-quick, partially hidden by the roadbed, and prepared to ford the creek. The orders they received were rather difficult to carry out. They were told to hold the gap but not to fire their guns unless advanced upon, and only then to use no more ammunition than necessary. They crossed an open field 500 to 600 yards wide, where they were greeted by muskets and artillery.[28] The 137th placed its left near an old barn, followed by the 102nd, 60th, and 149th, anchored on Chickamauga Creek. The hills on both sides were held by sharpshooters, and Ireland's brigade was caught in a deadly crossfire.

Goldthwaite opened his guns with telling effect. The 16th Alabama was ordered to counterattack and Govan's skirmishers sent Ireland reeling for cover behind the creek bed and outbuildings on the Jobe property. They had reached within 60 yards of the Confederate lines but could go no further. The Federals were able to regroup and return the fire around 11 o'clock as the 16th fell back among the trees. At this point the action stalled, turning into an exchange of rifle fire between the sharpshooters at the farm and Cleburne's hand-picked contingent of men armed with Whitworths.

---

[27] Report of John W. Geary, 15 December 1863, OR, ser. 1, vol. 31, pt. 2, p. 404–405.

[28] Report of David Ireland, 5 December 1863, OR, ser. 1, vol. 31, pt. 2, p. 438. Ireland lists the distance as "about half a mile"; report of Charles Randall, 4 December 1863, OR, ser. 1, vol. 31, pt. 2, p. 450. Randall estimates it at "500–600 yards."

The Federals still held a numerical advantage, and when they began to find their range Cleburne ordered Goldthwaite to unleash his guns. Ireland had little choice in the matter, but he bent his command back on itself at a 90-degree angle. One side faced White Oak Mountain, the other Taylor's Ridge.[29] The Confederates finally began to run low on ammunition, but Hooker gave them a brief respite while he paused to bring up his artillery.

The artillery did not appear until 12 o'clock, just as Cleburne received Hardee's dispatch allowing him the discretion to withdraw. Peter Snyder's 7th Arkansas took a position guarding the rear of the column until the first railroad bridge had been crossed. By the time he followed the rest of the division, the bridge was already on fire. Snyder's men waded the creek and moved down the railroad, where they joined the Confederates at Catoosa Station.[30]

Around noon St. John Liddell returned from the rear and took over the Arkansas troops on Taylor's Ridge, which had been directed so skillfully by Daniel Govan. The order from Hardee had just arrived and Cleburne began to fall back, but opinions differed as to the necessity of the movement at this particular time. Liddell had not been present on the field during the battle, and he believed that the Confederates had a strong position and could have inflicted further damage. In addition, he saw it as an opportunity for the Confederate supply wagons to put more distance between the two armies.

Cleburne, however, did not agree and Lucius Polk shared this view. He wrote:

> The enemy still continued moving over the railroad bridge in heavy column, and about one o'clock commenced moving rapidly to our right in two columns, one coming direct from the railroad bridge, and the other moving some three hundred yards beyond the foot of the ridge. This being reported to Gen. Cleburne, he ordered my command to withdraw. This move was made in perfect order. The enemy did not advance upon Taylor's Ridge until we had taken our position two miles in the rear.[31]

---

[29] Clark, *Catoosa County,* 237.
[30] Clark, *Catoosa County,* 239.
[31] Report of Lucius E. Polk, 3 December 1863, OR, ser. 1. vol. 31, pt. 2, pp. 760–61.

In retrospect, this was the wiser course of action. The original mission had been accomplished, and Cleburne was severely outnumbered. John C. Breckinridge and Joseph Wheeler had ridden forward to offer their assistance should it become necessary, and both men concurred with Cleburne's decision. After five hours the Rebels still held the gap, but pressure was mounting as fresh troops continued to appear. At 1:00 P.M. the artillery was withdrawn, the branches were replaced, and the cannon were dragged down by hand. The infantry filed off to the east in the direction of Dalton. Just as the Confederates left their position, Hooker's artillery arrived. By 2:00 P.M. the Federals had control of Ringgold, though skirmishers remained along the front to retard any pursuit. Cleburne took a new position 1 mile to the rear on a hill just east of the old Stone Church. Known as Dick's Ridge, rudimentary fortifications were constructed in anticipation of another assault. Hooker wanted no part of it, and after advancing to the eastern end of the gap he abandoned the idea. The Confederates were able to cook the first meal they had seen in three days.

On 28 November the Federals began to remove their wounded. Most were taken to hospitals in and around Chattanooga, but many were left on the ground. A freezing rain fell during the night, and the heavy casualties on the Union side left many men on the field who froze to death for lack of care. Two days later Cleburne sent in a request for a truce. He needed to bring back eight wounded and four dead who were still behind Federal lines.[32]

Of the 4,157 men he had taken into battle, Cleburne had lost 20 men killed, 190 wounded, and 11 missing, for a total of 221 casualties. Against this Hooker reported 65 killed, 424 wounded, and 20 missing, or 509 total casualties of the 15,190 who were actually engaged. However, Cleburne believed that Hooker's report substantially underestimated the actual losses. To place the loss in the context of a much larger battle, Hooker had suffered more casualties here at the hands of Cleburne than he had seen in his capture of Lookout Mountain only three days earlier.[33]

Hooker had been soundly beaten, but in the overall sense the Federal hold on this part of Georgia only grew stronger. The city of Chattanooga was secured, and with it came the supply lines from the Ohio River. While

---

[32] Philip D. Stephenson, "Reminiscences," in *Southern Historical Society Papers*, 52 vols. (Millwood NY: Kraus Reprint Co., 1977) 12:38.

[33] Joslyn, *Meteor Shining Brightly*, 91.

Cleburne received the thanks of the Confederate Congress for his performance on 27 November, the formal recognition was hardly commensurate with the value of his service. Perhaps the accolades would have been stronger had the politicians in Richmond born witness to the scene he left behind him. One soldier maintained: "Cleburne had had the doggondest fight of the war. The ground was piled with dead Yankees; they were piled in heaps… From the foot to the top of the hill was covered with their slain, all lying on their faces. It had the appearance of the roof of a house shingled with dead Yankees. They were flushed with victory and success…but their dead were so piled in their path at Ringgold Gap that they could not pass them."[34]

Cleburne knew exactly how close the Federals had come to destroying the Army of Tennessee. After the battle he praised their efforts: "To Brigadier-Generals Polk and Lowrey and Colonels Govan and Granbury, I must return my thanks. Four better officers are not in the service of the Confederacy."[35]

Historian Peter Cozzens echoed those sentiments, noting that "Seldom, in fact, was a unit commander in the Army of Tennessee better served by his subordinates than was Cleburne here at Ringgold Gap."[36] Cleburne recommended the promotions of Hiram Granbury and Daniel Govan to brigadier general. The nominations were ultimately confirmed and both men were to rank from 29 February 1864.

Following the battle, after the safety of the army was assured, Cleburne turned his attention back to Bragg and the North Carolinian's fitness to command. His assessment of the matter may well have been correct, but regardless of his exploits on the battlefield and his own opinion of a superior officer, it was a serious mistake to put his feelings down on paper. In reality it was a moot point, as Bragg resigned at his own request on 30 November. However, Cleburne's decision to express his views in the winter may have contributed to the controversy in the coming year. On 9 December Thomas Key, the artillery captain from Helena, came to Cleburne's headquarters along with Richard Goldthwaite. He kept a diary in which he wrote: "Lt. Goldthwaite and I visited Maj. Gen. Cleburne, who was unusually communicative. He was writing down his report of the Battle of Ringgold Gap, which he read to us. The general also read for our edification his diary

---

[34] Samuel R. Watkins, *Co. Aytch* (Dayton OH: Morningside, 1982) 110.

[35] Report of Patrick R. Cleburne, 9 December 1863, OR, ser. 1, vol. 31, pt. 2 p. 757.

[36] Cozzens, *Shipwreck of Their Hopes*, 377.

on the events.... His criticism on General Bragg and his military mis-management [sic] were quite severe."[37]

Cleburne's performance at Ringgold Gap was the moment at which he became known as the "Stonewall of the West." Printed in the Christmas Day issue of the Atlanta *Intelligencer*, the appellation was certainly well deserved. Prior to the battle he had been resigned to witness the destruction of his division. When the day was done, he had saved the Army of Tennessee. His tactical superiority at the point of attack would also stand him in good stead. Union soldiers began to realize that if they approached Cleburne's lines, they must be ready to receive a devastating fire that would inflict heavy casualties. They could proceed at their own risk.[38]

[37] Wirt Armistead Cate, ed., *Two Soldiers: The Campaign Diaries of Thomas J. Key, C.S.A. and Robert J. Campbell, U.S.A.* (Chapel Hill: University of North Carolina Press, 1938) 9 December 1863.

[38] *Atlanta Intelligencer*, 25 December 1863, in Mauriel P. Joslyn, ed., *A Meteor Shining Brightly* (Macon GA: Mercer University Press, 2000) 93.

10

THE PETITION

Many factors played a role in Patrick Cleburne's journey through the Civil War. He had reached his rank by merit, but through it all he remained subordinate to those above him who were saddled with lesser skills. With the exception of William Hardee, a string of superior officers fumbled their way through the Western theatre. The end result was a long list of casualties, one of whom was Cleburne.

In spring 1862 the Army of Tennessee was still under Beauregard's command. The Confederates had established their camp in Tupelo, but Beauregard's health was failing. For several months he had been suffering from a chronic bronchial infection. On 17 June he was replaced by the irascible Braxton Bragg. A change in commanders on the eve of a campaign was always difficult to implement, and the Confederates were planning a return into Tennessee. The army needed strong leadership to be successful, but they certainly did not get it.

On paper, Bragg's qualifications were sound. He had placed fifth in the West Point class of 1837, a group that also contained Joseph Hooker, Jubal Early, and John Sedgwick. Bragg had served as an artillerist in the Mexican War under Zachary Taylor, and the experience may well have shaped some of his later views. He had performed brilliantly at the battle of Buena Vista, and it was there that Jefferson Davis forged such high regard for Bragg's military acumen. Perhaps Davis's elevated opinion of his own ability clouded his judgment. The result was unwarranted confidence in a man with limited leadership skills.

Bragg lacked both imagination and creativity. As such he was unable to deviate from accepted practice, able neither to recognize nor foster enterprise in others. He was hindered by an intolerance of departure from rigid regulations, no matter how spectacular the result. John M. Daniel, editor of the *Richmond Examiner*, opined that he was a man "with an iron hand and a wooden head."[1]

---

[1] Glenn Tucker, *Chickamauga: Bloody Battle of the West* (1961; repr., New York: Smithmark, 1994) 79.

These defects in Bragg's personality hampered the performance of his troops. Strategically Bragg was capable, but he was unable to adjust to changing conditions and his plans rarely came to fruition.[2]

Bragg suffered horribly from ill health. His chronic bouts of dysentery, dyspepsia, and headaches must have contributed to his irritability, and he may have had a stomach ulcer as well. Emotionally he had a very difficult personality for a field commander. A quick temper caused him to blame others for his own mistakes, and he had a tendency to erupt into fits of rage. Though his strict sense of discipline was an asset, the entire army felt that he carried it too far. Men were repeatedly executed for seemingly minor offenses and as a result morale suffered. These soldiers had not seen many victories, and any display of anger only magnified their animosity.[3]

Despite all of his shortcomings, Bragg was not without ability. He had considerable talent for administration and organization. In retrospect, he may well have served the Confederacy better had he been assigned to a non-combat position in Richmond from the very beginning. Discontent with Braxton Bragg was not a phenomenon that appeared overnight; it had been building for months. Despite victories at Richmond and Perryville, the army headed south. Bragg selected an especially poor position in Murfreesboro and decided to retreat again. His generals had advised the move, albeit under difficult circumstances, but the effect on morale was tremendous. The march through seas of mud at Tullahoma brought more depression. Finally, the Confederates dealt the Federals a resounding defeat at Chickamauga only to be gripped by indecision.[4]

The army's confidence in him was gone, but Bragg lost the public trust as well. The men in the ranks almost expected to lose. Unlike the situation in Virginia, every setback was viewed as just another indication of Bragg's inability to command. The Army of Northern Virginia simply assumed they would win, and win every time. At this point in the war, they usually had.

---

[2] Peter Cozzens, *Shipwreck of Their Hopes* (Urbana: University of Illinois Press, 1994) 5.

[3] Philip D. Stephenson, "Reminisences," in *Southern Historical Society Papers*, 52 vols. (Millwood NY: Kraus Reprint Co., 1977) 12:34.

[4] Nathaniel C. Hughes, *General William J. Hardee: Old Reliable* (Baton Rouge: Louisiana State University Press, 1965) 81–82.

Even after the bloody stalemate at Sharpsburg, Robert E. Lee was never universally denounced as a dismal failure.

The morale in the West was quite different. In a letter dated 13 January 1863, Irving Buck wrote from Tullahoma:

> The feeling against General Bragg is very strong, with both officers and men since the late retreat, and I join with him [Cleburne] in wishing that General Beauregard may be sent to supersede him. I esteem General Bragg as a brave and gallant soldier, but no strategist. As a subordinate he will do very well, but cannot be trusted alone. The past six months have fully demonstrated this. Should he be removed, I hope he may be placed in some place where he may retrieve his lost glory. Public opinion is against him. My feeling toward him is that of pity—believing him to be a patriot—working to the best of his ability.[5]

Bragg was not indifferent to the undercurrent of frustration that plagued his army. Newspaper articles clamored for his release, and rumors began to surface that he would be replaced, perhaps by Beauregard or Kirby Smith. He was determined to get to the bottom of his troubles, which he mistakenly believed were confined to a small number of dissatisfied subordinates. On 11 January he sent a circular letter to Hardee, Breckinridge, Cheatham, and Cleburne in an attempt to determine the scope of his problems. Following the retreat from Stones River, Cleburne offered his own analysis: "They unite with me in personal regard for yourself, in a high appreciation of your patriotism and gallantry, and in appreciation of your great capacity for organization, but at the same time they see with regret, and it has also been my observation, that you do not possess the confidence of the army in other respects in that degree necessary to secure success."[6]

Throughout the year Bragg's army had been in a constant state of confusion. In September things really began to fall apart. On 25 September Bragg ordered Nathan Bedford Forrest to take his corps into East Tennessee to observe Burnside's movements around Knoxville. Bragg undoubtedly had a

---

[5] William P. Buck, "Headquarters' Staff: Cleburne's Division, Hardee's Corps," in Joslyn, ed., *A Meteor Shining Brightly*, 70.

[6] Tucker, *Chickamauga*, 81–82.

private agenda, and he intended to give Joe Wheeler a larger role in the army. The transparency of the directive was quickly revealed the next day, when Forrest was told to turn over all of his cavalry to Wheeler with the exception of one regiment and an artillery battery. In a desperate move to prevent Forrest from leaving the service altogether, Davis transferred him to West Tennessee and Mississippi. By 4 October the entire cavalry, with the obvious exception of Wheeler, was strongly against their commander. One day later Forrest learned of Bragg's machinations. The problem had been brewing for months, and it had finally become more than Forrest could take. On 7 October he exploded into Bragg's tent, shook his finger in the general's face, and raged:

> You commenced your cowardly and contemptible persecution of me soon after the battle of Shiloh, and you have kept it up ever since.... You robbed me of my command in Kentucky, and gave it to one of your favorites...in a spirit of revenge and spite, because I would not fawn upon you as others did.... Now the second brigade...in order to humiliate me, you have taken these brave men...from me. I have stood your meanness as long as I intend to. You have played the part of a damned scoundrel, and are a coward, and if you were any part of a man I would slap your jaws.... You may as well not issue any orders to me, for I will not obey them, and I will hold you personally responsible for any other indignities you may endeavor to inflict upon me. You have threatened to arrest me for not obeying your orders promptly. I dare you to do it, and I say to you that if you ever again try to interfere with me or cross my path, it will be at the peril of your life.[7]

Bragg was only beginning to purge his command of any malcontents he could find. He blamed Thomas Hindman and Leonidas Polk for mistakes at Chickamauga. He charged Hindman with disobedience of orders for his

---

[7] Thomas L. Connelly, *Autumn of Glory: The Army of Tennessee 1862–1865* (Baton Rouge: Louisiana State University Press, 1971) 240–41; John A. Wyeth, *Life of General Nathan Bedford Forrest* (New York: Harper & Brothers, 1899) 264–66; Wiley Sword, *Mountains Touched with Fire* (New York: St. Martin's, 1995) 65; Robert Selph Henry, *Forrest: First with the Most* (1944; repr., Wilmington NC: Broadfoot Publishing, 1991) 199. It has been suggested by one historian that this account is less than accurate, but given Forrest's volatile nature it is unlikely that he would have gone quietly.

failure at McLemore's Cove and censured Polk for not attacking promptly during the morning of 20 September. In an attempt to minimize the public reaction, both men were sent to Atlanta on 29 September with instructions to await further developments.

The dismal news forced Jefferson Davis to personally address the problems, just as he had done after Perryville and Stones River. He arrived at Marietta on 9 October and was a greeted by a petition to remove Bragg from his post. Dated 4 October, it was signed by eleven general officers as well as Colonel Randall Gibson, who was temporarily commanding Daniel Adams's brigade. There is little doubt that Longstreet and Buckner led the movement to oust Bragg, and compelling evidence suggests that Buckner was the actual author. His name appears first in the lower right section of the petition, in the place where a letter would normally be signed. Below his are the names of most of the signatories, whereas the left side contains the names of only two generals from Longstreet's corps. Both men had a motive for their actions. Longstreet had come to Tennessee with hopes of receiving command of the army, while Buckner had seen his Department of East Tennessee whittled down to nothing.

Davis held a private meeting with Longstreet. The general opened the discussion by suggesting that Joe Johnston take control of army, though given Longstreet's desire for that same posting the sincerity of this proposal is questionable at best. Davis listened to testimony for five days. A lack of confidence and the failure to pursue a beaten enemy following Chickamauga were the principal complaints. Regardless of the damage to the Confederate war effort, Jefferson Davis was determined to sustain the culprit. For Pat Cleburne, the ramifications of the decision were not immediate. As a major general in charge of a division in Hardee's corps, for the moment he was not the focus of the North Carolinian's displeasure. Bragg had turned his attention elsewhere.

In the face of obvious disaster, Davis was determined to support Bragg. He held to this position not so much out of respect for Bragg but because he felt he had no better alternative. Robert E. Lee was certainly qualified, but he had no intention of leaving the Army of Northern Virginia. Beauregard, Johnston, and Longstreet had been ruled out, and Davis could not bring himself to appoint a general of lower rank regardless of his ability.

Davis told St. John Liddell that the army needed to unify behind Bragg and quell the unrest. In keeping with many of the president's other decisions, the selection of Liddell as a calming influence over a group of men in need of reason could not have been worse. Liddell was simply too devious by nature to be given a task that required great diplomacy. He went to Bragg under the guise of friendship, but in the opinion of one historian it was more likely just to irritate him.[8] This approach was never going to work. After assessing the prospects of his endeavor, Liddell reported that "his mettle was up and beyond the control of dispassionate reason." He received a telling response that illuminated the inner workings of an army under Bragg: "General, I want to get rid of all such generals. I have better men now in subordinate stations to fill their places. Let them send in their resignations and I shall accept every one without hesitation."[9]

Much to Bragg's dismay, no apologies were forthcoming. Without them, he set about the task of removing his detractors. Even had he received the flood of resignations for which he hoped, Bragg would have seen that the rest of the army was not enamored with him either. The president left headquarters on 14 October, but before he departed he made it clear that the commanding general had the authority to reconfigure the Army of Tennessee. Bragg then put forth the specious argument that having too many brigades from one state under one officer put too great a burden on that general in the event of heavy losses. In reality this was a vehicle to undermine the loyalty in the anti-Bragg factions. Davis saw through the façade, but he approved it anyway.[10]

Bragg knew that he had won the battle, and he began to act. Harvey Hill had no strong political backing, nor did he enjoy a long friendship with Davis. As such, he was easily eliminated. With one general out of the way Bragg turned to Polk, Cheatham, Buckner, and Breckinridge, bent on the destruction of the strong blocks from Tennessee and Kentucky. Leonidas Polk had no intention of falling victim to incompetence. He stated that he would rather resign than serve under Bragg again.[11] Cheatham and Buckner saw their own commands shredded before their very eyes, carved up into so many pieces that their identities were completely torn apart. Thus far, the so-called reorganization was going smoothly.

---

[8] Cozzens, *Shipwreck of Their Hopes,* 24.
[9] Hughes, *Old Reliable,* 152–53.
[10] Cozzens, *Shipwreck of Their Hopes,* 24.
[11] Connelly, *Autumn of Glory,* 241.

Breckinridge, however, was another matter. Even though he was from Kentucky, he had not signed the petition. He was elevated to corps command but retained none of his original brigades. The new structure resulted in an army with three corps. Breckinridge had Stewart's old division, which had been reorganized, retaining only one of its original brigades. William Bate was awarded division command despite his performance at Chickamauga. Thomas Hindman was reinstated on 15 November to lead the third division.

Bragg had taken care of his most hated detractors, with the exception of Robert E. Lee's "war horse." Longstreet had a stronger resume than the others, but he did not escape unscathed. He kept his own corps, less Preston's division, which was broken up, and Walker's division, which was transferred to what had been Polk's command. Hood's division was given to Micah Jenkins while he was recovering from the wound he had received at Chickamauga. Lafayette McLaws took control of Longstreet's remaining division.

The more difficult task at hand was the creation of a third corps. Despite Bragg close friendship with Leonidas Polk, Polk had been relieved and it would be impossible for Davis to reinstate him. The president had decided to retain Bragg, but he believed that the dismissal of Polk was a mistake. He had to find some way of rectifying the situation without causing a public uproar. William Hardee had been assigned to Joseph Johnston's Alabama-Mississippi department, and he was a popular leader. Fortunately for Davis, Hardee was currently in Demopolis reviewing the troops under Carter Stevenson.

Shortly after Davis left, Bragg went to Vicksburg to meet with Johnston and Hardee. He hoped there were men available to send back to Tennessee, but Davis had another mission in mind. On the way, he went through Atlanta. He told Polk that he would remove the charges, restore his reputation, and send him to Mississippi to be a corps commander in Johnston's department. Davis would then bring Hardee back to Tennessee, where he would be given Polk's old corps. Hardee was elated at the transfer, and on 27 October he boarded a train for Tennessee.

The purpose in the new arrangement was not limited to tactics on the field of battle. Davis wanted Hardee to be a peacemaker as well. "The information from the army at Chattanooga painfully impresses me with the fact that there is a want there of that harmony, among the highest officers, which is essential to success. I rely greatly upon you for the restoration of a proper feeling, and know that you will realize the comparative insignificance of personal considerations when weighed against the duty of imparting to the all the efficiency of which it is capable."[12]

While Hardee now led four divisions, much of their cohesion had been lost. Cheatham was transferred from Polk to Hardee, but many of his Tennessee regiments were allocated among other commands. On 31 October he asked to be relieved. Cleburne's division contained only half of its original brigades, and a new division was created from brigades formerly led by Stewart and Buckner. These troops were given to Stevenson. W. H. T. Walker commanded the fourth division, which was comprised of his old Reserve Corps plus some troops from Cheatham.[13] Ironically, for all of the efforts directed against him, Polk suffered only minimal damage. He had been dismissed and sent to Atlanta, but Davis had dropped the charges against him and he was able to escape the clutches of Braxton Bragg.

Regardless of any attempts to salve the wounds within the Army of Tennessee, Bragg was a cancer Hardee could not remove. W. W. Mackall, Bragg's chief-of-staff, quit his post rather than become engulfed in a disaster. In a letter to his wife he described Bragg's commitment to the Cause: "his whole soul is in it, but he is as much influenced by his enemies as by his friends—and does not know how to control the one or preserve the other."[14]

The situation was spinning wildly out of control. Desertions continued at an alarming rate. St. John Liddell approached Bragg to request a transfer to Joseph Johnston's department, only to learn that he had been placed among a list of candidates to replace Mackall. George Brent, the assistant-adjutant-general, estimated that 2,149 men had walked away from the service in the months of September and October alone.

There had been considerable reshuffling within the Army of Tennessee. Bragg had attacked his enemies, divided their commands, reassigned them, and rendered their old divisions barely recognizable. He had taken his more powerful antagonists and dealt with them. Only one question remained: Patrick Ronayne Cleburne. He was the army's most talented infantry officer and Bragg knew it, having already recommended his promotion to major general.

---

[12] Dunbar Rowland, *Jefferson Davis, Constitutionalist: His Letters and Speeches*, 12 vols. (New York: J. J. Little & Ives Company, 1923) 6:71.

[13] Connelly, *Autumn of Glory*, 24.

[14] Nathaniel C. Hughes, ed., *Liddell's Record* (Dayton OH: Morningside, 1985) 155.

On the other hand, Cleburne had expressed a written vote of no confidence in January, then signed his name to a similar document in October. In this particular case, Bragg seemed to believe there might be some extenuating circumstances. Cleburne was very reserved, and he had never sought the limelight. He did not actively campaign against Bragg but merely recognized incompetence and tactfully expressed his views on paper. Bragg may have thought him more misguided than venomous. There were more obvious targets in Marietta, and for the moment Cleburne was unaffected.[15] That would change over the course of the following year.

By late October it had become clear that the siege of Chattanooga was not going to work, and it was well known that Burnside was in the general area. On 29 October Davis had remarked that Longstreet might send two divisions to monitor Federal actions, but this was merely mentioned in conversation. While the statement could never have been construed as an order, Bragg used it as such. The Union force in Bragg's front was estimated at between 80,000 and 90,000 exclusive of Burnside. After Longstreet departed, the Confederates would have only 36,000 men to oppose them.

Bragg's motives in sending Longstreet away were purely personal. Longstreet was at the heart of all of the unrest, and Bragg blamed him for the failure to seal off the Federal supply routes. After Davis had left the army, Longstreet returned to his old position as a wing commander. He occupied the area from Lookout Mountain to Chattanooga Creek. His relations with Bragg had soured to the point that Longstreet was almost completely isolated. The Federals had been reduced to one-quarter rations and the only route of supply was up the valley of Lookout Creek. According to Bragg, Longstreet failed to act decisively and shut down the avenue of relief. Longstreet countered that he sent numerous warnings to headquarters that went unheeded. Those arguments were weak, but the result of the feud was a constant conflict within the Confederate high command.[16] Regardless of his feelings toward Longstreet,

---

[15] Sword, *Mountains Touched with Fire,* 65–66.

[16] Gabor S. Boritt, *Jefferson Davis's Generals* (New York: Oxford University Press, 1999) 82; Steven E. Woodworth, *Jefferson Davis and His Generals* (Lawrence: University of Kansas Press, 1990) 156–57.

Bragg already had two divisions of infantry and two brigades of cavalry watching Burnside. The reassignment gave Bragg a convenient excuse to finally rid himself of an unrelenting headache.

Adding to the problem was the food supply. Quantities were always low and though Confederate soldiers rarely complained, the unrest had reached a crisis. Rations were short, butchers were corrupt, trains did not run, and inflation consumed the South. However, the problem went deeper. Corn and forage for the horses were not forthcoming; this had a detrimental effect on the artillery, as horses were constantly sent to the rear.

Clothing was scarce and poor in quality. A lack of tents, coats, and shoes combined with heavy rains led to a dramatic increase in disease. Under normal conditions, many of these hardships would have been borne by the rank and file. They understood this war, and all too well. However, many of these men had never experienced conditions so severe. Sam Watkins of the 1st Tennessee described their plight: " Never in all my life do I remember of ever experiencing so much oppression and humiliation. The soldiers were starved and almost naked, and covered all over with lice and camp itch and filth and dirt. The men looked sick, hollow-eyed and heartbroken, living principally on parched corn, which had been picked out of the mud and dirt under the feet of officers' horses. We thought of nothing but starvation."[17]

Aside from the hunger itself, perhaps the most frustrating aspect of their misery was the insanity of it all. While the troops and animals suffered terribly, Bragg stockpiled stores of commissary and quartermaster supplies, many of which were donated from home. He had set up supply depots at Tyner's Station, 7 miles away, and Chickamauga, only 4 miles distant.[18]

The series of disasters finally culminated in the cold shock of reality. Bragg realized that he had no chance of surviving the groundswell moving against him, so he fired off one last note to Davis. He was careful to criticize Breckinridge for his performance during the last week in November, claiming that Breckinridge was not merely unfit for duty but drunk as well. This charge was completely unsubstantiated by any other source, but the damage was done. Bragg proposed to replace Breckinridge with Hindman, even though he had been placed under arrest in the fall. He knew Hindman's commission as major general predated that of Breckinridge, so that for Hindman to arrive

---

[17] Samuel R. Watkins, *Co. Aytch* (Dayton OH: Morningside, 1982) 101.
[18] Cozzens, *Shipwreck of Their Hopes,* 28–29.

Breckinridge must go. With the end of his career as a field commander plainly in sight, Bragg requested to be relieved. On 30 November, Davis removed him.

Braxton Bragg had spent the year absorbed in his own troubles, constantly feuding with his generals, communicating back and forth with Richmond, and dodging Buckner's frequent letters. He failed to pay attention to the more pressing reports that would have told him Union troops were coming from Mississippi, under the helm of William T. Sherman.

11

THE GLASS CEILING

As the war dragged on, the effects of attrition on the Confederate forces were beginning to show. When a Union soldier fell, another man stepped forward to take his place. The Southerners were simply unable to replace their losses, and the disparity in numbers became more pronounced. Pat Cleburne recognized the need to properly utilize every available resource, but conventional appeals had produced minimal results. Desertion increased, as letters from home described increasing poverty. On 2 January 1864 Cleburne offered a shocking proposal.

Joseph Johnston had made his headquarters in Dalton, Georgia, at the home of Dr. James Black.[1] His corps and division commanders received an invitation from William Hardee to attend a meeting at 7:00 P.M. Present were Lieutenant-Generals Johnston and Hardee, along with Major-Generals Walker, Stewart, Hindman, and Stevenson. Frank Cheatham had been detained and was unable to participate. Patton Anderson and William Bate were the only brigadiers in attendance. Cleburne's division was stationed 7 miles northwest of Dalton at Tunnel Hill, and he rode to the meeting with his chief of staff Calhoun Benham.

After a few opening remarks Cleburne outlined the topic before bringing up several points that were not particularly noteworthy. The United States government had a much larger supply of manpower, and in addition they had a larger white population. He summarized his views: "the consequences of this condition are showing themselves more plainly every day, restlessness of morals spreading everywhere, manifesting itself in the army in a growing disregard for private rights, desertion spreading to a class of soldiers it never hoped to tamper with before, military commissions sinking in the estimation

---

[1] Howell and Elizabeth Purdue, in *Pat Cleburne Confederate General* (1973; repr., Gaithersburg MD: Olde Soldier Books, 1987), explain that at the time of the meeting the house belonged to Dr. Black. It was sold to the Huff family in 1886 (280).

of the soldier, our supplies failing, our finances in ruins. If this continues
much longer we must be subjugated."[2]

Everyone at the meeting was already painfully aware of the current
situation, but at this point Cleburne dropped a bombshell. He suggested that
the South should arm any slave who would fight until the end of the war.
They would receive their own freedom as well as that of their family.

Cleburne had already circulated a paper describing the idea above among
the general and field officers in his division. All four of his brigadiers, Daniel
Govan, Mark Lowrey, Lucious Polk, and Hiram Granbury, had come out in
support of the suggestion and eleven other men had actually signed it. Along
with Cleburne, the signatories were: Daniel C. Govan, Brigadier-General;
John E. Murray, Colonel 5th Arkansas; G. F. Baucum, Colonel 8th Arkansas;
Peter Snyder, Lieutenant-Colonel Commanding 6th and 7th Arkansas; E.
Warfield, Lieutenant-Colonel 2nd Arkansas; Mark P. Lowrey, Brigadier-
General; A. B. Hardcastle, Colonel 32nd and 45th Mississippi; F. A.
Ashford, Major 16th Alabama; John W. Colquitt, Colonel 1st Arkansas;
Richard J. Person, Major 3rd and 5th Confederate; G. Deakins, Major 8th
and 35th Tennessee; J. H. Collett, Captain Commanding 7th Texas; and J.
H. Kelly, Brigadier-General Commanding Cavalry Division.

In December Cleburne had also discussed the matter at length with his
staff. Irving Buck agreed with the conclusions but felt they had no chance of
acceptance. Slaveholders were very sensitive to the loss of their property, and
the South was not prepared for such a radical change. Furthermore, Southern
citizens who had not served in the armed forces could not fully appreciate the
need for such drastic legislation.[3] Leonard Mangum, Cleburne's old law
partner, also believed the concept was sound, but unlike Cleburne he had no
delusions as to its outcome.[4] Other responses were not as supportive. On 28
December Thomas Key stopped by the General's tent. Key commanded an
artillery battery in the division, but he had also been the editor of a newspaper
in Helena. Cleburne asked his opinion. Key felt that the idea was impractical
and would never be passed into law. Charles Swett, another artillery officer,
disliked the idea in principle but preferred the loss of the slaves to the loss of

---

[2] L. H. Mangum to Joseph M. Brown, *Kennesaw* (GA) *Gazette*, 1 June 1888, 2.

[3] "Negroes in Our Army," in *Southern Historical Society Papers*, 52 vols. (Millwood
NY: Kraus Reprint Co., 1977) 31:215–16.

[4] Mangum to Brown, *Kennesaw* (GA) *Gazette*, 1 June 1888, 2, 6.

the war.[5] Benham was shocked by the very suggestion. Strongly opposed to it, he tried unsuccessfully to convince Cleburne to abandon the proposal.[6]

Nevertheless, Cleburne felt it was his duty to introduce the idea regardless of the consequences. He held firmly to the belief that the war was for liberty, not slavery. With proper training and drill the Negroes would fight well, and he was prepared to lead them should it become necessary. The worst that could happen would be a court-martial and cashiering, whereupon he would enlist in the 15th Arkansas. If he were not allowed to command he would serve in the ranks.[7]

Cleburne had presented his feelings in earnest, but they were based on several assumptions, some more valid than others. He was convinced that the South would receive not only increased foreign recognition, but additional aid as well. England and France had withheld public support in part due to the issue of slavery. Unfortunately, he overestimated their inclination to become entangled in a conflict on the other side of the Atlantic Ocean. Europe could afford to wait. The Confederacy could have received meaningful assistance at several earlier points in the war, under far more favorable conditions. By January 1864, the Union was in control and any chance of foreign intervention had evaporated.[8]

With the extinction of the institution itself, the North would lose a valuable psychological weapon. After the publication of the Emancipation Proclamation, the Lincoln administration had used racial inequality to foster animosity among the Northern populace. It would be far more likely to reach an amicable settlement of the war without the cloud of slavery hanging over the negotiations. Here again, Cleburne did not grasp the fact that the Confederacy was not dealing from a position of strength. Abraham Lincoln's first priority was reunification of the nation, not emancipation of the slaves. Had every single slave been liberated, the war would have continued. In the presidential

[5] Wirt Armistead Cate, ed., *Two Soldiers: The Campaign Diaries of Thomas J. Key, C.S.A. and Robert J. Campbell, U.S.A.* (Chapel Hill: University of North Carolina Press, 1938) 16–19.

[6] Calhoun Benham, "Major Gen. P. R. Cleburne," *Kennesaw* (GA) *Gazette,* 5 May 1889, 2.

[7] "Negroes in Our Army," 216.

[8] Steve Davis, "That Extraordinary Document," *Civil War Times Illustrated* 16/8 (December 1977): 15; C. Vann. Woodward, *Mary Chesnutt's Civil War* (New Haven CT: Yale University Press, 1981) 525.

debates of 1860 Lincoln had declared that while he was opposed to slavery, he was not willing to grant negroes the privilege of citizenship. Cleburne was convinced that the prevailing Southern attitudes would have a decidedly negative influence on any discussions for surrender. As it turned out, the terms offered at Appomattox were quite lenient, but he could not have anticipated Grant and Lee.[9]

It had become apparent that the enticement of freedom had created a human resource for the North. The paper emphasized that the South had only one source of new recruits: the number of white males not currently in Confederate service. On the other hand, the Federal government could draw from its own population, which was greater than that of the South to begin with. They could also persuade slaves to enlist in the Union Army. As it was, the situation had deteriorated to the point where that segment of the population had almost become a network of spies. Given the Southern dependence on agriculture, their absence would have a profound effect on the economy as well. Finally, Washington could continue to conscript foreigners, a practice that had already been done in large numbers.

These points were essential, but there were still further advantages to be gained. Cleburne's proposal would completely eliminate the fanaticism that resulted from John Brown's raid. Initially, the attack on Harper's Ferry had created such an emotional upheaval that the people in the North overreacted. They would now examine the situation in a more rational light and realize their mistake. By 1864 there was growing sentiment that the list of casualties was excessive. Whether victorious at Gettysburg or defeated at Chickamauga, Union losses had been horrific. Many Northerners began to doubt the wisdom of the war's continued prosecution. Cleburne believed that the elimination of slavery would result in its end.

Slaves were in fact property and as such required a certain degree of protection. Due to their position within the household, they were on reasonably good terms with their owners. The adherents of the proposal held that without slavery free men would tend to gravitate back to the South. It was

---

[9] Paul M. Angle and Earl S. Miers, *Tragic Years, 1860–1865,* 2 vols. (New York: Simon & Schuster, 1960) 1:27–28. The debates between Abraham Lincoln and Steven Douglas took place on 18 September 1860 in Charleston IL and on 13 October 1860 in Quincy IL; Hudson Strode, *American Patriot, 1808–1861* (New York: Harcourt, Brace and Company, 1955) 311.

their home and they were familiar with it. When forced to choose, most of them would prefer to fight for their masters than serve in the Union Army. On the surface, these circumstances were an asset for the Confederacy. However, this particular point was not as simple as it looked. If captured by the North, a slave would be treated as a prisoner of war. If captured by the South, he could face either immediate re-enslavement or violent retribution. This made the decision much more difficult. Still, reinforcements would have both an immediate and long-term effect. Armies in the field would suddenly gain a numerical superiority in battle, as well as a reserve to exploit any weakness in the enemy. There had been many instances in which the Confederates had achieved early success but did not have enough men to press their advantage. By 1864 the Confederacy was reacting to Union movements. The influx of new recruits would provide the numbers to resume offensive operations. This argument presumed that not only would a large number of slaves remain in the South, but they would also enlist in the army. Neither expectation was certain.

Cleburne tried to point out that there would no longer be any embarrassment or vulnerability associated with the institution itself. A constant source of concern had been the fear of an insurrection much like the one John Brown had intended. This applied to slaveholders and non-slaveholders alike. It was an issue that had plagued the South for years, but in fall 1859 the problem had been magnified. From a military standpoint, the focus had shifted from the support of the Confederate war effort to the more immediate task of self-preservation. Without slaves there could be no such revolt, so the attention of the populace would return to Confederate independence. While he had a firm grasp of the inherent weakness in slavery, Cleburne made a serious mistake when he associated it with embarrassment. White control of the labor force had existed for generations and hardly encouraged analytical consideration of racial divisions.[10]

The proponents of Cleburne's memorial understood that a plantation was a ready base of supply for Northern recruits. This source of manpower was sure to disappear, as none of the slaves would fight for the Federal

---

[10] Carl H. Moneyhon, *The Impact of the Civil War and Reconstruction on Arkansas Persistence in the Midst of Ruin* (Baton Rouge: Louisiana State University Press, 1994) 60, Charles L. C. Minor, "That Old System of Slavery," *Baltimore Sun*, 14 June 1903; "Negroes in Our Army," 224.

government. In the event of an attack by the North, guides for future movements and reliable information about the geography of the area would cease to exist, thereby limiting the ability of the invaders to properly deploy their own troops.[11] This assessment did not accurately describe the present state of affairs. As Union tentacles stretched out across the South, the number of available slaves increased. It was illogical to believe that all slaves would remain true to their owner. The sight of black regiments in blue uniforms was certain to test their loyalty. By this point in the war, reliance on trained guides had become less important. Virtual control of the surrounding countryside relegated their absence to a minor inconvenience. A short delay in forward operations would have little effect on the final outcome.

The foundation of the entire proposal rested on the contention that there was nothing so sacred as the Southern pursuit of freedom. Cleburne looked at the Confederacy as one entity. He did not grasp the fact that the focus of the secession movement had never been on the creation of a new Federal government, but rather on the independence of each individual state. It would not be easy to persuade eleven governors to work together for a single purpose. They were loosely bound confederated states, not united states, and this was an extremely important distinction.[12]

Several of these assumptions were quite realistic, but taken as a whole this line of reasoning was wishful thinking at best. There is little doubt that a change would have taken place, but the entire reversal of current conditions was simply too much to expect.

The Army of Tennessee had not achieved the success of the forces in Virginia. This owed largely to their respective commanders, but the loss of men and land had had a devastating effect on the common soldier. Apathy and desertion were the results. The first attempt to increase Confederate numbers met with only partial success. Following defeats at Fort Henry, Fort Donelson, and Shiloh, the Congress passed a series of measures known collectively as the "Furlough and Bounty Act" that took effect on 16 April 1862. All white males between the ages of eighteen and thirty-five were to serve in the Confederate army. Men who had enlisted for twelve months would be retained for a three-

---

[11] "Negroes in Our Army," 224–25.

[12] Douglas S. Freeman, *R. E. Lee,* 4 vols. (New York: Charles Scribner's Sons, 1934–1936) 2:84–85; Jerrold N. Moore, *Confederate Commissary General* (Shippensburg PA: White Mane, 1996) 56.

year term or until the end of the war, whichever came first. Those who reenlisted would receive a sixty-day furlough and a bounty of $50. Officers were to be elected, not appointed, which would favor a popular incompetent over a skilled disciplinarian. As an additional incentive, men could choose not only their branch of service, but the company in which they served as well. This meant that if a soldier who was already in the army did not reenlist upon the expiration of his service, he was subject to immediate conscription. Naturally this took a horrible toll on morale.[13] There was limited desire to volunteer, and the requirements for military service were easy to circumvent. Without enough qualified state officers to enroll new men, substitution was rampant.[14] Worse legislation could not have been imagined.

It was obvious that more drastic reforms were required. In another attempt to solve the chronic shortage of manpower, Congress enacted a second set of laws effective 11 October 1862.[15] Authorities in Richmond proposed to create a large labor reserve by conscripting all able-bodied males under the age of forty-five. In addition, free Negroes as well as slaves were to be used in the army for non-combat roles. It was impossible for a nation at war to compete with private industry in providing an attractive wage, so military offices were to receive a prior right to labor. Substitution was abolished and conscription officers were to be assisted by state militia specifically trained for that purpose. Finally, legislation was to be passed that would retain any soldier whose enlistment was about to expire.

Despite some improvements, there was constant conflict between the policies in Richmond and individual state authorities. If details were formed from the army even more men would vanish from the ranks. If their absence was ignored morale would suffer and desertion would continue. This left the government in a quandary. Cleburne asserted that a change in the exemption status would only result in more soldiers under eighteen and over forty-five years of age. These groups were more likely to break down or fall ill, creating an additional burden for their officers. Moreover, if experienced planters

---

[13] Freeman. *R. E. Lee,* 25–26; John H. Reagan, *Memoirs* (New York, Neale Publishing Company, 1906) 118.

[14] Clifford Dowdey, *Lee* (Boston: Little Brown & Co., 1965) 335; James I. Robertson, Jr., *Stonewall Jackson* (New York: Macmillan, 1997) 675; Albert B. Moore, *Conscription and Conflict in the Confederacy* (1924; repr., Columbia: University of South Carolina Press, 1996) 131–32.

[15] Albert B. Moore, *Conscription,* 140–42.

enlisted in military service, the skilled management of the agricultural and manufacturing base would shift to the army and fewer goods would be produced at home. Each one of these conditions presented a difficult problem, but they were only small pieces of a larger puzzle. Cleburne's point was that even when taken together these solutions to the shortage of manpower would not result in a meaningful increase in Confederate forces.[16]

He presented his case as clearly as he could, but several objections remained. First was the notion that republicanism could not survive without the institution of slavery. Proponents of the suggestion disagreed. They preferred any form of government that supported Southern rights to one that was forced upon the South against its will. Cleburne felt that "as between the loss of independence and the loss of slavery, we assume that every patriot would give up the latter, giving up the Negro slave rather than be a slave himself."[17] He would soon discover that for many Confederates, this was an extremely difficult issue to resolve.

There remained the persistent argument that the white man could not perform hard labor in the fields, a dubious contention to be sure. The entire South was largely agricultural, yet only 10 percent of the Confederate army owned slaves. Of those, fully half of them had five slaves or less.[18] Many Southerners believed that slaves could not be spared from the fields. The economy was so dependent on agriculture that it was feared output would decline. It was simply unnecessary to remove so much of the labor force. Cleburne countered that many slaves were already occupied in non-farming roles and could easily be transferred to military service. Three years of war had proved that white men could withstand hardships far more severe than those on a plantation. In this instance Cleburne had a very strong case, but he was unable to quantify his opinion.

---

[16] "Negroes in Our Army," 221–22.

[17] Benham, "General Cleburne on Freeing the Negroes," *Kennesaw* (GA) *Gazette*, 1 June 1888, 6.

[18] Clifford Dowdey, *Death of a Nation: The Story of Lee and His Men at Gettysburg* (New York: Alfred A. Knopf, 1958) 45; Bruce Catton, *The American Heritage Picture History of the Civil War* (1960; repr., New York: Bonanza Books, 1982) 31; William J. Cooper, Jr., *Liberty and Slavery: Southern Policies in 1860* (New York: Alfred A. Knopf, 1983) 252; Charles C. Milham, *Gallant Pelham American Extraordinary* (Gaithersburg MD: Olde Soldier Books, 1987) foreword.

There also remained the belief that slaves would not work at all once they had attained freedom. The officers who had signed the document felt that wages would offer a tangible reward to those who were willing to work. However, the proponents of the paper did not fully appreciate all of the consequences of immediate emancipation. They understood the possible military benefits, but the sudden addition of so many freemen would flood the labor market. Furthermore, a slave did not understand the concept of wages and salary, so he was unable to evaluate his own economic worth. No doubt some would have been more industrious than others, but this part of Cleburne's proposal most surely would have brought mixed results. Without consideration of any harm to their argument, Cleburne's adherents added that "wise legislation" must also be passed. Dependence on political wisdom was risky, and the Confederate Congress was never noted for its prescience.

Finally, immediate freedom would foster disaffection for the Southern Cause. Cleburne's supporters stated that excitement was preferable to apathy. Slavery would seem less important when contrasted with the yoke of white oppression.[19] They recognized that the United States was fighting for more than just slavery, but they also believed that the government in Washington wanted to establish sectional supremacy and a more centralized government, thereby depriving the South of its rights and liberties. This particular point was fundamental to the cause of the war itself. The conflict between states' rights and a centralized government had not gone away. While this difference still existed, the years of war had ravaged the heart of the Confederacy. Cleburne's argument was weak. He asked the South to either accept disinterest or embrace discontent. Neither was very desirable.

Cleburne anticipated the doubt that the slaves would actually fight, so he cited several examples throughout history in which they had. The helots of Sparta fought against their masters, and at the naval battle of Lepanto galley slaves had been promised their freedom in an attempt to defeat the Mohammedans. Slaves at St. Domingo had resisted French troops and Jamaicans held the mountains against their masters for 150 years.[20] The prospect of freedom was the necessary inducement to persuade the black

---

[19] Stephen E. Ambrose, "By Enlisting Slaves, Could the South Still Win the War?" *Civil War Times Illustrated* 3/9 (January 1965): 20; Minor, "That Old System of Slavery," 314–18.

[20] "Negroes in Our Army," 226.

population to enlist. While historically accurate, these examples had little impact on the men before him.

These statements serve to illustrate the critical nature of the problems within the Confederacy. But Patrick Cleburne's vision was not limited to the present. He gave a great deal of thought to future generations. In his opinion, subjugation would mean that "the history of this heroic struggle will be written by the enemy; that our youth will be trained by Northern school teachers; will learn from Northern school books their version of the war; will be impressed by all the influences of history and education to regard our gallant dead as traitors, our maimed veterans as fit objects for derision. It means the crushing of Southern manhood, the hatred of our former slaves, who will be our secret police."[21]

The officers were momentarily stunned. No one could have foreseen such a radical notion. W. H. T. Walker was absolutely furious. He asked for a copy of the paper, as well as permission to forward it to Jefferson Davis. Unwisely, Cleburne granted both requests. Everyone in the room understood that if this became known it would cause a deafening public outcry. They all agreed to keep silent, with the exception of Walker. He decided to solicit other views as to the wisdom of Cleburne's ideas, then send the information to the president.

Hindman came out in support of the measure, claiming that Walker was in violation of privacy agreements when he decided to send the document to Richmond. He would answer any questions "at the proper time" but not "under compulsion of this sort." Hindman was quite willing to cooperate when he said that "if my superiors order a response, I will give it." Though it was not necessary to inform the officers present, he made it very clear that Walker was not his superior.[22]

Cheatham had not been able to attend the meeting, but Bate told Walker that he sided with Cleburne as well. Cheatham refused to answer Walker's request on the grounds that the proposal was not an official document. He shared Hindman's view that this was a private matter and should remain private. Neither man had voiced the opinion Walker was seeking. An honest account of their responses would certainly weaken his arguments in Richmond. Walker was loyal to Braxton Bragg, but the advantages of this allegiance were suddenly slipping away. He had already blamed Bragg's

---

[21] Ambrose, "By Enlisting Slaves," 16–21.

[22] Davis, "Extraordinary Document," 16.

downfall on his detractors, which included Frank Cheatham. His failure to immediately oppose the paper only heightened Walker's frustration.[23]

William Hardee knew Cleburne better than anyone in the room and had great respect for his judgment. Though he did not publicly endorse the proposal, he seemed favorably disposed to the idea. Along with the other officers, he discussed alternatives in which the slaves could be utilized without being armed. In perhaps a tacit sign of support, he never did respond to Walker's request.

Carter Stevenson differed only slightly from Hardee's view but also felt that slaves had great value in non-combat positions. He was a moderate and sought a more realistic answer to the current crisis. Along with Hardee, Stevenson had the most pragmatic approach to the entire question. He suggested "using the Negro as teamsters—pioneers—laborers on roads and fortifications—cooks for soldiers & servants for hospitals." His outlook did not contain the enthusiastic naivete of Cleburne and avoided the emotional hostility of Walker.

Bate, Anderson, and Stewart were firmly against the idea. William Bate thought that arming the slaves would create such an uproar among the white soldiers that the army would simply cease to exist. He stated that "our situation requires no such remedy" and deemed the very idea "hideous and objectionable." He expressed these views to Walker when he said, "I regarded at the time, and do now, the seductive argument with which it is interwoven, as the rose beneath which, the serpent of Abolitionism is coiled." Like most Southerners he was steadfastly opposed to emancipation, and he was afraid to destroy the barriers between the races.[24]

Patton Anderson agreed. He felt that agitation of the population on the issue "would shake our governments, both state and Confederate, to their very foundations, if indeed it did not tear them up by the roots." If the slaves were actually armed he predicted an even worse result, asserting that "Southern society would become but an earthly pandemonium."[25] In a 14 January letter

---

[23] B. F. Cheatham to W. H. T. Walker January 10 1864 Huntington Library, San Marino, California; Christopher Losson, *Tennessee's Forgotten Warriors: Frank Cheatham and His Confederate Division* (Knoxville: University of Tennessee Press, 1989) 137.

[24] Davis, "Extraordinary Document," 16–18.

[25] Richard M. McMurry, "Patton Anderson: Major General C.S.A.," *Blue and Gray* 1/2 (October/November 1983): 15.

to Leonidas Polk, he repeated his opposition to the paper, stating that "if this thing is once openly proposed to the Army the total disintegration of that Army will follow in a fortnight…." He continued, "and not the least painful of the emotions awakened by it was the consciousness which forced itself upon me that it met with favor by others beside the author in high station then present." Yet Anderson faced a personal dilemma. In his mind, while it was out of the question to arm the slaves, the virulent criticism of Cleburne was equally unwarranted. With clear admiration he described Cleburne as "one of our bravest and accomplished officers."[26]

A. P. Stewart had two objections. First he denounced the proposal itself, describing it as "at war with my social, moral and political principles."[27] Like Walker, he was unable to reconcile the demand for additional troops with the traditions of his past. He also addressed the morale of the Confederacy as a whole. The adoption of Cleburne's ideas would foster a defeatist attitude that was "at best discouraging, and at worst seditious."[28]

The differing statements of each man provide great insight into their personal feelings on the institution of slavery, as well as the wisdom of the memorial before them. Most of the opposing responses were relatively consistent and seemed to accurately reflect the prevailing sentiment at the time. It appeared as though there were a common recognition of a serious problem and simply honest disagreement as to the proper solution.

The one exception belonged to W. H. T. Walker, and it was his persistence that did the most damage to Pat Cleburne. His reaction was far more emotional than any other, and he repeatedly violated Johnston's orders to keep the matter quiet. There has been some speculation that, far beyond a difference of opinion, he had an ulterior motive in discrediting Cleburne. He certainly expended a great deal of energy in the defeat of a suggestion that would never have been seriously considered in the first place.

What then did Walker have to gain by his outburst? From the standpoint of promotion, both Cleburne and Cheatham outranked him. Both

---

[26] US War Department, comp., *The War of the Rebellion: A Compilation of the Official Records of the Union and Confederate Armies*, 128 vols. (Washington, DC: Government Printing Office, 1880–1901) ser. 1, vol. 52, pt. 2, p. 598–99.

[27] Sam D. Elliott, *Soldier of Tennessee* (Baton, Rouge: Louisiana State University Press, 1999) 168.

[28] Davis, "Extraordinary Document," 18.

men held a commission as major general that predated that of Walker. Cleburne had far more talent.[29] Cheatham had a longer and better record. Walker had handled a few small opportunities with success, but Cleburne had made a magnificent stand on Missionary Ridge and then saved Hardee once again at Ringgold Gap. Next to Cleburne, Cheatham led the most reliable troops in the Army of Tennessee. On the right flank at Perryville, he drove the Federals back over a mile and captured three field pieces. He had attacked over difficult terrain against larger numbers. In short, advancement by Cleburne or Cheatham could be earned by their performance on the field of battle. Walker would have to work behind the scenes.

Logically, Walker should not have had any chance at all to be promoted over either man. However, the Georgian held one advantage that was very important to Jefferson Davis, Braxton Bragg, and Joseph Johnston. He was a West Point graduate who had served in the regular army. Cleburne was from Ireland, and while Cheatham had fought in the Mexican War, he was a farmer and politician with no formal military training.

Hardee was their mutual corps commander and had high regard for Cleburne, but Walker's family had a long social history with the Johnstons. Walker was a vocal supporter of Braxton Bragg, while Hardee, Cleburne, and Cheatham were against him. It is interesting to note that the responses to Cleburne's plan were remarkably similar to the opinions put forth in the 4 October petition to remove Bragg from the army. Following the battle of Chickamauga, the Union forces had retreated to the confines of Chattanooga. They were soundly beaten, weakened in battle, driven from the field, and largely demoralized. Many of the senior Confederates urged a rapid pursuit to finally eliminate the Army of the Tennessee. Bragg paused, allowing the enemy time to regroup. His vacillation broke down the confidence of the army. Frustration mounted in what seemed to emerge as a pattern of squandered opportunities. Finally it was suggested that Bragg step down from his position and turn over the leadership to a more aggressive general. The officers present split into two camps. Those who had opposed Bragg came out

---

[29] Russell K. Brown, *To the Manner Born: The Life of General William H. T. Walker* (Athens: University of Georgia Press, 1994) 203; Peter Cozzens, *No Better Place to Die* (Urbana: University of Illinois Press, 1990) 34; Wiley Sword, *Embrace an Angry Wind* (New York: St. Martin's, 1995) 18; Robert Selph Henry, *Forrest: First with the Most* (1944; repr., Wilmington NC: Broadfoot Publishing, 1991) 390.

in favor of Cleburne while his supporters took the opposite stance. Ironically, Bragg was actually pleased with Cleburne's suggestion. He knew it would never be adopted and would weaken the stature of the petitioners against him.[30]

In Walker's case, these peculiar circumstances may have outweighed his other shortcomings. Neither Davis nor Bragg had the vision to appreciate genius. They made their decisions according to accepted practice and went strictly by the book. A West Point graduate was an inherently superior soldier. The promotions in 1864 from major general to lieutenant general bear this out. John B. Hood, A. P. Stewart, and Stephen D. Lee had all served in the United States Army. None of them possessed Cleburne's ability. Another man who shared Cleburne's fate was Nathan Bedford Forrest. He was a truly remarkable officer who should have been made a lieutenant general much earlier in the war. Davis denied him that rank until February 1865. Cleburne was not even an American, and Forrest had been a planter and slave trader before the war. Their backgrounds did not sit well in Richmond.

Despite these advantages, if he were to have any chance at all Walker had to stay in the good graces of Richmond. This could be problematic. In 1861 he had abruptly resigned from the army due to his failure to receive a promotion to major general. After the first battle of Manassas, Joseph Johnston, P. G. T. Beauregard, and G. W. Smith recommended that a reorganization of the Confederate forces was necessary. Prior to that engagement all brigades reported directly to the head of the army. All three generals felt it would be more efficient to adopt a traditional structure in which brigades reported to divisions and divisions reported to corps commanders. This change would require more generals. Seven men were under consideration and Walker headed the list. In addition to Walker, the names of W. W. Mackall, Earl Van Dorn, James Longstreet, Mansfield Lovell, Thomas J. Jackson, and W. H. C. Whiting were submitted to the president. Jefferson Davis did not quite agree with the need for expansion, but he acquiesced in part. On 7 October he conferred the rank on Longstreet, Jackson, and Lovell. Four days later Edmund Kirby Smith was also promoted.

On 22 October the military structure was altered again, this time in order to conform more closely to state lines. Not only did Walker fail once

---

[30] Judith Lee Hallock, *Braxton Bragg and Confederate Defeat*, 2 vols. (Tuscaloosa: University of Alabama Press, 1991) 180.

more, but the Louisiana brigade he had personally trained was taken from him. It was given to a junior colonel, Richard Taylor of Louisiana. Walker knew quite well that Taylor was the brother of President Davis's first wife. The offer of a Georgia brigade to replace the loss was no consolation.[31]

This series of events was too much for Walker's pride to bear. On 27 October 1861, he recorded his thoughts in a letter to Secretary of State Judah Benjamin. He listed his own accomplishments, service, and sacrifice, pointing out that he had been passed over by men who were younger and had not attended West Point.[32] Furthermore, he was from Georgia whereas Lovell was from New York, and there was simply no justification for the transfer of his own brigade to a junior officer. He could no longer submit to the insults of Jefferson Davis and resigned in disgust.[33]

By 1864 Walker was desperate, still consumed by the desire to become a lieutenant general. He had been brought back into the army in 1863 by Joseph Johnston in a futile attempt to save Vicksburg. It was a plea for help created by the urgency of the moment, not the result of any inherent qualities Walker possessed. On 4 July Vicksburg capitulated, so there had been no glory there. He was an angry man, frustrated by his failure to receive an honor he never deserved.[34] It would take a cataclysmic event for someone of his stature to attain that rank, but Patrick Cleburne had opened a window of opportunity and W. H. T. Walker was going to walk through it.

By 10 January Walker had collected as many responses as possible, whereupon he asked Joe Johnston to forward the information to Richmond using conventional procedures. Johnston refused, as he did not wish to become embroiled in a matter of such controversy. Walker took the matter into his own hands and two days later wrote the following note to President Davis: "The gravity of the subject, the magnitude of the issues involved, my strong

---

[31] Brown, *To the Manner Born,* 111.

[32] Walker was in the class of 1837. Longstreet, Lovell, and Van Dorn graduated from West Point in the class of 1842, Smith in 1845, and Jackson 1846. Whiting had also graduated in 1845, compiling the highest record at the institution up until that point. Mackall did not receive a promotion at that time. Walker was referring to Richard Taylor, who had entered Harvard and then transferred to Yale, where he graduated in 1845.

[33] Brown, *To the Manner Born,* 108–12.

[34] Walter Brian Cisco, *States Rights Gist: A South Carolina General of the Civil War* (Shippensburg PA: White Mane Publishing Co., 1991) 119; Losson, *Forgotten Warriors,* 139.

convictions that the further agitation of such sentiments and propositions would ruin the efficacy of our Army and involve our cause in ruin and disgrace constitute my reasons for bringing the document to the Executive."[35]

Perhaps disturbed by Johnston's refusal to assist him, on 16 January Walker wrote Davis a second letter. He explained:

> My excuse for sending the communication of Genl. Cleburne direct to you is that the Commanding Genl. of the Army of Tennessee declined for reasons satisfactory to himself to permit me to forward it through the regular official channel. My excuse for sending it at all is that I honestly believe that the propagation of such sentiments in our army will ruin our cause and that it is my duty to lay the document before the Chief Magistrate of the country. I have written a note to the Hon. H. V. Johnson requesting him to hand the sealed package to you and requested him to inform me of its safe delivery. The contents of the package he is not acquainted with.[36]

The response from Davis was evasive. Like many of his decisions during the war, it was inconsistent. He did acknowledge that there was a shortage of manpower and claimed to be in favor of reform, but he did not have the courage to act decisively. He revealed the politician within when he described a dire situation yet proposed only a half-hearted remedy that would never solve the problem. He knew exactly what the public would accept, and he had no intention of instigating a social revolution. He responded, "No effort must be spared to add largely to our effective force as promptly as possible. The sources of supply are to be found in restoring to the army all who are improperly absent, putting an end to substitution, modifying the exemption law, restricting details, and placing in the ranks such of the able-bodied men now employed as wagoners, nurses, cooks and other employees as are doing service for which the Negroes may be found competent."[37]

After deliberate consideration of Walker's correspondence, Davis replied that "while recognizing the patriotic motives of its distinguished author, I deem it inexpedient, at this time, to give publicity to this paper, and request

---

[35] OR, ser. 1, vol. 52, pt. 2, p. 595.
[36] Civil War Collection, Huntington Library, San Marino, California.
[37] "Negroes in Our Army," 221.

that it be suppressed."[38] On 23 January, Davis wrote him directly, stating: "I have concluded that the best policy under the circumstances will be to avoid all publicity.... If it be kept out of the public journals, its ill effects will be much lessened."[39] Naturally this was very disappointing. Cleburne asked his aide, Captain Buck, to destroy all of the copies with the exception of the one Walker had sent to Davis.

Jefferson Davis was still very worried that the contents of the document would somehow be revealed. He was not content to settle the matter with a few words of advice to Walker. He wanted to be sure there would be no further discussion of the matter. Davis directed Secretary of War James A. Seddon to give Johnston clear instructions regarding the policies in Richmond. On 24 January Seddon wrote, "...The motives of zeal and patriotism which have prompted General Walker's actions are...fully appreciated...."[40] Johnston received Seddon's message on 31 January. He told Cleburne to make sure that none of the field officers mentioned the paper either. Johnston now understood the party line and tried to wash his hands of the whole matter. He replied on 2 February, reporting that "none of the officers to whom the memorial was read favored the scheme."[41] He would distort the truth to save his reputation, but he never did abandon Cleburne's idea.

The government in Richmond made every effort to suppress the publication of the memorial, but they were not entirely successful. Several officers who were not present at the conference offered their own opinions on the subject. John C. Breckinridge sided with Cleburne. He was somewhat familiar with the contents, as he had both read and endorsed the paper on 17 December. On 28 December he stated that he was in favor of raising 300,000 black troops. In early January he had gone to Richmond on leave, in part to raise support for another invasion of Kentucky, but he had many friends in the capital as well. Despite an active social schedule he was still engrossed with the shortage of manpower in the Army of Tennessee. On 19 January 1864, the famous diarist Mary Boykin Chesnut recorded that Breckinridge had

---

[38] "Negroes in Our Army," 217.
[39] Dunbar Rowland, *Jefferson Davis, Constitutionalist: His Letters and Speeches*, 12 vols. (New York: J. J. Little & Ives Company, 1923) 159–60.
[40] OR, ser. 1, vol. 52, pt. 2, p. 606.
[41] OR, ser. 1, vol. 52, pt. 2, p. 608–609.

informed her of Cleburne's ideas. He had a positive view of the proposal but felt it was premature.[42]

By this time many people in the North had become weary of the war. The unification of the nation was very important and the institution of slavery was odious, but there was little desire to see sons of Ohio die for Negroes in Alabama. Perhaps the most telling commentary came from General Ulysses S. Grant. In his *Memoirs* he stated that "anything that could have prolonged the war a year beyond the time that it finally did close, would probably have exhausted the North to such an extent that they might then have abandoned the contest and agreed to a separation."[43]

In a post-war article written for the *Kennesaw Gazette*, Joseph M. Brown agreed but observed that Cleburne's proposal came way too late. In his book *Advance and Retreat*, General John B. Hood wrote, "[Cleburne] was a man of equally quick perception and strong character, and was, especially in one respect, in advance of many of our people. He possessed the boldness and wisdom to earnestly advocate at an early period of the war the freedom of the Negro and enrollment of the young and able-bodied men of that race. This stroke of policy and additional source of strength to our armies would, in my opinion, have given us our independence."[44]

On the other hand, States Rights Gist was not only on Walker's side but a staunch ally of Braxton Bragg as well. Gist felt that Bragg had been mistreated by the earlier petition to remove him. On 27 February he had written the North Carolinian to congratulate him on his new appointment as Davis's military adviser. Bragg responded by sending a message through Gist to Walker, praising "my old and true friend" on winning the battle against the "Abolition Party of the South." He added that "I should like to know as a matter of safety the secret history of the treason and the names of the traitors."[45] Gist received Bragg's letter on 8 March and replied one day later. He was

[42] William C. Davis, *Breckinridge Statesman Soldier Symbol* (Baton Rouge: Louisiana State University Press, 1974) 403; Brown, *To the Manner Born,* 202.

[43] Ulysses S. Grant, *Personal Memoirs of U. S. Grant,* 2 vols. (New York: Charles L. Webster & Company, 1885) 2:167.

[44] John B. Hood, *Advance and Retreat* (1880; repr., Edison NJ: Blue and Gray Press, 1985) 296.

[45] Braxton Bragg to States Rights Gist, 27 February 1864, Braxton Bragg Papers, Western Reserve Historical Society, Cleveland OH, from microfilm edition at University of West Florida, Pensacola FL.

extremely pleased with the suppression of Cleburne's proposal and gave the following assurance to Bragg that Walker would communicate to him directly: "It is really a rich affair, and I am delighted beyond expression to know that the traitors will meet with their just deserts at the hands of the powers that be." He added, "You will see that Hindman is one of the chief offenders and, I think, the most dangerous man of all."[46]

Howell Cobb was against the entire concept. In a letter from Macon dated 8 January 1865, he explained:

> I think that the proposition is the most pernicious idea that has been suggested since the war began. You cannot make soldiers of slaves or slaves of soldiers. The moment you resort to this your white soldiers are lost to you, and one reason why this proposition is received with favor by some portion of the army is because they hope that when the Negro comes in they can retire. You cannot keep white and black troops together, and you cannot trust Negroes alone. They won't make soldiers, as they are wanting in every qualification to make one. Better by far to yield to the demands of England and France and abolish slavery and thereby purchase their aid than to resort to this policy, which would lead to certain ruin and subjugation.[47]

Joseph Wheeler was outraged as well. He wrote Bragg on 14 February 1864, claiming that Cleburne would have been hanged "in five minutes" if he had proposed such a change in Wheeler's home town before the war. For many officers, Cleburne's memorial simply cut too far into deeply ingrained traditions.[48]

The single remaining question was the mind of Jefferson Davis. Did he still harbor resentment over Walker's abrupt resignation in 1861? Years had passed, but Davis did not forgive easily. Walker had told Davis what he wanted to hear, but could he rely on the president's support? Davis liked

---

[46] States Rights Gist to Braxton Bragg, 9 March 1864, Bragg Papers, Western Reserve Historical Society, Cleveland OH.

[47] John C. Stiles, "Confederate States Negro Troops," *Confederate Veteran* 23/6 (June 1915): 246–47.

[48] Wheeler to Bragg, 14 February 1864, Frederick M. Dearborn Papers, Harvard University. Wheeler was born in Augusta, Georgia.

Bragg and Bragg liked Walker, but how much weight did Bragg's endorsement carry? These were all issues Walker needed to resolve. Even if Davis did support him, the coveted promotion to lieutenant general was far from certain.

Other suggestions had been made before, but the comprehensive plan Cleburne offered had never been submitted. Even before the bombardment of Fort Sumter, the general concept had been discussed. C. B. New, a planter on the Mississippi River, sought permission to arm his own slaves. He was very concerned that flatboaters from the Northwestern states would pillage his property, and he seemed to have had no reservations about a revolt.[49] In Virginia, C. M. Hubbard of James City suggested to Governor Letcher that slaves might be used as laborers and "in any other way that the safety of the country might require."[50] On 17 July 1861, farmer William S. Turner from Helena had written a letter to then-secretary of war Leroy P. Walker. Turner asked if "Negro regiments…are offered, of course by white men" could be "received" for Confederate service. The government refused.[51]

On 3 April 1862, an article published in the New Orleans *Daily True Delta* suggested the enlistment of 100,000 men into the armed services.[52] Later that month, a group of planters from Sunflower County, Mississippi, petitioned Governor Pettus to consider using slaves as soldiers.[53]

There was growing support for change in Alabama as well. The 2 September issue of the Montgomery *Weekly Mail* recommended that the state legislature consider the employment of slaves not only as cooks and teamsters, but as soldiers as well. The legislature admitted that the state had been forced into a very difficult position by the Northern enlistment of slaves. However, the nature of the war had changed, and it would be advisable to adapt to different circumstances.[54]

One week later, the paper was more emphatic. Quoting the Jackson *Mississippian*, the *Mail* criticized the wisdom of bondage itself. The following

---

[49] New to Pettus, 14 January 1861, Mississippi Archives, Jackson MS, series E, no. 56.

[50] OR, ser. 1, vol. 51, pt. 2, p. 47.

[51] OR, ser. 4, vol. 1, p. 482.

[52] *New Orleans Daily True Delta*, 3 April 1862, in Bell I. Wiley, *Southern Negroes, 1861–1865* (New Haven, CT: Yale University Press, 1938) 149.

[53] Wiley, *Southern Negroes*, 149; Mississippi Archives, series E, no. 56.

[54] Robert F. Durden, "The Gray and the Black," *Montgomery* (AL) *Weekly Mail*, 2 September 1862, 32–35.

column appeared on 9 September: "...we must either employ the Negroes ourselves, or the enemy will employ them against us. While the enemy retains so much of our territory, they are, in their present avocation and status, a dangerous, element, a source of weakness...."[55]

It was apparent that President Lincoln intended to use involuntary servitude as both a social and a military weapon against the South. Therefore, the paper argued, the Confederacy "must thwart the enemy in this gigantic scheme, at all hazards, and if nothing else will do it—if the Negroes cannot be made effective and trustworthy to the Southern cause in no other way, we solemnly believe it is the duty of this Government to forestall Lincoln and proceed at once to take steps for the emancipation or liberation of the Negroes itself. Let them be declared free, placed in the ranks and told to fight for their homes and country."[56]

Up to this point, Richmond had dismissed such ideas without the slightest consideration. On 24 November 1863, Seddon had stated, "our position with the North and before the world will not allow the employment as armed soldiers, of Negroes."[57] Robert E. Lee, however, had written the authorities several times, endorsing that black recruitment:

> I should prefer to rely on our white population; but in view of the preparation of our enemy it is our duty to provide for a continuous war, which, I fear, we cannot accomplish with our present resources.... I think, therefore, that we must decide whether slavery shall be extinguished by our enemies and the slaves used against us or use them ourselves at the risk of the effects which may be produced upon our soldiers' social institutions. My own opinion is that we should employ them without delay.[58]

For Cleburne, the responses in Richmond from Jefferson Davis and Braxton Bragg decided the matter. However, even in the capital opposition was not unanimous. Less than one month earlier, on 21 December, Judah

---

[55] "Employment of Negroes in the Army," *Jackson Mississippian*, as quoted in *Montgomery* (AL) *Weekly Mail*, 9 September 1862.

[56] Durden, "The Gray and the Black," 30.

[57] OR, ser. 4, vol. 2, p. 941.

[58] Stiles, "Negro Troops," 246.

Benjamin had expressed the pragmatism of Cleburne and Lee: "It appears to me enough to say that the negro will certainly fight against us if not used for our defense. There is no other means of swelling our armies than that of arming the slaves and using them as an auxiliary force. I further admit that if they fight for our freedom they are entitled to their own."[59]

If advice from Lee had no effect, Cleburne's opinion carried little weight. Even after its rejection the logic remained sound. Johnston believed that with minor alterations he could persuade Davis to accept a similar plan. He offered to employ males in non-combat positions as cooks, teamsters, laborers, and the like. He estimated that this would release 10,000 to 12,000 men in the army at Dalton.[60] Johnston knew that additional legislation would have to be passed before the measure could be enacted, and he emphasized the urgency of the matter. A bill authorizing the use of freemen and up to 20,000 slaves was finally passed on 17 February 1865, but the measure was a weak one. It gave the responsibility of organizing the slaves to the Bureau of Conscription, but the jurisdiction remained unchanged. Officers could impress them only after consultation with the state authorities. The Bureau explained that Johnston could use only those free Negroes who were currently available, nothing more. The result was that the Army of Tennessee received only negligible assistance and Johnston's vision of more concrete improvements never materialized.[61]

What then, were the true motives behind Walker's persistent efforts to not only oppose but also discredit his opponents? The answer seems to lie somewhere between jealousy and sincerity. Bragg's characterization of Cleburne and Cheatham as "traitors" is simply incomprehensible. Walker was a patriot who believed in the Cause. He was a dedicated officer, determined to do his best to achieve independence for the Confederacy. However, there is no comparison in the military ability of Walker, Cleburne, and Cheatham. Walker had seen a steady stream of other generals promoted while he languished in the pool of his own mediocrity. It is quite probable that the proposal to free the slaves was merely the fuse to a keg of powder just ready to explode.

---

[59] Stiles, "Negro Troops," 246.

[60] Gilbert Govan and James Livingwood, *Joseph E. Johnston: A Different Valor* (1956; repr., New York: Smithmark, 1995) 245.

[61] Govan and Livingwood, *Different Valor,* 245.

For Pat Cleburne, the decision to release his paper was a momentous one.
It is widely accepted that, next to Nathan Bedford Forrest, he had the most
innate military ability of any general officer in the Western theatre.[62] While his
reasoning was sound, he had misgauged the mood of the South. He owned no
slaves and may have had a good deal of difficulty understanding the feelings of
those who did. He had approached the issue from the standpoint of military
logic. Cleburne saw the struggle in simplistic terms, but his vision was clear.
There was a goal, and every effort must be made to reach it. He had little
doubt as to the proper course of action. Arrayed against this was the social
order of the Deep South. Stewart summarized Cleburne's greatest obstacle
when he stated that the proposal was "at war with my social, moral and
political principles." This belief was by no means restricted to the Confederate
Army. The values of the Confederacy were expressed very clearly before the
war even began. Keziah Brevard, who kept a diary in Charleston, wrote on the
subject of the manumission of the slaves. In an entry dated 13 October 1860,
she exclaimed, "…what can we do with them?—free such a multitude of half
barbarians in our midst—no—no—we must sooner give up our lives than to
submit to such degradation.…" She echoed these sentiments on 9 November,
following the election of Abraham Lincoln: "Oh, My God! This morning
heard that Lincoln was elected—I had prayed that God would thwart his
election in some way & I prayed for my *country*—Lord we know not what is to
be the result of this—but I do pray if there is to be a crisis—that we all lay
down our lives sooner than free our slaves in our midst—no soul on this earth
is more willing for justice than I am, but the idea of being mixed up with free
blacks is *horrid*."[63]

This general mindset was too much to overcome. Irving Buck
understood the ramifications of the plan far better than Cleburne. He believed
that after Cleburne's suggestion, advancement would become difficult. In
spring 1864 Jefferson Davis gained a series of opportunities to appoint
lieutenant generals in the Army of Tennessee. First, after Breckinridge was

---

[62] Glenn Tucker, *Chickamauga: Bloody Battle of the West* (1961; repr., New York:
Smithmark, 1994) 182; Nathaniel C. Hughes, *General William J. Hardee: Old Reliable*
(Baton Rouge: Louisiana State University Press, 1965) 214; Henry, *First with the Most,*
390; Cozzens, *No Better Place to Die,* 34; Sword, *Embrace an Angry Wind,* 24.

[63] John Hammond Moore, *A Plantation Mistress on the Eve of the Civil War: The Diary
of Keziah Goodwyn Hopkins Brevard, July 1860–April 1861* (Columbia: University of
South Carolina Press, 1993) 39, 49.

relieved on 15 February and ordered to Richmond, Davis appointed Thomas
Hindman, despite his difficulties with Braxton Bragg in the fall.

The next opportunity came abruptly with Leonidas Polk death at
Kennesaw Mountain on 14 June. Alexander P. Stewart was the senior officer in
Polk's corps; he assumed command on 23 June. Stewart had fought well at
Shiloh, contributing to the surrender at the Hornet's Nest.[64] Like Cleburne,
he took heavy casualties in that bloody battle, and like Cleburne he improved
with time. At Chickamauga he pushed back the Federal center on 19
September, capturing over 200 prisoners and 12 pieces of artillery.[65] On 20
September he occupied the right of Longstreet's command, which forced the
breakthrough in the Union lines.

Stewart had also experienced failure. Following the Confederate retreat
from Murfreesboro, Bragg moved south toward Tullahoma. The Federals
pursued, advancing along several lines. Stewart was positioned behind
Hoover's Gap, 11 miles southeast of Murfreesboro. On 24 June 1863,
Union cavalry under John T. Wilder attacked and seized the gap, but Stewart's
men were too far back to contest the advance. The nearest Confederates
belonged to William Bate, some 4 miles away near the village of Beech Grove.
Not only was the brigade out of position, but many of its officers were absent
at a Masonic picnic.[66] Stewart was simply unprepared. He ordered Bate to
attack the Federals at the south end of the gap, but they did not reach the field
until late in the afternoon.[67] The concentrated fire of Wilder's repeating rifles
made Bate believe that he was facing a much larger force. Still, he threw wave
after wave of his troops into the gap, losing one fourth of his strength.[68] At the
end of the day Hoover's Gap was in Union hands and the Confederates
continued their retreat to Tullahoma.

In the fiasco at Missionary Ridge Stewart was badly outnumbered. His
troops fought as well as possible, but they did not have sufficient strength to

---

[64] Elliott, *Soldier of Tennessee,* 39–42.

[65] Report of Alexander P. Stewart, 15 October 1863, OR, ser. 1, vol. 30, pt. 2, p. 362–
63.

[66] Thomas L. Connelly, *Autumn of Glory: The Army of Tennessee 1862–1865* (Baton
Rouge: Louisiana State University Press, 1971) 126.

[67] Report of Bushrod Johnson, 12 July 1863, OR, ser. 1, vol. 23, pt. 1, p. 602; report of
William B. Bate, 15 July 1863, OR, ser. 1, vol. 23, pt. 1, p. 611.

[68] Glenn W. Sunderland, *Lightning at Hoover's Gap* (New York: Thomas Yoseloff,
1969) 40–42.

secure the Confederate flank. When Jesse Finley's Floridians collapsed on Stewart's right, he had no choice but to fall back. He was placed in an untenable position by the faulty dispositions of Braxton Bragg and John Breckinridge. Cleburne was in a similar predicament and held out long enough for Hardee, Stewart, and the rest of the army to escape. Two days later, Cleburne repeated his performance at Ringgold Gap.

A. P. Stewart had proved himself a fine officer. Generally, his troops had given a good account of themselves. He did not, however, possess the combat record of Cleburne, and Cleburne's appointment as major general preceded Stewart's by almost six months. Still, when Cleburne's memorial had been offered in January 1864, the Tennessean was emphatic in his opposition. He had graduated from West Point in the class of 1842, and his commanding officer thought highly of him. Johnston wired Davis on 14 June that "it is essential to have a Lt. Genl immediately to succeed Lt. Genl Polk. I regard Maj. Genl Stewart as the best qualified of the Maj. Genls of this army. Time is important."[69] Stewart received the promotion.

This note raises yet another curious point. Jefferson Davis and Joseph Johnston had been at odds since the beginning of the war. Davis had submitted a list of nominees to Congress for the rank of full general. He placed Johnston fourth, behind Samuel Cooper, Albert Sidney Johnston, and Robert E. Lee. Johnston was insulted. He believed that due to his rank as a United States quartermaster general prior to the war, he should have been first in line. This was clearly a debate over a technicality and should never have been an issue at all. Neither man worked to solve the problem, and their relationship began to deteriorate. Yet, on this one point, Davis took counsel of Johnston's advice.

During the campaign for Atlanta, the Confederates were at a serious disadvantage. The Army of the Cumberland alone outnumbered Johnston's entire force. He had few alternatives, constantly falling back and then probing for a weakness in Sherman's advance. In all probability, a gradual retreat was the wisest course of action. Grant was making no progress in Virginia, Union losses were heavy, and if Sherman could be stopped in Georgia, Lincoln's reelection might be in jeopardy. Davis could not appreciate this fact, nor did he approve of the defensive tactics. Johnston was removed on 18 July, only

---

[69] Johnston to Davis, 14 June 1864, Officers File, RG 109, National Archives, Washington, DC.

two days before the battle of Peachtree Creek. Davis wanted an aggressive, offensive-minded general, and he had one close at hand.

John Bell Hood graduated from West Point in the class of 1853. His rise through the ranks was nothing short of meteoric. He was promoted to brigadier general to rank from 3 March 1862. Based on his prior service, this was premature. He had been a dependable regimental commander, but Jefferson Davis promoted him over two senior colonels, James Archer of the 5th Texas and William T. Wofford of the 18th Georgia. Neither man had attended West Point.[70]

It was after Joseph Johnston's wounding at Fair Oaks that Robert E. Lee took center stage. The next several weeks saw the Army of the Potomac slowly make its way up the Peninsula until it paused at the outskirts of Richmond. The gravity of the situation was not lost on anyone; the Federals had to be stopped. On 25 June the armies fought a small engagement at Oak Grove followed by a much larger battle at Mechanicsville. Hood vaulted into prominence for his role in the battle of Gaines's Mill, which took place on 27 June. The contest was bitter and cooperation on the Confederate side was lacking. The day wore on and the armies pounded away at each other, taking heavy losses. As darkness approached, no progress had been made. The Confederacy could not afford a stalemate this close to the capital. Lee searched for Hood and quickly explained the situation. Along with troops under Evander Law, Hood's Texans rushed forward and broke the Union lines. In desperate fighting the Confederates pushed the Federals from the field, but again the casualties were horrendous. Hood and Law lost roughly 25 percent of their forces, but this was a battle the Confederates simply had to win.[71] If Richmond had fallen, the war would have ended at that point. Instead, George McClellan began to retreat.

At the battle of Second Manassas, Hood moved through Thoroughfare Gap on 28 August, taking the lead in Longstreet's advance. The next day he continued forward in the direction of Manassas Junction, bringing up his two

---

[70] Richard M. McMurry, *John Bell Hood* (Lexington: University Press of Kentucky, 1982) 35; Gabor S. Boritt, *Jefferson Davis's Generals* (New York: Oxford University Press, 1999) 86.

[71] Stephen W. Sears, *To the Gates of Richmond* (New York: Ticknor & Fields, 1992) 241; H. J. Eckenrode and Bryan Conrad, *James Longstreet Lee's War Horse* (1936; repr., Chapel Hill: University of North Carolina Press, 1986) 70.

brigades[72] on Jackson's right. They formed across the Warrenton Turnpike and at right angles to it. Before sunset Hood made a forward reconnaissance and was attacked by Rufus King. Hood responded and after half an hour King withdrew. On 30 August they continued to press the attack and hit the Union left with tremendous force. Hood swept into their flank and Lee's army drove the Federals back toward Washington. Hood had shown consummate skill in handling the movement of his troops, but he revealed a trait that would resurface later in the war with far more serious consequences. He was a tremendous fighter, but he took very heavy losses.[73] On 29 August the 5th Texas alone had lost 225 men, more than any other regiment in the army.[74] These were casualties the Confederates could ill afford.

Another promotion soon followed. Hood became a major general to rank from 10 October 1862. When the Army of Northern Virginia confronted the Federals at Gettysburg, Hood commanded a division in Longstreet's corps. On 2 July he advocated an attack around the south side of Round Top, taking it in the flank and rear. Longstreet refused and ordered Hood to adhere to Lee's original plan of an attack along the Emmittsburg Road. Conditions on this part of the field had changed, and Lee should have been notified. Longstreet's obstinance prevented Hood from fighting the battle he wanted.[75] What the outcome of Hood's proposal would have been is debatable, but it certainly had enough merit to warrant considerable speculation by current historians.

John B. Hood had participated in every major battle in the Eastern theatre and had met with considerable success. The Texans attained a reputation exceeded only by the Stonewall Brigade. However, while his courage and aggression were without question, his regard for his men was suspect. He was not well versed in strategy and had little grasp of reconnaissance. He simply attacked, and with reckless abandon.[76] Robert E.

---

[72] His own, under William T. Wofford, as well as W. H. C. Whiting's brigade.

[73] Connelly, *Autumn of Glory*, 431.

[74] John J. Hennessy, *Return to Bull Run: The Campaign and Battle of Second Manassas* (New York: Simon and Schuster, 1993) 405.

[75] Douglas S. Freeman, *R. E. Lee*, 4 vols. (New York: Charles Scribner's Sons, 1934–1936) 3:97–98; Hood, *Advance and Retreat*, 57–59; Albert Castel, *Decision in the West* (Lawrence: University of Kansas Press, 1992) 58.

[76] Mary B. Chesnutt, *A Diary from Dixie* (1905; repr., New York: Random House, 1997) 319; Douglas Freeman, ed., *Lee's Dispatches to Jefferson Davis, 1862–1865* (New York: G. P. Putnams's Sons, 1957) 282; Hennessy, *Return to Bull Run*, 289.

Lee expressed his views in a dispatch to Jefferson Davis shortly before Hood replaced Joseph Johnston. On 12 July 1864 he wrote: "It is a bad time to release [relieve] the commander of an army situated as that of Tenne. We may lose Atlanta and the army too. Hood is a bold fighter. I am doubtful as to other qualities necessary."[77]

Far too often, Hood initiated the action with a frontal assault. This consistently resulted in excessive casualties, which were finally brought to an end by the slaughter at Franklin. It may be said that Hood fought very well as a brigadier and his division was excellent in Longstreet's corps, but he did not possess the mental acuity, military genius, or administrative capacity to lead the army in Atlanta.[78] From the time he replaced Joseph Johnston to his resignation on 23 January, his performance was simply disastrous.

By comparison, Pat Cleburne did not have similar chances for victory. Hood served under Lee and Longstreet. Cleburne fought under Bragg and Hood. The Texans had been instrumental in the victories at Gaines's Mill and Second Manassas, but Cleburne's performances at Missionary Ridge and Ringgold Gap were no less spectacular and were conducted under far greater adversity. Hood was able to achieve great victories, but at tremendous cost. Cleburne suffered heavy losses at Shiloh but seemed to learn from his early mistakes. In fact, many of his casualties took place after his greatest successes and he had outdistanced his support. Such was the case at both Perryville and Stones River. In assessing the two men prior to the Atlanta campaign, Albert Castel wrote, "Hood is a superb combat leader; in the entire Confederate Army only Cleburne matches him."[79]

What factors influenced Jefferson Davis to promote Hood over Cleburne? What really separated the two men? Hood did not have a better combat record, and he had taken many more casualties. His troops were more famous but not any better than Cleburne's. When placed side by side, the men reveal two striking differences. First, Hood went to West Point. Cleburne was Irish, and his service in the British Army meant nothing in Richmond.

---

[77] Freeman, *Lee's Dispatches*, 282.

[78] Grady McWhiney, *Attack and Die* (Tuscaloosa: University of Alabama Press, 1982) 73; Freeman, *Lee's Dispatches*, 282.

[79] Castel, *Decision in the West*, 60.

Second, there can be no doubt that Cleburne's proposal to arm and free the slaves did him irreparable damage.[80]

In his book *Jefferson Davis and His Generals*, Steven Woodworth offers a further analysis of Davis's actions of 1864. He contends that Cleburne's alliance with Hardee did him no favors where the subject of John B. Hood was concerned. In a pointed analysis, Woodworth criticizes the president's judgment during 1864, noting that the choice of Joe Johnston to replace Bragg was made only as a last resort. He continues: "A related error was choosing Hood rather than Stewart or, better, Cleburne to fill the vacancy of Corps commander in the Army of Tennessee.... Cleburne would have been more satisfactory in every respect and might have proved to be a superior army commander after Johnston's failure."[81]

Mangum expressed his views in a letter to the former governor of Georgia, Joseph M. Brown. He noted that "Cleburne was the most popular and esteemed general in the army in December of 1863, specifically due to the recent results around Chattanooga. Why was he denied promotion? Hood did not have as good a record." In a comment on the promotions earned by Hood and Stewart, Mangum held that these were positions Cleburne "should have occupied—would have occupied in all human probability but for doubts engendered by this very suggestion."[82] It is ironic that not only did Hood praise the idea in his *Memoirs*, but Davis eventually adopted it anyway.

Regardless of personal convictions as to the impact Cleburne's memorial may have had on any subsequent promotions, it is clear that his views were not well received in the capital. Harsh criticism from the government was not restricted to Jefferson Davis. From Lownesboro, Alabama, Braxton Bragg wrote a letter to Brigadier General Marcus J. Wright, asserting that "Great sensation is being produced...by the Emancipation project of Hardee, Cleburne, Cheatham & Co. It will kill them."[83] His caustic attitude was a harbinger of the promotions to come.

---

[80] Sword, *Embrace an Angry Wind*, 18–22; Hughes, *Old Reliable*, 214.

[81] Steven E. Woodworth, *Jefferson Davis and His Generals* (Lawrence: University of Kansas Press, 1990) 302.

[82] T. O. Moore, "Anecdotes of General Cleburne," *New Orleans Picayune*, 2 July 1893, [PAGES]; L. H. Magnum to Joseph M. Brown, 7 May 1888, *Kennesaw* (GA) *Gazette*, 1 June 1888, 2–3.

[83] Bragg to Marcus J. Wright, 6 February 1864, Marcus Joseph Wright Papers, Southern Historical Collection, University of North Carolina, Chapel Hill NC.

With the appointment of John B. Hood to lead the Army of Tennessee, it was necessary to name another corps commander. Frank Cheatham served in a temporary capacity, but the army needed a permanent replacement. Perhaps more clearly than any other, the appointment of Stephen D. Lee illustrates the fact that Pat Cleburne was never going to become a lieutenant general. Though capable, Lee's background was not even with the infantry. He had enlisted as an artillery officer in Hampton's Legion. Prior to the battle of Second Manassas he had not distinguished himself, though he had provided timely artillery support for Hood at Eltham's Landing. At Second Manassass he served in Longstreet's corps and placed his artillery on Hood's left, in the center of the Confederate line. As Porter and Heintzelman massed to attack Jackson, they moved across Lee's line of fire. He raked their lines and did considerable damage.[84] Once again, he had fought well in support of Hood.

This may have influenced Davis's decision to give Lee corps command in 1864.[85] Less than three weeks after the action at Manassas, the armies moved to Sharpsburg. Lee's men fought valiantly against difficult odds, although Longstreet gives him only passing mention in his *Memoirs*.[86] On 6 November 1862 he was appointed Brigadier General. He moved to the Western theatre to direct the guns at Vicksburg. The inability of Joseph Johnston and John Pemberton to work together certainly affected Lee's performance. After the surrender he was exchanged, and on 3 August 1863 he was promoted to major general. He changed branches of service and took control of the cavalry in the Department of Mississippi, Alabama, West Tennessee, and East Louisiana. Lee received a subordinate with far greater ability: Nathan Bedford Forrest.

The greatest controversy during the career of Stephen D. Lee came on 14 July 1864 at Harrisburg, Mississippi. Union forces under A. J. Smith had taken a strong position facing west, with their left flank refused. Lee believed that the Federals must be attacked immediately. As a subordinate, Forrest was compelled to obey orders, but there is considerable doubt that he actually agreed with them. He may well have wanted to strike, but not here, and not

---

[84] Report of Stephen D. Lee, 2 October 1862, OR, ser. 1, vol. 12, pt. 2, p. 577–78.

[85] Herman Hattaway, *General Stephen D. Lee* (Jackson: University Press of Mississippi, 1976) 115.

[86] James Longstreet, *From Manassas to Appomattox* (1895; repr., Philadelphia: J.B. Lippincott Company, 1896) 243; Hattaway, *Stephen D. Lee,* 60.

against this formation.[87] The contest was a one-sided affair and the
Confederates lost over 1,300 men, Smith less than 700. Lee lost control of the
action and failed to coordinate all of the men at his disposal. After the battle he
summoned several officers to his quarters. Forrest was boiling with anger. He
stormed into the room, sitting in silence as the others reviewed the events of
the day. Finally, Lee turned to him and asked, "General Forrest, do you have
any ideas on the subject?" Forrest replied, "Yes, sir, I've always got ideas, and
I'll tell you one thing, General Lee. If I knew as much about West Point tactics
as you, the Yankees would whip hell out of me every day." With great effort he
continued, "I've got five hundred empty saddles and nothing to show for
them."[88]

Lee assumed command of Hood's corps on 27 July, one day before the
engagement at Ezra Church. He was familiar with all three branches of the
army, but his most valuable service had occurred with the artillery. His
combat record did not approach Cleburne's, and Cleburne outranked him.
Lee had, however, attended West Point. He was appointed lieutenant general
to rank from 23 June 1864.

Robert E. Lee had watched Hood's performance in Virginia and
recognized his faults. Hardee had seen him in the West and had similar
misgivings. Prior to a pair of very serious wounds, Hood had been physically
impressive, standing 6-foot-2 with long blonde hair. Mentally he was limited,
placing forty-fifth in a class of fifty-five at West Point and earning 196
demerits in the process. He was gallant but rash. Hardee had no aspirations to
lead the entire army, but he could not in good conscience serve under a man
like Hood.[89] He resigned on 23 September and the corps was given to
Cheatham, though he did not become a lieutenant general.

Of all of the chances for promotion during 1864, this one has received
the most attention. Throughout the careers of so many general officers,
controversies abound. Some of these are born from particular circumstances
that are unable to be substantiated. A charge or rebuttal may well have

[87] Jack Hurst, *Nathan Bedford Forrest: A Biography* (New York: Alfred A. Knopf, 1993)
203; Edwin C. Bearss, *Forrest at Brice's Cross Roads* (Dayton OH: Morningside Bookshop,
1997) 199; Henry, *First with the Most*, 316.

[88] Andrew Lytle, *Bedford Forrest and his Critter Company* (New York: McDowell,
Obolensky, 1960) 312–15.

[89] Boritt, *Jefferson Davis's Generals*, 85; Connelly, *Autumn of Glory*, 208; Castel,
Decision in the West, 423.

occurred after the death of one of the principals, rendering debate impossible and sources incomplete. Of particular curiosity in the case of Patrick Cleburne is the assertion by John Bell Hood that Hardee recommended the advancement of Cheatham over Cleburne during the middle of the Atlanta campaign.

Many valid points can be made both for and against either man. Several of their attributes are quite similar. The quality of their troops was very high, though Cleburne generally receives higher marks from present-day analysts. Cheatham had been superb at Perryville, Chickamauga, and Kennesaw Mountain, as had Cleburne at Stones River, Missionary Ridge, Ringgold Gap, and Pickett's Mill. They were each close at hand, so there would have been no delay in command due to travel from another theatre. Neither man had attended West Point. Both had acted in a limited capacity as corps commander, and though brief in both cases, Cheatham did have more experience in this role. Cleburne was Hardee's favorite, best, and most reliable subordinate, yet Hood certainly held Cheatham in high esteem. In the assessment of these factors the comparison is very even, and no clear advantage appears in either direction.

However, there were other points on which the men were far apart. In Cleburne's favor he had better-drilled soldiers, and Cheatham's wide repu0-tation as a hard drinker gave Cleburne a much stronger grade on moral grounds. In what should be the most important consideration, while Cheatham had a fine combat record, Cleburne's was definitively stronger. Though these were advantages in Cleburne's favor, this was hardly the end of the story.

There was also their experience prior to the Civil War. While not overly impressive in Richmond's eyes, an American farmer and politician who had fought in the Mexican War was better than an Irishman in the 41st Regiment of Foot who had struggled against a national potato famine. In addition, Cheatham had been a politician and knew how to work with the Confederate Congress; Cleburne, on the other hand, had neither the knowledge nor the desire to approach his counterpart in that area. Finally, Cheatham outranked him.

These were insurmountable advantages. There did not appear to be any jealousy between the two men, but realistically Cleburne could not have expected to receive that particular promotion.[90] Once again Cleburne was denied. In just five months a corps had changed hands four times. Each time

---

[90] Losson, *Forgotten Warriors,* 196; McMurry, *John Bell Hood,* 137–38.

the finest infantry officer in the army was passed over.[91]

It would seem hard to imagine that Pat Cleburne would really take over a corps when Frank Cheatham was available, but that is not the issue. The question at hand is not whether Cheatham was promoted, and it does not concern the opinion or reaction of Hood, Davis, Bragg, Cheatham, or Cleburne. It is simply this: did William J. Hardee actually recommend Cheatham over Cleburne?

Based on the professional relationship between Hardee and Cleburne, this seems very doubtful. At Stones River Hardee watched Cleburne roll up the Union right while Cheatham stalled in the center. When Buckner was transferred Cleburne received his command. At Missionary Ridge it was Cleburne who held off Sherman; two days later Cleburne saved the army again while Cheatham headed south with Braxton Bragg. Over the course of the war Hardee had also witnessed success at Shiloh, Richmond, and Perryville and, most recently, a resounding victory at Pickett's Mill.

It is also an indisputable fact that Hood hated Hardee and blamed him for the defeats at Peachtree Creek, Leggett's Hill, and Jonesboro. Cleburne was Hardee's principal lieutenant. In the middle of September he wrote two letters to President Davis concerning the opening in the Army of Tennessee. On 13 September he advocated the following: "…it is of the utmost importance that Hardee should be relieved at once. He commands the best troops in the army. I must have another commander. Taylor or Cheatham will answer…."[92]

Four days later he reiterated his opinion but altered it slightly to focus on Frank Cheatham. "…Please appoint Cheatham to command Hardee's corps. This change will promote the efficiency of the army. If Hardee is relieved Cheatham takes command by seniority of rank."[93] All of this is a matter of record. Cheatham was promoted. Hood advocated it. Davis approved it. But none of this addresses the actual question, again, did Hardee recommend it?

The real difficulty with Hood's comments is that they are unsubstantiated by any other source, and upon examination many of his assertions seem quite contradictory. It is clear that Hood blamed Hardee for many of the army's troubles and wanted to get rid of him. Why would he take Hardee's

[91] Thomas Robson Hay, "Pat Cleburne Stonewall of the West," in Irving A. Buck, *Cleburne and His Command* (1908; repr., Wilmington NC: Broadfoot Publishing, 1995).

[92] OR, ser. 1, vol. 39, pt. 2, p. 832.

[93] OR, ser. 1, vol. 39, pt. 2, p. 842.

advice on anything? Hood and Davis did confer with Bragg on the matter, and earlier in the war Bragg had endorsed Cleburne's promotion.[94]

The only claim that indicates Hardee recommended Cheatham comes from Hood himself. Hood's memoirs were not published until 1880, seven years after Hardee had died. His post-war writings are clearly biased in his own favor, and any later statement to the effect that Cleburne was Hardee's true preference would have cast considerable doubt on both Hood's judgment and his honesty. Without concrete evidence to the contrary, it simply cannot be determined what, if anything, William Hardee really said. His rejection of Cleburne's ability to command is possible, but not very likely.

Hood's biographer, Richard M. McMurry, asserts that Cleburne was victimized by the strife within the Confederate government. Commenting on the promotions of both Lee and Cheatham, he wrote:

> Lee had many desirable qualities, but he was even younger than Hood and had had less experience commanding large bodies of troops than the Texan had had when he was given a corps the preceding winter. Perhaps it would have been better to have chosen Patrick R. Cleburne as the army's new lieutenant general. Indeed, one wonders why Hood and Hardee chose Cheatham rather than Cleburne as the division commander best qualified to lead a corps. Cleburne was a victim of the internal politics of the army, which did so much to make it impossible for anyone successfully to command the Army of Tennessee.[95]

The 15 August 1864 edition of the New York *Herald* quoted the Charleston *Daily Courier* in an assessment of Cheatham's promotion: "Cheatham is only a fighter, not a general, and a better horse jockey than either. Cleburne, who has been raised to the rank of Major-General against a great deal of opposition, is perhaps the best man in Hood's army at this time, at least possessed of more of the sterling qualities of a man and experience as a soldier."[96]

---

[94] Losson, *Forgotten Warriors,* 197.

[95] McMurry, *John Bell Hood,* 137.

[96] *Charleston Daily Courier,* 15 August 1864.

While this no doubt criticizes Cheatham too harshly, the fact remains that the commentaries of the day supported Cleburne in overwhelming fashion. To attribute the sequence of promotion solely to seniority would be a mistake. Hood ranked Cleburne, but Cleburne ranked Stewart and Lee, and Cheatham's commission as major general preceded not only Cleburne, Stewart, and Lee but Hood as well. Hood, Stewart, and Lee had graduated from West Point; Cleburne had not. Cleburne had authored the proposal to arm and free the slaves. His talent clearly exceeded the men above him. Unfortunately, he could only watch their promotions from a distance. With Jefferson Davis and Braxton Bragg in Richmond, he had gone as far as he could go.

As the year progressed, Cleburne's memorial gained supporters. On 17 October a convention was held in Augusta, Georgia, in order to assess the state of the Confederacy. Governors William Smith of Virginia, Zebulon B. Vance of North Carolina, Joseph E. Brown of Georgia, A. C. Magrath of South Carolina, and Charles Clark of Mississippi offered a resolution that stated that "the course of the enemy in appropriating our slaves who happen to fall into their hands to purposes of war, seems to justify a change of policy on our part."[97] They did not, however, envision the changes Cleburne had suggested. He knew the South was losing the war. He knew that partial solutions would never solve a problem of this magnitude, and he fervently believed that strong moral principles grounded his proposal. It was only just to offer freedom to a man who was willing to fight for it; therefore freedom was the proper inducement. Cleburne was sincere when he stated that "the very magnitude of the sacrifice itself, such as no nation has ever voluntarily made before, would apal [sic] our enemies, destroy his spirit and his finances, and fill our hearts with a pride and singleness of purpose which would clothe us with new strength in battle."[98]

The private from Ireland had the skill to become a general in America. Pat Cleburne would soon give his life for a cause he thought was just. He learned to read the face of Dixie, but he could not see its soul. Many opinions were offered both for and against this proposal. Some arguments were weaker than others. Regardless of the reader's view as to what effect this measure might have had on the outcome of the war, the fact remains that the South needed men. It may well have failed, but the idea was never attempted.

---

[97] Purdue and Purdue, *Pat Cleburne Confederate General,* 275.
[98] "Negroes in Our Army," 225.

12

ATLANTA

When the campaign for Atlanta began, the Army of Tennessee had a new commander. With Bragg's resignation Jefferson Davis was forced to name a replacement. The position was offered to Hardee, but he declined. He agreed to assume temporary control in December, but only with the understanding that he would yield to a permanent successor. The lack of a suitable candidate created a problem in Richmond. Robert E. Lee would never leave Virginia, and Davis found both Beauregard and Longstreet unacceptable. Despite their mutual dislike, Davis realized that Joseph Johnston was the only lieutenant general available.[1] The Virginian arrived on 27 December and took command one day later.

He found the army in disarray. Though their confidence had been destroyed under Bragg, Johnston gave the men in the ranks new hope. Private Sam Watkins described his personal reaction to the appointment: "He was the very picture of a general. But he found the army depleted by battles; and worse, yea, much worse, by desertion. The men were deserting by tens and hundreds, and I might say by thousands. The morale of the army was gone. The spirit of the soldiers was crushed, their hope gone. The future was dark and gloomy. They would not answer at roll call. Discipline had gone. A feeling of mistrust pervaded the whole army."[2]

In winter quarters there was little military activity, but the new year began with a celebration. Joseph Hardee had fallen in love with Mary Foreman Lewis of Demopolis, Alabama, and the twenty-six-year-old accepted his proposal of

---

[1] Albert Castel, *Decision in the West* (Lawrence: University of Kansas Press, 1992) 29–31; William J. Hardee to Samuel Cooper, 30 November 1863, OR, ser. 1, vol. 31 pt. 3, pp. 764–65; Steven E. Woodworth, *Jefferson Davis and His Generals* (Lawrence: University of Kansas Press, 1990) 302.

[2] Samuel R. Watkins, *Co. Aytch* (Dayton OH: Morningside, 1982) 111–12; J. P. Austin, *The Blue and the Gray* (Atlanta: Franklin Printing and Publishing Co., 1899) 118–19; Philip D. Stephenson, "Reminiscences," in *Southern Historical Society Papers*, 52 vols. (Millwood NY: Kraus Reprint Co., 1977) 12:39.

marriage. The ceremony would take place on 13 January at the home of the bride's brother, Major Ivey Lewis of the Jeff Davis (cavalry) Legion. In perhaps the greatest honor he could bestow, Hardee asked Cleburne to be the best man. The two men departed for Alabama and on their way they stayed at the home of Cleburne's old friend, Charles Nash. Qualified physicians were in short supply, so Dr. Nash had been placed in charge of the Confederate Marine Hospital in Selma.

Several officers were present at the service, one of whom was Robert Tarleton, a lieutenant stationed at Fort Morgan in Mobile Bay. His twenty-four-year-old sister Susan was the maid of honor. Tarleton was not completely unfamiliar with Cleburne's career, as he had been a friend of Leonard Mangum's since they were at Princeton together. After the festivities concluded, the party boarded a steamboat on the north edge of town for a trip down the scenic Tombigbee River. The west bank was lined with evergreens in stark contrast to the high bluffs above the opposite shore. While the general was most certainly impressed by the grandeur surrounding him, he was most captivated by Miss Tarleton. The national upheaval seemed to make romance impossible, but it was here that their courtship began.

The experience was quite a change from the dreary routine of a camp in the Confederate Army. For one day life was filled with paneled sleeping quarters, an elegant dining room, luxurious halls, and thick carpets. In the aft portion of the boat a grand piano stood among gilded mirrors. The voyage itself lasted only twenty-four hours, but Cleburne remained in Mobile for eleven days. He stayed at the Battle House Hotel, where he could walk to the Tarleton home along broad streets lined with magnolias. The house was a two-story structure that sat at the corner of St. Louis and Claiborne streets, with a private garden in the back. The sympathies of the household were divided. Susan's father had come to the South from New Hampshire, and while he was not an active supporter of the Northern war effort, he was a Unionist at heart. The remainder of the family was strongly Confederate, and Patrick was always a welcome guest.[3]

On Saturday afternoon, 23 January, a "grand review" of the forces in Mobile was conducted. Several thousand infantry were accompanied by cavalry and artillery for the two-and-one-half hour procession down Government

---

[3] Howell and Elizabeth Purdue, *Pat Cleburne Confederate General* (1973; repr., Gaithersburg MD: Olde Soldier Books, 1987) 285–86.

Street. Along with their staff officers, Cleburne and Dabney Maury rode past each regiment as they came to "present arms." The visit made a lasting impression on the city. The Mobile *Daily Advertiser and Register* noted, "The appearance of the hero of Ringgold Gap is not easily forgotten."[4]

Cleburne's absence was short-lived, and only one week later he was back at Tunnel Hill.[5] In a letter to his sister dated 9 February 1864, Irving Buck painted a picture of a new man: "Gen. Cleburne...says he had a wonderful time. Rumor says that he lost his heart with a young lady in Mobile. He has been in a heavenly mood and talks about another leave, already."[6]

On 4 February John B. Hood arrived in Dalton to take charge of Hindman's corps. Hindman had taken the corps after Bragg's departure, although he had hoped to be reassigned to the Trans-Mississippi department. He tendered his resignation, but when Davis refused to accept it he returned to his former position.[7]

The time spent in Alabama had been a welcome respite from military matters, but upon his return Cleburne faced a serious problem. Many of the three-year men's terms were about to expire and the Army of Tennessee could ill afford to lose them. Federal gunboats had seized control of the Mississippi River, and there were soldiers from Texas and Arkansas who had not heard from their families in over a year. Speculation was rampant, then gave way to images of poverty and hardship. Pat Cleburne, however, was a true leader. His strength of character and single-mindedness of purpose had a profound effect upon his men. Despite uncertainty at home and grim prospects in Georgia, every man in the division reenlisted.[8]

---

[4] *Mobile Daily Advertiser and Register,* 23 January 1864, 2; *Mobile Daily Advertiser and Register,* 24 January 1864, 3.

[5] Purdue and Purdue, *Pat Cleburne Confederate General,* 286.

[6] Irving Buck to Lucie Buck, 9 February 1864, Buck Papers, Southern Historical Collection, University of North Carolina, Chapel Hill.

[7] Diane Neal and Thomas W. Kremm, *Lion of the South: General Thomas C. Hindman* (Macon GA: Mercer University Press, 1993) 191–92; John B. Hood, *Advance and Retreat* (1880; repr., Edison NJ: Blue and Gray Press, 1985) 67–68.

[8] William J. Hardee, "Biographical Sketch of Major-General Patrick R. Cleburne," *New Orleans Times Picayune,* 12–19 July 1903, in *Southern Historical Society Papers,* 52 vols. (Millwood NY: Kraus Reprint Co., 1977) 31:151–65; Thomas R. Hay, "The South and the Arming of the Slaves," *Mississippi Valley Historical Review* 6/1 (June 1919): 39–40.

The relative quiet of the winter months allowed Cleburne to refine some of his earlier ideas. During this time his contingent of sharpshooters became more organized under the leadership of Lieutenant A. B. Schell. The corps had its own wagon and reported directly to division headquarters, bypassing lengthy channels of communication. The elite assignment was both dangerous and prestigious. Casualties were high but losses were quickly filled. A shipment of Whitworths had arrived from England, and along with sixteen Kerr rifles that had been manufactured in Macon, Cleburne was able to fully equip forty-six marksmen.[9]

On 3 February Sherman had taken over 20,000 men from Vicksburg in an attempt to capture Meridian. The town itself had a population of only 800 inhabitants, but it contained repair shops, barracks, an arsenal, and several warehouses full of military supplies. In addition, railroad connections ran to Selma and Mobile. At the same time, Sherman ordered William Sooy Smith to bring 7,000 additional troops down from Memphis. The idea was to drive Leonidas Polk out of the theatre altogether, and just as Sherman had hoped, the bishop reacted to the threat by retreating to Demopolis. The Federals entered Meridian on 14 February with very little opposition. From Joseph Johnston's perspective the sheer weight of numbers would shortly overwhelm the Army of Mississippi, so on 22 February Hardee's corps was sent to Dalton where they boarded trains bound for Alabama.[10]

The Federal plans soon began to fall apart. With only 2,500 men, Forrest intercepted Smith and drove him back to Memphis. This caused Sherman to cancel the advance, and he returned to Vicksburg. When Polk learned that the danger had passed he sent word to Hardee that reinforcements were no longer necessary. Polk had acted promptly, but by the time the information was received Cleburne's division had become strung out over a very large area. Some of his men were still in Dalton while others had made it all the way to Montgomery. It was decided to concentrate at one point, and by 25 February they had reassembled in Atlanta.

The opening of the Atlanta campaign centered on a topographical formation in North Georgia known as Rocky Face Ridge. The ridge itself ran north and south, broken by three gaps that offered access to the east. Its sharp

---

[9] Irving A. Buck, *Cleburne and His Command* (1908; repr., Wilmington NC: Broadfoot Publishing, 1995) 201.

[10] Castel, *Decision in the West*, 49.

rise extended 14 miles in length, with Dalton only 3 miles from its center. Three miles to the northwest, the Western and Atlantic Railroad passed through Mill Creek Gap. Roughly equidistant but to the southwest was Dug Gap. Further south was Snake Creek Gap, the possession of which would place Sherman on the Confederate flank.[11] Johnston recognized the vulnerability of the position and had already fortified the ground from Rocky Face east to Crow Valley.[12] Jacob Cox described the surrounding terrain from the Union position:

> The eastern barrier of this region is Rocky Face Ridge, a continuous wall of quartz rock with precipitous faces, flanked on the west by a subordinate ridge, through which, at Tunnel Hill, the railway pierces and runs southeasterly through a gorge in Rocky Face known as Mill Creek Gap, the towering sides of which are called the Buzzard's Roost. Mill Creek winds southeasterly five or six miles after passing the gap and flows into a branch of the Connesauga River, a tributary of the Oostenaula. Dalton lies about a mile south of Mill Creek; through it, and upon the same side of the Connesauga, the railway passes, Tilton and Resaca being the neighboring villages and stations, the latter at the crossing of the Oostenaula, and about twelve or fourteen miles from Dalton. Rocky Face extends some three miles north of Mill Creek Gap, or a little further than Tunnel Hill, where it breaks into smaller hills.[13]

George Thomas was in Chattanooga and directed Union movements in Sherman's absence. He learned of Hardee's detachment and on 24 and 25 February drove in Confederate outposts. Federal troops attacked the area in front of Mill Creek Gap near Dalton but when they were repulsed Thomas was convinced that Johnston held the area in force. Against this display of strength he felt that he had no choice but to fall back to his base.

---

[11] Purdue and Purdue, *Pat Cleburne Confederate General,* 291–92.

[12] Richard M. McMurry, "Resaca: 'A Heap of Hard Fiten,'" *Civil War Times Illustrated* 9/7 (November 1970): 4–15.

[13] Jacob D. Cox, *Atlanta* (1882; repr., Wilmington NC: Broadfoot Publishing, 1989) 29–30.

Hiram Granbury's brigade was the first to return from Alabama, so on the night of 25 February the men were sent to the foot of the mountain. Granbury advanced just after sunrise, but when he discovered that the enemy camps were abandoned, he rejoined the rest of the division at Mill Creek, 3 miles east of Dalton on Middle Spring Road. Cleburne remained there for two months, during which time there were some changes in command. Ranking from 29 February, Granbury and Govan were promoted to brigadiers general. Govan took the Arkansas troops as St. John Liddell was transferred to the Trans-Mississippi. Granbury assumed control of the Texans while James Smith recovered from the severe wound he had suffered at Missionary Ridge.[14]

Jefferson Davis believed that the wisest course of action to ensure the safety of Georgia was to mount a campaign that would drive the Federals back into Tennessee. In order to accomplish his objective he needed an aggressive general who would be willing to fight, but Johnston continued to sound a note of caution. He maintained that the army was not prepared to begin offensive operations, and he pointed out that when he arrived he could put only 36,000 men in the field.[15]

Hood, on the other hand, was trying to persuade Davis that the army was strong enough in its present condition. William Hardee had already served at the head of the army, and he did not share Hood's enthusiasm. In a 17 December letter to Samuel Cooper, he painted a disappointing picture:

> To…enable this army to take the field, re-enforcements are necessary…an increase in the strength of this command would enable the commanding general to take the field, and by celerity of movement to avail himself of the dispersion of the enemy's forces, to strike an opportune blow upon his weakest line of resistance with our masses; or should he concentrate and advance our general commanding would oppose to him an active and vigorous resistance. But in our present condition it is necessary to avoid a general action….[16]

---

[14] Buck, *Cleburne and His Command*, 202–203.

[15] Nathaniel C. Hughes, *General William J. Hardee: Old Reliable* (Baton Rouge: Louisiana State University Press, 1965) 181.

[16] US War Department, comp., *The War of the Rebellion: A Compilation of the Official Records of the Union and Confederate Armies*, 128 vols. (Washington, DC: Government Printing Office, 1880–1901) ser. 1, vol. 31, pt. 3, p. 839–40.

Although Hardee did not specify the numbers at hand, even Bragg expressed reservations about the army's offensive capabilities. He wrote Davis on 2 December in the following language: "Let us concentrate all our available men, unite them with this gallant little army, still full of zeal and burning to redeem its lost character and prestige, and...if practicable, march the whole upon the enemy."[17]

Not only did these evaluations of the army's condition support Johnston's assertions over the next several months, but they also endorsed the approach Johnston would take throughout the campaign until he was replaced in July. This was hardly well received in Richmond, but in light of the fact that the Confederates had taken heavy losses at Chickamauga and Chattanooga, the president decided to be patient. However, as the weather improved Johnston's reluctance to move caused mounting frustration. By March it seemed as if the numbers should have increased substantially, yet Davis saw nothing but requests for more men.

There was a very fundamental difference in the philosophies of the two men. Johnston had always favored the health of his men over the occupation of land. He pointed out that a defeat north of the Tennessee River would destroy his army, but if he experienced a setback in Georgia the troops could simply fall back along the Western and Atlantic Railroad to Atlanta. On the other hand, Davis insisted that all territory must be held. This disagreement provided Hood with the opportunity to advance his own aims.

While Johnston and Davis were occupied with each other, Hood was busy composing letters. On 7 March he wrote the President:

My Dear Sir: I have delayed writing to you so as to allow myself time to see the condition of this army. On my arrival I found the enemy threatening our position. I was, however, delighted to find our troops anxious for battle.... We should march to the front as soon as possible, so as not to allow the enemy to concentrate and advance upon us. The addition of a few horses for our artillery will place this army in fine condition. It is well clothed, well fed, and the transportation is excellent and the greatest possible quantity required.

---

[17] OR, ser. 1, vol. 52, pt. 2, p. 568.

I feel that a move from this position, in sufficient force, will relieve our entire country.... I sincerely hope and trust that this opportunity may be given to drive the enemy beyond the limits of the Confederacy.... He is at present weak, and we are strong.... I am eager for us to take the initiative, but fear we will not do so unless our army is increased.[18]

Three days later he wrote a similar note to Secretary of War James Seddon: "My Dear Sir:... I am an earnest friend to the President and am ever willing to express to him my ideas in regard to the approaching campaign.... I am very much pleased with the condition of our army, as I expressed to the President. After the enemy concentrates his forces our chance of success will be in having an opportunity to strike him in case he should divide his forces. But we have a sufficient number of troops, if thrown together, to defeat his entire army...."[19]

These letters played right into the wishful thinking that was so prevalent in the capital. Hood was able to convince Davis that the problem was one not of logistics but with the commander in charge. On 13 April he penned another note, this time to Bragg. Although it was marked "Private," Hood must have known that it would reach the president's desk.

My Dear General: I received your letter, and am sorry to inform you that I have done all in my power to induce General Johnston to accept the proposition you made to move forward. He will not consent, as he desires the troops to be sent here and it is left to him as to what use should be made of them.

I regret this exceedingly, as my heart was fixed upon our going to the front and regaining Tennessee and Kentucky. I have also had a long talk with General Hardee. While he finds many difficulties in the way of our advancing, he is at the same time ready and willing to do anything that is thought best for our general good. He has written a long letter to the President, which will explain his views, &c....[20]

---

[18] OR, ser. 1, vol. 32, pt. 3, p. 606–607.
[19] OR, ser. 1, vol. 32, pt. 3, p. 606.
[20] OR, ser. 1, vol. 32, pt. 3, p. 781.

Hood's sentiments were no doubt strengthened in March in a letter written by William Pendleton following an evaluation of the artillery. It was addressed to Johnston, but it is unlikely that the letters existence was unknown in Richmond. After a series of generally positive remarks, Pendleton ended, " In conclusion, my belief is decided that your artillery, thus adjusted and well commanded, will prove greatly efficient and powerfully contribute to the great victory which this army is, by the blessing of Providence, destined, I trust, to achieve at no distant day."[21]

The tone of Hood's communications was not one of a subordinate under Joseph Johnston, but rather the communications sought to persuade Jefferson Davis that the actual state of the army was a good one; but for the want of a proper leader, victory was within his grasp. Despite Hood's protests to the contrary, his actions clearly indicated that he was after control of the army.[22]

Despite superior talent, Pat Cleburne had no such aspirations. His simple modesty endeared him to his men, and while the high command suffered from internal dissent the rank and file gave him one of his most prized possessions. On 18 April his cherished 15th Arkansas presented him with a ceremonial sword that had come through the blockade from Bermuda. Every man contributed to the extravagant purchase, which Irving Buck described in *Cleburne and His Command* as "a fine Damascus blade in polished steel scabbard, the hilt bearing the device of a shamrock, and the belt rings and bands being solid gold, as was a plate, on the scabbard, surmounted by the 'Harp of Erin' upon which was the simple inscription 'To Major-General P. R. Cleburne, from his old regiment, Fifteenth Arkansas.'"[23]

The Confederates had attempted to strengthen their forces over the winter, but there was still a grave disparity in numbers. According to the returns of 30 April, Johnston could put only 43,887 men in the field. He listed his strength as follows: Staff and Engineers: 596, Hardee's corps:

---

[21] OR, ser. 1, vol. 32, pt. 3, p. 684–86.

[22] Thomas L. Connelly, *Autumn of Glory: The Army of Tennessee 1862–1865* (Baton Rouge: Louisiana State University Press, 1971) 321–22.

[23] The account given by Captain Buck was written in 1908, at that point his memory may have been in error. His version of the presentation has been accepted in good faith by other historians, however the author has chosen to rely upon the diary entry of R. D. Smith, an artillerist in Polk's brigade who actually witnessed the ceremony. His eyewitness account is well documented and all information is courtesy of the Atlanta History Center, which is currently in possession of the sword.

19,311, Hood's corps: 19,201, Cantey's division, currently in Rome: 1,543, Cavalry: 2,419, Artillery Reserve: 817, for a total of 43,887. After this report was prepared, Mercer's 63rd Georgia regiment joined the army with 814 effectives. The 37th Mississippi was currently en route to the army, though it had not yet arrived. Its strength was estimated at "about 400." The Army of Tennessee was now divided into two corps, one under Hardee and the other under Hood, who had been promoted to lieutenant general on 1 February, to rank from 20 September. The cavalry was given to Joe Wheeler. With the arrival of Leonidas Polk's corps from Mississippi, as well as several smaller units, Johnston would have roughly 63,000 men on hand, but they were not all in camp until the middle of May.[24] As of the same date, Sherman listed an effective force of 110,123 men of all arms. Within one month the number would grow by another 3,000.

Rocky Face Ridge

By the beginning of May Sherman realized that the campaign for Atlanta was about to begin. He looked to the south and assessed the situation. Rocky Face Ridge was an imposing sight. It stood 1,500 feet high, with sheer walls on the western side that were almost perpendicular. However, an appearance of strength masked the true weakness of the position. The north end of the ridge was open, so while it was very difficult to assault from the west, a Union force moving from Tennessee would encounter no significant obstructions. The penetration of any one of the gaps would almost certainly capture the railroad.[25]

Dalton itself was well fortified and essentially impregnable, but the Confederate line was not a strong one. Snake Creek Gap opened up into Sugar Valley only 6 miles from Resaca. The Western and Atlantic Railroad ran parallel to the ridge, not perpendicular to it. While this sheltered the railroad from attack, it also disguised Federal movements from Johnston's observation and kept the tracks within easy striking distance. This geographical weakness made Dalton easy to turn, even though it was heavily fortified. Johnston

---

[24] Confederate field returns, 30 April 1864, Robert Underwood Johnston and Clarence Clough Buel, eds., *Battles and Leaders of the Civil War,* 4 vols. (1884–1887; repr., Secaucus NJ: Castle Books, n.d.) 4:281–82.

[25] William R. Scaife, *The Campaign for Atlanta* (Atlanta: Civil War Publications, 1993) 7.

compounded his error by failing to defend Snake Creek Gap. His chief-of-staff, W. W. Mackall, contended that the mistake was due to "disobedience of orders," but he did not volunteer the name of the guilty party. Some evidence suggests that he may have been referring to Wheeler, particularly his poor reconnaissance during the spring.[26] Regardless, the disposition of his forces made it clear that either Johnston was unaware of the gap's location or he did not consider it a liability. Either explanation would have been inexcusable.[27]

The campaign for Atlanta was unsurpassed in its dependence upon the railroads. Once the Federals left Chattanooga, they could no longer depend upon the Tennessee River as a source of provisions. During the winter great stores were stockpiled in Nashville while Chattanooga had been turned into a forward base of supplies, but the Union army was still heavily exposed to any disruption in their rear. Lee, Johnston, Hardee, and Polk urged Davis to give Forrest the latitude to destroy Sherman's communications, but the president overreacted to activity in Memphis and Forrest was sent into West Tennessee.

Sherman constantly worried over the safety of the railroad. His high regard for the former slave trader was expressed in a letter to Secretary of War Edwin Stanton: "...Forrest is the devil, and I think he has got some of our troops under cower. I have two officers at Memphis who will fight all the time—A. J. Smith and Mower. The latter is a young brigadier of fine promise, and I commend him to your notice. I will order them to make up a force and go out to follow Forrest to the death, if it costs ten thousand lives and breaks the Treasury. *There will never be peace in Tennessee until Forrest is dead.*"[28]

On 7 May the Federal advance began in earnest. Johnston responded by spreading his forces. A. P. Stewart's division placed his left flank in Mill Creek Gap and extended his lines to the north until he met Frank Cheatham at the end of Rocky Face Ridge. Carter Stevenson and Thomas Hindman encamped along the Cleveland Road in Crow Valley, east of Cheatham's

---

[26] Connelly, *Autumn of Glory*, 338.

[27] Richard M. McMurry, "The General's Tour: The Atlanta Campaign: Rocky Face to the Dallas Line, the Battles of May 1864," *Blue and Gray* 6/4 (April 1989): 17–18.

[28] Andrew Lytle, *Bedford Forrest and his Critter Company* (New York: McDowell, Obolensky, 1960) 304–305; Robert Selph Henry, *Forrest: First with the Most* (1944; repr., Wilmington NC: Broadfoot Publishing, 1991) 307.

division. South of the gap William Bate's division held the ridge, with W. H. T. Walker and Pat Cleburne in reserve around Dalton.[29]

Although he had his opponent pinned in an untenable position, Sherman had problems of his own. The political ramifications of the campaign were enormous. It was imperative for the Federals to win at Atlanta, as sentiment was growing in the North for a peaceful end to a horrible tragedy. While Sherman had to deliver a victory, Johnston had merely to avoid a loss. He could afford to stall for time. Making matters worse, many of the Federal three-year enlistments were about to end as well, and the will to fight among the rank and file was beginning to evaporate. By this point the soldiers were thinking of their return home. They had little desire to risk their lives in a war they never understood in the first place.

George Thomas had received orders to "threaten Buzzard Roost," the colloquial name for the high walls of Mill Creek Gap. Finding it well protected, he was unable to attack. Johnston correctly supposed that Sherman would have to advance along the lines of the Western and Atlantic, so the Confederates dammed the creek. This formed a lake over the only passage through the gap. The steep sides were lined with infantry supported by massed artillery. On the north end of Rocky Face 4 miles from Dalton another line of fortifications connected the ridge with high ground overlooking the East Tennessee Railway. The works then turned again to protect the east side of town.

Thomas recognized the futility of a direct assault and had already told Sherman that the position might be turned by sending McPherson through Snake Creek Gap. He pointed out that this would offer a route to either Resaca or Calhoun and force Johnston to leave his fortifications. Six miles to the south, Geary's division of Hooker's XX Corps moved from Trickum to Dug Gap. His immediate orders were to attack the gap, but the mission was twofold. He was to take the gap if possible, but equally important was the goal to occupy the Confederates so that they could not shift any troops to oppose McPherson.[30]

John Geary made his approach just before 4:00 P.M. and sent two brigades into the 6-mile passage. Charles Candy led 2,846 men on the left

---

[29] Connelly, *Autumn of Glory*, 334; Cox, *Atlanta*, 38; Castel, *Decision in the West*, 129–30.

[30] Cox, *Atlanta*, 31–32.

with 1,762 Yankees under Adolphus Buschbeck on the right. Though the Confederates were heavily outnumbered, the difficult terrain negated the Union advantage. It forced Candy and Buschbeck together and greatly reduced the power of the assault. They reached the summit twice but were forced back each time.[31]

Despite the setbacks, Geary still felt it was possible to secure the area before more Confederates could arrive. He sent the 33rd New Jersey to a location half a mile to the south, which appeared to be undefended. They came upon a sheer wall of rock, but on their left they found a more accessible incline. Rifled artillery shelled the crest of the ridge and the 33rd was able to reach the top. Loud cheers encouraged their comrades, but when they tried to break the lines for a third time they were handily repulsed. Both sides were beginning to struggle. The Federals had not been able to capture any ground, and the Rebels were badly fatigued and almost out of ammunition. The gap was held by only two regiments of Arkansas dismounted cavalry from D. H. Reynolds's brigade, along with 800 dismounted troopers from Warren Grigsby's 9th Kentucky. In total, the Confederates numbered only 1,050 men while Geary had 4,500.[32]

Reinforcements, however, were on the way. Cleburne and Hardee rode ahead of Granbury and Lowrey's brigades. They saw the danger and sent orders to Granbury to bring his men forward at the double-quick. Followed by Lowrey, the Texans quickly took control of the gap and allowed the cavalry to fall back down the slope. The Federals continued to lob shells onto the ridge but without any noticeable effect. Soon darkness fell and the first actual fight of the campaign came to a close. The Confederates had managed to stave off disaster. A breakthrough at this point could well have turned Johnston's flank and resulted in a calamitous defeat. Instead, Dug Gap was in Southern hands and casualties had been very slight. Their losses were estimated at "less than twenty" while Geary reported 357.[33] The next morning Cleburne moved to the western base of the ridge and threw out his pickets. While no battle took

---

[31] Report of John W. Geary, 15 September 1864, OR, ser. 1, vol. 38, pt. 2, p. 115.

[32] Castel, *Decision in the West,* 133–34.

[33] Robert H. Dacus, "Reminiscences of Company H, First Arkansas Mounted Rifles," in *Echoes of Glory,* Larry M. Strayer, and Richard M. Baumgartner, eds., (Huntington WV: Blue Acorn Press. 1991) 69–70; report of John W. Geary, 15 September 1864, OR, ser. 1, vol. 38, pt. 2, p. 114–17; report of Daniel Cameron, 16 July 1864, OR, ser. 1, vol. 38, pt. 3, p. 720–21.

place, he was able to bring in his wounded and capture some small arms that had been discarded during Geary's retreat.[34] Johnston finally learned that two Federal corps had moved to Snake Creek Gap. He sent Hood, along with parts of Cleburne's, Walker's, and Hindman's divisions, to return to Resaca. Johnston continued to adjust his forces, and one day later Hood was ordered back to Dalton while Cleburne and Walker remained at Tilton.[35]

Although Cleburne's timely arrival had held off Geary, the Federals still had the upper hand. The badly broken ground rendered the area virtually uninhabitable and dense woods lined the walls, creating a dark, narrow pass some 5 miles long. It provided an opening to the rear of Johnston's entire army, yet inexplicably it was not defended. McPherson would have liked to bring his troops together, but as many were still en route he gave orders to attack in the morning. Sherman's overall plan was to cut off Johnston from Atlanta, thereby eliminating his base of supplies. The Federals were moving nicely on Snake Creek Gap, but he wondered why they had not encountered more resistance. He feared that Johnston had left only a small force near Dalton in order to strike McPherson when he was most vulnerable.[36]

Upon hearing that McPherson held a strong position in the east mouth of Snake Creek Gap, Sherman ordered Howard's IV Corps to hold Johnston in place at Dalton while he sent the remainder of McPherson's army forward. At first glance this was one of the greatest opportunities of the entire war, as the Yankees had approached the passage undetected. However, McPherson believed that he did not have the necessary support, so he hesitated and fell back to consolidate his forces. Had he continued it is quite likely that the Army of Tennessee would have been either captured or destroyed. Objectively, he did not know the strength of Johnston's army, where it was located, or the nature of the terrain; there were no reinforcements; and he knew that if he were trapped the entire campaign could be lost. Sherman was devastated, but upon reflection he was forced to admit that McPherson had chosen the wiser course of action.

At 1:00 A.M. on 10 May, Cleburne was directed to move to the junction of the Sugar Valley and Dug Gap roads. When he arrived he received additional orders to move toward Resaca, but by this time the Confederates

---

[34] Report of Daniel Cameron, 16 July 1864, OR, ser. 1, vol. 38, pt. 3 p. 720–21.
[35] Connelly, *Autumn of Glory*, 340; McMurry, "Resaca," 10.
[36] Castel, *Decision in the West*, 135.

were far apart. Grigsby had been sent to Snake Creek Gap while the 1st and 2nd Arkansas remained at Dug Gap. Cleburne took Granbury and Lowrey and moved to within 1 mile of Resaca, where he waited three hours before receiving further orders to return to his original position. Govan and Polk joined him and they made camp at sundown.[37]

In response to McPherson's aggression, Cleburne moved along the Sugar Valley Road in the direction of Resaca. Johnston was still unsure of Sherman's intentions, so he instructed Hood to leave the town and rejoin the rest of the army. However, at 9:00 A.M. he received a report from his cavalry stating that the Federals were moving on Resaca in force. Johnston ordered Hood to retrace his steps and alerted Cleburne to be ready to move in that direction. Cheatham was to prepare his troops to shift from Rocky Face Ridge and replace Cleburne at Dug Gap. Upon Hood's report that there was no activity in the area, Johnston cancelled his orders and Cleburne remained where he was.[38]

Sherman was hoping to force an immediate retreat but Johnston refused to panic. He knew that he held interior lines, and the narrow width of Snake Creek Gap would prevent a rapid advance. The Confederates remained at Dalton until the evening of 12 May, when the infantry and artillery were withdrawn. The cavalry formed the rear guard and did not leave until the next morning.[39] Close to 10:00 A.M. the Rebels moved from Dalton to Resaca, where Johnston placed his army in a semicircle anchored on two rivers. Leonidas Polk's corps held the left, aligned on the Oostenaula. Hardee held the center with Hood on the right, resting his flank on the Connesauga. The Federals did manage to advance in front of Polk, but the action that day was little more than skirmish fire.

Resaca

Cleburne's division formed the center of Hardee's line with Bate on his right and Cheatham on his left. The army went into position along the crest of a hill and breastworks were constructed. In their front was a valley several hundred yards wide. Using considerably poor judgment, Cleburne decided to

---

[37] Report of Daniel Cameron, 16 July 1864, OR, ser. 1, vol. 38, pt. 3 p. 720–21.

[38] Connelly, *Autumn of Glory,* 340; Castel, *Decision in the West,* 145–46.

[39] Buck, *Cleburne and His Command,* 210.

examine the heavily wooded ground in his front on foot. It was quickly occupied and the Confederates were very fortunate Cleburne was not captured.

The action opened at 6:00 A.M. and spread along the entire front. The principal thrust came against Hindman's division, but the Yankees continued to bring up reinforcements in front of Cleburne. They took high ground and the artillery opened fire. Federal officers shouted encouragement, reminding the men that just as they had stormed Missionary Ridge, they could take this position as well. All of their exhortations were in vain. Despite a series of repeated attempts, the Federals were unable to break Cleburne's line.[40]

The Confederate position at Resaca was almost impregnable in the face of a frontal attack, but it did have one weakness. The Connesauga and Oostenaula rivers were at their backs, allowing a relatively small force to dictate Johnston's movements. Sherman soon discovered his advantage and sent Thomas Sweeny's division across Lay's Ferry. This would be the Union strategy throughout the campaign. They would hold the Confederates in place with a presence in their front, then throw an equally strong force on the flank that would compel Joe Johnston to retreat.[41]

The Federals had superior numbers, but their preparation was careless. A cavalry reconnaissance revealed that the Union left was "in the air," and Johnston determined that it was feasible to encircle their flank. The series of retreats had opened the Western and Atlantic to the enemy, and it was imperative to prevent it from falling into Sherman's hands. Johnston ordered Hood to take Stewart's and Stevenson's divisions along with four brigades from the center and left. The attack commenced at 6:00 P.M., and before dark the Federals had been driven off the railway.[42]

The line was finally stabilized when reinforcements arrived, but the encouraging results persuaded Johnston to continue the effort the next day. His plans changed very quickly. After nightfall Confederate pickets on the far left were driven in. Johnston received a report that the Federals had already passed around him and crossed the Oostenaula River near Lay's Ferry.

---

[40] Report of Patrick R. Cleburne, 16 August 1864, OR, ser. 1, vol. 38, pt. 2, p. 721–22.
[41] Buck, *Cleburne and His Command,* 211–12.
[42] Joseph E. Johnston, "Opposing Sherman's Advance to Atlanta," in Robert Underwood Johnston and Clarence Clough Buel, eds., *Battles and Leaders of the Civil War,* 4 vols. (1884–1887; repr., Secaucus NJ: Castle Books, n.d.) 4:265.

He reacted swiftly and dispatched W. H. T. Walker to the crossing while he cancelled the order to Hood. On 15 May there were sharp exchanges on both flanks, but the center was a duel of musketry. The left of Cleburne's division was subjected to exceedingly accurate fire, as it ran across an open hill. A very shallow rifle pit provided the only protection, and its depth forced the troops to lie flat, as any rise of a head would bring certain death. Increasing darkness brought an end to the battle of Resaca, and the losses were heavy. Though estimates vary, the total casualties numbered approximately 12,000 men, with an advantage to the South.[43]

Calhoun

Once the Federals established a base across the Oostenaula, Johnston's current position was no longer an option. Cleburne's division crossed the river at 10:00 P.M. by the trestle bridge and halted at midnight only a few miles from Calhoun. At sunrise they formed a line of defense with the right near the railroad tracks and the left on a wagon road to the south. At this point Sherman presented the Confederates with a real opportunity. He made the mistake of splitting his forces, exposing each wing to attack. One part of the army crossed the Oostenaula west of Calhoun while another followed Johnston south from Resaca. Although the river placed the Federals in jeopardy, Johnston chose not to act.

At 11 o'clock Cleburne was directed to shift to the left and rear in order to meet a Federal detachment that was threatening Walker's right. Lucius Polk's brigade held the front, with Granbury behind him. Govan formed *en echelon* on Polk's right, with Lowrey on a hill between Oothkaloga Creek and the Oostenaula River. Polk soon came in contact with skirmishers and was able to deliver an enfilading fire into the right flank. It was extremely effective but short-lived. After only a few rounds Cleburne received word that the Federals were moving in force on Calhoun, so he was ordered to pull back across the creek and into the town. Johnston continued to seek a position for defense

---

[43] McMurry ("Resaca," 48) places Union losses at 939 killed, 5,696 wounded and 170 missing, for a total of 6,805. Confederate casualties amounted to 531 killed, 3,259 wounded and 1,464 missing, for a total of 5,254, and a combined loss of 12,059 men. Scaife (*Campaign for Atlanta*, 23) offers a more general number of 12,000 men, allowing for numerous incomplete reports.

which would allow him to neutralize Sherman's numerical advantage, but thus far he had been disappointed.

Cleburne pulled his division back around 5:00 P.M. Granbury deployed on a wooded hill above the creek while Polk took a position on the right along the creek's bottom. Rifle pits were constructed for the infantry along with epaulements for an artillery battery. Govan and Lowrey were moved further south on the Adairsville Road but the Federals did not approach, allowing the Confederates eighteen hours of peace. Hampered by poor maps, Johnston was still unable to find an acceptable position. Early the next morning the army moved 8 miles to Adairsville in search of more favorable ground, and in hindsight it seemed almost as though Johnston never intended to fight at Calhoun. Cleburne moved out at 1:00 A.M. and stopped 2 miles north of town.[44]

Adairsville

By 17 May Johnston had learned of another opening. Sherman had weakened his army even further and detached more of his troops to Rome. Hardee had already started to skirmish with the Yankees who had taken ferries over the Oostenaula, and it was less than 6 miles from his position to the crossings at Resaca. Johnston could hold the Federals above the river and attack west of town.

Unfortunately for the Confederates, Johnston was still focused on defense. At 3 o'clock in the afternoon the Federals appeared in force on the railroad from Calhoun. Cheatham's division was placed along the crest of a ridge with Cleburne to the left of the road and 800 yards in the rear. Polk and Granbury formed his first line with Lowrey and Govan in support. Between Cheatham and Cleburne was an open field crossed by thick, swampy water. On Cleburne's left lay a more substantial creek, forming his weakest point. He constructed rifle pits and placed one of Lowrey's regiments on the far side of the stream. The Federals attacked Cheatham, and though his preparations had been thorough Cleburne was not involved.

As a defensive position Adairsville did show some promise. The town was surrounded by a series of ridges, many of which were over 900 feet high. The valley of Oothkaloga Creek ran through the defile, and a survey by

---

[44] Report of William S. Stewart, 6 July 1864, OR, ser. 1, vol. 38, pt. 3, p. 723.

Confederate engineers had determined that the north end was narrow enough
to control the Union approaches. Nevertheless, opinions differed as to the
proper course of action. Hardee believed that the present location was a strong
one, while Hood suggested a retreat south of the Etowah. Johnston could not
make up his mind, so he devised an alternate plan. During the night the
Confederates fell back once again, and on the march Johnston divided his
army. Where the troops left Adairsville the turnpike and the railroad split
apart. The Atlanta Road continued to the southeast until it reached Cassville,
12 miles in the distance. The railroad veered off in a southwesterly direction
toward Kingston, also 12 miles away, where it turned abruptly to the east and
completed a triangle that connected Kingston and Cassville. Hood and Polk
took the former route and reached their destination close to noon, while
Hardee accompanied the baggage train to Kingston. If Sherman decided to
follow both columns, the Federals would end up over 7 miles apart in very
mountainous country. Any communication would be lost and neither force
could assist the other.

Cassville

Hardee placed Cheatham in the lead, followed by Bate, Walker, and
Cleburne. Skirmishers protected the rear of the column, but they abandoned
their position too soon and Cleburne's rear was thrown open to attack.
Fortunately, a heavy fog had moved in during the night. While the retreat was
slow, pursuit was impossible. Cleburne left Lucius Polk at Kingston and
moved his three remaining brigades to within 2 miles of Cassville, where they
arrived early in the morning.[45]

When the Confederates set up behind the town their lines faced west,
roughly 1 mile behind it. Hardee held the left, with Polk in the center and
Hood on the right. Hood and Polk held high ground, but Hardee's corps
trailed off toward the railroad tracks. The Federals continued to follow, and by
this time Lucius Polk had rejoined the rest of the division. Cleburne crossed
the Western and Atlantic at right angles, with Walker on his right.
Ambulances and ordnance trains were sent to the rear in preparation for a
general withdrawal, made necessary by a concentration of artillery in Walker's
sector. The Georgians were particularly exposed and took heavy fire. On the

---

[45] Report of William S. Stewart, 6 July 1864, OR, ser. 1, vol. 38, pt. 3, p. 723.

night of 20 May, Johnston's orders called for a shift over the Etowah to a line on the south bank at the head of Allatoona Pass. Cleburne crossed over a bridge to Willford's Mill on Pumpkin Vine Creek, where he remained until 23 May. The Confederates established a new position over a mile away and began to fortify.[46]

Confederate actions at Cassville are open to debate. Allegedly, Johnston ordered Hood to attack the Federal left as they focused their attention on Polk. Hood advanced in a timely manner, but after marching a short distance he halted his corps. He claimed there were Federals on his flank that would threaten the safety of the army's rear. He knew that if the Confederates were encircled they would be destroyed. Johnston contended that Hood was never in danger, although there were Federal cavalry detachments as well elements of Hooker's XX Corps operating in the general area. In post-war arguments Johnston attempted to prove that Hood had thrown away a great opportunity, and Hood expended a like amount of energy to maintain his innocence.[47]

On 23 May Confederate cavalry located the enemy and discovered that Sherman was moving across the Etowah near Stilesboro. Johnston responded by ordering the army to intercept Sherman at Dallas, and the Confederates halted on a front that ran from Dallas to New Hope Church. Hood's corps remained in Allatoona while Hardee moved 8 miles to the west, giving him the extreme left of the line. Leonidas Polk took his command to Lost Mountain, halfway between Hood and Hardee. One day later Hardee and Polk pitched their tents on the road from Stilesboro to Atlanta, with Hood 4 miles from New Hope Church on the Allatoona Road. Cleburne continued, moving his division through New Hope Church until they reached Powder Springs.[48]

New Hope Church

On 25 May Cleburne retraced his steps. Just east of Dallas, Hood's corps was placed with its center at the church. Polk formed on his left and Hardee continued the line until it reached the Atlanta Road. At dark Cleburne

---

[46] Report of William S. Stewart, 6 July 1864, OR, ser. 1, vol. 38, pt. 3, p. 723.

[47] Richard M. McMurry, "Cassville," *Civil War Times Illustrated* 10/8 (December 1971): 8, Joseph E. Johnston, "General Joseph E. Johnston's Campaign in Georgia," *New Orleans Picayune*, 22 October 1893, in *Southern Historical Society Papers*, 52 vols. (Millwood NY: Kraus Reprint Co., 1977) 21:314–18.

[48] Connelly, *Autumn of Glory*, 354.

received orders to go to New Hope Church, where Hood had been fighting for several hours. He was unable to make any progress and collided with Walker's division, bringing his movement to a halt. He was forced to bring his men back into camp, and around 10:30 P.M. they went into bivouac.

Hooker hit the center of Hood's corps in a fierce rainstorm less than two hours before sundown, but each wave was thrown back with heavy loss. Much of the damage was done by A. P. Stewart's artillery, and the repulse gave the Rebels time to dig earthworks in the wet clay. By the next morning scouts had returned from Cleburne's front to report that the Federals had shifted to the northeast during the night. Light skirmishing on 26 May allowed Sherman to establish contact with his adversary, but Hooker's assaults had been costly. He had lost 3,000 men, the Confederates roughly 900.[49]

Cleburne got orders to stay in place until 4:00 A.M. on 26 May, then move to Lemuel Maulding's farmhouse on the Dallas-Atlanta Road. He reached the property at 6:30 that morning, but Johnston worried that the Federals would try to turn his right and seize the Western and Atlantic. Sherman knew that if Johnston overreacted he could move in either direction and flank the Confederates, and the prize would be his. Johnston was in fact deeply concerned about just such a movement. He transferred Cleburne to Hood's corps on a temporary basis. Cleburne moved his division to the far right of the army in support of Thomas Hindman and went into position before sundown.[50]

Pickett's Mill

Despite Johnston's efforts, the danger had not passed and the right flank was still quite vulnerable. The assignment at Pickett's Mill was simply to secure the Confederate right and prevent any movement that would force Johnston to evacuate. Cleburne had to hold a narrow front in a dense forest and protect the communications with Atlanta. After an examination of the ground it became obvious that due to the thick vines and heavy undergrowth, troops could not be moved quickly from point to point. In response Cleburne

---

[49] William Key, *The Battle of Atlanta and the Georgia Campaign* (New York: Twayne Publishers, 1958) 27; Philip L. Secrist, "Scenes of Awful Carnage," *Civil War Times Illustrated* 10/3 (June 1971): 5; Jeff Dean, "The Battle of Pickett's Mill," *Blue and Gray* 6/4 (April 1989): 29.

[50] Report of Patrick R. Cleburne, 16 August 1864, OR, ser. 1, vol. 38, pt. 2, p. 724.

organized details and cleared paths from each brigade to the rear, as well as to the adjoining brigade. These preparations stand in stark contrast to Bragg's lethargy on Missionary Ridge.

The men began to prepare fortifications and the work continued into the night. Lucius Polk held the left of Cleburne's division with Charles Swett's Mississippi artillery. One section of Thomas Key's Arkansas battery joined Polk's right with Govan's brigade. Earlier in the day Cleburne had sent Govan forward to watch the movements of the Federal columns, and at 11:00 A.M. he reported that they were shifting toward the Confederate right. Cleburne left skirmishers three-quarters of a mile in his front and brought Govan back into a series of rifle pits. The formation was extended by two 12-pounder Napoleons, also under Key. At 4:00 P.M. he ordered Granbury to form on Govan and the Texans moved forward at the double-quick. To their right was an open field; in front was a road leading north. A sharp defile ran east and west and from a position 200 yards west of Granbury, Key's guns and Govan's infantry could pour an enfilading fire on any approaching Federals.[51] Mark Lowrey and William Quarles held their brigades in reserve behind Granbury's right, with a cornfield in their front. In his official report, Cleburne described the ground: "…in front of Granbury's left was a deep ravine, the side of which next to Granbury was very steep, with occasional benches of rock, up to a line within 30 or 40 yards of Granbury's men, where it flattened into a natural glacis. This glacis was covered with trees and in most places with thick undergrowth."[52] One thousand dismounted cavalry led by John H. Kelly held the remainder of the line.[53] By 3:00 P.M., however, his skirmishers had been driven in by Federal cavalry as they moved past Pickett's Mill Creek.[54]

The Federals opposing Cleburne were under the overall command of Oliver Otis Howard. He had Thomas Wood's division of his own IV Corps in the center, with Richard Johnson's division of the XIV Corps on his left. Nathaniel McLean's division of the XXIII Corps was deployed near a wheat

---

[51] Morton E. McInvale, *The Battle of Pickett's Mill: Foredoomed to Oblivion* (Atlanta: Georgia Department of Natural Resources, 1977) 80–82; Dean, "Pickett's Mill," 31.

[52] Report of Patrick R. Cleburne, 16 August 1864, OR, ser. 1, vol. 38, pt. 2, p. 724–25; Alexis Cope, *The Fifteenth Ohio Volunteers and Its Campaigns, 1861–1865* (Columbus OH: self-published, 1916) 111.

[53] William R. Scaife, *The Battle of Pickett's Mill: A Critical Blunder* (N.p., 2004) 7.

[54] McInvale, *Pickett's Mill*, 81.

field on the right flank, but the main thrust would take place in Wood's sector. The brigades formed in two parallel lines, each one in two shoulder-to-shoulder ranks along a front 400 yards wide. William Hazen's troops would lead the attack with William Gibson behind, followed by Frederick Knefler. Hazen's first line was comprised of four Ohio regiments: from his left to right, the 124th, 93rd, 41st, and 1st. The 23rd Kentucky, 6th Indiana, and 5th and 6th Kentucky regiments made up his second line. In theory Howard had developed a sound plan of attack, but the Union effort was in trouble before it began. At 4:30 Hazen was ordered to advance, but he moved forward unsupported. Colonel Benjamin Scribner of Johnson's division thought he was supposed to support Gibson, not Hazen, and he waited until 5:00 P.M. before he moved. As a result, Hazen's protection on his left was gone, and if there was any confusion during the attack he might lose Gibson as well. Given the terrain, this was almost certain.[55]

Lieutenant Ambrose Bierce, Hazen's topographical engineer, recorded the details of their advance:

> In less than one minute the trim battalions had become simply a swarm of men struggling through the undergrowth of the forest, pushing and crowding. The front was irregularly serrated, the strongest and bravest in advance, the others following in fan-like formations, variable and inconstant, ever defining themselves anew.... The color bearers kept well to their front with their flags, aslant backwards over their shoulders. Displayed, they would have been torn to rags by the boughs of the trees. Horses were all sent to the rear; the general [Hazen] and staff and all the field officers toiled along on foot as best they could.[56]

When Hazen emerged from the woods, the trenches exploded and his brigade took heavy losses very quickly. He was caught in a trap. With Lowrey and Quarles on his left and Granbury and Key on his right, his lone brigade received a devastating fire as the men struggled through the ravine. Hazen continued to send couriers to the rear for support only to see them shot down

---

[55] Scaife, *The Campaign for Atlanta,* 7; Dean, "Pickett's Mill," 29–30.

[56] Ambrose Bierce, *Ambrose Bierce's Civil War* (1956; repr., Washington, DC: Regnery, Gateway 1988) 43.

or lose their way in a virtual jungle of closely packed trees shrouded in a thick blanket of smoke. As the battle wore on and ammunition grew thin the Federals tried to fall back, but the hailstorm was so destructive that many were unable to withdraw. Bierce continued his narrative:

> The battle, as a battle, was at an end, but there was still some slaughter that it was possible to incur before nightfall; and as the wreck of our brigade drifted back through the forest we met the brigade [Gibson's] which, had the attack been made in column, as it should have been, would have been but five minutes behind our heels, with another [brigade] five minutes behind its own. As it was, just forty-five minutes had elapsed, during which the enemy had destroyed us and was now ready to perform the same kindly office to our successors.[57]

Gibson however, was not entirely at fault. The impenetrable terrain had prevented any coordinated advance, and his brigade became hopelessly confused. As they struggled up the hill they took fire from their right as well as from their front. Pinned down, they finally had no choice but to retreat. Battle reports from the action reveal the carnage; Gibson lost 681 men, Hazen 487, and Knefler 301.[58]

Purely by chance, the Federal left was in much better shape. Instead of acting in support, Hazen's second line veered off their course and created a front much longer than originally envisioned. While the Ohioans came under attack, the line now extended into the cornfield beyond Granbury's right. The Yankees moved ahead with the 6th Indiana in the center, flanked by the 23rd and 5th Kentucky. They could not see any earthworks, and Kelly's dismounted troopers were the only Confederates in view. Skirmishers hit Kelly opposite the mill, but as soon as Scribner made contact Wheeler sent a regiment of William Humes' brigade in on Kelly's right.[59]

Scribner drove in Humes and took the ground on Granbury's flank. Some of the Federals had actually penetrated 40 yards into the Confederate

---

[57] Dean, "Pickett's Mill," 33.
[58] Castel, *Decision in the West*, 241; Dean, "Pickett's Mill," 33.
[59] McInvale, *Pickett's Mill*, 86.

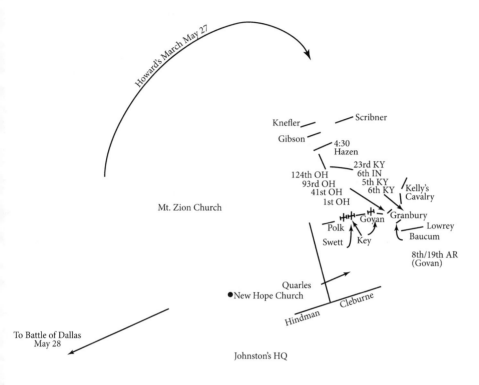

Howard's March May 27

Knefler ———— Scribner
Gibson
4:30
Hazen
23rd KY
6th IN
124th OH   5th KY
93rd OH   6th KY   Kelly's
41st OH   Cavalry
1st OH
Mt. Zion Church   Granbury
                    Goyan
              Polk   Lowrey
              Swett Key   Baucum

                                8th/19th AR
                                (Govan)

Quarles
●New Hope Church
                    Cleburne
              Hindman

To Battle of Dallas
    May 28

              Johnston's HQ

Scale
0_____1 Mile

rear. Granbury needed help, and quickly, so he sent word to Govan for reinforcements. Having failed to obey Howard's orders to advance, McLean was still hidden in the woods and had offered little assistance. As a result, Govan was able to send George Baucum with the 8th and 19th Arkansas (consolidated) to Granbury's relief. The movement was correct but insufficient, as the Federals were still strong enough to pass Baucum's right. Cleburne sensed the problem and brought up Lowrey's brigade from its reserve position. He moved 1 1/2 miles to the east, mostly at the double-quick, where the 33rd Alabama joined Baucum's charge. The slight resistance had suddenly become quite substantial.

Captain Charles Briant of the 6th Indiana described the effect of Lowrey's arrival:

> I thought this meant mischief, and broke at the top of my speed to the left, down the line toward the creek [Pumpkin Vine Creek], passing to the bluff beyond the extreme left of the Twenty-Third Kentucky. From here I could see no help anywhere; but this rebel column had passed by our left, down the creek, and were just coming into the field at the mouth of the ravine [in the cornfield], and in five minutes more time would have been completely in our rear. I instantly gave the order to retreat....[60]

The area on Granbury's right was the closest the Federals would come to a victory. They poured a frontal and oblique fire into the Rebels. Though both Baucum and Lowrey were driven backwards, they managed to reform. When some of the Confederates fell back, others construed it as an actual retreat and it appeared as though the right flank was about to be turned. Cleburne moved Quarles's 48th Tennessee regiment to the front, but as soon as they discovered that the line had not been broken they were moved back behind Lowrey, still in reserve.[61]

This victory had been delivered by the persistence of John Kelly's dismounted cavalry. Kelly had positioned his men along Little Pumpkin Vine Creek in two lines southwest of Pickett's Mill. When Scribner advanced his left across the creek, Kelly's men were able to enfilade his lines and bring the

---

[60] Dean, "Pickett's Mill," 31–34.
[61] Dean, "Pickett's Mill," 33.

Yankees to a halt. Unaware that Hazen needed support, Scribner went into action against Kelly. He received no help from any of Richard Johnson's other two brigades and threw three regiments across the stream. The weight of numbers finally forced Kelly to pull back, but he had been able to stall for time, which was critical as daylight began to fade.

By 7:00 P.M. both Howard and Wood had come to the conclusion that further assaults were pointless. Their casualties covered the ground. In an attempt to bring his men back into Union lines, Wood ordered Knefler to move forward. The men were only to retrieve the wounded and were not to initiate a counterattack. Belatedly, the Federals on the left had driven Kelly from the hill. They were able to form on Knefler's flank and, although the lines were finally connected, it was too late to win the field. Knefler finally retired around 10:00 P.M.[62]

Sporadic fire broke out but nothing of any consequence occurred. Most of the fallen soldiers were left on the field. Jagged ground and dense undergrowth combined with a lack of ambulances prevented their recovery. While the Federals had been soundly defeated, the two sides remained no more than 100 feet apart. Cleburne wanted Granbury to send out skirmishers to feel the enemy's position, but this was impossible until the front had been cleared. Granbury asked permission to move forward and secure the area and Cleburne consented. As the Texans charged down the hill he brought up Walthall's brigade from Hindman's division and filled the gap in the line. Reports of the action in the darkness are mixed, but after a short exchange the Federals attempted to retreat and many more prisoners fell into Southern hands.[63]

The fighting in close quarters resulted in a staggering ratio of killed to wounded. A. J. Gleason of the 15th Ohio described the field as a "slaughter pen." Under normal circumstances there would have been approximately one man killed to every five wounded. At Pickett's Mill, however, Wood's division lost roughly one killed to every two and one-half wounded. Scribner's losses were not fully reported, but the Federals lost around 1,600 men in the battle. Cleburne reported 85 men killed and 363 wounded, though this does not

[62] McInvale, *Pickett's Mill,* 92.
[63] Dean, "Pickett's Mill," 34.

include the returns from Kelly's division.[64] Wood reported total casualties of 1,457 men in his division. Hazen had 87 men killed, 326 wounded, and 54 missing, for a total of 467. Gibson lost 102 men killed, 426 wounded, and 153 missing, for a total of 681. Knefler reported casualties of 21 killed, 169 wounded, and 111 missing, for a total of 301. Scribner also stated in his battle report that his two right regiments suffered severely. The 78th Pennsylvania lost 5 men killed and 44 wounded while the 37th Indiana lost 13 men killed and 40 wounded, for an additional loss of 102.[65] Private Edward Bourne of Govan's 3rd Confederate recorded his thoughts: "It was a bloody fight, and one could walk upon dead Yankees for a long distance down our front. Behind one large tree in front of Granbury's Brigade, I counted a number of dead—thirty-two, as I recall it."[66] Norman Brown, a member of the 24th Texas cavalry (dismounted), wrote: "...here I beheld that which I cannot describe, and which I hope to never see again, dead men meet the eye in every direction and in one place I stoped [sic] and counted 50 dead men in a circle of 30 feet of me." Private Silas Crowell of the 93rd Ohio recalled a conversation between an officer and William Hazen. The general was asked simply "where is our brigade?" Hazen wept and replied, "Brigade, hell, I have none. But what is left is over there in the woods."[67]

The following are merely two observations of many made one day later by soldiers on the Southern side. From the 43rd Mississippi, Columbus Sykes could not believe his eyes: "I walked over the battlefield in Cleburne's front yesterday evening. The Yankee loss was terrific—the spectacle was revolting— the ground was almost literally covered with their dead." A lieutenant in Granbury's brigade surveyed the field. The sunlight "revealed a sight on that hill side that was sickening to look upon. All along in the front of the center and left of our brigade the ground was literally covered with dead men. To look upon this and then the beautiful wild woods, the pretty flowers as they drank in the morning dew, and listen to the sweet notes of the songsters in

[64] A. J. Gleason, diary. 27 May 1864; John M. Harrell, *Confederate Military History*, 12 vols., ed. Clement A. Evans (Atlanta: Confederate Publishing Company, 1899) 10:367.

[65] Report of Benjamin F. Scribner, 7 August 1864, OR, ser. 1, vol. 38, pt. 1, p. 596.

[66] Gleason, diary,; Edward Bourne, "Govan's Brigade at New Hope Church" *Confederate Veteran* 31/3 (March 1923): 89.

[67] Norman D. Brown, ed., *One of Cleburne's Command* (Austin: University of Texas Press, 1980) 88; Silas Crowell, "The Generals Wept," *National Tribune* (Washington, DC), 31 December 1896.

God's first temples, we were constrained to say, 'What is man and his destiny, to do such a strange thing?'"[68]

Dallas

Howard had failed to win that battle, but his efforts produced valuable results. On 3 June the XXIII Corps was able was able to gain a lodgment on Cleburne's flank and Johnston was forced to withdraw from the Dallas-New Hope line. To the Union, the results at New Hope Church and Pickett's Mill were very discouraging, so much so that Sherman neglected to mention the defeats in his *Memoirs*. He decided to move his infantry back to the east and sent his cavalry ahead in order to capture Allatoona Pass, which would give the Federals control of the railroad south of the Etowah River. Johnston ordered Hardee to reconnoiter the Dallas line, so Bate was sent to hold the far left of the formation with Jackson's cavalry on his flank.

On the afternoon of 28 May, Hood was directed to march around the Confederate right at night and attack the Federal flank at dawn. Polk and Hardee would follow in successive attacks, but Hood sent a message to Johnston in the morning that the defenses were too strong to be assaulted.

Opposing Bate's troops was the XV Corps under John Logan. They were strongly entrenched in front of Dallas, with William Harrow's division on the right, Morgan Smith in the center, and Peter Osterhaus on the left. The Rebels advanced, and although they were able to capture the guns of the 1st Iowa battery, they were not able to carry the works. The orders to attack were not properly distributed and the disjointed attempts never had a chance. Bate reported a loss of 677 men, Logan 379.[69]

On 29 May Cleburne's division was ordered "to the left." They got into position next to Bate around 11:00 P.M. and now formed the far left of the army. Around 1:00 A.M. skirmish fire opened, then the Federals opened their artillery on Bate. The noise awakened Cleburne, but the shells did little damage. The men went into line awaiting an assault, but the darkness brought both sides to their senses. They realized that a general engagement would have to wait.

---

[68] Columbus Sykes to "My Dear Darling," 29 May 1864, Kennesaw National Military Battlefield Park, Kennesaw GA; R. M. Collins, *Chapters from the Unwritten History of the War between the States* (St. Louis: Nixon-Jones Printing Co., 1882) 215.

[69] Scaife, *Campaign for Atlanta,* 34–36.

The next day Sherman began a very slow movement and continued to ease his lines to the northeast at roughly 1 mile per day. Cleburne was transferred back to the other end of the army, and the Confederates simply mirrored Union movements. By 4 June it became apparent that Sherman was heading for the railroad, so Johnston moved southeast in order to protect Atlanta.[70]

Sherman gave his men five days of rest before he issued the orders to move out. He expected Johnston to continue his retreat and fall back to a position on the Chattahoochee River, 14 miles south of Marietta. There was occasional skirmishing on 10 June, but with their focus still on Bate the Yankees kept sliding to the east.[71]

Cleburne remained in his position until 13 June. Along with an aide, he rode to the north end of the Confederate lines at the top of Pine Mountain. Artillery fire passed overhead, far too close for his liking. He turned and said, "Let's get out of this. I have seldom known one to go where he had no business but that he got hurt."[72] One day later his cold prophecy became reality. Bate had been under pressure for four days, and on the morning of 14 June, Johnston, Hardee, and Polk rode to the summit to assess the situation. Several batteries opened fire and a shell fragment tore through Polk's chest from left to right, killing him instantly. William W. Loring temporarily assumed corps command, though A. P. Stewart was quickly named to the post, to rank from 23 June.[73]

Gilgal Church

The new line began at Lost Mountain, skirted the north end of Kennesaw Mountain, and crossed the railroad. When Johnston extended his lines there were simply not enough men to present a concentrated front, so the Confederate flank ended at this point. Cleburne was stationed on the northwest edge of the hills near Gilgal Church, located at the intersection of

---

[70] Purdue and Purdue, *Pat Cleburne Confederate General,* 328–29.

[71] Richard M. McMurry, "Kennesaw Mountain," *Civil War Times Illustrated* 11/8 (January 1970): 22.

[72] Buck, *Cleburne and His Command,* 223.

[73] Key, *The Battle of Atlanta,* 33.

the Burnt Hickory-Marietta and Acworth-Sandtown roads.[74] On 15 June there was a sharp engagement with Daniel Butterfield's division just southwest of Pine Mountain. Three brigades of Hooker's XX Corps marched down the Sandtown Road, while further west John Schofield sent eight brigades from the XXIII Corps toward Cleburne's left in an attempt to catch the Rebels in a pincer movement. The Federals stopped 1,000 yards north of the Confederate position. The first line of defense overlooked the flood plain of Allatoona Creek and the approaches on the road.[75]

William Ward's brigade held the Union right, on the east side of the Sandtown Road. He formed a line of battle as the Confederates came into view. The Federal advance reported a strong Confederate position some 500 yards in the distance, but Butterfield refused to believe the reports. Even though it was late in the day he directed Ward to attack. Confederate skirmishers were partially concealed in a wooded section past the plain, and he received orders to drive them out. Ward sent the 102nd Illinois to develop the position, but Butterfield soon added the 105th Illinois and the Rebels fell back. With eighteen field pieces at their disposal, they had deployed on higher ground behind the crossroads and used wood from the building to strengthen the fortifications.

At dusk the 79th Ohio held the left, with the 70th Indiana on their right. Cleburne's skirmishers slowly retired, drawing the Yankees after them. When they reached their own lines the earthworks burst into flame as musketry and canister plowed through the Union ranks. The Hoosiers were more exposed than the 79th and took heavy losses. The Federals tried to return the fire, but they were unable to reform and fired wildly in Cleburne's general direction. As darkness began to fall, the 70th Indiana was relieved by the 85th Indiana and 19th Michigan, who received the same treatment. Major Elia Griffin, in command of the 19th, was mortally wounded when a bullet pierced his chest.

On Ward's left, John Geary had tried to turn Cleburne's right and was actually able to approach the works. However, after a brutal fight in close quarters he was turned away, losing 500 men. By the end of the day neither

---

[74] The church is sometimes erroneously called Golgatha or Hardshell Church in Union accounts.

[75] Sydney Kerksis, "Action at Gilgal Church, June 15–16, 1864," in Sydney C. Kerksis, ed., *The Atlanta Papers* (Dayton OH: Morningside Books, 1970) 833.

Ward nor Geary had made any progress whatsoever, ammunition was running low, and the Federals had expended some 30,000 rounds without any tangible result. Finally Butterfield issued the orders to entrench, a welcome relief. Trees were cut throughout the night and at dawn the Confederates were confronted by three lines of works, bringing the action to a close.

Once again Cleburne had soundly bested his opponent, but once again a lack of numbers prevented him from realizing a meaningful victory. Combined, the Federals lost some 650 men on 15 June while the strong breastworks had kept Confederate casualties to approximately 250.[76] Still, the defeat at Gilgal Church was only a momentary setback. Schofield had too many men for Cleburne to contain, and he had reached a position where he could enfilade the Confederate flank. The Yankees now controlled both the Dallas and Burnt Hickory roads. Johnston was forced to turn Hardee's corps to the west, while Loring and Hood remained facing north. This created a weak point between Hardee's right and Loring's left, causing Johnston to begin work on a new line of earthworks much closer to Marietta. At 10:00 P.M. on 16 June, Hardee's four divisions evacuated their trenches and fell back to low bluffs on the east bank of Mud Creek. The division stretched from Kennesaw Mountain southward to a point between the Dallas and Burnt Hickory roads. The Federals attempted to follow, but when they arrived they found that the water had risen and the pursuit was checked.[77]

While the army was safe, Cleburne's division was not. Late in the afternoon on 17 June, Lucius Polk's command was shelled by artillery and his horse was shot from under him. Polk's leg was badly crippled, and he was never fit for field duty again. Shortly thereafter, the brigade was dismantled and divided among several other units. Johnston retreated again one day later. The infantry left at 11:00 P.M., leaving only a rear guard in place until 1:00 A.M. The men trudged through horrible weather, and the left wing was swung back another 2 miles. It was still raining, the roads were very poor, and the Confederates began to fortify again.[78] Hardee was still on the left, Loring in the

---

[76] Dennis Kelly, "The General's Tour: Mountains to Pass, A River to Cross," *Blue and Gray* 6/5 (June 1989): 17–18.

[77] McMurry, "Kennesaw," 22–23.

[78] Kelly, "Mountains to Pass," 20. Polk's brigade sent the 1st and 15th Arkansas to Govan and the 5th Confederate to Smith. The 2nd Tennessee went to Tyler's brigade of

center, Hood on the right. There were several days of skirmishing, but Sherman was intent on turning the Confederate left and shifted his troops accordingly. Most of McPherson's army was moved to face Kennesaw Mountain. South of the Burnt Hickory Road his right met Thomas's left, while Schofield moved all the way around the formation until his troops constituted the Federal right.

Kolb's Farm

When the Confederates pulled back from the mountains northwest of Marietta, Sherman assumed they were in full retreat. His conclusions were premature, but he ordered Schofield to push toward the Chattahoochee River. On 20 June the XXIII Corps began to head south along the Sandtown Road. Hooker's troops completed a similar movement that forced Johnston to transfer Hood to the left side of the army.[79] The orders were issued, and on the night of 21 June Hood was in motion.

Early in the morning Hooker marched east toward Marietta. He placed his right near Valentine Kolb's farm and connected his corps with Schofield, 4 1/2 miles southwest of the town.[80] Captured prisoners revealed that Hood was massing his forces to their east, so the Yankees began to entrench. Hood came upon skirmishers and, without telling Johnston, decided to attack. Hooker and Schofield brought up reinforcements and the Confederates were repulsed with ease.[81]

Hooker had placed Butterfield on his left in front of Hardee, but nightfall ended the contest and neither side was engaged on this part of the field. The results at Kolb's Farm ran decidedly in favor of the Union. Hood suffered 1,000 casualties in his ill-conceived assault while Hooker lost only 300 men.[82] In addition, this relatively minor action allowed the XXIII Corps

---

Bate's division, and the 48th Tennessee was given to Quarles's brigade of Walthall's division.

[79] Wilbur G. Kurtz Sr. Collection, MSS 130, box 34, folder 7, Atlanta History Center, Atlanta GA.

[80] Wilbur G. Kurtz Sr. Kurtz Collection, box 5, folder 2, Atlanta History Center, Atlanta GA.

[81] McMurry, "Kennesaw," 23.

[82] Kelly ("Mountains to Pass," 24) estimates Hooker's losses at 350 men.

to continue south on the Confederate flank and eventually contribute to Johnston's evacuation of his position on Kennesaw Mountain.

After the battle at Kolb's farm both sides went back into their trenches. Sherman had three options, one of which was simply to stay where he was. Obviously this was unacceptable, but he could also continue to attempt to flank Johnston's left. While this tactic had some appeal, Sherman realized there were other considerations, and not of a military nature. The fall elections were not far away. Ulysses S. Grant had failed in his attempt to capture Richmond, and it did not appear likely that he would defeat Robert E. Lee. Sherman would have to deliver a victory, and a powerful one at that. The risks were high, but the stakes were enormous. Against his better judgment, Sherman decided to attempt a frontal assault at Kennesaw Mountain. By nature he preferred to maneuver, but he had spent a very frustrating spring trying to lure Joe Johnston out of position. This particular move, if successful, would ensure a Republican victory in November and return Abraham Lincoln to the White House. He would have to try it.

Kennesaw Mountain

The country northwest of Marietta was very rugged, as white men had taken it from the Cherokees only thirty years earlier. Running roughly northeast to southwest, Brush Mountain, Pine Mountain, and Lost Mountain formed a line 5 miles long. Between the town and this formation of peaks lay Kennesaw Mountain. In the early part of June, Johnston held a position that ran from one end to the other and contained a salient in the center. The left was held by cavalry, the center and right by Hardee's and Loring's corps, respectively. Hood took a reserve role close to Loring.[83]

Pine Mountain was held by William Bate. Wet weather throughout the month had worked to the Confederates' advantage, as it slowed the pursuit and gave the Rebels time to prepare fortifications. The process itself was an arduous one. No roads existed, so the artillery was hauled up the mountain by hand. Ammunition chests were removed and squads of 100 men per gun were detailed to complete the work.

Sherman issued the orders for the movement to begin at 8 o'clock on the morning of 27 June. McPherson would feint north of Marietta and deliver his

---

[83] Kelly, "Mountains to Pass," 9; McMurry, "Kennesaw," 20.

main assault on the southern end of Kennesaw Mountain. Thomas would advance south of the Dallas Road while Schofield threatened Olley's Creek in order to attack Hood near the Powder Springs Road. The Army of Tennessee would be led by the very reliable XV Corps belonging to John Logan. He would march along the Burnt Hickory Road and attempt to force a break between W. H. T. Walker's division on Hardee's right and Samuel French of Loring's corps, which held Pigeon Hill.

At 6:00 A.M. demonstrations began to occupy the Confederate right. Two hours later to the southwest, the advance got under way. The Yankees emerged from heavy timber and thick swamps to hit Walker. In vicious hand-to-hand fighting nine of eleven Georgians in one rifle pit were killed by the bayonet. After a brief exchange the Southerners were forced from their positions, but not before 150 men fell captive. Despite their early success the Federals still had several hundred yards to go before reaching the main line, and they would have to work their way through trees, rocks, and brush that had been placed in their way. The impediments slowed their progress, and when they began to break apart it became clear that the effort would not succeed. There was little choice but to fall back and regroup.[84]

Thomas probed for a weak point and finally settled on a sector called the "dead angle," which would later become known as Cheatham Hill. Jefferson Davis's division of the XIV Corps was to attack the salient held by Cheatham. Further north, John Newton's division of the IV Corps would strike Cleburne's command, which was strongly posted in a line of trenches.

After a short advance Newton's brigades came upon a gulch cut by a small stream. They were able to find some momentary shelter but soon came under heavy fire. Newton had decided to pack his lines very closely in order to achieve maximum effect at the point of impact. They were placed in "closed columns of divisions," or two companies abreast and five companies deep. As they neared the Confederates they went into formation. This was not an easy maneuver to execute in open drill, but the Federals now faced the difficult task of performing it on the battlefield. Smoke hung over the ground; trees and vines interrupted the advance; and the Union pickets unleashed only one volley before quickly retreating. Still, Cleburne waited. At 40 yards the cannon erupted with telling effect. As John Gillespie of the 78th Ohio described it,

---

[84] McMurry, "Kennesaw," 24–28.

the leaves and bushes had been stripped "so that they looked as naked as though a furious hailstorm had passed over them."[85]

Although the flag of the 27th Illinois made it to the top of the breastworks, the men met stubborn resistance from the 1st and 15th Arkansas and were unable to force a breakthrough. Their guns ignited the dry grass, leaving many of the wounded Federals in grave danger of being burned alive. Lieutenant-Colonel William Martin of the 1st Arkansas leaped to the parapet with a white handkerchief and called for a truce in order to allow the Yankees to remove their wounded. After a brief pause in the action, the contest resumed.

On Cleburne's left Frank Cheatham had similar success. The Federals were in the process of crossing a small stream when a sudden volley rang out and six officers from one Ohio regiment fell to the ground. The musketry caused enough confusion, but Cheatham's artillery opened and any semblance of organization was lost. As the Yankees turned in one direction they received fire from another. Without any recourse they charged. Some of the Federals actually made it into the works, but they were quickly killed or captured. Cheatham Hill had held. Lieutenant Ralsa Rice of the 125th Ohio recalled, "at point-blank range for grape and canister, in solid column, company front, no troops could endure such a slaughter." Sergeant John Brubacker of the 86th Illinois later wrote that he fell injured, "as did seven shot dead and 14 wounded who lay in a heap around me." The casualties revealed that the Confederates were holding firm here too. Cleburne lost 11 men and Cheatham 194, while Federal estimates ran as high as 1,000 casualties. Precise figures are extremely difficult to obtain for the entire action at Kennesaw Mountain, but in total the Federals lost some 3,000 men, the Confederates roughly 750.[86]

While McPherson and Thomas had failed, Schofield was having better luck. The XXIII Corps had begun to demonstrate on 26 June and after some success Sherman ordered Schofield to continue to press the attack the next day.

[85] John Gillespie, letter, 28 June 1864, *The Ohio Soldier* 1/19, 24 December 1887

[86] Ibid.. Ralsa C. Rice, "Memoir: Three Years of Service with the 125th Ohio, Opdycke's Tigers," *National Tribune Scrapbook*, vol. 2 (Washington, DC: National Tribune) 76–77, 93–108; Connelly, *Autumn of Glory*, 359; John Brubacker, letter, *Echoes of Glory*, Larry M. Strayer, and Richard M. Baumgartner, eds. (Huntington WV: Blue Acorn Press. 1991) 178.

Schofield moved out and his right actually reached a point that was closer to the Chattahoochee River than was Johnston's left.

Despite the failures on 27 June, Sherman continued to look south. McPherson had been in position on the Union left, followed by Thomas and Schofield. At 4:00 A.M. on 2 July, McPherson pulled his troops out of line and marched across the formation. The Army of the Ohio now held the center. Once this movement was accomplished, Johnston was forced to abandon his defenses and fall back toward Atlanta.[87]

The Change

By the middle of July Davis had seen enough of defensive warfare. He discounted the strength of the opposing armies and grew impatient as the Confederates continued to retreat. It seemed as if there were always a chance to attack, but Joe Johnston was unwilling to strike a decisive blow. Despite the fact that a battle might be imminent, Davis chose to relieve his commander—a serious mistake in the middle of a campaign. When John B. Hood assumed control of the army on 18 July, the Confederates were stunned.

Richard Taylor wrote, "Certainly no more egregious blunder was possible than that of relieving him from command in front of Atlanta."[88] Among the rank and file, Hood's reputation as a vicious fighter had preceded him. R. M. Collins described a feeling of general disgust: "The boys all threw down their cards and collected in little groups discussing the new move they were all dissatisfied, but soon dismissed the whole with the remark h--l will break loose in Georgia sure enough now…. Hood was a bull-dog fighter from away back, and President Davis could not have suited General Sherman better, had he commissioned him to have made the appointment."[89]

In a letter to his sister, Colin Dunlop wrote: "General Hood commands in place of Genl. Johnston you have no idea what gloom is cast over the Army when we heard of the change." Ellison Capers of the 24th South Carolina stated that "the loss of the commanding general was felt to be irreparable."[90]

---

[87] McMurry, "Kennesaw," 29–33.

[88] Richard Taylor, *Destruction and Reconstruction* (New York: Appleton & Co., 1879) 44.

[89] Collins, *Unwritten History,* 226.

[90] Colin Dunlap to sister, 13 August 1864, Kurtz Collection, box 13, folder 9, Atlanta History Center, Atlanta GA.

Charles Nash pointed out that Cleburne had little confidence in the appointment and attempted to explain his friend's concern. "Cleburne believed that the death warrant of the Confederacy had been sealed when Joseph E. Johnson [Johnston] was removed to give place to a leader who had nothing but courage and dash to recommend him. Had the mantle of leadership fallen on Cleburne, instead of Hood, the army of the South would have gained a victory that would have ensured far better terms of surrender than was secured by this mad rush after military fame."[91]

The Federal officers were surprised as well and could hardly believe their good fortune. They had great respect not only for Johnston's ability, but for his judgment as well. They had been rid of a man who had offered considerable resistance and rewarded with an opponent they knew quite well. Howard, McPherson, and Schofield had attended West Point with Hood, and Thomas had served with him prior to the war. They admired his courage and combative nature but understood that he was rash. It was clear that the Confederates were going to attack, but the generals were quite confident that Hood would make a mistake.[92]

Comments from the Federal side illustrate the relief they felt at the change. Oliver Otis Howard wrote: "Just at this time, much to our comfort and surprise, Johnston was removed, and Hood placed in command of the Confederate army. Johnston had planned to attack Sherman at Peach Tree Creek, expecting just such a division between our wings as we made."[93] Sherman added:

> At this critical moment the Confederate Government rendered us a most valuable service. Being dissatisfied with the Fabian policy of General Johnston, it relieved him, and General Hood was substituted to command the Confederate army. Hood was know to us to be a "fighter."… The character of a leader is a large factor in the game of

[91] Charles E. Nash, *Biographical Sketches of Gen. Pat Cleburne and Gen. T. C. Hindman, together with Humorous Anecdotes and Reminiscence of the Late Civil War* (Little Rock AR: Tunnah and Pittard, 1898) 159.

[92] Cox, *Atlanta*, 148. Hood, Schofield, and McPherson were in the class of 1853, Howard graduated in 1854.

[93] Oliver Otis Howard, "The Struggle for Atlanta," in Robert Underwood Johnston and Clarence Clough Buel, eds., *Battles and Leaders of the Civil War,* 4 vols. (1884–1887; repr., Secaucus NJ: Castle Books, n.d.) 4:313.

war, and I confess I was pleased at this change, of which I had early notice…. I was willing to meet the enemy in the open country, but not behind well-constructed parapets.[94]

In his memoirs, Grant provided the following analysis: "Johnston's tactics in the campaign do not seem to have met with much favor, either in the eyes of the administration in Richmond, or the people in that section of the South in which he was commanding. The very fact of a change in commanders being ordered under such circumstances was an indication of a change of policy, and that now they would become the aggressors—the very thing our troops wanted." He added: "I was as happy as if I had reinforced Sherman with a large army corps…. My own judgment is that Johnston acted very wisely; he husbanded his men and saved as much of his territory as he could, without fighting decisive battles in which all might be lost."[95]

The removal of Joseph Johnston had serious repercussions in the life of Patrick Cleburne. The constant retreats had disappeared, but so had the deliberate consideration of an actual campaign. Instead, the army received a determined leader who would certainly attack but failed to grasp the implications of an unwise decision. Cleburne was extremely apprehensive at the change in command. He had confided to several friends: "We are going to carry the war into Africa, but I fear we will not be as successful as Scipio was."[96]

Peachtree Creek

Hood decided to strike Thomas as he was crossing Peachtree Creek. On 20 July he placed A. P. Stewart on the left of his line, followed by Hardee, Cheatham, and G. W. Smith's Georgia state militia. Hardee placed George Maney on the left, then Walker and Bate, with Cleburne in reserve. The attack was ordered to take place *en echelon*, starting with Bate's division. The

---

[94] William T. Sherman, "The Grand Strategy of the Last Year of the War," in Robert Underwood Johnston and Clarence Clough Buel, eds., *Battles and Leaders of the Civil War*, 4 vols. (1884–1887; repr., Secaucus NJ: Castle Books, n.d.) 4:253.

[95] Ulysses S. Grant, *Personal Memoirs of U.S. Grant*, 2 vols. (New York: Charles L. Webster & Company, 1885) 2:167; Robert McElroy, *Jefferson Davis*, 2 vols. (New York: Harper & Brothers, 1937) 2:416.

[96] Nash, *Biographical Sketches*, 160.

Confederates encountered two problems. First, Bate's front was confronted by heavy undergrowth and he was unable to find the enemy. Furthermore, the Federals had arranged their defenses in an arc so that their closest brigades were in front of Walker, not Bate. The Georgian made the first contact but was handily repulsed, and Hardee ordered Cleburne and Maney to come forward. Just as both divisions began to move, Hardee received word from Hood that Wheeler was in trouble in Decatur. One division must be shifted to his support, and Cleburne was removed from the action. With his corps thus diminished, Hardee had no choice but to cancel his attack.

Hood intended for the attack to begin at 1:00 P.M., but McPherson had reached Decatur with ease. Logan's artillery opened up 20-pounder Parrott guns and began to shell the city, forcing Cheatham to shift to his right. Hood wanted him to move only one division front but Cheatham moved too far. This resulted in a delay while Hardee closed the gap. Poor execution stalled the attack until 4:00 P.M., and by the middle of the afternoon Thomas was across Peachtree Creek.[97]

The entire affair had been badly managed by both Hood and Hardee. Neither man had allowed enough time for the attack to materialize, and Hardee's best division, Cleburne's, was held in reserve until it was removed from the battle altogether. The piecemeal, uncoordinated assaults all along the front combined with the tardiness of the movement to guarantee failure and resulted in losses of some 4,800 men for the Confederates against only 1,700 for Thomas.[98]

Leggett's Hill

On the afternoon of 20 July, Wheeler's cavalry had engaged McPherson on the east side of Atlanta. The men extended the Confederate line southward past the Georgia Railroad until they had outdistanced the Federals by three-quarters of a mile. Wheeler's horsemen held the top of a low rise, soon to be known as Leggett's Hill. Though the elevation was not particularly great, the hill commanded the surrounding area and as a result held a great deal of importance. The eastern face was severe, but the gentle north and south slopes offered easy access to an ascending army. The crest ran for just over one-

---

[97] OR, ser. 1, vol. 38, pt. 3, p. 698.

[98] J. C. Foster to C. E. Custis, Kurtz Collection, box 3, folder 7, Atlanta History Center, Atlanta GA. There are slight variations among estimates.

quarter of a mile long.[99] However, cavalry would not be able to withstand an infantry attack. At midnight they were replaced by Cleburne's division. Cleburne left one regiment north of the railroad and brought the rest of his men to Wheeler's relief.

Govan's brigade was the first to arrive, followed by Lowrey and Smith. Maney was actually part of Cheatham's corps, but on 22 July he would fight under Hardee's direction. The night was exceptionally dark, making it was very difficult to form proper lines. The cavalry attempted to prepare fortifications, but as the troopers were not used to this type of labor, the entrenchments were far from ideal. At daybreak the Confederates saw the weakness in their design. They had no protection in front of them, the Federals held higher ground, and their left would be badly exposed to an enfilading fire. Skirmishing began at dawn, and shortly after 9 o'clock Sam Adams of the 33rd Alabama was struck down by a sharpshooter.[100]

Francis P. Blair recognized the significance of the hill and sent Mortimer Leggett's division forward with Giles Smith on his left. Federal artillery northeast of Cleburne opened up at 7:00 A.M. and inflicted heavy casualties, particularly in James Smith's brigade. The Texans lost 140 men "in a matter of minutes." In total, he saw 47 men killed, 120 wounded, and 19 captured at the hands of decidedly accurate enemy fire. Of the eighteen men in the 18th Texas Cavalry, seventeen were lost in a single shot. Although Smith was a veteran of the bloody battles at Shiloh, Murfreesboro, and Chickamauga, he wrote that he had never seen "such accurate and destructive cannonading."[101]

The remaining cavalry had no defensive works, and the Federals stormed the heights from the east and southeast. The Rebels feared they would be surrounded and the right flank gave way. Dismounted, the 24th and 25th rallied, and along with Govan and Lowrey, they recaptured 200 yards of the ground. Cleburne placed sharpshooters in the woods and enfiladed the Union right, but Leggett responded with a contingent of howitzers and drove the Confederates off of the hill for good. The XVII Corps had suffered 728 casualties to only 300 for Cleburne, but the Federals controlled Leggett's Hill. The city of Atlanta was less than 2 miles from their artillery.

---

[99] Prior to this battle the rise was known simply as Bald Hill. For purposes of clarification and consistency, it is referred to in this book as Leggett's Hill.

[100] Buck, *Cleburne and His Command*, 232–33.

[101] Report of James D. Smith, 5 August 1864, OR, ser. 1, vol. 38, pt. 3, p. 746.

On the morning of 21 July Hood had not fully digested the reports from the previous day, but he decided to attack McPherson east of Atlanta. Govan reacted to the order to march to Decatur and attack the following day: "After having bivouacked about an hour within the entrenchments of Atlanta on the night of the 21st instant, I received an order to move at 12:30 upon the McDonough Road, and marched accordingly. My men had been much wearied by the operations of the 20th, the subsequent moving and entrenching on the Augusta Railroad, and the fight of the 21st, and the loss of another night's rest was a heavy tax upon their powers of endurance."[102]

According to Hood, Hardee's corps was relatively fresh and had been able to rest almost all day on 21 July. Therefore, his corps was chosen to lead the next day's action. This estimation does not appear to be accurate. In his official report, Hardee referenced Hood's comments while describing the activities during and after the battle of Peachtree Creek: "...no mention is made in General Hood's report of the fight made by Cleburne on the 21st, which [Hood] described as the 'bitterest of his life...' He added, '...my troops had been marching, fighting and working the night and day previous, had had little rest for thirty-six hours.'"[103]

Cleburne's brigadiers offered similar statements, strongly refuting Hood's assertions. Lowrey and Smith gave the following accounts of 21 July: "My men had had neither sleep nor rest for two days and nights, and under the rapid marching...and under the oppressive heat, many good men fell completely exhausted and could go no farther.... Owing to the long march the night before and the heavy fire it had been subjected to throughout the previous day, the brigade was much worn and exhausted when it went into action."[104]

Hood states that Hardee was to march "at dusk," but the infantry, cavalry, and artillery that had been designated for the assignment were not all in one place. They could not be drawn into Atlanta until after dark, and Cleburne could not extricate himself from enemy fire until 10:00 P.M. His division was ordered to move at 1:00 A.M. on 22 July. In a letter written the following day, Hardee reflected: "I marched in line for two miles through a dense forest

---

[102] Report of Daniel C. Govan, 30 July 1864, OR, ser. 1, vol. 38, pt. 3, p. 737.

[103] OR, ser. 1, vol. 38, pt. 3, p. 699.

[104] Report of Mark P. Lowrey, 29 July 1864, OR, ser. 1, vol. 38, pt. 3, p. 731–32; report of James A. Smith, 15 August 1864, OR, ser. 1, vol. 38, pt. 3, p. 747.

where I could not see ten paces. Of course it was impossible to keep an alignment.[105]

Hardee was to leave the trench lines at Peachtree and Spring streets and march through Five Points, almost to South River. He would then turn northeast along the Fayetteville Road, then east and north again until he reached the left flank of the Union army. He would attack at dawn while Wheeler hit the Federal wagon trains in Decatur. In total, the march would be 15 miles. Wheeler would send two divisions of cavalry and Cheatham would head due east, trapping McPherson in a vise.[106]

Hardee's assignment was next to impossible. Shortly after dark the Confederates began their circuitous march in an effort to find the Union left. When Hardee reached the Bouldercrest Road he was joined by Cleburne's division, which had been pulled back into the city's inner defenses after fighting all day around Leggett's Hill. Cleburne's men were famished. They had been heavily engaged without any food or water, and now they were subjected to a night march. The sun had disappeared, but it was still very hot as the men slowly made their way through a dense forest riddled with vines and thick undergrowth. The broken ground forced the columns to make frequent stops to readjust alignment, but the journey had only begun.

The troops turned northwest on the Fayetteville Road and reached a fork. Without accurate maps, Hardee was forced to make a difficult decision. He sent Cleburne and Maney to the left, while Bate and Walker continued toward Decatur. After a march of over a mile, Hardee changed his mind. The columns were shifted to a road that ran parallel to Cleburne. This appeared as if it would bring more concentration to the point of attack, but in reality it placed the Confederates too far west to gain the Federal rear.

The Confederates were not moving very smoothly, but Blair's corps was in fact quite vulnerable to this type of a flanking maneuver. Giles Smith had placed William Hall and Benjamin Potts in a line facing south. Though he had turned Hall's brigade east again to create a formation in the shape of a fishhook, the division was still dangerously exposed as Hall's left was "in the air." McPherson reacted swiftly and began to bring up troops from Dodge's

---

[105] T. B. Roy, "General Hardee and the Military Operations around Atlanta," in *Southern Historical Society Papers,* 52 vols. (Millwood NY: Kraus Reprint Co., 1977) 8:358–60; Hughes, *Old Reliable,* 226–28.

[106] T. B. Roy to Patrick R. Cleburne, 21 July 1864.

XVI Corps. He placed John Morrill's brigade half a mile behind Smith's left and at a right angle to him. During the morning of 22 July he extended the line with Thomas Sweeny's division. By the time Hardee actually attacked, he was facing strong fortifications instead of the open flank he had expected.

William Bate led the advance and moved along the east side of Sugar Creek toward the center of Sweeny's division. The men were hit by shells and halted halfway across the valley in their front. They charged, only to be caught in a murderous crossfire of canister from the 14th Ohio battery's six Rodmans. Bate's weak response ended in complete failure, and for all intents and purposes he was no longer a factor in the battle.

Walker reached Sugar Creek, where against the advice of his guide he decided to turn to the west. The young man explained that his route would be blocked by a large body of water known as Terry's Mill Pond. The pond was 10 feet deep and a mile wide. When Walker came upon it his troops were forced to change their march again. The first contact of the day was made at 12:15 P.M. when Walker and Bate ran into Sweeny's pickets. Walker finally negotiated the water and crossed the creek. He approached the crest of another ridge and rode ahead of his troops to assess the situation. He scanned the terrain, and as he raised his field glasses a sniper brought him to the ground. His death dealt a devastating blow to the division, but after another delay Hugh Mercer took command.

The action that morning had been constant, and the Federals had taken a beating. A gap half a mile wide had developed between John Morrill and Giles Smith. McPherson knew he needed to close it, and quickly. He sent William Strong toward Blair's corps, where he met Smith. Strong gave him instructions to hold his ground; reinforcements were on the way. Strong returned and reported large numbers of Confederates moving in that direction. McPherson was eating lunch when he heard the sounds of an attack. He galloped to the south and found a hill that provided a clear view of Dodge's right flank. When he saw the hole in his defenses, he brought Hugo Wangelin's brigade south from Logan's corps and closed the line.

The popular thirty-five-year-old ventured too far forward. The Confederates signaled for him to surrender, but McPherson merely raised his hand and turned his horse. Corporal Robert Coleman set his sights, and with one shot through the lung the general was dead. Command of the Army of Tennessee was given to Logan. The appointment infuriated Joe Hooker. Never

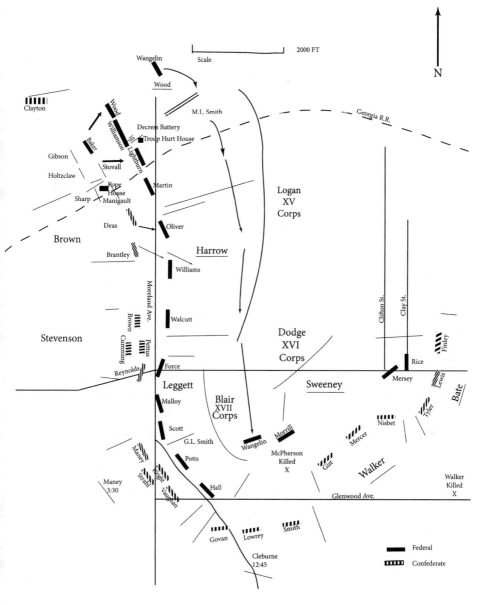

2000 FT

Scale

N

Wangelin

Wood

Clayton

M.L. Smith

Georgia R.R.

Wood

Williamson

Decress Battery

Troup Hurt House

Baker

Lightburn

Gibson

Stovall

Holtzclaw

Martin

Rope House

Sharp

Manigault

Logan
XV
Corps

Deas

Oliver

Brown

Harrow

Brantley

Williams

Moreland Ave.

Walcutt

Clifton St.

Clay St.

Finley

Brown

Dodge
XVI
Corps

Stevenson

Pettus

Cumming

Rice

Reynolds

Force

Mersey

Sweeney

Lewis

Leggett

Bate

Malloy

Blair
XVII
Corps

Tyler

Scott

Nisbet

G.L. Smith

Wangelin

Morrill

Mercer

Maney

Potts

McPherson
Killed
X

Gist

Walker

Wright

Strahl

Maney
3:30

Vaughan

Hall

Walker
Killed
X

Glenwood Ave.

Govan

Lowrey

Smith

Federal

Cleburne
12:45

Confederate

Attack on Legget Hill
July 22, 1864

lacking admiration of his own ability, Hooker felt he should have received the promotion. He offered his resignation. Sherman was only too happy to be rid of his troublesome lieutenant, and the XX Corps was handed to Henry Slocum.

Belatedly, Hood realized that Hardee was not going to reach beyond the Union flank. He ordered Cheatham forward, but the corps did not move until 4:00 P.M.[107] The lack of coordination among the Confederates was costly. Had Cheatham and Hardee attacked simultaneously, the results may have been very different. As it was, McPherson was able to shift additional troops and barely seal the breach Cleburne had created.

John B. Hood was standing on the second floor of a two-story farmhouse in Oakland cemetery, watching Cheatham's attack. Maney advanced at 3:30, followed by the rest of Cheatham's corps. The Federals were strongly posted, and despite a series of furious charges by Carter Stevenson's division the Rebels were unable to break the defenses. While Stevenson was turned away on the south end of the front, Brown and Clayton had more success. Clayton was able to pierce the works in some places, and the center of Brown's division swarmed over the lines. Arthur Manigault's brigade took heavy artillery fire, but the Graycoats regrouped and charged again. Followed by Jacob Sharp's Mississippians, they captured four guns and pushed the Federals for half a mile. The Confederates turned north and routed four regiments of Joseph Lightburn's brigade, but their day was not yet over. They continued on to the Troup Hurt property and took the house along with four 20-pounder Parrott guns of Battery H, 1st Illinois Light Artillery, commanded by Francis DeGress.

John Logan witnessed the action and brought up reinforcements. Manigault had done considerable damage, but Logan's task was not as difficult as it appeared. Despite their success, Brown's division was ordered to withdraw and by 5 o'clock Logan's sector was secure. Manigault was livid. In post-war writings he revealed his frustration:

> … a message had been sent to the Division Commander by both
> Sharp and myself, to say that we could make our position good and
> hold them, when an order came to retire quickly, as the enemy was

---

[107] Scaife, *Campaign for Atlanta,* 64.

moving in large masses on our left flank and rear, and to delay would cause the loss or capture of the forces engaged. There was nothing left to do but obey, and I never saw men obey an order so unwillingly. They were fully conscious of having distinguished themselves, and wanted to bring off the artillery they had so gallantly captured. They believed that the place could be held, and that as soon as dark set in, the guns could be moved with little difficulty.[108]

While Cheatham's attack had begun to stall Hardee was faring much better, despite moving through what Daniel Govan termed "almost impassable undergrowth." The Confederates drove Giles Smith's entire division back to Leggett's Hill. In the process they captured eight guns of the 2nd Illinois and 2nd US Artillery, along with the entire 16th Iowa infantry regiment. Morrill was swept up in the assault and driven back as well.[109] Govan continued, hitting Potts in the left flank. He captured two guns and several hundred prisoners, but in doing so his left and right became separated. The Federals had constructed sound fortifications of logs and earth, with an abatis in front. In combination with some of Smith's Texans Govan poured over Hall's left. The Federals were in serious jeopardy, and at 5:00 P.M. the Confederates mounted the final attack of the day. As Cleburne attacked from the south and east, Maney struck from the west. The Union flank crumbled. If the entire corps collapsed, Hood's attack would succeed and the destruction would be irreparable. Unfortunately for the Confederates, numbers and position told the story. Even though Giles Smith had been defeated, Leggett was posted on higher ground and backed by artillery. The combat was hand to hand and a final repulse was inevitable. Lowrey came up on Govan's right, but the Confederates were only able to hold their position until nightfall allowed them to withdraw. Although Govan had captured eight cannon he lost three-quarters of his field officers, including Colonel John Murray of the 5th Arkansas. The Federals had been fighting on the defensive and the numbers reflect it. Cleburne captured 1,600 men, 8 field pieces, 4 colors, and large

[108] Scaife, *Campaign for Atlanta*, 67.
[109] Scaife, *Campaign for Atlanta*, 62.

quantities of stores and equipment, but in the process he lost almost 1,400 men, over half of his total forces engaged.[110]

At the same time James Smith advanced and pushed the Federals over a mile, driving them back in confusion. His men had become widely scattered, but they carried three lines of temporary works before reaching an open field where they found Union entrenchments. Smith was able to attack Blair from the east and actually forced the Yankees to jump to the other side of their trenches to defend their position. James Smith had outdistanced the Confederates on his flanks, so he sent a staff officer to ask for reinforcements. His brigade was caught in the crossfire and all of the regimental commanders but one were either killed, wounded, or captured. Faced with such overwhelming numbers, he was compelled to retreat. Smith was wounded and taken from the field. Due to the heavy casualties the command fell to a lieutenant-colonel, R. B. Young of the 10th Texas. The Rebels were awfully disorganized and some were captured, but they had taken two colors and fifteen pieces of artillery. In a very incomplete report, Smith estimated his losses as 23 men killed, 100 wounded, and 75 captured or missing, for a total of 198.[111]

Mark Lowrey had been in the center of Cleburne's division but somewhat to the rear, 500 yards behind Smith. Although he was unable to see more than 50 yards ahead of him, he moved forward around 4:00 P.M. and, along with Govan, got into action with Giles Smith south of Leggett's Hill. He made it to the rifle pits, but his losses were staggering. Entire rows fell in the first volley as his lines were torn apart. In vicious hand-to-hand fighting Govan lost 578 men and was forced back as well. Colonel Harris Lampley of the 45th Alabama stormed the parapets of the 15th Iowa, exhorting his men forward. He was easily captured, and when he looked behind him he saw that his regiment simply ceased to exist.[112]

In the assaults of 22 July Cleburne achieved the greatest success. His right brigade, under Smith, fought through John Morrill and was able to turn to his left and attack Blair from the east. On Smith's left Govan captured a six-

[110] John W. Fuller, "A Terrible Day: The Fighting before Atlanta, July 22, 1864," *National Tribune* (Washington, DC), 16 April 1885, [**PAGES**]; report of Daniel C. Govan, 30 July 1864, OR, ser. 1, vol. 38. pt. 3, p. 740.

[111] Report of James A. Smith, 15 August 1864, OR, ser. 1, vol. 38, pt. 3, p. 747.

[112] Buck, *Cleburne and His Command,* 239.

gun battery. He charged two lines of earthworks and pierced the lines but was driven back in a counterattack by William Hall. Govan's right still overlapped Hall's left, and his persistence captured two guns and several hundred prisoners.

Hardee failed to accomplish his mission, but the fault lay with Hood. The Confederates were moving over unfamiliar ground in the dark, hoping to pass the Union flank, yet they were uncertain of its location. Had all four divisions stayed on the Fayetteville Road, it is quite likely that they would have turned the Federal left. However, Hood was just too far away to manage the battle effectively. Sherman was able to shift his troops more quickly, and he averted disaster on more than one occasion simply by his ability to send more men to the point of impact. The line had held, but for much of the afternoon the outcome hung in the balance. Strong described the ferocity of the assault: "It seemed that every mounted officer of the attacking column was riding at the front of or on the right or left of the first line of battle. The battle from half past three was desperate and bloody in the extreme, and the result was extremely doubtful until late in the day. Our lines were broken and pierced in several places, and batteries and regimental colors were lost and won again and again."[113]

Ezra Church

The armies were in almost constant contact on 22 July, and the casualties were horrendous. The Federals lost roughly 5,500 men, the Confederates almost 8,000.[114] On 27 July Stephen D. Lee replaced Cheatham in command of Hood's old corps, and Sherman began to withdraw his left. Cleburne was placed in reserve 2 miles due east of Atlanta, and his division headquarters were established a few hundred yards behind the lines in an old stone house. It stood on a rise in the ground, surrounded by a grove of oak trees. Federal artillery shelled the position from time to time, but no damage was done until Cleburne and his staff sat down to dinner the next day. A shell exploded right above the table and fragments showered in all directions. Calhoun Benham was struck near the corner of his right eye. The wound continued to his ear, but fortunately it did not pierce the skull.

---

[113] Buck, *Cleburne and His Command,* 244.
[114] Castel, *Decision in the West,* 411–12.

On 3 August the division moved from its position east of the city to a new location north of it. Generally, Cleburne shifted his lines each day to conform to Sherman's movements. On 9 August Cleburne's left reached a point only 2 miles from East Point, and over the next week the group continued slowly toward the town.

The next ten days witnessed nothing of importance aside from sporadic skirmish fire, but this period of time provides a significant illustration of Patrick Cleburne's character. While the division was near East Point, Confederate scouts captured a Federal cavalry officer. He was a member of the 6th Kentucky and an aide to Jacob Cox. The next morning, Cleburne learned that when the well-dressed young man had been sent to the provost guard, he was robbed of his hat, boots, and blanket. Cleburne was furious, but he was unable to identify the guilty party. He gave the young man an extra hat and one of his own two blankets. As Irving Buck revealed in his book *Cleburne and his Command*, the generosity and compassion was later repaid in kind:

> Upon the surrender at Greensboro, North Carolina, the writer with several comrades separated from the bulk of the army, moving south, and had to cross the country to our homes in Virginia. We were destitute of money or subsistence. Learning that General Cox was in command, I rode to his quarters, and upon announcing my late position was most courteously received. When I referred to the capture of Lieutenant Coughlan the general said that after exchange the lieutenant had spoken of the kind treatment received from Cleburne, and he further informed me that the young officer had been killed near the gin house at Franklin, Tennessee; which was close to the spot where Cleburne fell. Upon explaining my needs, General Cox directed his commissary to fill our wagon (we were fortunate enough to have secured one out of the army wreck) with hardtack, bacon, sugar and coffee. This afforded our party good living during the twelve days overland journey to our homes, as the sugar and coffee were current exchange for eggs, milk, and butter from the farmhouses we passed.[115]

Utoy Creek

---

[115] Buck, *Cleburne and His Command*, 249.

The Federal armies controlled Atlanta, but two rail lines into the city still remained. A successful attack between Whitehall Tavern and East Point would destroy the Atlanta and West Point Railroad along with the Macon and Western, cutting off the remaining avenues of supply. Hood established a new line along the Sandtown Road with its left flank refused around a hill that overlooked Cascade Springs. William Bate occupied the ground facing north with his lines running across the Willis Mill Road, while Cleburne was held in reserve near the home of Robert Baugh.[116]

Early in the morning of 6 August, Schofield had ordered Cox to advance. Skirmishers moved south across a valley and easily drove in Confederate pickets. At 10 o'clock Cox directed James Reilly to attack the west end of the ridge, where the Rebels appeared to be entrenched.

Although a strip of timber below the ridge offered some protection, it also prevented Reilly from gaining a clear view of the surrounding terrain. The initial movement was successful, but as the Federals passed through the woods they emerged in front of a cleared area where the Confederates had cut down trees during the night. The obstructions proved effective, and the attackers had considerable trouble. William Bate's artillery opened fire and shredded the Union ranks. The Northerners approached to within 25 yards of the fortifications but were unable to advance any further. Reilly lost 306 men killed, wounded, or missing, while Bate reported total casualties of "fifteen to twenty." Ironically, the 8th Tennessee (Union) suffered severely. Of the 160 men the regiment took into battle, 95 went down.

The Federals continued to try to turn Bate's left. Heavy rain and impending darkness eliminated another direct assault, but under the sheer weight of numbers Bate had to withdraw. On the next day the XXIII Corps cautiously moved forward, only to discover that the Confederates had abandoned their position. Schofield continued down the Sandtown Road until he came upon a new line of works extending further to the south. Recalling painful memories of their recent experience, the men constructed entrenchments and made no attempt to advance. The XIV Corps threw up fortifications as well, but not before engaging the Confederate outer lines in a pointless attack that cost them 400 men.[117]

---

[116] Scaife, *Campaign for Atlanta*, 101.

[117] Castel, *Decision in the West*, 459–60.

Jonesboro

By the time the Confederates reached Jonesboro, the army had changed considerably. The string of costly defeats had completely changed its face. William Hardee assumed overall control of the entire sector, including the corps under Stephen Lee. Cleburne led Hardee's corps and Mark Lowrey now commanded Cleburne's division, with his brigade going to Colonel John Weir. Hugh Mercer's troops had been given to Cleburne in July; they were also led by a colonel, Charles Olmstead. A similar number of changes occurred in Bate and Cheatham's divisions as well, with John Brown and George Maney leading their respective commands.

Sherman was clearly frustrated. Despite his constant pounding and a series of Confederate retreats, he still had not taken the city. On 25 August he sent Slocum's XX Corps back to Atlanta and ordered the remainder of his army to begin a wide flanking movement to the west and south. They would cut the railroads to Macon and West Point far below the immediate defenses, and without his supply lines Hood would be forced to evacuate. On 30 August Howard accomplished his task, severing the Atlanta and West Point at Red Oak and Fairburn.

Hood was slow to grasp the danger, but on the same day he sent Hardee's corps under Cleburne's direction to Jonesboro followed by Lee's corps, still under Hardee. The weary Butternuts began to move long after dark. They trudged through East Point and Rough and Ready, 26 miles south of Atlanta. At 3:00 A.M. Brown's division encountered Federal pickets, but Hardee had no desire to initiate a fight in the dark. The column continued to the east, a move that caused a serious delay. It was not until the middle of the afternoon that Hardee's troops were in place.[118]

After a debilitating march through the night without any food, the troops arrived to find that on 30 August the Yankees had occupied Jonesboro. The Federal line in front of Hardee ran roughly northeast to southwest. John Logan's XV Corps deployed on the east side of the Flint River, while across the water the XVI Corps continued the line with two divisions under John Fuller and Montgomery Corse.

The Confederate left was anchored on the river, which ran parallel to the Macon and Western Railroad at Jonesboro. Cleburne placed his division

---

[118] Scaife, *Campaign for Atlanta*, 108.

behind a ravine with the water to his left, Brown's division to his right, and Maney behind Brown. Granbury held the left with Weir in the center, Olmstead on the right. Govan was in reserve behind Olmstead. Lee formed on Hardee's right with his line extending to the railroad north of Jonesboro.

Cleburne's corps was to swing gradually to the right, while Lee would move in mirror image and pivot to his left. Hopefully this would trap the Federals in the middle. Lee was instructed to await the sound of Cleburne's guns and then press the attack. With Lowrey in command, Cleburne moved at 3:30 in the afternoon and found Judson Kilpatrick's dismounted cavalry strongly posted behind fence rails in an open field. The Federals quickly fled, but some of them formed and made a brief stand to allow the remainder to escape. Lowrey's advance was falling behind schedule.

Federal artillery still played upon the Rebels, and without orders Granbury charged across the water to capture the battery. Weir and Olmstead soon followed and drove the Yankees from another line of works, but their advance created a large gap between Olmstead's right and the left of Brown's division. Govan was brought forward, but the sounds of Granbury's initial attack had reached the ears of Stephen Lee. Mistakenly, he thought that the actual battle was under way and by 2:20 P.M. he had begun to move. The disjointed efforts had no cohesion whatsoever. Hardee was forced to call off the action and try to reorganize. Lowrey realized that the Confederates had advanced too far and were unsupported. He brought them back across the river and ordered Govan to align his right flank on Lee's corps while he brought the other three brigades into line as quickly as possible.

On the night of 31 August, Hood directed Hardee to withdraw Lee at 2:00 A.M. and send him back to Atlanta. The plan's logic lay in the belief that the bulk of Sherman's army was still in front of Atlanta. In reality, Slocum's XX Corps was the only Federal force still in the city. At 1:30 A.M. Cleburne was ordered to move to the right. He placed Olmstead on the left next to Brown, followed by Weir, Granbury, and Govan.

The first of September brought yet another mistake from John Bell Hood. Without assessing the situation at Jonesboro, he had recalled Lee to Atlanta. The city was weakly held by A. P. Stewart's corps and a contingent of Georgia Militia, but the addition of one corps made no difference in the city and Lee's corps's removal weakened Hardee.

Hardee's line was stretched to the breaking point. The Confederates faced west, on the western side of the Macon and Western. During the night Maney had been replaced by John Carter, who held the left with Brown in the middle and Lowrey on the right. From left to right, Lowrey spread out Olmstead, Weir, and Granbury. The numbers were so overwhelming that the right of the line was bent back to face north; this section was held by Govan's brigade. This unusual formation created a salient between Granbury's right and Govan's left. Staring straight at Hardee were three Federal corps, with three more in supporting distance.

When the attack began at 4:00 P.M., the Confederates had little chance. Daniel Govan held the most vulnerable point in the fishhook, and his brigade was quickly overrun. The general was captured along with 8 pieces of artillery and 600 men. Remnants of several brigades held off the Federals until dark, but Hardee was forced to retreat once again. At 11:00 P.M. Cleburne withdrew to Lovejoy Station, 6 miles to the south. The Confederates attempted to throw up breastworks, but before these were completed the Federals struck the center of Cleburne's division. They drove in the skirmishers and got to within 250 yards of Lowrey's brigade, but Lowrey was able to hold on for the moment.[119] Every inch of ground had been hotly contested, but the brief stands were in vain. Hardee finally sent a message to Hood with news that the town had been captured. The two days had been very costly to both sides. The Federals lost 3,237 men while the Confederates lost 3,705, along with any hope the South may have had of holding Atlanta.

With Hardee at Lovejoy Station, Stewart in Atlanta, and Lee strung out in between, Hood was forced to abandon the city. The withdrawal began at 5:00 P.M., and the destruction quickly followed. Since the local populace had no protection whatsoever from either Federal soldiers or Confederate vandals, Mayor James Calhoun rode down Marietta Street searching for someone in authority. He met a reconnaissance party from Slocum's corps, and after a short conversation he learned that William Ward was the closest general officer. On behalf of the citizens, Calhoun wrote the following note: "Sir: The fortune of war has placed Atlanta in your hands. As mayor of the city of Atlanta I ask protection for non-combatants and private property."[120]

The Army of Tennessee had been decimated. After the battle of New Hope Church, Johnston had been able to field roughly 45,000 effective infantry; Hood could now put barely 23,000 into action. He had lost 12,500

---

[119] Buck, *Cleburne and His Command,* 258.
[120] Scaife, *Campaign for Atlanta,* 112–13.

men killed or wounded, plus an undetermined number of captured or deserted. Federal reports indicated some 13,000 men were taken prisoner during the campaign. The losses, however, went far beyond men. Much like Albert Sidney Johnston at Nashville, Hood had waited far too long to ensure the safety of his supplies. Twenty-eight carloads of ammunition were destroyed, along with eighty-one cars and five locomotives. Thirteen siege guns, large quantities of quartermasters stores, and ordnance equipment were left behind. Commissary stores were thrown open to the public and the streets erupted in chaos. Battles would rage until April, but when the Atlanta campaign finally came to an end, Lincoln was assured of the White House and the war was over.[121]

By noon the Union flag flew over city hall, and on 3 September Sherman wired Henry Halleck: "So Atlanta is ours, and fairly won."

---

[121] Alex E. Spence to parents, 6 September 1864, in Mark K. Christ, *Getting Used to Being Shot at: The Spence Family Civil War Letters* (Fayetteville: University of Arkansas Press, 2002).

13

SPRING HILL

"The best move in my career as a soldier I was
thus destined to behold come to naught."[1]

The Confederates continued to retreat. Stephen Lee was encamped around
Jonesboro, with A. P. Stewart at East Point. Cleburne's division withdrew
from Jonesboro at 11:00 P.M. on 1 September and arrived at Lovejoy Station
early the next morning. One mile east of the station they formed a line facing
north and began to dig breastworks. The Federals sent in a strong party of
skirmishers, supported by two additional lines. They advanced to within 250
yards but could go no further and fell back to Jonesboro. The center of
Cleburne's division, commanded by Mark Lowrey, took most of the
casualties.

Over the next two days, Stewart and Lee joined Hardee and the army was
reunited. Sherman began to withdraw into the safety of Atlanta on 6
September, and on the 8th Hardee's corps moved back into Jonesboro. One
day later a truce was placed in effect in order to exchange some 2,000
prisoners, one of whom was Daniel Govan. It was at this point that Sherman
issued his infamous order, instructing the remaining citizens of Atlanta to
evacuate, and a series of exchanges between the commanding generals began:

> General:—I have deemed it to the interest of the United States that
> the citizens now residing in Atlanta should remove, those that prefer it
> to go South, and the rest North. For the latter I can provide food and
> transportation to points of their election in Tennessee, Kentucky, or
> further North. For the former I can provide transportation by cars as
> far as Rough and Ready, and also wagons; but, that their removal may
> be made with as little discomfort as possible, it will be necessary for

---

[1] John B. Hood, "The Invasion of Tennessee," in Robert Underwood Johnston and
Clarence Clough Buel, eds., *Battles and Leaders of the Civil War,* 4 vols. (1884–1887; repr.,
Secaucus NJ: Castle Books, n.d.) 4:432.

you to help the families from Rough and Ready to the cars at Lovejoy's. If you consent, I will undertake to remove all the families in Atlanta who prefer to go South to Rough and Ready, with all their moveable effects, viz., clothing, trunks, reasonable furniture, bedding, etc., with their servants, white and black, with the proviso that no force shall be toward the blacks, one way or another. If they want to go with their masters or mistresses, they may do so; otherwise they will be sent away unless they be men, when they may be employed by our quarter-master. Atlanta is no place for families or non-combatants, and I have no desire to send them North if you will assist me in conveying them South....[2]

Hood was outraged, but he had no recourse in the matter. On the tenth of the month he responded:

General:—Your letter of yesterday's date, borne by James M. Ball and James R. Crew, citizens of Atlanta, is received. You say therein, 'I deem it to be to the interest of the United States that the citizens now residing in Atlanta should remove,' etc.... I do not consider that I have any alternative in this matter.... And now, sir, permit me to say that the unprecedented measure you propose transcends, in studied and ingenious cruelty, all acts ever before brought to my attention in the dark history of war. In the name of God and humanity, I protest, believing that you will find that you are expelling from their homes and firesides the wives and children of a brave people.[3]

The month of September was marked by disappointment for Pat Cleburne. Unwilling to serve under John B. Hood, Hardee resigned and was transferred to the Department of South Carolina and Florida. His departure had a devastating effect on the men in the ranks, but it hit Cleburne hardest of all. With only a few brief interludes he had served under Hardee during the entire war. He was so distraught that he considered relinquishing his commission as major general in order to serve as a staff officer in Hardee's new

[2] John B. Hood, *Advance and Retreat* (1880; repr., Edison NJ: Blue and Gray Press, 1985) 229–30.

[3] Hood, *Advance and Retreat,* 230.

command. Cleburne's relations with Hood had become strained. He should have been promoted to lead Hardee's corps, but Hood still blamed Hardee for many of his own failures at Atlanta. Furthermore, Jefferson Davis was now beginning to appreciate the foresight of Cleburne's proposal to arm the slaves, and promotion to lieutenant general would only serve to validate the logic he had so steadfastly opposed. As a result, the corps was given to Frank Cheatham, though he remained a major general.

With the failure of Hood's aggressive assaults around Atlanta, the Confederates had few options left. Although they were seriously outnumbered, Hood believed that another successful drive into Tennessee might cause Sherman to ease the pressure in Georgia. On 18 September the army began to move west in the direction of the West Point Railroad, which it reached at Palmetto the next day. The troops deployed with the right flank east of the railroad and the left near the Chattahoochee River. Six days later Davis visited the army to ascertain its true condition. He tried to encourage the troops, and in consultation with his corps commanders he emphasized the importance of disrupting Sherman's supply lines at Chattanooga and Nashville. It simply was not possible to attack the entrenchments around Atlanta, but he hoped to draw Sherman north of the city. If he were defeated the Confederates might invade the Volunteer State, but Hood was clearly instructed to keep his army within striking distance of the enemy, regardless of which direction he might take.[4]

On 29 September he sent two divisions to Nashville under George Thomas, as well as another to Rome. On the same day Hood put his army in motion. On 1 October they crossed the Chattahoochee on pontoon bridges at Pumpkin Town and Phillip's Ferry where they went into bivouac, 8 miles north of Pray's Church. The next day Cleburne's division was at Powder Springs, only 12 miles southwest of Marietta.

The night was spent near Flint Hill Church before the Army of Tennessee continued northward through a series of small towns. By 3 October the main body was within 4 miles of Lost Mountain. Stewart was directed to move upon Big Shanty, and two days later Samuel French attacked at Allatoona Pass. The position was heavily fortified, and though French was able to pierce

---

[4] US War Department, comp., *The War of the Rebellion: A Compilation of the Official Records of the Union and Confederate Armies*, 128 vols. (Washington, DC: Government Printing Office, 1880–1901) ser. 1, vol. 39, pt. 2, p. 862.

the lines in several places, he was turned away with heavy loss. He learned that Federal forces were attempting to move behind him, so he fell back to Lost Mountain with the rest of Stewart's command.

By the tenth of the month they had reached Coosaville, 10 miles southwest of Rome, and arrived in Resaca on 12 October, destroying track along the Western and Atlantic Railroad as they went. One day later the Rebels surrounded the Federal outpost at Dalton. General Hood demanded a surrender and Cleburne's division was brought to the front in case any hostilities broke out. Without any other options, the garrison capitulated and no shots were shots fired. The victory was decisive and 751 men were lost to capture.[5]

The Confederate operations north of Atlanta were not enough to lure Sherman into a pitched battle, despite his superior numbers, so Hood decided to fall back to his supply base at Gadsden, Alabama. On 20 October Cleburne was camped in the town, his men finally able to rest and recuperate. From Hood's viewpoint, the movements in North Georgia were a success. Sherman detached a force of some 65,000 infantry and artillery plus 2 divisions of cavalry to protect his lines.[6] While this was encouraging, the Confederates were still vulnerable. Hood could not afford to remain idle, only to watch Sherman's army gain strength; he believed that the time was right to invade Tennessee. Although it was not his idea, Davis supported the campaign.[7] The capture of Nashville would deal the Federals a serious blow, as well as establish a base for future operations. With possession of the capital Hood could move north into Kentucky and threaten Cincinnati, or the troops could turn east in an attempt to join Robert E. Lee in Virginia.

On 21 October the army headed north toward Guntersville, but when it was learned that heavy rains had pinned Forrest in West Tennessee, Hood decided to keep going and connect with Forrest in Florence. One week later skirmishers from Cleburne and Bate's divisions conducted a minor demonstration against Union positions in Decatur. No significant action took place, but the Federals were held in place and the Confederates resumed their march. They began to enter Tuscumbia on 29 October and the situation there

---

[5] Report of Lewis Johnson, 17 October 1864, OR, ser. 1, vol. 39, pt. 1, p. 720.

[6] Hood, *Advance and Retreat*, 263.

[7] Thomas L. Connelly, *Autumn of Glory: The Army of Tennessee, 1862–1865* (Baton Rouge: Louisiana State University Press, 1971) 476–79.

was not at all as Hood had expected. Despite the urgency of the mission, sufficient supplies had not arrived and the pontoon bridges had not been completed. The army was forced to wait nine days.

Perhaps the campaign was just too ambitious. The bridges across the Tennessee River had been laid on the first of November, but the Confederates waited while commissary officers worked to assemble the twenty-day supply of rations Hood had requested. The Army of Tennessee was forced to depend on the run-down Memphis and Charleston Railroad for all of its needs. Part of the line had been destroyed, so provisions had to come overland by wagon from the railhead, 15 miles west of Tuscumbia. The supply system was so broken down that Confederate officials struggled to provide one day of food, much less accumulate a surplus. Finally, the weather could not have been worse. Constant rain turned the roads to mud and washed away many of the railroad bridges, creating a logistical nightmare that only added to Hood's difficulties. Cheatham's corps finally reached Florence late at night on 13 November, but A. P. Stewart did not arrive until the twentieth. The Confederates began their march from Florence on 19 November. Cheatham crossed the river in a snowstorm on 21 November, arriving in Rawhide at 5:00 P.M. that afternoon.

Cleburne's division covered 12 miles on 21 November, and despite the bitter weather the army made good time. By 25 November all three corps had converged on the Mount Pleasant Road. Lee was just beyond Mount Pleasant, Cheatham 5 miles south of it, and Stewart to the east in Henryville. Two days later they had reached the Warfield home, 3 miles south of Columbia. Cheatham placed his right flank on the Duck River and his left on the Pulaski Turnpike.

On 26 November Cleburne was marching on a road that ran by Ashwood, 6 miles from Columbia. There the Confederates passed the small Episcopal church and cemetery of the Polk family. A beautiful red brick building in the Gothic style, its walls and sharp-pointed roof were covered with ivy. Even on a dreary November day, flowers and shrubbery were still in bloom, framing a classic structure that stood among a grove of tall magnolias. Thomas Foster, a captain in Granbury's brigade, wrote in his journal that it was "the prettiest place I have ever seen in my life." Cleburne stopped to admire the beauty around him. No doubt his thoughts went back to a more peaceful time, to a life with Susan, when he turned and said, "It would not be hard to die if one could be buried in a spot such as this."[8] Only light skirmishing marked 27 November as the Rebels took their positions around the south side of Columbia, but on the next day the real work began. The army made preparations to advance, and bridges were thrown across the Duck River.

John Schofield led a force of 24,000 men at Pulaski, Tennessee.[9] He was unsure of Hood's intentions, but as early as 21 November he had received cavalry reports that the Confederates were approaching. Even without any additional information, Schofield did not want to remain in Hood's front. He had already received orders from George Thomas in Nashville to delay the Confederates but not bring on a general engagement. Rumor had it that Hood had 40,000 men, although this overstated his actual strength by about 8,000. Schofield became alarmed at the enemy advance and ordered a retreat. He decided to cross the Duck River, putting it between him and the pursuing Confederates. The cavalry was charged with guarding all of the crossings but they overlooked Davis's Ford, the point at which Pat Cleburne would cross.[10] Cleburne's infantry consisted of four brigades, under Lowrey, Govan, Granbury, and James A. Smith, but Smith, along with Thomas Key's battery, was detached to protect the supply train. He did not rejoin the army until 6 December.

The Confederates made their camps on the southern approaches to Columbia. Lee's corps occupied the southwest, Stewart the center, and Cheatham the southeast. On Sunday, 27 November, Cleburne's division was headquartered 2 miles from Columbia. Schofield had ordered its evacuation the day before, but due to heavy rain it was not completed until the following evening. The Confederates spent Monday night constructing pontoon bridges. On 29 November the race for Spring Hill continued.

The battle, or lack thereof, at Spring Hill was without question one of the most contentious episodes of the entire war. A major factor contributing to the difficulty in understanding the events that transpired was the fact that so many participants on the Southern side were killed the next day at Franklin. Cleburne, Granbury, Strahl, Gist, and Adams lost their lives on the field

---

[8] Thomas Y. Cartwright, "Franklin: The Valley of Death," in Mauriel P. Joslyn, ed., *A Meteor Shining Brightly* (Macon GA: Mercer University Press, 2000) 182.

[9] Alethea D. Sayers, "The Last Campaign," in Joslyn, ed., *Meteor Shining Brightly*, 154.

[10] Sayers, "Last Campaign," 156.

while John Carter received a mortal wound, rendering the battle reports inconclusive. Out of the ashes of the multiple failures within the Confederate high command came a series of charges and rebuttals. Hood lashed out at all of his generals, but he vented most of his wrath at Frank Cheatham.

Cleburne's division was up before daybreak and crossed the Duck River at Davis's Ford with Mark Lowrey in the lead.[11] The Confederates marched east along an old wagon road through clusters of cedars. Cleburne led the advance, followed by William Bate, John Brown, and A. P. Stewart's corps. Edward Johnson's division of Lee's corps had been temporarily transferred, and his infantry brought up the rear. Combined, they had seven divisions with roughly 20,000 men.[12]

Schofield had already received permission from Thomas to fall back if he were endangered. In anticipation of an attack he had issued orders to send 2 divisions from David Stanley's corps and 800 wagons to Spring Hill. However, during the morning his cavalry delivered ominous news. They feared that the Confederates might try a flanking maneuver on the forces between the Duck River and Rutherford's Creek. Schofield rescinded his order and recalled Nathan Kimball, leaving only George Wagner's division moving north. He entered Spring Hill shortly after noon with just over 5,600 men.[13] The nearest Federal troops to Wagner were Kimball's men, 7 miles south of Luther Bradley's brigade at Rutherford's Creek. Even after the departure of Wagner and Kimball, the larger part of the army was still in front of Stephen Lee. Wagner's third brigade, under Bradley, had made it into Spring Hill by 2:00 P.M., although the wagons were still entering the town two hours later.[14]

---

[11] Howell and Elizabeth Purdue, *Pat Cleburne Confederate General* (1973; repr., Gaithersburg MD: Olde Soldier Books, 1987) 393.

[12] J. P. Young, "Hood's Failure at Spring Hill," *Confederate Veteran* 16/2 (January 1908): 32. According to Young, Cleburne and Brown combined had 6,785 men, Bate had 2,100, Forrest roughly 5,000, Stewart and Johnson combined had 10,700. The Confederates had 25,021 men on the field, with Lee's two divisions in supporting distance. Wood, Cox, and Kimball were 7 to 10 miles away.

[13] OR, ser. 1, vol. 45, pt. 1, p. 1133. Weekly Report of Effective Force of the Department of the Cumberland 28 November 1864 gives Wagner's total as 5,689 men. Stanley Horn (*The Army of Tennessee* [Norman: University of Oklahoma Press, 1952] 32) places the number slightly lower, at 5,500.

[14] Report of Luther P. Bradley, 5 December 1864, OR, ser. 1, vol. 45, pt. 1, p. 268–69.

The Federals deployed in a semicircle on the east side of Spring Hill. Emerson Opdycke arrived about 12:30 P.M. and faced northeast, with John Lane on his right. Situated on a knoll three-quarters of a mile south of town, Bradley's 2,000-man brigade completed the line. The slight elevation provided an open view of the field but there was a gap of half a mile between his left and Lane's right. Barricades of fence rails were quickly erected and the Federals placed thirty-four artillery pieces in position.[15]

During the morning hours Forrest had pressed the Union cavalry back to a point 5 miles east of Spring Hill. This made James Wilson think that the Confederates would bypass Spring Hill and Franklin in order to press on to Nashville. As he fell back to protect the approaches, Forrest suddenly turned west. At noon he made contact with skirmishers and David Stanley heard the gunfire, so he hurried Opdycke's brigade forward at the double-quick, only minutes ahead of Forrest's Graycoats.

Hood established his headquarters at Absalom Thompson's house, 500 yards west of Rally Hill Road and 2 miles south of Spring Hill. Here he received some conflicting information. Forrest told him that there had been skirmishing over an extended front, indicating that part of Schofield's army had passed the Confederates and had already reached Spring Hill. However, Hood had also seen several reports from couriers stating that most of the Union Army was still at the Duck River opposite Stephen Lee.[16] This left Hood in a state of uncertainty. He was sure that the Federals were spread out, but where was the main body?

Hood's first move was to place Cheatham's corps between them, and he was ordered to move his infantry in two parallel columns along the Rally Hill Road. Cleburne faced west toward the Columbia-Franklin Pike.[17] Bate would follow and face west as well, while Brown would advance on the east side of the road.

The plan was not only a logical one, it was a very good one. Hood believed that his location behind the river had given Schofield a false sense of

---

[15] William R. Scaife, *The Campaign for Tennessee* (Atlanta: Civil War Publications, 2003) 22.

[16] John K. Shellenberger, *The Battle of Spring Hill, Tennessee, November 29, 1864* (Cleveland OH: Arthur H. Clark Company, 1913) 100–103; John B. Hood, "The Invasion of Tennessee," 4:431.

[17] Scaife, *The Campaign for Tennessee*, 22.

security. He would hold the Federals at Columbia with a strong demonstration by Stephen Lee while he took the rest of his army around their left flank. They would cross the Duck River 3 miles behind the Union lines, block the pike at Spring Hill, and then destroy Schofield between them. The Army of Tennessee would then have a clear road to Nashville, the campaign's ultimate objective. Such was Hood's original intent, but he would soon change his mind. He explained his plans to Cheatham and Cleburne. Upon reaching the field, Cleburne was to attack immediately without waiting for any reinforcements. Bate and Brown would support Cleburne while a portion of Stewart's corps would move northwest, take control of the pike, and then turn south toward Columbia.[18] According to Captain John Shellenberger of the 64th Ohio infantry, the plan would have worked well "if it had been carried out, in the orders to Cheatham's divisions."[19]

Hood gave the following account of the afternoon:

Thus I led the main body of the army to within about two miles and in full view of the pike from Columbia to Spring Hill and Franklin. I here halted about 3 p.m., and requested General Cheatham, commanding the leading corps, and Major-General Cleburne to advance to the spot where, sitting upon my horse, I had in sight the enemy's wagons and men passing at double-quick along the Franklin Pike. As these officers approached I spoke to Cheatham in the following words, which I quote almost verbatim, as they have remained indelibly engraved upon my memory ever since that fatal day: "General, do you see the enemy there, retreating rapidly to escape us?" He answered in the affirmative. "Go" I continued "with your corps, take possession of and hold that pike at or near Spring Hill. Accept whatever comes, and turn all those wagons over to our side of the house." Then I turned to Cleburne and said "General, you have heard the orders just given. You have one of my best divisions. Go with General Cheatham, aid him in every way you can, and do as he

[18] Young, "Hood's Failure," 25; Robert Selph Henry, *Forrest: First with the Most* (1944; repr., Wilmington NC: Broadfoot Publishing, 1991) 387–88.
[19] Shellenberger, *Battle of Spring Hill,* 102–103.

directs." I added "Go and do this at once. Stewart is near at hand, and I shall have him double-quick his men to the front."[20]

Hood rode with Cheatham and arrived at Rutherford's Creek at 3:00 P.M., 2 1/2 miles south of Spring Hill. Without asking Forrest to reconnoiter the area, Hood gave Cheatham the following verbal orders: "Cleburne was to advance across the creek on the Rally Hill Pike and proceed to Spring Hill. He would march on the west side of the road and parallel to it. Once there, he was to communicate with Forrest, determine the position of the enemy and attack immediately. Cheatham would remain with Bate and send him toward a farm which belonged to Nathaniel Cheairs. Hood would direct Brown's division from his position at the creek."[21]

Brown soon discovered that a crossing of Rutherford's Creek would not be practicable on the east side of the stream, so he moved to his left where he found Bate preparing to ford. However, just as Brown was about to begin his advance, States Rights Gist's brigade and half of Otho Strahl's were detached for picket duty, to be relieved by orders of the commanding general. This removed much of Brown's striking power, reducing his division to only 2,750 men. After reaching Rutherford's, Brown was instructed to march north in the direction of the Caldwell property. Once the men reached the vicinity of the house they changed direction to the left and reached the Rally Hill Turnpike near a toll-gate 1 1/2 miles from Spring Hill. Brown moved his division 500 yards and threw his right flank across the road, with his left extending westward until it was 600 yards from Bradley's position.[22]

A. P. Stewart reached Rutherford's Creek between 3:00 and 4:00 P.M., just as Brown was crossing. A staff officer from Hood told him an attack was to be made, and Stewart fully expected to be hurried forward in support. He received orders to do so at 6:00 P.M., but as he approached Spring Hill another aide arrived and halted his corps. Stewart would be held south of Rutherford's Creek until 9:00 P.M.[23]

---

[20] Hood, *Advance and Retreat*, 284–85.

[21] James D. Porter, "Spring Hill and the Battle of Franklin," *Confederate Veteran* 12/7 (July 1904): 342.

[22] James D. Porter, *Confederate Military History*, 12 vols. (Atlanta: Confederate Publishing Company, 1899) 8:148–51; Young, "Hood's Failure," 31.

[23] Report of Alexander P. Stewart, 3 April 1865, OR, ser. 1, vol. 45, pt. 1, p. 712–13.

Shortly before 4:00 P.M. Cleburne began to approach Bradley. Hood was with him to witness the opening attack. Cleburne placed Mark Lowrey on the right, Daniel Govan in the center, and Hiram Granbury on the left. The moment Lowrey arrived in position, he formed a line of battle and moved forward. On his right was Luther Bradley's brigade, situated on the knoll and supported with artillery. His formation curved in a southwesterly direction toward the turnpike, with the left end anchored by the 79th Illinois. The 51st Illinois, 15th Missouri, and 65th Ohio completed the line. Bradley threw out the 64th Ohio as skirmishers and brought up the 42nd Illinois to protect his right flank.

At 4:15 Cleburne attacked. Lowrey moved through a wooded area, and when he came out he found his brigade within range of the 42nd Illinois. The 42nd, along with the 64th Ohio and one battery of artillery on the east side of the pike, delivered an enfilading fire that caused Lowrey to change front and call up Govan in support. Together they opened a furious counterattack, driving the Federals back at the point of the bayonet. Cleburne dispatched Mangum with orders to bring up Granbury. He was to advance in a line parallel to the pike and 200 yards east of it. Bradley's men were largely inexperienced, and without any help on their flank the rest of the brigade collapsed. The front line of infantry had been destroyed, but as they fell back they passed through a ravine and uncovered eight guns of their own artillery. The cannon erupted, and fire from their front and flank checked Cleburne's advance. The action was brief, lasting only until 4:30, but the Confederates had become disorganized. To make matters worse, a house had been set on fire by Union artillery. Govan and his adjutant rushed into the building and managed to save the family, but the heroic actions disrupted what little continuity Cleburne had left. He was in the process of reforming when around sunset he got the order to halt.

Bate did not see Cheatham at the moment he arranged his line of battle, but Hood was present. Bate had left Cleburne and headed south on the Rally Hill Pike until he reached Bate's position. Hood would send Bate forward so that Cheatham could place him properly on the field. Under Hood's direction, he formed on the west side of the road.[24] The lines were established in an identical formation as Cleburne, but half a mile to the south. This was a crucial point in the action at Spring Hill. It was here that Hood changed his

---

[24] Report of Nathan Bedford Forrest, 24 January 1865, OR, ser. 1, vol. 45, pt. 1, p. 753.

mind and altered the original battle plan. Instead of assisting Cleburne, Hood now directed Bate to assume the role that was earlier given to Stewart. Bate would now secure the pike and turn toward Columbia. Stewart's corps and Johnson's division would remain on the south side of Rutherford's Creek to protect the roads to Murfreesboro in case Schofield attempted to escape.[25] Hood and Bate were alone, and neither Cheatham nor Cleburne was aware of the conversation so assumed that Bate would support Cleburne. Cheatham had left Bate and ridden 1 mile, but just as Cheatham brought his horse to halt he saw the end of Cleburne's command disappear over a hill. He brought Bate's division forward and sent the men over the same ground on Cleburne's left.

Soon after Cheatham heard the guns on Cleburne's right, Brown arrived on the Rally Hill Pike. Cheatham instructed him to march around the hills in his front and form on Lowrey's brigade. As he was sending Brown into position, Cheatham received a message from Cleburne confirming that his right flank had been attacked with heavy losses. It was close to 4:30 P.M. when Cheatham began to move Brown forward, and shortly after 5:00 he was in position.[26] He arranged his lines behind Cleburne and at a right angle to him. While Cleburne and Bate faced west, Brown faced almost due north.

At 6 o'clock Brown was ordered to attack, but he sent word back to Cheatham that the battle would be a disaster, as the Federal line extended beyond his right flank by several hundred yards. Not only were Gist and Strahl absent, but to make matters worse Brown had no cavalry or artillery support. After conferring with his brigadiers he decided to wait for further instructions. Cheatham ordered him to throw back his right and attack. At that moment Cleburne appeared, announcing that he had adjusted his lines. Upon hearing this Cheatham ordered Brown to connect his left with Cleburne.

Brown may have had reservations about the Federals in his front, but Cheatham was unconcerned. Hood had reassured him that A. P. Stewart was "near at hand" and would provide immediate support. Unfortunately, not only was Stewart not "near at hand," but Hood had given him specific orders to remain on the south side of Rutherford's Creek. Cheatham told both Cleburne and Brown that he would ride to Bate and direct his movements.

---

[25] Purdue and Purdue, *Pat Cleburne Confederate General,* 396.
[26] Scaife (*The Campaign of Tennessee,* 23) places the time at 5:30 P.M.

Cheatham said that he had already sent Lieutenant Schell to order Bate to stop his advance and form on Cleburne's left. The attack would be made from right to left and begin at the sound of Brown's guns. As Cheatham reflected, "I immediately rode to the left of my line for that purpose." On his return he received a message from headquarters directing him to attend a meeting at the Thompson house.[27]

Joseph Vaulx, an aide on Cheatham's staff, recounted a slightly different story. He claimed that as Cheatham rode to the left, he kept repeating, "Why don't I hear Brown's guns?" Brown had discovered that he was outflanked and sent word to Cheatham that any attack would be senseless. Cheatham met Hood's couriers and upon hearing their report remarked, "If that is the case, then come with me to General Hood and tell him what you have told me." Hood replied in substance, "If that is the case, do not attack, but order your troops to hold the position they are in for the night."[28] While the overall picture is similar, there are certainly some discrepancies.

On 24 October 1881, John Brown wrote the following from St. Louis:

> When near Rutherford's Creek, learning that a crossing was not practicable east of the road, I changed the direction of the march to the left into the road, and found Bate's Division preparing to cross the stream. After reaching the north bank of the stream I was ordered to pursue the road leading in the direction of the Caldwell place, while Cleburne's and Bate's divisions moved at an angle to the left, but, before reaching the Caldwell house, I was ordered to change the direction of my columns to the left, and we reached the Lewisburg or Rally Hill pike, near the toll-gate, a distance of one and one-half miles from Spring Hill. This was within an hour or an hour and a half of sunset. I could distinctly see the enemy in force both of infantry and artillery, at Spring Hill, but I did not, and perhaps could not, at that point, see either troops or wagons moving along the Columbia pike.... I formed my line as speedily as worn troops could move, and, after throwing forward a skirmish line, advanced four hundred or five

[27] B. F. Cheatham, "Lost Opportunity at Spring Hill," in *Southern Historical Society Papers*, 52 vols. (Millwood NY: Kraus Reprint Co., 1977) 9:525–27; Horn, *Army of Tennessee*, 29–31; Young, "Hood's Failure," 31–33.

[28] Young, "Hood's Failure," 33–35.

hundred yards, when I discovered a line of the enemy thrown out of Spring Hill, across and threatening my right flank, and I then discovered for the first time that General Forrest's cavalry, which I had been assured would protect my right, had been ordered to another part of the field, leaving me without any protection on my right flank or support in my rear. I had neither artillery nor cavalry, and was left in a position where I must meet with inevitable disaster if I advanced on Spring Hill. A hasty consultation with my brigade commanders resulted in a determination to suspend the advance and confer with the corps commander. I need not remind you [B. F. Cheatham] that in a very few minutes you were on the field and fully approved of what had been done, as also did General Hood a little later, when he directed that the attack should be delayed until the arrival of Generals Stewart and Gist, and in the meantime that the whole command should be held under orders to advance at a moment's notice. General Stewart's corps came up later and went into bivouac on the stream in rear of my right, where it remained until the following morning. I received no further orders that evening or during the night to advance or change my position.[29]

Cheatham, Bate, and Cleburne were unaware of Hood's conversation with Brown—all they knew was that Brown was silent. It was close to 7:00 P.M. when Cheatham went to Hood to inform him that Brown was outflanked, but it was not until 8:30 that Hood sent a staff officer to Stewart with orders to align his troops on Brown's right.[30] According to Joseph Cummings of Hood's staff, Cheatham explained Brown's situation and offered his opinion as to the wisdom of a night attack. Hood refused to hear any excuses. He said he would send an officer to bring Stewart up on Brown's right, but he sought and received assurance from Cheatham that Stewart's arrival would secure the pike. Hood then announced that everything else could wait until morning. Cheatham, absolutely stunned, wrote: " I was never more astonished than when Gen. Hood informed me that he concluded to postpone the attack until daylight. The road was still open—orders to remain quiet until

---

[29] Cheatham, "Lost Opportunity," 9:537–38.
[30] Purdue and Purdue, *Pat Cleburne Confederate General,* 403; Sayers, "Last Campaign," 166–67.

morning—and there was nothing to prevent the enemy from marching to Franklin."[31]

Hiram Granbury continued toward the pike and Wagner knew he was in trouble. He began to rush reinforcements to the front. Granbury pushed Emerson Opdycke's 36th Illinois back through a section of guns belonging to a Pennsylvania battery. He tried to connect his Texans with the rest of the division, but to do this he had to endure the fire of eighteen guns posted on the ridge southwest of Spring Hill. Cleburne now became aware of more Federals on his right. John Lane had moved his 26th Ohio to Bradley's assistance and changed his front to support the battered left flank.[32]

Marching unopposed, Granbury had reached his objective and was less than 100 yards from the road. By 6:30 it was completely dark, but he knew that Bate was trying to connect with his left. Within fifteen minutes his men could hear the muffled sounds of Thomas Ruger's division and one brigade under Walter Whitaker as they moved steadily along the pike. When the Confederates heard the muffled sounds of Ruger's Yankees, many of them thought the Union column was Bate's men, moving northward in an attempt to find Granbury's left flank. R. M. Collins reported that "pretty soon we heard troops moving over beyond the fence." Some one said that it was Bate's division "tiering" to the left. Others said it was a body of Federal troops. Granbury's adjutant went to investigate, but he was captured and never returned. At 7:30 Ruger had passed, but only after Cleburne had been ordered to pull back Granbury. To the south William Bate had had some difficulty searching for Granbury, but by 8:00 they had joined their lines.[33]

Despite the proximity of Cleburne's division to the turnpike, Joseph Bostick of Cheatham's staff arrived with instructions to halt until further orders. None came, and at nightfall Cleburne's division went into bivouac, still facing the road. The results of Cleburne's assault were heavily in his favor, but the casualties were not. Bradley reported a loss of 198 men in the attack, while his casualties were approximately 500.[34] According to Mark

[31] Cheatham, "Lost Opportunity," 9:526.
[32] Young, "Hood's Failure," 31–33. These guns were from Battery A, 1st Ohio Light Artillery, 4 guns; Battery G, 1st Ohio Light Artillery, 6 guns; Battery B, Pennsylvania Veteran Volunteers, 4 guns, and Battery M, United States Artillery, 4 guns.
[33] Purdue and Purdue, *Pat Cleburne Confederate General,* 404.
[34] Report of Luther P. Bradley, 5 December 1864, OR, ser. 1, vol. 45, pt. 1, p. 268–69.

Lowrey, almost all of the Confederate losses came from his brigade, with the exception of five or six wounded and one or two killed in Govan's command. The brief stand by the 42nd Illinois played a major role in the failure of Hood's plan. It caused Cleburne to turn north, and although he drove Bradley from the field in a very short period of time he turned his attention away from the pike, which was the more important objective.

William Bate faced a similar problem. His division had continued until it reached the Cheairs property. Cleburne had already engaged the enemy, and when he changed his line of attack he was unable to see the action along the pike. Rolling hills separated the divisions and they began to drift further apart. Bate's skirmishers opened fire on the head of the Federal column, which temporarily threw the Federals into confusion. They scattered, but the momentary success did not last long. At 5:30 P.M. Lieutenant A. B. Schell arrived with an order from Cheatham directing him to stop his advance and link his division with Cleburne's left.[35] Cheatham had ascended high ground to observe Cleburne's division and was not aware of Hood's earlier conversation with Bate. Despite the directive to halt, Bate had reached his objective. He was reluctant to give up ground already won. In order to confirm the order he sent a messenger to the Thompson house, where Cheatham was with Hood. Bate stated that he "occupied a good position" to defeat the Federals. He was only 100 yards from the turnpike when Ruger passed his lines.[36]

In Hood's presence, Cheatham responded with a peremptory order for Bate to move to his right and unite with Granbury, or Cheatham would have him arrested. Bate withdrew, though with considerable difficulty. It took some time, but by 8:00 the Confederates had joined their forces. This meant very little. By that time Ruger was already gone, and shortly after 9 o'clock Bate went into bivouac.[37]

Bostick's note ordered Cleburne to halt "until receiving further orders." The troops were extremely frustrated at the order to stop when they were so close to victory. Granbury could have easily taken the turnpike, but Cleburne was compelled to abandon the position. Daniel Govan wrote: "Had we not

---

[35] Horn, *Army of Tennessee,* 29.

[36] Cheatham, "Lost Opportunity," 9:540; Henry, *First with the Most,* 392; Sayers, "Last Campaign," 164.

[37] Shellenberger, *Battle of Spring Hill,* 142.

been halted and made a determined advance, we could in 20 minutes have captured or destroyed Schofield [Wagner] together with 800 wagons and his artillery and planted our army firmly on the pike."[38]

In a report from Leonard Mangum, Pat Cleburne echoed those sentiments precisely, but he mistakenly placed the failure's blame on Bate. He was not aware that Hood had changed Bate's line of advance. Mangum recorded Cleburne's words: "The arrest of his movement on the turnpike was a bitter disappointment to General Cleburne and he expressed himself very forcibly in regard to the failure [of Bate] that caused it."[39]

Cleburne was constrained by the instructions to wait for Brown's guns, but they never opened. William Bate had a serious dilemma on his hands. His first order came from the commanding general, explicitly instructing him to reach the pike and turn south. Now Cheatham sent a different order that halted his movements, instead sending him to Cleburne's left. Bate chose to do nothing, and decided to seek some confirmation from Cheatham.[40]

> This order of Cheatham must have been given in ignorance of that of General Hood to Bate, as a continuation of the movement then in progress would have caught in flank the Federal column at that time moving on the pike, completely blocked the way, and stopped the passage through Spring Hill of Schofield's forces retreating from Columbia and compelled them to form line and remain until morning in that position, with two corps and a division on his flank and front, and Lee with two divisions on his flank and rear.[41]

The Confederate cavalry had been fighting on foot almost continuously throughout the day, and the men were almost out of cartridges. Forrest rode to Hood to informed him of the situation. Hood told Forrest that Cheatham held the pike, but Forrest explained that he did not. Hood then asked Forrest if he could hold it until he got Cheatham into position. Forrest replied that

---

[38] Govan to George A. Williams, [?] June 1906, in Irving A. Buck, *Cleburne and His Command* (1908; repr., Wilmington NC: Broadfoot Publishing, 1995) 270–76.

[39] J. C. Brown to B. F. Cheatham, 24 October 1881, in Cheatham, "Lost Opportunity," 9:538–39.

[40] Purdue and Purdue, *Pat Cleburne Confederate General,* 404.

[41] Buck, *Cleburne and His Command,* 267.

Chalmers and Buford had no ammunition, but Jackson would try to check the retreat. As Hood heard no musketry, he assumed that the Confederates held either the town or the pike. He claimed that he sent word to Cheatham, instructing him to attack at once. "Cheatham was ordered to attack the enemy at once vigorously *and* get possession of the pike, and, although these orders were frequently and earnestly repeated, he made but a feeble and partial attack, failing to reach the point indicated. Had my instructions been carried out there is no doubt that we would have possessed the road."[42]

Along with Edward Johnson's division, A. P. Stewart had been ordered to remain on the south side of Rutherford's Creek to protect the escape routes to Murfreesboro. He was of the opinion that four divisions was a much larger force than necessary in order to accomplish Hood's purpose, and he decided to investigate. Shortly after 6:00 P.M. he rode ahead of his corps and found Hood sitting by a fire at the side of the road. He was to leave one division south of the creek, move forward, and go into line on Brown's right flank. Hood ordered him to place his right flank across the pike beyond the town, with his left "extending down this way." This would place Stewart's corps behind Cheatham with his right continuing past Brown's division. Hood furnished him with a local guide, but in an attempt to find a shortcut he took a wrong turn that cost a great deal of time. At 9:00 P.M. Stewart arrived at the Caldwell home, which happened to be Forrest's headquarters.

While the two men were talking, a staff officer from Cheatham's corps arrived with orders that he claimed had come from General Hood. He explained that the body of Stewart's command had been halted, which puzzled Stewart, as the order came from member of Cheatham's staff not Hood's. Stewart thought it was possible that Hood had changed his mind, so he inquired whether the aide had seen Hood more recently than he had. The young man replied that he had, and that the reason he was sent was that he had gone over the ground with Brown during daylight hours. Stewart thought it best to comply, and they continued toward Spring Hill until they came upon Brown. He pointed out that his right flank extended away from the pike, not toward it. Stewart recognized that a mistake had been made and allowed his men to go into bivouac.

---

[42] Report of John B. Hood, 15 February 1865, OR, ser. 1, vol. 45, pt. 1, p. 652–56; emphasis added.

Despite the importance of the battle, Hood had gone to bed early that night. Stewart and Forrest awakened him at 10:00 P.M. Stewart told Hood that his men had halted for the night, whereupon Hood told him to let them rest. Hood turned to Forrest and asked whether or not he could block the road with his cavalry. At this point Forrest replied that Buford and Chalmers were out of ammunition, but Jackson had captured a supply during the day and would "do his best in an emergency."[43] While Forrest was talking with Hood, Bate entered and informed the commanding general that his movements had caused a cessation of the movement on the turnpike; however, due to his receipt of Cheatham's order to halt he had not crossed it. Bate was very apprehensive about so much traffic passing the Confederate lines, but Hood replied that "it made no difference now, as General Forrest has just left and assured me that he holds the pike."[44] Forrest had said nothing of the sort. Two-thirds of his cavalry had no bullets, and he said only that Jackson would "do his best." This was a guarantee only in Hood's mind.

After Bate departed a private arrived and informed Hood that the Yankees were escaping. He stated that he had been behind enemy lines and seen the Federals greatly confused. The roads to Franklin were blocked by baggage wagons and gun carriages. Hood could not confirm any of the reports, as he had already retired when he was told that troops were marching along the turnpike. Without getting out of bed, he sent A. P. Mason, his chief of staff, to deliver the orders to Cheatham to advance on the road. The next day, Mason admitted that he never sent the message; Isham Harris verified Mason's account: "On the march to Franklin, Gen. Hood spoke to me, in the presence of Maj. Mason, of the failure of Gen. Cheatham to make the night attack at Spring Hill, and censured him in severe terms for his disobedience of orders. Soon after this, being alone with Maj. Mason, the latter remarked that 'Gen. Cheatham was not to blame about the matter last night. I did not send him the order.' Porter asked him if he had told Hood that. He had not."[45]

Hood went to sleep well behind Confederate lines while his subordinates were passing orders back and forth, yet he maintained, "I could not succeed in arousing the troops to action." Captain John Inglis of the 3rd Florida disputed this contention, reporting, "We lay down early in the afternoon near

---

[43] Report of Alexander P. Stewart, 3 April 1865, OR, ser. 1, vol. 45, pt. 1, p. 712–13.

[44] Henry, *First with the Most*, 393; Young, "Hood's Failure," 42.

[45] Porter, "Spring Hill," 343.

Spring Hill, saw Schofield [Wagner] pass by—our men begging to fight—never saw men so anxious." Hood placed a great deal of the blame on the divisions under Brown and Cleburne. It should be noted that when they fought Lane's and Bradley's troops the next day they attacked with devastating effect. At Spring Hill, both divisions had specific orders to stop their advance before they reached the turnpike. Hood's assertion that he was unable to persuade these men to attack is simply not believable.

After Bate returned from his conference with Hood, Cleburne offered a suggestion since both Cleburne and Bate understood what was happening, even if Hood and Cheatham did not. "Bate, suppose you and I report to General Hood under arrest and leave our divisions under the commands of our brigadiers, and before we get back they will have whipped the Yankee army." After some consideration, they decided not to pursue such a radical measure.[46]

Edward Johnson had been assigned temporarily to Cheatham's corps. At 11:00 P.M. Hood ordered him to take his division and report to Cheatham. Major Bostick was then directed to place Johnson on the extreme left, next to Bate. He was to deploy his troops across the turnpike and use whatever force necessary to prevent enemy troops from marching toward Spring Hill. Bostick returned at midnight and reported that he heard stragglers heading north on the pike.

While Bostick was discussing this with James Porter, Cheatham's chief-of-staff, a courier from Hood's headquarters delivered a note from Mason. The message explained that General Hood had just learned that there were still some enemy soldiers passing along the road in front of Cheatham's left, and "the Commanding General says you had better order your picket line to fire on them."[47] Cheatham differed considerably and offered his own version of the facts: "This suggestion that I had better order my pickets to fire on stragglers passing in front of my left was the only order, if that can be called an order, that I received from General Hood after leaving him at his quarters early in the night, when he had informed me of his determination to wait until daylight to attack the enemy."[48]

---

[46] Young, "Hood's Failure," 25.
[47] Cheatham, "Lost Opportunity," 9:527.
[48] Cheatham, "Lost Opportunity," 9:527.

Cheatham read the note and sent Bostick to order Johnson to take whatever measures necessary to cut off any stragglers. Johnson objected to being "loaned out," asking why Cheatham did not use one of his own divisions, but at length he obeyed. Together Bostick and Johnson rode to the front. They returned to Cheatham at 2:00 A.M. on 30 November and reported that everything was quiet, but by this time the Federals were all in Spring Hill.

The head of the remaining three divisions had begun to pass Cleburne at 10:45, and by 2:00 A.M. the rear of Schofield's command had in fact entered the town. When dawn broke the army was headed to Franklin.[49] Hood was incensed. He began to point fingers, but Schofield was still in striking distance, and the Confederates moved out. After the defeat at Franklin, Cheatham and Hood turned their attention toward their own vindication given the events at Spring Hill. Again, Cheatham took issue with opposing views: "On the morning of the 4th of December, I went to the headquarters of Gen. Hood, and, referring to his note and criticism that had evidently been made by some one, I said to him: 'a great opportunity was lost at Spring Hill, but you know that I obeyed your orders there, as everywhere, literally and promptly.' Hood did not dissent."[50]

During the aftermath of the events surrounding the debacle on 29 November, Hood sent a series of telegrams to Secretary of War James Seddon. The letters were marked by inconsistencies, and Hood refused to assume any responsibility for the failure. The first was sent on 7 December: "I withdraw my *recommendation* in favor of the *promotion of Major-General Cheatham* for reasons which I will write more fully." Two followed the next day: "General G. T. Beauregard, *Macon, Ga.*: A good *Lieutenant General* should be sent here at once to *command the corps now commanded by Major General Cheatham.*... I have no one to recommend for the position." And later: *Major General Cheatham* made a failure on the 30th [29th?] of November *which will be a lesson to him.* I think it best he should remain in his position for the present. I withdraw my telegrams of yesterday and today on this subject." Seddon received one final telegram on 11 December: "Major General Cheatham has frankly confessed the great error of which he was guilty, and attaches much blame to himself. While his error lost so much to the country, it has been a

[49] Purdue and Purdue, *Pat Cleburne Confederate General,* 404–407.
[50] Porter, "Spring Hill," 344.

severe lesson to him, by which he will profit in the future. In consideration of this, and of his previous conduct, I think that it is best that he should retain for the present the command he now holds."[51]

Hood claimed that he sent word to Richmond revoking his recommendation to deny Cheatham's promotion; he explained that prior to these telegrams Cheatham had come to Hood and admitted his error, which had cost the Confederacy the chance of a brilliant victory. Hood then said he withdrew his objection in the belief that "inspired with an ambition to retrieve his shortcomings Cheatham would prove in the future doubly zealous in the service of his country."

Not to be outdone, Cheatham stated that had he received the following note from Hood on 13 December, absolving him from any blame in the affair: "I do not censure you for the failure at Spring Hill. I am satisfied that you are not responsible for it. I witnessed the splendid manner in which you delivered battle at Franklin on the 30th ult [sic]. I now have a higher estimate of you as a soldier than I ever had. You can rely upon my friendship."[52]

Cheatham said he attached no importance to the note and subsequently lost it in North Carolina. One would think he would have kept it at all costs. None of these accounts appear particularly credible, but regardless of their sincerity, the one fact that remains irrefutable is that Frank Cheatham never admitted any failure on his own part. Why Hood felt it necessary to write three letters in two days to justify a decision that governed the fate of an entire corps is difficult to explain. Equally puzzling is how Cheatham managed to lose the one piece of evidence that would have cleared his name in a sequence of events he must have known would remain steeped in controversy.

The following statements from the generals involved all corroborate Cheatham's version of events. They were written in 1881, a year after the publication of Hood's *Advance and Retreat*.

Chancellor's Office, University of Mississippi, Oxford, Miss., February 8, 1881—*Captain W. O. Dodd, Louisvlle, Ky.* My Dear Sir: I will say, however, that on that occasion General Hood was at the front with Cheatham's and Forrest's troops, and should have compelled the execution of his orders. I was not allowed to cross Rutherford's Creek

[51] Hood, *Advance and Retreat*, 289–90; the words in italics were in cipher.
[52] Cheatham, "Lost Opportunity," 9:534.

until dark. When I reached the creek, riding in advance of my troops, Cheatham's Corps was crossing. A staff officer of his informed me that an attack was to be made. I expected to be hurried forward to support the attack. Instead, I was ordered to form in line of battle *before crossing* the creek, and about at right angles to it. This, in my poor judgment, was the fatal error. My impression is that Cheatham and his officers thought themselves in great danger of being outflanked and crushed. Had they known my command was coming up to their support, it is likely they would not have hesitated to make the attack. When, about dusk, I received orders to move across the creek, and rode forward to find the Commanding General, he complained bitterly that his orders to attack had not been obeyed. But *he was there himself.* I asked him why he had halted me at Rutherford's Creek. He replied that he confidently expected Cheatham would attack and rout the enemy; that there was a road leading to Murfreesboro on the other side of the creek. He wished me there to prevent the escape of a routed foe in that direction. Here, I think, was the error. Johnson's Division of Lee's Corps was with me. That division, reinforced if necessary by one of mine, would have been sufficient to guard that road. The rest of my command should have been pressed forward to reinforce Cheatham and Forrest. I have a note from General Hood, written after we moved round into North Carolina, fully exonerating me from all censure on that occasion.

Very sincerely yours, Alex. P. Stewart[53]

Blue Mountain, Tippah County, Miss., November 8, 1881.— *** After I made the attack my command was not struck in flank by the enemy, as you seem to have understood from General Cheatham, and I only had to make a slight change of direction, by swinging my left round, which was done without much confusion. As I drove the enemy from his rail protection, a command of the enemy was left in line on my right, and I saw demonstrations by the officers which led me to believe they were attempting to charge me in flank. I reported this to General Cleburne, and he moved against them with Govan's

[53] Alexander P. Stewart to B. F. Cheatham, "The Lost Opportunity at Spring Hill,: 9:534-36. ; emphasis original.

Arkansas brigade. The only trouble I had with these fellows on my right was to give them a few shots from my right flank to keep them demoralized; and as their flank was to my flank they could not have charged us without changing front, and as I was in full view of them I watched them. I did not see the enemy's wagons during the day. Rather, I should say, I do not remember if I did.

Yours truly, M. P. Lowrey[54]

General Bate recounted the events in a letter to Cheatham:

> After you [B. F. Cheatham] had ordered me to retire my lines so as to align my right with Cleburne's left, and the order obeyed, skirmishers placed, pickets posted and the men sleeping on their arms in line of battle—it being then a late hour, between 10 and 12 o'clock at night—I, accompanied by a staff officer and one or more couriers, did go to General Hood's quarters, at a farmhouse, and made known to him the situation in my front an what had occurred there that evening and night, the same and substance, as shown in my official report, forwarded through your office soon thereafter, a copy of which I suppose you have.
>
> Upon my arrival at his quarters I found General Hood in conference with General Forrest, consequently I waited some time for an interview. I informed the General about having, about dark, come near to, in line of battle, and commanded, with my skirmish line, the turnpike south of Spring Hill, and caused a cessation in the movements of wagons, horsemen, etc., which were passing; but I did not pass on to the turnpike and sweep toward Columbia as you [J. B. Hood] had directed me to do, because just at that time I received an order from my corps commander, General Cheatham, to halt and align the right of my division with the left of Cleburne's, which I declined to do until I received a second order to the same effect, and then I did so.
>
> General Hood replied in substance: "It makes no difference now, or it is all right anyhow, for General Forrest, as you see, has just left and informed me that he holds the turnpike with a portion of his

---

[54] Cheatham, "Lost Opportunity," 9:536.

forces north of Spring Hill, and will stop the enemy if he tries to pass toward Franklin, and so in the morning we will have a surrender without a fight." Hood added, "We can sleep quiet tonight."[55]

Cheatham was collecting his forces for a strike on Spring Hill itself, while Hood was concentrating on the possession of the turnpike and Schofield's troops back in Columbia. In any discussion of the battle of Spring Hill, numerous questions abound. Many different Confederates played a role in the dramatic escape of the Union Army, but all of the testimony ultimately goes to the heart of one basic question: Was the disaster at Spring Hill the fault of John B. Hood, or was Frank Cheatham the larger culprit?

Perhaps it is best to consider the events in the order they occurred. The first issue that must be resolved is the extent to which Hood was able to view the Columbia-Franklin Turnpike. Hood maintained that he was with Cheatham at 3 o'clock. Hood pointed to the pike asked, "Do you see the Federal columns marching along the pike?" Hood also states that Cheatham replied that he did, but it would have been impossible to see the turnpike from Hood's position. A topographical study performed by the Tennessee Valley Authority made the following conclusion: "It is a geographical fact, determined by an actual visit to the place, and by reference to a current TVA topographical map indicating a considerably higher elevation [40 feet] of intervening terrain, that Hood could not have seen the road from there."[56]

Cheatham described this account of the events as "total fiction," and observations from both the Union and Confederate armies agree with Cheatham's version. John Shellenberger stated that Hood could see nothing of what was going on in Spring Hill, and Cheatham claimed that not only was there never any movement of enemy troops on the turnpike at 3:00 P.M., but the pike was not visible from the point where Hood claimed he was stationed.[57]

Mark Lowrey supported Cheatham with the following statement: "I did not see the enemy's wagons during the day. Rather, I should say, I do not

---

[55] William B. Bate to Cheatham, 29 November 1881, in Cheatham, "Lost Opportunity," 9:534.

[56] David E. Roth, "The General's Tour: The Mysteries of Spring Hill," *Blue and Gray* 2/2 (November 1984): 26.

[57] Shellenberger, *Battle of Spring Hill*, 143.

remember if I did." The movement of Wagner's division and 800 wagons was not an insignificant detail a general officer would easily forget. Hood stated that he observed the turnpike at 3:00 P.M. Luther Bradley reported that the last of the infantry arrived in Spring Hill at 2:00 P.M., though the wagons were still moving along the pike. It is not likely that Hood referred to wagons and mules when he said, "General, do you see the enemy there, retreating rapidly to escape us?"

In his letter written in 1881, Brown agreed with Lowrey: "I could distinctly see the enemy in force both of infantry and artillery, at Spring Hill, but I did not, and perhaps could not, at that point, see either troops or wagons moving along the Columbia pike."[58]

If Hood actually did see Federal columns (Wagner) heading north past Cheatham's corps, why would he tell Cheatham that the attack could wait until morning? During the late-night meeting at his headquarters, Bate informed Hood that troops (by now Ruger's division and Whitaker's brigade) were marching along the pike. Hood gave no indication that he had seen any troops earlier in the day. Having had no confirmation of Bate's report, he hesitated. His only response was to send Mason to Cheatham with advice to fire on enemy pickets. If he had already seen Wagner at 3:00 P.M. and believed there were Yankees on the pike at 11:00 P.M., he would have feared that Schofield's entire army was escaping.

In addition to differing accounts regarding the visibility of the road, there is also a discrepancy in testimony concerning the possession of it. At his headquarters Hood told Forrest that Cheatham held the pike. Forrest clearly explained that this was not the case. Hood then asked whether Forrest could hold it. Despite Forrest's reply that two-thirds of his cavalry had no ammunition but that Jackson would "try to hold it," Hood immediately told Bate that Forrest had sealed the road to Franklin.

A major factor in Cheatham's decision to send Brown forward with only half of his division was the knowledge that A. P. Stewart's corps would add enough weight to the attack to destroy any force that overlapped Brown's flank. This certainly was not conjecture or wishful thinking on Cheatham's part. Hood had told him, in person, that Stewart was on the field. Hood had also told Stewart, in person, to remain on the south side of Rutherford's Creek.

---

[58] Cheatham, "Lost Opportunity," 9:529.

Hood was the army commander, but did he supervise the actions of his subordinates? If one is to believe Hood's version of the events as they unfolded, then Hood stood on the edge of his greatest opportunity of the war—the possibility to redeem himself, salvage his reputation after a series of catastrophic mistakes at Atlanta, and, in his own words, witness "the best move in my career as a soldier I was thus destined to behold." Hood correctly believed that the larger Union force was not at Spring Hill but rather closer to Columbia. His couriers had delivered several reports to this effect, and he had personally instructed William Bate to strike the Columbia-Franklin Pike then turn south in order to eliminate any realistic chance of escape. For the same reason he held A. P. Stewart on the south side of Rutherford's Creek.

Presented with such an opportunity to destroy Schofield and prevent the Federals from reaching Nashville, he retired early and went to sleep. The following quote from Hood would be an explanation for his thought process, but it is no excuse for his absence from the field: "Had I dreamed for one moment that Cheatham would have failed to give battle, or at least take a position across the pike and force the enemy to assault him, I would myself have ridden to the front and led the troops into action."[59]

Physically, John Bell Hood was a broken man. He had lost his right leg at Chickamauga and the use of his left arm at Gettysburg. He had been strapped in the saddle for much of the day, and the extent of his medication is unknown. It is possible that he had been taking laudanum, or liquid opium. Laudanum was commonly used by both sides, but Confederate access to medical supplies was very limited and became more so as the war progressed. Purely military considerations, for both munitions and equipment, had always taken precedence over requests from physicians. These conditions may well have been a factor in Hood's behavior at Spring Hill, yet the preponderance of evidence still suggests that he should have been awake.

Hood may have thought the battle was won as soon as he sent Mason to Cheatham with what he believed were orders to attack. However, this did not ensure that Cheatham would either receive or obey the orders. As Mason himself stated that he did not deliver the orders, and as Cheatham said he never received them, this was not a case in which Cheatham had them in hand and refused to attack. The only inference one could draw is that Hood thought

---

[59] Hood, "The Invasion of Tennessee," 4:431.

his note to Cheatham was a direct order and Cheatham did not regard stragglers as a serious threat.

All of this would lead one to believe that Hood was clearly at fault. However, there are many questions concerning Cheatham's behavior as well. Perhaps the most puzzling was his reaction to Bate's report that there were Federals on the turnpike. Cheatham was with Hood when that news arrived, and he clearly understood the importance of preventing Schofield from reaching Thomas, yet he threatened to have Bate arrested if he did not comply with the order to join his division with Cleburne.

Closely connected to this question is why Cheatham told Bate and Cleburne to halt when both divisions were so close to the pike. Had they been allowed to continue, either division would have taken and held the pike with ease. Wagner's force was too small to be any deterrent; Cleburne, Bate, and Forrest were very close to the turnpike; Stewart and Brown were within supporting distance; the larger part of the Union Army was in front of Stephen Lee; and the Federals were outnumbered to begin with.

Hood failed to control the movements of his subordinates, but did Cheatham do any better? He directed Brown to begin an attack, to be followed by Cleburne, then Bate. He had a plan in his mind, but he failed to see it completed. As far as Cheatham was concerned, the key to his final advance was the forward movement of Brown's division. He may well have intended to start Brown forward when he was intercepted by Hood's couriers. However, if this were true he could have told Hood that an attack was under way, ridden back to Brown, and supervised an assault that undoubtedly would have succeeded.

Some writers have asserted that the Union Army was never in any real danger, as there were alternate routes they could have taken to bypass Spring Hill altogether and arrive in Franklin uncontested. The best evidence in addressing this particular question comes not from overconfident Confederates, nor from modern-day scholars equipped with current maps of the area, but from Federal soldiers who recorded the events as they saw them.

David Stanley was so concerned about the fate of the wagons that he suggested they be burned. Noting the presence of Forrest's cavalry as well as infantry at Spring Hill and Columbia, he added: "Thus we were threatened and attacked from every direction, and it was impossible to send any reinforcements to Bradley's Brigade, which had become engaged, lest in so doing we should expose the train and artillery park to destruction."[60]

Henry Stone, a member of Thomas's staff, observed: "A single Confederate brigade, like Adams, or Cockrell's or Maney's—veterans since Shiloh,—placed squarely across the pike, either south or north of Spring Hill, would have effectually prevented Schofield's retreat, and daylight would have found his whole force cut off from every avenue of escape."[61]

Thomas Wood wrote: "It was necessary to move the troops rapidly and silently through Spring Hill to avoid a night attack on a column from an entire corps of four divisions—Cheatham's, which lay encamped within 800 yards of the road. The effect of a night attack on a column en route would have been, beyond a doubt, most disastrous."[62]

Captain Shellenberger of the 64th Ohio felt that by 3:30 P.M. "the situation of our army had become so critical that nothing short of grossest blundering on the part of the enemy could save it from a great disaster, and there was a fine possibility of destroying it."[63]

Stewart's local guide got lost despite living in the area. There was no guarantee that the Federals would get any guide at all. Furthermore, they were thoroughly unfamiliar with the area, Wilson's cavalry had been driven from the field, and with the exception of Wagner's men, who were already in Spring Hill, they would have had to navigate their way in the dark. Based on Union observations, there was never any consideration of alternate routes, regardless of whether or not they existed.

Aside from Hood and Cheatham's actions, did their lieutenants contribute to the Union escape? Cleburne had attacked aggressively, driving Bradley from his position in a brief period of time, yet he turned north and failed to take possession of the turnpike. This could be construed as a failure, but he was unexpectedly attacked and received enfilading fire from Bradley's brigade. When his own assault was cancelled by Cheatham, he was out of options.

---

[60] Report of David S. Stanley, 25 February 1865, OR, ser. 1, vol. 45, pt. 1, p. 114–15.

[61] Henry Stone, "Repelling Hood's Invasion of Tennessee," in Robert Underwood Johnston and Clarence Clough Buel, eds., *Battles and Leaders of the Civil War*, 4 vols. (1884–1887; repr., Secaucus NJ: Castle Books, n.d.) 4:446.

[62] Report of Thomas J. Wood, 10 January 1865, OR, ser. 1, vol. 45, pt. 1, p. 119–26.

[63] Shellenberger, *Battle of Spring Hill*, 101.

Bate, like Cleburne, had reached a position that would have controlled the turnpike but was also directed to stop. He had been instructed by Hood to take the road, then by Cheatham to turn and connect his right flank with Cleburne. He did try to confirm the instructions to halt, but after Cheatham's peremptory order he was compelled to withdraw or face certain arrest.

Should A. P. Stewart have moved forward and supported Brown's right? Had Stewart been present in the afternoon, perhaps the attack would have been made in concert by overwhelming numbers; Wagner would have been routed and Schofield would have been crushed between Columbia and Spring Hill. However, Stewart had specific orders from Hood to remain at Rutherford's Creek and was not ordered to advance until 9:00 P.M. When he finally did receive permission to support the attack, his guide became lost in the woods.

Nathan Bedford Forrest dominated the cavalry action for much of the day, but he has been faulted for his inability to secure the road from Spring Hill to Franklin. Realistically, could he have been expected to contain his adversary when Buford and Chalmers had no ammunition? If he had devoted his attention to the control of Thompson's Station much earlier in the day and held it with dismounted cavalry, Wilson's troopers would have been turned loose. Again, there is little room for criticism.

The one general officer whose performance seems to be in doubt is John Brown. His movement was the signal for the entire attack to begin, and his failure to initiate the action caused Cleburne and Bate to remain idle. Brown was left without half of his division, and he thought that if he advanced he would be outflanked. He reported this to Cheatham, who told him to refuse his right flank and attack anyway. Cheatham was confident that Brown would have support, as Hood had repeatedly said that Stewart was close at hand. Quite the opposite was true, but Cheatham had no way of knowing that Brown would have to act alone. Even if he had no orders, as he contends in his own reports, he showed very little initiative. With Stewart's entire corps supposedly on his flank, Brown's advance would not have entailed a great degree of risk.

Very different points of view concern the question, "Did Cheatham give Brown the orders to attack?" Judge J. P. Young, who at that time was serving as a member of Forrest's cavalry, made an extensive study of the battle and believes that he did. If he did not order Brown to attack, why did he leave the scene and ride to Bate? Why did he keep asking, "Why don't we hear the guns?" Why didn't Cleburne attack on his own? Cleburne was noted for his enterprise. He knew Bate was on his left, and he thought he had Stewart within supporting distance. Young's conclusion is that the only reason Cleburne and Bate did not attack was that they were awaiting the sound of Brown's guns.

Other views support Brown's version of the battle. James Chalmers and John Brown were on friendly terms, and Chalmers was riding on Brown's right. He asked, "Why didn't you attack?" to which Brown replied, "I have no orders." In a gentle reprimand he pointed out that he had attacked at Shiloh, under similar conditions, in order to "seize an opportunity." Unmoved, Brown repeated, "I would prefer to wait for orders."

Late in the afternoon Captain H. M. Neely, the assistant-adjutant-general to John Carter, and Major John Ingram rode out well in front of the Confederate lines, where they found Federal troops on the pike. They went back to Carter to inquire why there was no attack. He replied that he did not know; he was not in command. The two men continued until they reached Brown, to whom they asked the same question. He replied simply, "I have no orders."[64]

Much of the focus in the unending controversy surrounding Spring Hill concerns the actions of the generals, but overshadowed by the stream of accusations between Hood and Cheatham is the role played by A. P. Mason. Regardless of the fact that Hood should have made sure Cheatham received an order of that importance, the fact remains that it was not delivered.

Several rumors further darken the murky picture of what really happened at Spring Hill, all of which are unsupported speculation. Still, the rumors are interesting enough to perpetuate their discussion. One story is that Frank Cheatham was drunk and unable to effectively discharge the duties of command. Major Joseph Vaulx, an aide on Cheatham's staff, wrote: "I was with Gen. Cheatham when he was giving his orders to Gen. Brown. The charge that he was intoxicated is false. I never saw him more self-possessed than on that afternoon. He gave his orders in a very plain and explicit manner His words expressed just what he wanted, in such a manner that no doubtful construction could be given them."[65]

---

[64] James Dinkins, *1861–1865 Recollections and Experiences in the Confederate Army* (Dayton OH: Morningside, 1975) 232.

[65] H. M. Field, *Bright Skies and Dark Shadows* (New York: Charles Scribner's Sons, 1890) 216.

Former governor Porter confirmed this version of events: "I was with Cheatham during the entire day from Columbia to Spring Hill, and he was not only *not* intoxicated, but I am positive that he did not taste nor see a drop of liquor of any kind."[66]

Another is that John Brown was drunk and therefore failed to obey Cheatham's order to advance. The success of the entire attack depended on Brown's prompt, aggressive assault. Therefore Cheatham must have covered up the fact due to their close friendship. If Chalmers's account is true, the exchange between Brown and Chalmers would lead one to believe that Brown might have been mistaken, lazy, unclear about his orders, or perhaps even cowardly but not drunk.

According to another account, Cheatham failed to give the attention to detail necessary to properly manage the battle because he was away from the field at Jessie Peters's house. James Wilson offered this claim in his *Memoirs*, though only in the form of hazy innuendo. Obviously he was not an eyewitness to any activity there, but he may have repeated a story that had existed since Earl Van Dorn had been murdered by her husband. Certainly she was not averse to frequent visits from Confederate officers, but Cheatham's presence on other parts of the field throughout the day and evening is well documented, making an extended absence from his troops appear unlikely.

Finally, one story suggests that none of the Confederate officers were to blame, because the entire battle was won for the Union through the actions of a spy who infiltrated Confederate lines. This particular tale is perhaps the most amazing of all. J. D. Remington, a member of Emerson Opdycke's brigade, claimed to have secured a Confederate uniform and undermined Southern efforts by preventing information from reaching the various generals involved. Judge Young emphatically stated that "the whole story is manifestly a pipe dream."[67] By 1:00 P.M., Forrest had 5,500 cavalry crossing the area between Opdycke's brigade and the Confederate lines. He would have had to traverse ground in broad daylight through Chalmers and Buford's divisions. At the time skirmish fire was being exchanged, so he would have had to cross a battlefield undetected. Remington asserted that he met Hood and Cheatham as they were directing the advance, when in fact Hood had ridden forward with

---

[66] Field, *Bright Skies,* 216; emphasis original.

[67] J. P. Young, "Remington and Gen. Hood at Spring Hill," *Confederate Veteran* 22/3 (March 1914): 126–28.

Cleburne while Cheatham was back at Rutherford's Creek. Remington goes on to say that he notified Hood that he had just come from Forrest, who told him that he had left one division to annoy the enemy and taken the rest of his command to Thompson's Station to secure the pike at that point. From Hood's position, Chalmers, Buford, and Forrest were all within immediate eyesight.[68] Given these conditions, it would seem that this account has no basis in fact.

In consideration of whether the ultimate failure lay with Hood or Cheatham, the author has chosen to disregard their attacks on each other and rely instead upon corroborating testimony from other sources. A. P. Stewart, who was relatively unblemished in the flurry of accusations, stated that "the failure at Spring Hill was General Hood's fault.... The remedy was entirely in his own hands."[69] Throughout the war, Hood did exhibit a distinct tendency to blame others for his own mistakes.

According to Captain Shellenberger, the primary cause of Hood's failure was apparently lack of confidence in his generalship on the part of some of his subordinates. They had been dissatisfied with Hood's appointment to command the army, and their dissatisfaction had been greatly increased by the failure of his attacks on Sherman's lines in front of Atlanta. With the poor opinion they held of his ability, they could not give to any of his plans that wholehearted, unquestioning support that affords the best guarantee of success.[70]

After all of the controversy has been distilled, these facts remain: Hood was the commanding officer; he was present on the field with two corps and one division; and the enemy, even when concentrated, was outnumbered. The Confederates had two options, either one of which would have been very effective. They could have attacked Spring Hill directly and taken possession of the town. Allowing for the fact that A. P. Stewart was at Rutherford's Creek, Hood still had Cheatham's entire corps plus Forrest's cavalry. Wagner's lone division would not have been able to offer any meaningful resistance, and Schofield would have been trapped between the Confederates at Columbia and those at Spring Hill. In addition to the Federals facing Stephen Lee, this option would have captured Wagner as well.

---

[68] Young, CV 22/3 (March 1914): 126.

[69] Buck, *Cleburne and His Command*, 276.

[70] Shellenberger, *Battle of Spring Hill*, 47.

Hood could also have taken the pike below the town. Bate and Cleburne would have had almost no opposition had they merely continued moving to the west. Forrest, Brown, and Stewart would most certainly have arrived in support before Schofield could extricate himself from Lee's attacks. Again, with the exception of Wagner, the entire army would have been destroyed.

The following analysis may be the most succinct:

> Simple as his plan was, they all failed to grasp the importance of getting possession of the pike and, Cleburne excepted, they all acted as if they were anticipating a repetition of the disastrous experience that had followed the attacks on Sherman. The promptness with which Cleburne turned and rolled up Bradley's brigade, when so unexpectedly assailed on his own flank, was the only vigorous action shown by any of them after crossing Rutherford's Creek; and, no doubt, if Cleburne had not been stopped by Cheatham's order, he would have gone on until he reaped the full measure of success made so easily possible by the faulty situation of our army.[71]

---

[71] Shellenberger, *Battle of Spring Hill,* 188.

14

FRANKLIN

John Bell Hood left Spring Hill with a bitter taste in his mouth. Despite his own mistakes he blamed not only Frank Cheatham, but his lieutenants as well. Constrained by the orders of their superiors, Brown, Cleburne, and Bate bore little blame for the result at Spring Hill, but they led Cheatham's divisions and thus were held accountable. Cleburne was incensed. He believed the charges were so unfounded that he demanded a court of inquiry to clear his name. The mounting frustration at the head of the army was an ominous portent of things to come.

At dawn on 30 November, the Confederates received the order to march to Franklin. A. P. Stewart would lead, followed by Cheatham. Lee did not reach Spring Hill from Columbia until 9:00 A.M., so he was given a supporting role. Only 12 miles away, the town lay on the south bank of a sharp bend in the Harpeth River, which borders it on three sides. Overlooking the river on the northeast side of the town was Fort Granger, held by Thomas J. Wood's division of the Union IV Corps. It was nothing more than an earthen enclosure, but its strategic location provided an excellent view of the field below. John Schofield placed Giles Cockerill's battery of long-range rifled guns in a position to dominate the open plain in front of the breastworks. While Schofield was in overall command of the army, he directed the forces north of the river and gave Jacob Cox temporary control of the troops on the south side.

Franklin had only 900 white residents in 1861,[1] but the town offered excellent means of transportation. One turnpike originally ran from Nashville to Franklin, but in 1832 it had been extended to Columbia. From the southeast the Lewisburg Pike made its approach before turning north as it neared the river. Between the Lewisburg Pike and the Harpeth River was a cut where the tracks of the Tennessee and Alabama Railroad went all the way to the

---

[1] Wiley Sword, *Embrace an Angry Wind* (New York: St. Martin's, 1995) 165.

Alabama state line. From the southwest another route came from nearby Carter's Creek.

Each one of these arteries played a part in the action that afternoon, but the focal point of the battle was the ground along the Columbia Turnpike. It ran due north and just before reaching the plain it crossed a range of hills through a gap 2 miles south of town. To the right of the pike stood Breezy Hill, a low rise one-quarter of a mile wide. Just across the road was Winstead Hill, high and rounded. From there the formation curved northwest for a mile and a half to Carter's Creek Pike. One mile north of Winstead Hill was a small, rocky eminence known locally as Privet Knob but also referred to as Merrill Hill. It had an elevation of 100 feet, and clusters of cedars dotted the eastern slopes.[2]

The Federals marched along the Columbia Pike and entered Franklin throughout the morning. The men worked feverishly and by noon had erected strong fortifications, 5 feet high in some places. Thick headlogs were placed on top of the dirt, leaving only a 3-inch gap large enough for a rifle to protrude.[3] The task at hand was a formidable one, but some construction had been started two years earlier and parts of the line remained. From one bank of the Harpeth to the other was a distance of 1 1/2 miles, and the Federals placed 17,000 men inside the works.[4] In front of the walls they dug a ditch 4 feet wide and 3 feet deep. The field before them was relatively open, but near the Lewisburg Pike a thorny hedge of osage orange provided ideal material for defensive warfare. The Yankees cut the branches and dragged them into position in front of their trenches, creating an impenetrable abatis.[5] Generally, the Federal line was crescent shaped. It was centered around the brick home of Fountain Branch Carter. Along with servants' quarters and a smokehouse, the building was just west of the turnpike. Just 80 yards away on the other side of

---

[2] Isaac Shannon, "Sharpshooters with Hood's Army," *Confederate Veteran* 15/3 (March 1907): 124–25.

[3] Hardin P. Figuers, "A Boy's Impressions of the Battle at Franklin," *Confederate Veteran* 23/1 (January 1915): 5; James Lee McDonough, "The Mysteries of Spring Hill," *Blue & Gray* 11/1 (September 1984): 24; L. G. Bennett, and William Haigh, *History of the 36th Illinois Volunteers* (Aurora IL: Knickerbocker & Hodder, 1876) 659.

[4] Sword, *Embrace an Angry Wind,* 164.

[5] Thomas Y. Cartwright, "Franklin The Valley of Death," in Mauriel P. Joslyn, ed., *A Meteor Shining Brightly* (Macon GA: Mercer University Press, 2000) 176–77.

the road stood the family's large cotton gin, but the building was quickly dismantled.

The Union left was anchored on the railroad cut and as the earthworks passed the gin they veered to the northwest and created a salient. The two-gun battery of the 6th Ohio established their position at the angle, commanded by Lieutenant Aaron Baldwin. From Baldwin's position the fortifications continued west until they found the only break, an opening just wide enough to permit the passage of the turnpike. Cox deployed the four guns of the 1st Kentucky to protect the gap. In back of the Kentuckians was one section of the 1st Ohio Light Artillery, and east of the smokehouse were four Napoleons of the 20th Ohio. Altogether Cox placed twenty-six pieces of artillery along his front with twelve more in reserve. Ninety yards south of the house the line continued west, then turned sharply northwest again to reach Carter's Creek Pike. This part of the property contained a dense thicket of locust trees, although these were soon cut down.

Jacob Cox understood the strategic importance of the road. He placed two rows of Federals in a shallow depression behind the works, then added a third rank in a retrenched position 50 yards to the rear. Cox was only a brigadier general, but on 30 November he directed the XXIII Corps, assigning his own division command to James Reilly. Reilly placed his right flank near the turnpike with John Casement on his left. Israel Stiles led the third brigade and secured his own left on the railroad. The remainder of the IV Corps completed the Union forces south of the river, commanded by David Stanley. George Wagner's Second Division held the area along the Columbia Turnpike; his troops would face the opening assault. Wagner had Emerson Opdycke, John Lane, and Joseph Conrad at his disposal. All six brigades were about to be placed at the very center of some of the most horrific slaughter of the entire war.

At 11:00 A.M. Stanley issued orders to occupy the high ground south of Franklin. In addition to his own troops, Wagner received Walter Whitaker's brigade from Nathan Kimball's division. Whitaker took possession of Winstead Hill and began to prepare breakfast while Conrad and Lane did the same on Breezy Hill. Opdycke was used as a rear guard. All seemed quiet until Confederate cavalry suddenly appeared. Opdycke had spent the entire morning sparring with Forrest, placing his men in defensive positions, skirmishing, and then falling back, only to repeat the process. Small arms fire broke out, but mounted cavalry was not going to make any headway against four brigades of infantry. By 12 o'clock the remainder of the Union Army had arrived in Franklin itself and Whitaker was withdrawn. There was no particular danger, but with his departure Winstead Hill was vacant, leaving Wagner somewhat isolated. He began to worry that he could be outflanked, so around 12:15 he withdrew Conrad and Lane as well. Within half an hour the Second Division was strung out for over a mile along the Columbia Pike.

At this point confusion began to emerge within the Union high command. George Thomas was in Nashville. He had exchanged a series of telegrams with Schofield. Thomas wanted him to delay the Confederates as long as possible but not to act too aggressively. Accordingly, Schofield gave Stanley specific instructions. He was to relieve Opdycke, hold both hills until nightfall, and then move the entire army across the Harpeth River after dark.

Unfortunately, Wagner did not receive any communication from Stanley until 12:30. His position had just been abandoned and he knew he would have to countermarch. As Emerson Opdycke was the last to leave the area, he would be the first to return. When he reached the heights he scanned the southern approaches. The view was not a pleasant one. Opdycke saw two Confederate columns advancing in force. To his left, A. P. Stewart's men were moving along the Lewisburg Pike. Right in front of him Frank Cheatham's corps headed straight up the Columbia Pike, with John Brown' s division in the lead. Pat Cleburne and William Bate were close behind.

Wagner knew his position was untenable. Cheatham was beginning to form and he would easily be outflanked by Stewart, so he decided to withdraw. Around 2:00 P.M. the Federals descended the hills and headed toward Franklin once again.[6] Although the safer course was a direct retreat into the confines of the army, Wagner remembered that he was still to delay Hood as long as possible. He ordered Lane to halt and take a position on the south side of Privet Knob. In addition to infantry, Lane arranged a section of 3-inch rifled guns under Lieutenant Milton Mitchell. Satisfied for the moment, Wagner continued on with Opdycke and Conrad. Less than a mile from the fortifications he ordered Conrad to deploy east of the pike, although the 15th Missouri actually went into line on the opposite side of it. Wagner sent out the 79th, 51st, and 42nd Illinois, followed by the 64th and 65th Ohio. The purpose was merely to stall for time; Wagner never intended for Conrad to actually fight. As soon as Opdycke arrived he would simply connect his left

---

[6] Sword, *Embrace an Angry Wind,* 171–76.

with the Missourians, and Hood would be forced to deal with Wagner's division before he attacked Cox and Stanley.[7]

This seemed like a reasonable plan, but Opdycke would not comply. His men had suffered the most at Spring Hill, and he had been used as the rear guard on the march to Franklin. When Schofield led the rest of the army to safety, he was still marching along the turnpike. Whitaker sat down on one hill while Conrad and Lane had breakfast on the other. In Opdycke's mind the entire army was well rested, but his men had yet to boil coffee. The order to form one more front line of defense was more than he could bear, and he would have none of it. With complete disregard for his superior, Opdycke refused to stop. The two men continued to argue but Wagner could not persuade his obstinate lieutenant to obey. The First Brigade finally found an open spot of ground 200 yards north of Fountain Carter's house and stacked their arms around 2:30.

With Lane still at Privet Knob, Conrad by the side of the road, and an uncooperative Opdycke behind the lines, Wagner was desperate. He rode back to the house for a conference with Jacob Cox. Cox attempted to placate him with the reassurance that the force in their front was merely a feint. The real thrust would surely come in a flanking maneuver as Hood would try to gain the Federal rear.

Kind words from his commanding officer failed to sooth Wagner's fragile nerves. At 2:00 p.m. Lane sent a message to Wagner. The Confederates were still advancing and had passed Winstead Hill. Both flanks were in serious danger. Lane tried to delay the Rebels as long as he could with his skirmishers and Mitchell's artillery, but he was soon pulled back to a position across from Conrad. As Cheatham's divisions marched along the pike, these were the first Yankees they would face. Wagner had followed Schofield's general directions, but the decision to place two brigades 600 yards in front of the main line was a poor one. This section of land was an uncultivated cotton field, and as such there were no trees or rocks that might afford some degree of protection. The men attempted to throw together broken rails and dirt, but with only a few shovels it was impossible to construct sound entrenchments.

Hood had arrived in Franklin around noon with the van of Stewart's corps and established his headquarters 1 mile south of Winstead Hill at the

---

[7] Jacob D. Cox, *The Battle of Franklin* (1897; repr., Dayton OH: Morningside, 1983) 76.

home of William Harrison. With his crutch strapped to his saddle he rode to the top. After a hasty reconnaissance he ordered Stewart to pass around Breezy Hill. He was to march 1 1/4 mile to the Lewisburg Pike, then turn north. In addition to his own infantry corps, he would also receive cavalry support. The orders were clear but their execution wasted an opportunity for the South. Wagner had evacuated both hills, and there were no Confederates to take possession of them. Stewart was gone, Forrest was with him, and Cheatham had not arrived. By the time Cheatham did appear, Wagner had returned. Still, Hood was unconcerned. Schofield had not offered any meaningful resistance at Spring Hill and was retreating once again. In Hood's opinion the escarpments appeared to be poor in quality and temporary at best. One more thrust would force the Yankees back across the river. Hood had made up his mind, and the Confederates must press the attack.

While the Confederates were forming their lines, Hood assembled his generals for a conference of war. Cleburne, Cheatham, and Forrest pointed out the open terrain and fortified position of the Federals, but their objections fell on deaf ears.[8] Cleburne had ridden forward ahead of his infantry in order to examine the ground. He arrived at Winstead Hill shortly after noon. While he waited for his men to form, he ascended to the summit, placed his binoculars on a stump, and surveyed the entrenchments. He said merely that "they are very formidable" and wrote down a few brief observations. An examination of that notebook would be invaluable, but Cleburne was killed only a few hours later and it was never recovered. He was firmly opposed to the idea of a frontal assault and stated that it was "a terrible and useless waste of life."[9]

Frank Cheatham, who had also been to the crest of Winstead Hill, came to the same conclusion. He returned to Hood and said, "I don't like the looks of this fight; the enemy has an excellent position and is well fortified." Unmoved, Hood replied, "I prefer to fight them where they have had only eighteen hours to fortify, than to strike them at Nashville, where they have been strengthening themselves for three years."[10]

Forrest was speechless. He had instantly recognized the weakness in the plan. He proposed a flanking maneuver in which he would take his cavalry

---

[8] Cartwright, "Franklin," 173.

[9] Irving A. Buck, *Cleburne and His Command* (1908; repr., Wilmington NC: Broadfoot Publishing, 1995) 290.

[10] Buck, *Cleburne and His Command,* 280.

through Holly Tree Gap, an opening in the hills east of Franklin. The Nashville Turnpike ran through the pass only 4 1/2 miles from Hood's present position. This would place the Confederates between Schofield and Nashville. Forrest believed that his suggestion was quite feasible, as Hood was just as close to the gap as Schofield.[11] However, with no inclination to deviate from his original plan, Hood only replied that Forrest's cavalry would support the frontal attack.

Despite the protests, Hood laid out his dispositions for the battle. The heaviest weight of the alignment fell upon the Union left. From the river to the Columbia Pike, Hood had placed four divisions of infantry and two of cavalry. The longer line, from the Carter house to Carter's Creek Pike, received only two divisions of infantry and one cavalry division. Stewart would mass his corps in the woods on the east side of the field, then strike near the railroad. Cleburne and Brown would attack in the center over open ground and make their assault in the direction of Fountain Carter's house. Bate would move north, pivot on his right, and attack along the Carter's Creek Pike. Forrest would divide his cavalry, with two divisions on Stewart's right and the third supporting Bate.

There is considerable speculation, not without merit, that this alignment contained an ulterior motive. Hood could easily have had A. P. Stewart's corps screen Cheatham. This would allow more time for Cheatham to advance undetected as he passed through heavy undergrowth in the rear of the Confederate lines. As it was, by sending Stewart to the east Cheatham appeared in plain sight of Federal skirmishers on top of the hills.

Hood was still immersed in the fiasco at Spring Hill, and he sought desperately to lay the blame on Cheatham's corps. He had convinced himself that many of those soldiers had reservations about charging well-fortified positions and preferred to fight defensively behind breastworks of their own. Therefore, the attack must be made by Brown and Cleburne. The inevitable casualties would only rid the army of men with questionable courage. Was the order a means of intentional punishment? Perhaps. A misguided message to the rest of the army? Most certainly.[12] In his memoirs *Advance and Retreat*, Hood wrote: "The discovery that the Army, after a forward march of one hundred and eighty miles was, still, seemingly, unwilling to accept battle

---

[11] Sword, *Embrace an Angry Wind*, 179.
[12] Sword, *Embrace an Angry Wind*, 177.

unless under the protection of breastworks, caused me to experience grave concern. In my inmost heart I questioned whether or not I would ever succeed in eradicating this evil. It seemed to me I had exhausted every means in the power of one man to remove this stumbling block in the Army of Tennessee."[13]

Hood's memoirs were published in 1880. Whether this statement was a self-serving justification for a dismal military failure, or merely an honest assessment of the situation by a general unable to adjust his tactical approach to the conditions in front of him, is largely irrelevant. The words provide great insight into the mind of John Bell Hood. It is clear that he never considered the use of maneuver to induce Schofield to fight on Confederate terms. With a particular vision of the battle in mind, he gave Cleburne the following verbal instructions: "Form your division on the right of the pike with your left resting on the same. General Brown will form on your left with his right resting on the pike. You will connect with Stewart on your right." He continued, "give orders to your men not to fire a gun until you drive the Federals from the first line of works in your front. Then press them and shoot them in the backs while running to the main line. Then fix bayonets, and break the enemy line at all hazards."[14] Finally he added, "Experience has proved to you that safety in…battle consists of getting in close quarters with your enemy. [Captured] guns and colors are the only unerring indications of victory. The valor of troops is easily estimated…by the number of these secured."[15]

Conceptually, Hood certainly had designs on Nashville. After the war Daniel Govan related that Hood had stated, "[I]f we take Franklin, we will take Nashville, which is the key to the independence of the Southern Confederacy."[16] Hood had also stated that while the Union center was strong, the flanks were weak. Given the fact that the ultimate objective was in fact

---

[13] John B. Hood, *Advance and Retreat* (1880; repr., Edison NJ: Blue and Gray Press, 1985) 290.

[14] Howell and Elizabeth Purdue, *Pat Cleburne Confederate General* (1973; repr., Gaithersburg MD: Olde Soldier Books, 1987) 419.

[15] US War Department, comp., *The War of the Rebellion: A Compilation of the Official Records of the Union and Confederate Armies*, 128 vols. (Washington, DC: Government Printing Office, 1880–1901) ser. 1, vol. 38, pt. 5, p. 909.

[16] Daniel C. Govan to Irving A. Buck, 3 September 1907, in Buck, *Cleburne and His Command*, 290–91.

Nashville, this should have given even more weight to the idea Forrest had in mind. Hood was a fighter, not a thinker, and the focus of his concentration was Frank Cheatham, not John Schofield. The limits of his mental capacity were soon to show.

Cleburne understood that these orders most probably sealed his fate. He knew that a frontal assault was doomed to failure, as the Confederates faced an extremely strong position. Yet he was a soldier, and an order must be obeyed. Allegedly he replied, "General, I will take the works or fall in the attempt."[17] The source for this quotation is reliable, but given the circumstances of that day it must certainly be called into question. Cleburne met with his brigade commanders just before the battle. Daniel Govan noticed that he was "greatly depressed." He emphasized the need to carry the works with the bayonet. Govan easily grasped the futility of the order, remarking, "Well, General, few of us will ever return to Arkansas to tell the story of this battle." The reply was poignant: "Well, Govan, if we are to die, let us die like men."[18]

Up to this point the Confederates had been largely concealed by the high ground south of Franklin, but around 2:45 P.M. they began to form their lines. Although the battle plan was poor, Hood had 20,000 men at his disposal. Unfortunately, he did not know how to use them. Most of the artillery was still with Lee and there were only two batteries on the field. Instead of massing what little firepower he had, Hood gave one to each corps. With Union guns at Fort Granger as well as in Franklin, the South was clearly overmatched.

Hood could hardly have chosen a more unfavorable position from which to attack, as the ground afforded no protection whatsoever. From the base of Winstead Hill, the plain stretched some 2 1/4 miles to the Carter house. It was unobstructed save for the hedge of osage orange near the railroad cut, the remnants of the locust trees close to the Carter house, and the cedars on the

---

[17] Mangum relates this experience in the *Kennesaw Gazette,* 15 June 1887, 3. He had serious doubts as to the accuracy of this version of the conversation. He knew the general quite well and felt it quite out of character. From the information currently available, it would seem highly unlikely that Cleburne responded in this manner, but this was related by Dr. Daniel Linthicum, the chief surgeon of Cleburne's division. He stated that he had just arrived and heard both men, and it is the Linthicum version that appears in the *Gazette.*

[18] Govan to Fullerton, 22 May 1894 box 1, folder 1, War Department Commission Papers, Chickamauga and Chattanooga National Military Park, Chattanooga TN.

side of Privet Knob. Every part of the field over which the Confederates would advance was in clear sight of the enemy, not only from the Carter property but from Fort Granger as well.[19] The men in the ranks had a foreboding sense of the fight to come. Some exchanged personal belongings, while others sought the counsel of their chaplain.

From Winstead Hill Cleburne rode to the top of Breezy Hill, where he summoned his brigadiers for a council. They were to form on the east side of the pike with their lead regiments just below the crest of Breezy Hill. Cleburne anticipated deadly artillery fire, so he asked, and received permission, to form in columns of brigades. This would present as narrow a front as possible and allow rapid deployment without confusion when the men came within range of small arms fire. While the lines were forming he rode forward to the crest of Privet Knob, where he had a clear view of the works only 1 mile away. When he arrived, he realized he had left his field glasses behind. A Confederate sharpshooter, John Ozanne, took the long telescope from his rifle and handed it to the general. Cleburne rested it on a stump and surveyed the field. "They have three lines of works," he said, "and they are completed."[20]

The common soldier had no need for binoculars or elevation; he understood that this battle was going to be a serious mistake. The men could see the breastworks, they knew the Federal Army had not taken many casualties at Spring Hill, and it was painfully obvious that the ground in front of them was wide open to artillery. J. C. Dean of the 3rd Mississippi spoke for thousands of his comrades when he said that "even the men in the ranks knew this was going to be very bloody."[21]

It took over an hour to form and the advance began very close to 4 o'clock. One regiment was thrown out in front of each division to act as skirmishers. All of the troops received explicit orders not to stop for any reason until they had reached the breastworks. Cleburne was drawn up in "double columns at half distance." Granbury placed his left along the

---

[19] M. H. Dixon, diary, 30 November 1864, Carter House Archives, Franklin TN; W. E. Preston, "Memories of the War," *Confederate Reminiscences and Letters, 1861–1865,* 22 vols. (Atlanta: Georgia Division of the United Daughters of the Confederacy, 1995) 14:143–45.

[20] Shannon, "Sharpshooters," 124–25.

[21] J. C. Dean, "The Battle of Franklin," *Confederate Veteran* 7/1 (January 1899) 27.

Columbia Pike with Govan to his right and Lowrey in reserve. Just across the
pike was John Brown's division, with George Gordon closest to the road. At
4:00 P.M. Cheatham dropped a signal flag from Winstead Hill. Cleburne's
division surged forward, and his distinctive blue battle flag rose high among
the red banners with the St. Andrews cross. The advance was in perfect order,
and the earth seemed to crawl toward the Federal lines. The Union Army
watched a grand spectacle unfold as Hood's entire force was laid out before
them, bands playing, regimental colors flying in the wind, and the sun
shining on 20,000 bayonets.

The view of the field was truly magnificent. Dr. G. C. Phillips, senior
surgeon of the 22nd Mississippi, accompanied another physician to high
ground above the plain. He gazed down at a large bowl with the small town of
Franklin in its center. As the Confederates were forming their lines, he told
his colleague that "during this time the ground was perfectly still; no sound
jarred upon the ear to disturb the beautiful and apparently peaceful scene."
Hood and his staff rode up to a position not far from where the two men were
sitting. Dr. Phillips continued, "I do not like this quietness. It is ominous,
and I fear our men are going to be annihilated."[22]

The view from the breastworks evoked similar emotions. As Captain Levi
Scofield described it,

> It was a grand sight, such as would make a lifelong impression on
> the mind of any man who could see such a resistless, well-conducted
> charge. For the moment we were spellbound with admiration,
> although they were our hated foes; and we knew that in a few brief
> moments, as soon as they reached firing distance, all that orderly
> grandeur would be changed to bleeding, writhing confusion, and that
> thousands of those valorous men of the South, with their chivalric
> officers, would pour out their life's blood on the fair fields in front of
> us.[23]

---

[22] Wiley A. Washburn, "Cleburne's Division at Franklin," *Confederate Veteran* 13/1
(January 1905): 27–28; G. C. Phillips, "Witness to the Battle of Franklin," *Confederate
Veteran* 14/6 (June 1906): 261–62, Figuers, "A Boy's Impressions," 5.

[23] Stanley Horn, *The Army of Tennessee* (Norman: University of Oklahoma Press,
1952) 400.

Cleburne's division was led by his skirmishers, but from Conrad's position it appeared as if the Confederates were attacking in double lines. Around 4:10 Mitchell's artillery opened up at 400 yards, but by this time Mitchell was already under pressure from the sharpshooters on Privet Knob. The crews quickly called for grape and canister—solid shot would do them little good. Despite their anxiety, Mitchell waited; he knew the Confederates were not close enough. Thus far, the rifled cannon had been ineffective and momentary holes in the ranks were easily filled. The Confederates were getting closer, and in overwhelming numbers.

The Federals were so preoccupied with the swarming tide in front of them that they failed to notice the Confederates to their left, who were swiftly moving along the Lewisburg Pike. Henry Guibor's Missouri battery unlimbered and fired a shot directly over Mitchell's guns. The next one fell just short, and Captain John Shellenberger knew that a third shot was sure to find its mark. Mitchell had already seen two of his men killed and five wounded, and he knew he had to withdraw regardless of the consequences. He fired a few rounds of canister and then hitched up his horses. He covered the ground to the Union lines at full speed, but Conrad and Lane were stunned. They had been left on an island without any help, they were heavily outnumbered, and their artillery support had just fled the field.

It was just over a mile between Cleburne and Wagner's forward brigades, and it took only fifteen minutes to cover the open ground. Cleburne advanced to within 400 paces of Conrad and halted. Here they shifted from columns of brigades into two lines of battle. They waited for the order to charge, then sprinted for the Yankees. George Gordon was not about to be outdone by Hiram Granbury, and his battle-hardened veterans ran just as quickly on the other side of the pike.

As the Confederates neared the works, Fort Granger went into action. Cockerill's battery exploded and did particular damage between the Lewisburg and Columbia turnpikes. The guns opened as Cleburne was about 300 yards from Conrad. The Confederates had massed their troops and gaps began to appear. At 100 yards Conrad and Lane opened fire. The Rebels recoiled under the shock but quickly recovered and resumed their advance. Both brigades frantically tried to reload, but Cleburne was too close to allow it. His men were on Conrad in a matter of seconds, shouting, "Follow them into the works!"[24]

The placement of Wagner this far forward saved many of Hood's men. Had Wagner been stationed much further back, the Confederates could easily have been killed before they ever approached musket range. The artillery in Franklin was useless, as the Federals own men shielded the attack. Wagner was quickly overrun, and Cheatham's corps took very few casualties until they were within 50 yards of his line. At that point Jacob Cox released the power in the trenches. Later, in 1891, General Gordon described the scene. At the unveiling of a memorial shaft in Helena, he spoke in honor of his fallen comrade: "The army of columns moved steadily, a front of at least two miles...they halted 400 paces from the Federals. When 'charge' was ordered the Federals fired one volley and then ran.... sustaining but small losses ourselves, until we arrived within about one hundred paces of their main line and stronghold, when it seemed to me that hell itself had exploded in our faces."[25]

As the gray lines advanced, Jacob Cox looked out over the center of the field. He saw Cleburne and Brown and observed: "They were seen coming in splendid array. The sight was one to send a thrill through the heart, and those who saw it have never forgotten its martial magnificence."[26]

Milton Mitchell was not the only target of Confederate of artillery. At the moment he unleashed his guns, a shell struck the back of the Carter house just above the porch. The Confederates were closing quickly; Conrad and Lane knew they could not hold out much longer. Combined they had less than 4,000 muskets to hold off 8,000 screaming Rebels. Both men sent couriers back to Wagner, repeatedly imploring him to pull them back. From his position Jacob Cox expected both brigades to retire at any moment. They were filled with green troops, heavily outnumbered, and about to be flanked.[27]

---

[24] Washburn, "Cleburne's Division," 27–28.

[25] George W. Gordon, "Dedicationof His Monument to His Memory at Helena, Arkansas," 10 May 1891, in *Southern Historical Society Papers*, 52 vols. (Millwood NY: Kraus Reprint Co., 1977) 18:260–72.

[26] James D. Porter, "Spring Hill and the Battle of Franklin," *Confederate Veteran* 12/7 (July 1904): 341–49.

[27] OR, ser. 1, vol. 45, pt. 1, p. 1133; W. W. Gist, "The Other Side at Franklin," *Confederate Veteran* 24/1 (January 1916): 14.

It seemed incomprehensible to allow Conrad and Lane to remain in their present position, but Wagner was adamant. They would stand and fight. At this point disaster stared the Yankees in the face. Wagner rode frantically back and forth in an attempt to steady his lines. Perhaps a measure of panic set in, as there is little else to explain his reasoning. Despite rumors that Wagner was drunk, General Cox's well-documented account of the battle of Franklin makes no such allusions, although Cox was highly critical of Wagner's performance. Just as the couriers turned around, Mitchell appeared. With a face blackened by powder, one of the gunners turned to Levi Scofield and said, "Old hell is let loose, and coming [in from] out there."[28]

The pursuit was desperate, and Brown and Cleburne charged forward right on the heels of the Federals. Conrad had been easily flanked by the speed of A. P. Stewart, but it was actually Granbury's brigade that caused his line to collapse. After fifteen minutes the Yankees began to disintegrate under Cleburne's attack, exposing Lane.[29] Many of the men were new recruits with little training or experience, and what appeared to be a decisive blow against a poorly supported position quickly turned into a rout. Two entire brigades streamed down the pike and converged on the gap in the entrenchments. One of Cleburne's officers described the chase: "We go right after them, yelling like fury, and shooting at them at the same time. The yanks [were] running for life and we for the fun of it, but the difference in the objects are so great that they out run us, but lose quite a number of their men before they get [away]."[30]

According to a Northern account, the entire episode resulted in a "butcher's bill" as horror-stricken men unseasoned in battle all rushed to the same point. Some were killed by the Confederates, others trampled to death by their own friends. There were so many bodies in such close quarters that they fought with bayonets, clubbed muskets, and anything they could find.[31] Union soldiers blamed the disaster on poor generalship. They realized that Conrad and Lane should never have been placed so far in front of the Union lines. Offensively they were no impediment to either Cleburne or Brown, and

---

[28] Sword, *Embrace an Angry Wind,* 190.

[29] In their own individual reports, each general claimed that the other left the field first, but most independent sources indicate that Conrad was the first to retreat. See also L. G. Bennett, and William Haigh, *History of the 36th Illinois Volunteers* (Aurora IL: Knickerbocker & Hodder, 1876) 650.

[30] Sword, *Embrace an Angry Wind,* 192.

[31] Sword, *Embrace an Angry Wind,* 193.

from a defensive standpoint they were a liability to their own men behind the earthworks. Both infantry and artillery were forced to remain silent until the Yankees cleared the field. The rank and file understood the misfortune they were dealt at the hand of a poor commander, but the Confederates were soon to suffer an identical fate at the hand of John B. Hood. It would be far more costly.

The infantry could not hold their fire any longer. Cleburne was only 50 yards from the entrenchments when the barricades exploded in flames. The Confederates were so close that they dropped like leaves. The east side of the turnpike was held by Jim Reilly's division, and Reilly had placed the four guns of the First Kentucky battery next to the pike opposite Granbury. As the trenches continued they made an abrupt angle toward Cleburne. This line was held by two Ohio regiments, the 100th by the road and the 104th on their left. The cotton gin was next, with the two guns under Baldwin in front of what remained of the building. Both infantry regiments dissolved under the weight of the charge. Cleburne captured the battery closest to the pike, as well as about 110 yards of the line. They turned the pieces at the Federals, but the friction primers had been removed and so the guns were useless.

For five minutes a vicious hand-to-hand combat ensued. Hiram Granbury charged ahead of his brigade, yelling, "Forward, men, forward! Never let it be said that Texans lag in the fight." Almost immediately thereafter, a minie ball entered his cheek and passed through his head, killing him instantly. The Confederates almost took Baldwin's position as well but were stopped as they entered the embrasures. The gunners were forced to use sponge staves, picks, and axes, but they managed to hold the line. The Union faced complete disaster, but Jacob Cox had some reserves close at hand. John White's 16th Kentucky infantry held the area next to the pike between Baldwin's battery and the retrenched line, a distance of only 65 yards. A frantic staff officer rushed up to tell him that the front had caved in. Along with Lawrence Rousseau's 12th Kentucky on his left, White rushed forward to stem the tide. Rousseau's advance swept the 8th Tennessee (Union) along as well, quickly followed by the 175th Ohio. Some of the Rebels paused at the sight of the charge, and many of them were captured.

The Federals' failure to hold their center created a gap for Gordon and Granbury. Gordon's right had drifted across the road so that their brigades began to mix together. The two generals conferred repeatedly in an attempt to straighten their alignment. It would seem impossible to survive the rain of lead, but Cleburne charged into the smoke with the rest of his men. When he was roughly 80 yards from the ditches, his horse was shot from under him. James Brandon, a nineteen-year-old escort from Mississippi, gave up his own mount, but as Cleburne began to rise the animal was killed. Cleburne continued on foot, waving his kepi to direct his men. He simply had no chance of survival. Some 50 yards from the lines he fell with a single bullet through the chest, nearly missing his heart.

The Confederates, not realizing that their leader had fallen, broke through near the gap. For a short time they controlled the area by the Carter house and tried to form around the front of the buildings. Prisoners were taken, but there was no time to send them to the rear. The gains were short-lived, as Emerson Opdycke rushed into action. His troops were lounging around the house, but they quickly rushed into the breach. The charge was not made in a single, straight line but the penetration was stopped. The action raged for about twenty minutes before the Rebels fell back.[32]

The Confederates were relentless, but they were not strong enough to push through so many reinforcements. They were driven into the ditch, where the equivalent of trench warfare ensued. Soldiers on both sides had no choice but to hold their weapons above their heads and fire. The troops along the pike were badly disorganized, but the confusion grew as Stewart became engaged on their right. The hedges in his front pushed him into Cleburne's division. Some of Gordon's division became separated as well and blended into Granbury. They were all pinned below the earthworks, unable to advance or retreat; to lift one's head would mean certain death. The numbers along the point of attack offered little hope, as the Federals stood five and six men deep at the gin.[33]

Charge after charge could not take the trenches. Regimental flags made it to the top of the parapets but could go no further. Union soldiers counted over a dozen assaults, each turned away with heavy loss. Once they reached the ditch, the design of the fortifications began to wreak havoc. The salient at the cotton gin provided a forward position for artillery, and despite the attempts to break the lines the 6th Ohio battery was still firmly under Baldwin's control.

---

[32] Report of David S. Stanley, 25 February 1865, OR, ser. 1, vol. 45, pt. 1, p. 116; Cox, *Franklin*, 98, 115.

[33] Dixon, diary, 30 November 1864, Carter House Archives, Franklin TN.

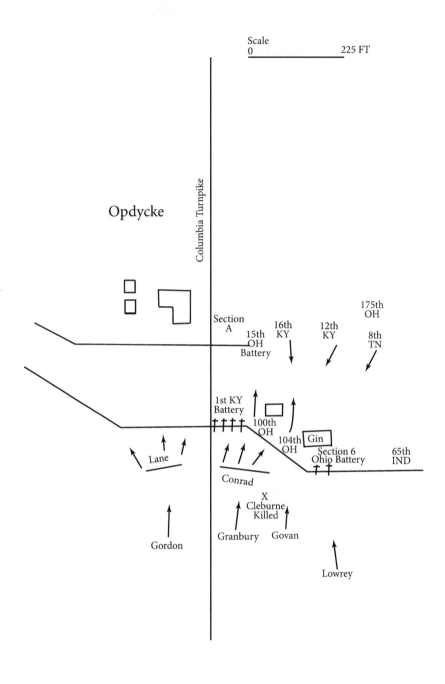

Scale
0   225 FT

Columbia Turnpike

Opdycke

Section
A
15th   16th   12th   175th
OH   KY   KY   OH
Battery   8th
                                     TN

1st KY
Battery
                 100th
                 OH
                     104th   Gin
                     OH   Section 6   65th
Lane   Ohio Battery   IND

Conrad

                 X
                 Cleburne
                 Killed
Gordon   Granbury   Govan

                         Lowrey

Pinned where they were, lead rained down on the helpless men. Baldwin turned his guns to the west and poured a devastating fire along the lines. He fired double and triple canister charges into swarming Confederates at point-blank range as they tried to storm the walls. Across the turnpike more cannon fired straight down the line from the opposite direction. The dead bodies were so thick that at one point that they had to be dragged aside merely to service the guns.[34]

The Confederate position was hopeless. Their left and right had melted into the center, their artillery was useless, and they faced Yankees on three sides. The center of the field was the key to the battle, but by 5:00 P.M. Cleburne and Granbury were dead and Brown was wounded. Cleburne's division had enough problems, but their plight was made even worse by Stewart's earlier success. His corps had moved rapidly up the Lewisburg Pike and did not have to contend with any natural obstructions. On the other hand, while Wagner's troops had been easily overrun, they did offer some degree of resistance that caused a short delay along the Columbia Pike. As a result Stewart made contact much sooner than Cheatham, and any possibility of a simultaneous assault was lost. The Federals at the railroad cut fought behind the impassable hedge of osage, and no greater impediment could have been imagined. Without any cohesion and in front of a mass of piercing needles, Stewart's men were easily turned away. This allowed the men in the works to turn their attention to Cleburne, and they raked his lines with deadly effect. James Barr, an orderly from the 65th Illinois regiment, wrote: "I never saw men put in such a hellish position as Cleburne's Division was in for a few minutes at Franklin. The wonder is that any of them escaped death or capture."[35]

Not only were the Confederates trapped before the earthworks, but they had used up most of their ammunition. They were forced to search among piles of lifeless bodies just to find cartridges. The gunfire finally began to subside around 9:00 P.M., by which time both sides were completely spent. The night filled with the agonizing cries of the wounded, many buried beneath dead comrades. Between 11 o'clock and midnight the Federals fell back across the Harpeth River and began their march to Nashville.

---

[34] Washburn, "Cleburne's Division," 27–28.

[35] Wiley Sword, "The Other Stonewall," *Civil War Times Illustrated* 36/7 (February 1998): 44.

Of the major generals on the Confederate side, Cleburne had been killed and Brown wounded. Among brigadiers, Hiram Granbury, States Rights Gist, Otho Strahl, and John Adams lay dead on the field; F. M. Cockrell, Arthur Manigault, William Quarles, and T. M. Scott were wounded. Brigadier-General John C. Carter was wounded, but mortally, and on 10 December he died. Finally, Brigadier-General George W. Gordon had been captured. The battle of Franklin cost the Confederacy the services of two major generals and ten brigadiers, but the damage to the Army of Tennessee ran much deeper. Regimental commands were decimated; on 30 November twenty-three colonels, eleven lieutenant-colonels, ten majors, and nine captains were lost. Every captain on this list was the ranking officer when he fell.[36]

Casualties in Cleburne's division are difficult to determine, as Granbury was also killed. We do know that in addition to losing Cleburne and Granbury, four regimental commanders were killed and three more were wounded. The best evidence for divisional losses can be taken from medical reports made after the battle. On 18 December Federal forces returned to Franklin and the hospitals fell into Union hands. Estimates revealed that there were 1,750 Confederates buried on the field, 3,800 wounded, and 702 captured, for total casualties of 6,252. This number did not include slightly wounded men or those who may have been listed as missing. There are slight variations among other sources, but it is reasonable to assume that the South lost close to 6,300 men at the battle of Franklin.[37]

It is interesting to compare the casualties at Franklin with those at Gettysburg, where George Pickett lost 21 percent of his men. A. P. Stewart lost 28 percent of his troops, Cheatham 35 percent. The heaviest losses fell upon Cleburne's division, which had a casualty rate of 52 percent. William W. Gibson, a private in the 6th Arkansas, wrote, "The 6th and 7th (consolidated) went into the fight with 357 men, fifty-five answered the roll. In my company

[36] Cox, *Franklin*, 214; Robert Selph Henry, *Forrest: First with the Most* (1944; repr., Wilmington NC: Broadfoot Publishing, 1991) 399–400; OR, ser. 1, vol. 45, pt. 1, p. 684–86. Confederate losses, by rank, are as follows: major generals: one killed, one wounded; brigadier generals: four killed, four wounded, one mortally wounded, one captured; colonels: six killed, fifteen wounded, two missing; lieutenant-colonels: two killed, nine wounded; majors: three killed, five wounded, two missing; captains: two killed, three wounded, four missing. The totals are eighteen officers killed, thirty-eight wounded, eight missing and one captured, for a total of sixty-five.

[37] Cox, *Franklin*, 211.

every man engaged was killed, wounded or captured." [38] The Carter family had sought refuge in their cellar, and when Fountain Carter emerged from hiding he found his property strewn with Confederate casualties. In addition to the wounded, he counted fifty-seven dead in the door yard alone.[39]

John B. Hood has received a great deal of criticism for his order to charge the works, but he made several other mistakes as well. First of all, the Confederates attacked before the entire army was on the field. Not only did Lee have an additional corps of infantry,[40] but he had almost all of the artillery as well. An assault without any type of bombardment defied military logic. Hood made his own assessment of the conditions and still decided to attack a strongly fortified position. Whether his own estimation of the works was faulty or he sought to teach Cheatham a lesson is open to debate, but most probably both factors played a part in his decision. Either one by itself would have been reason enough to avoid a frontal assault.

Perhaps Hood intended to orchestrate a complicated three-pronged assault, but in effect he created three separate battles, with Bate on the left, Brown and Cleburne in the center, and Stewart on the right. Not only did the greatest concentration of troops attack the osage orange, but also they were closest to the artillery at Fort Granger. This accentuated the terrible confusion in the center, as the unfavorable terrain pushed everyone together and obliterated any semblance of organization. Again, this could have been avoided with proper reconnaissance. Hood ignored the advice of Forrest, Cheatham, and Cleburne, each of whom had made a more thorough examination of the field. All three men believed that regardless of any form the final orders might take, the worst possible plan was the very one Hood selected.

Even if the Federal position had been properly evaluated, Hood was still not compelled to attack. It should have been obvious that the better idea was Forrest's suggestion to interpose the Confederate Army between Schofield and Thomas. Clearly the proper strategy would have been to flank the Union left. For his part, John Schofield never wanted to give battle at Franklin in the first

---

[38] W. W. Gibbons to Mrs. John McGavock, 26 February 1900, Carter House Archives, Franklin TN. W. W. Gibbons was a private in Company E, 6th Arkansas infantry.

[39] H. M. Field, *Bright Skies and Dark Shadows* (New York: Charles Scribner's Sons, 1890) 244. James H. M'Neilly, "Franklin-Incidents of the Battle," *Confederate Veteran* 26/3 (March 1918): 116–18.

[40] According to Irving Buck (285), Lee had 7,852 infantry in his corps.

place. The rising waters of the Harpeth had destroyed the main bridge to
Nashville. A smaller bridge had been partially burned and the pontoon boats
he had requested had not arrived. In effect, his army was trapped. He would
have been forced to try to protect the supplies and communications with
Nashville, but even the most efficient retreat possible would not have been
able to prevent Forrest from gaining his rear.[41] Mark Lowrey attempted to
describe the brutality of the charge:

> I brought up my brigade and under the most destructive fire I
> witnessed, I threw my brigade into the outside ditch of his massive
> works, and my men fought the enemy across the parapet. Up to this
> time, about half my men had fallen, and the balance could not scale the
> works. It would have been certain death or capture to every one of
> them. I went on my horse to within thirty feet of the works, where I
> had my horse wounded, and I saw that nothing more could be done. I
> went to the rear, and began the work of gathering up the fragments of
> our division.[42]

Captain James Dinkins added: "In many instances, Confederates and
Federals lay across each other, and there was one case where a Confederate and
a Federal were found together in the ditch, the Confederate grasping the
Federal's throat."[43]

The Federals believed that Hood's tactics were not only tragic, but
astounding as well. Comparing the relative strengths of each army, David
Stanley noted the following in his battle report: "In view of the strong position
we held, nothing appeared so improbable as that they would assault. I felt so
confident in this belief that I did not leave Gen. Schofield's headquarters until
the firing commenced."[44]

Tillman H. Stevens, a private in the Union Army, concluded:

---

[41] Bennett and Haigh, *36th Illinois,* 647; Henry, *First with the Most,* 397.

[42] Cartwright, "Franklin," 179.

[43] James Dinkins, *1861–1865 Recollections and Experiences in the Confederate Army*
(Dayton OH: Morningside, 1975) 238–39.

[44] Report of David S. Stanley, 25 February 1865, OR, ser. 1, vol. 45, pt. 1, p. 115.

To my mind, the battle of Franklin was the most disastrous of all the battles in the great war. The loss in generals exceeded that of any two great battles, not barring Gettysburg and Chickamauga. The loss in our front between the Lewisburg Pike and the Columbia Pike was the greatest ever known on a line of that length. Within 300 yards Adams, Scott, Cleburne, and Granbury all went down, along with thousands of their men, good and true as ever marched to battle. While I scarcely ever refer to the matter, yet I have a pardonable pride in the fact that I was a humble member of the brigade that could and did stop a host led by such invincible spirits as Adams, Scott, Cleburne and Granbury, and the lesser lights, but who had hearts just as brave as their superiors, and, if opportunity offered, would rise to the full stature of their indomitable leaders.[45]

On 16 January 1865, Sergeant Ambrose Remley of the 72nd Indiana Volunteers wrote his family:

We came through Franklin. That must have been one of the severest battles of the war. Our works were in the shape of a half circle and the rebels had to charge over an open field and I never saw graves thicker on the battlefield. All over the fields here and there was three or four or five graves and close to our works the graves could be counted by the hundreds. And all the housses [sic] in the town of Franklin was filled with rebel wounded. I hear there was twenty seven hundred wounded rebels there when we came through.[46]

A member of the 36th Illinois offered this opinion of Hood's conduct: "Disappointed and enraged at the dislodgement of his forces from the works, Gen. Hood organized a second assault, and with unparalleled recklessness and disregard of life, again and again hurled his solid columns upon the entrenchments."[47]

---

[45] Tillman H. Stevens, "'Other Side' in Battle of Franklin," *Confederate Veteran* 11/4 (April 1903): 165–67.

[46] Medical reports file, Carter House Archives, Franklin TN.

[47] Bennett and Haigh, *36th Illinois*, 657.

The comments from different perspectives carry a similar tone, generally one of disbelief that the battle ever occurred. Jacob Cox offered a more analytical, though no less damaging, view of Hood's performance: "His exasperation at what he regarded as a hair's breadth escape on our part from the toils in which he thought he had encompassed us at Spring Hill had probably clouded his judgment. He blamed some of his subordinates for the hesitation which he seems himself to have been responsible for, and now, in an excitement which led him astray, he determined to risk everything upon a desperate assault."[48]

John B. Hood had accomplished virtually nothing in his futile attempt to break the Union lines. His frustration with the lost opportunity at Spring Hill, his inability to reconnoiter ground in front of him, and his penchant for bloody frontal assaults led to an unforgivable disaster. The South had lost the services of twelve general officers, and an already broken command would never recover. Hood led his men north with great victory on his mind, only to shatter his once-proud army on the rocks of Tennessee.

And Pat Cleburne had disappeared.

---

[48] Cox, *Franklin*, 85.

EPILOGUE

As in many accounts of an historical event, the details of Pat Cleburne's death have become somewhat distorted. Only a few witnesses were capable of providing firsthand information, and while the remainder certainly may have been well intentioned, their distance from the location of his body has been plainly revealed by the errors in their reports.

John McQuaide, a private in the 1st Arkansas, wrote the following undated article, which appeared in the Vicksburg *Herald*:

> ...I and two others were the first to discover his dead body at early dawn, the next morning. He was about forty or fifty yards from the works. He lay flat on his back, as if to sleep, with his military cap partly over his eyes. He had on a new gray uniform, the coat of the sack or blouse pattern. It was unbuttoned and open; the lower part of his vest was unbuttoned. He wore a white linen shirt which was stained with blood on the front part of the left side, or just off the abdomen. This was the only sign of a wound I saw on him, and believed it was the only one he had received...[1]

In a letter written on 26 January 1893, Reverend Thomas Markham, the chaplain in Featherston's Mississippi brigade, added the following evidence:

> Dear Friend: Our brigade (Featherston's of which I was chaplain) ambulance was in my charge. It was just after daylight in the gray of the morning. The men were in the act of lifting General Adams' body into the ambulance, when you rode up and reported that General Cleburne's body lay on the field. The ambulance was at once driven to the spot indicated by you. His body was placed beside that of General Adams' and both taken to Colonel McGavock's residence. The two were placed together on the lower gallery, perfectly protected and cared for until their friends removed them. Your recollection of the position

---

[1] John McQuaide, *Vicksburg Herald*, n.d., Old Court House Museum, Vicksburg, Mississippi, Whitaker scrapbook, 179.

of their bodies on the field, when Cleburne was discovered by you, and Adams by me, agrees with mine in every particular.[2]

Despite the reliability of these eyewitnesses, a different version lists no fewer than forty-nine bullets that riddled Cleburne's body, his horse gallantly leading his master over the Union parapets. Perhaps the image of a general on foot, surrounded by smoke as he led his men into battle, was not as romantic as that of a dashing equestrian charging over trenches, minie balls crashing around him. However, the fact remains that Pat Cleburne died roughly 50 yards in front of the earthworks. Lost in this description of his death is the detail surrounding the position of his horse.[3] The location of any horse is irrelevant, with respect to Cleburne. At the moment of his death Cleburne was on foot, and the two horses that were actually with him during the battle were both shot from under him.

There was little opportunity to attend to the fallen generals in the manner they deserved. Cleburne, Granbury, and Strahl were placed on the front porch of Carnton, the home of Mrs. John McGavock. Next to them were the bodies of Colonel R. B. Young, Granbury's chief-of-staff, and Lieutenant John Marsh, an aide to Otho Strahl. Adams was a native of Nashville but had married a girl at Pulaski, Tennessee, where he was buried on 1 December. Given the date of his burial, it is most likely that he remained at Carnton only long enough for his body to be cleaned and dressed.[4]

Close to 11:00 A.M. on 1 December, the bodies of Cleburne, Granbury, and Young were brought by wagon to Columbia, Tennessee. Cleburne was placed in a walnut coffin in the home of Dr. William J. Polk.[5] At 3:00 P.M. on 2 December, Dr. Charles Quintard officiated at a funeral for the three men, then they were buried at Rose Hill cemetery next to Strahl and Marsh.

---

[2] Irving A. Buck, *Cleburne and His Command* (1908; repr., Wilmington NC: Broadfoot Publishing, 1995) 293.

[3] Both Hardin P. Figuers ("A Boy's Impressions of the Battle at Franklin," *Confederate Veteran* 23/1 [January 1915]: 5) and (James H. M'Neilly, "Franklin—Incidents of the Battle," *Confederate Veteran* 26/3 [March 1918]: 117–18) state that Adams was found with his horse on the parapets. This may explain some confusion among different sources.

[4] Campbell Brown, "The Myth of the 5 Dead Rebel Generals," *Civil War Times Illustrated* 8/5 (August 1969): 14–15.

[5] Thomas Y. Cartwright, "Franklin: The Valley of Death," in Mauriel P. Joslyn, ed., *A Meteor Shining Brightly* (Macon GA: Mercer University Press, 2000) 180–81.

Lucius Polk was outraged to discover that they had been placed in a potter's field between rows of blacks and Federal soldiers. With the aid of the chaplain they were taken to the cemetery of St. John's Church, near the Polk family home at Ashwood. Cleburne, Granbury, and Strahl were subsequently laid to rest in their hometowns, though Young and Marsh were not moved.[6]

The State of Arkansas later claimed Cleburne's remains and removed them to Helena. On 29 April 1870, Cleburne was reburied there, placed beneath an elegant monument erected by the Ladies Memorial Association.[7] The tribute was truly deserved.

[6] Ezra Warner, *Generals in Gray* (Baton Rouge,: Louisiana State University Press, 1992) 296; Brown, "5 Dead Rebel Generals," 14–15. Strahl was moved to Dyersburg TN and Granbury is buried in Granbury TX named in his honor

[7] Buck, *Cleburne and His Command,* 291; R. B. Young file, Carter House Archives, Franklin TN.

BIBLIOGRAPHY

Primary Sources

Bevens, William. *Reminiscences of a Private.* Fayetteville: University of Arkansas Press, 1992.

Blakemore Diary. Tennessee State Library and Archives. Nashville, Tennessee.

Boyd, Cyrus F. *The Civil War Diary of Cyrus F. Boyd.* 1953. Reprint, Iowa City: State Historical Society of Iowa, 1976.

Branch, Mary Jones Polk. *Memoirs of a Southern Woman "Within the Lines."* Chicago: Joseph G. Branch Publishing Co., 1911.

Braxton Bragg Papers, Western Reserve Historical Society, Cleveland, Ohio, from microfilm edition at University of West Florida, Pensacola, Florida.

Buck, Irving A. *Cleburne and His Command.* 1908. Reprint, Wilmington NC: Broadfoot Publishing, 1995.

Cate, Wirt A., editor. *Two Soldiers: Campaign Diaries of Thomas J. Key C.S.A. and Robert J. Campbell U.S.A.* Chapel Hill: University of North Carolina Press, 1938.

Chesnut, Mary B. *A Diary from Dixie.* 1905. Reprint, New York: Random House, 1997.

Christ, Mark K. *Getting Used to Being Shot at the Spence Family Civil War Letters.* Fayetteville: University of Arkansas Press, 2002.

Patrick R. Cleburne Collection, Special Collections, University of Arkansas, Fayetteville, Arkansas.

Cleburne Family Letters. Carter House Archives, Franklin, Tennessee.

Collins, R. M. *Chapters from the Unwritten History of the War between the States.* St. Louis: Nixon-Jones Printing Co., 1882.

Frederick M. Dearborn Papers, Harvard University.

Dinkins, James. *1861–1865 Personal Recollections and Experiences in the Confederate Army.* Dayton OH: Morningside Bookshop, 1975.

Dixon, Munford. H. Diary. Carter House Archives, Franklin, Tennessee.

Doubleday, Abner. *Reminiscences of Forts Sumter and Moultrie.* New York: Harper & Brothers, 1876.

Duke, Basil. *Reminiscences of General Basil W. Duke.* Garden City NJ: Doubleday, Page & Co., 1911.

Dunlop, Colin to sister, 13 August 1864. Carter House Archives, Franklin, Tennessee.

Folmar, John Kent. *"From that Terrible Field": Civil War Letters of James M. Williams.* Tuscaloosa: University of Alabama Press, 1981.

Foster, J. C. to C. E. Custis, 1 May 1900. Carter House Archives, Franklin, Tennessee.

Fowler, J. A. Letter. Carter House Archives, Franklin, Tennessee.

Fuller, John W. "A Terrible Day: The Fighting before Atlanta July 22, 1864," *The National Tribune* [Washington, DC], 16 April 1885.

Gibson, William W. to Mrs. Colonel John McGavock, Franklin, Tennessee, 26 February 1900. Carter House Archives, Franklin, Tennessee.

Jeremy F. Gilmer Letters. Southern Historical Collection, Manuscripts Division, University of North Carolina, Chapel Hill, North Carolina.

Gordon, John B. *Reminiscences of the Civil War.* New York: Charles Scribner's Sons, 1904.

Daniel C. Govan Papers. Southern Historical Collection, Manuscripts Division, University of North Carolina, Chapel Hill, North Carolina.

Govan, Daniel C. to Jas. Fullerton, 22 May 1894, folder 1, box 1, War Department Park Commission, series 8 Atlanta Campaign, Chickamauga Chattanooga National Military Park.

Grant, Ulysses S. *Personal Memoirs of U. S. Grant.* 2 volumes. New York: Charles L. Webster & Company, 1885.

Hallock, Judith Lee, editor. *The Civil War Letters of Joshua K. Callaway.* 2 volumes. Athens: University of Georgia Press, 1997.

William Hardee Papers. Alabama Department of Archives and History, Montgomery, Alabama.

Hood, John B. *Advance and Retreat.* 1880. Reprint, Edison NJ: Blue and Gray Press, 1985.

Hughes, Nathaniel C., editor. *Liddell's Record.* Dayton OH: Morningside, 1985.

Johnston, Joseph E. *Narrative of Military Operations.* 1874. Reprint, Millwood NY: Kraus Reprint, 1981.

Wilbur G. Kurtz Sr. Collection. Atlanta History Center, Atlanta, Georgia.

Longstreet, James. *From Manassas to Appomattox.* 1895. Reprint, Philadelphia: J. B. Lippincott Company, 1896.

Will T. Martin Papers. Chickamauga Chattanooga National Military Park, Chattanooga, Tennessee.

Medical Reports Folder. Carter House Archives, Franklin, Tennessee.

Moore, John Hammond, editor. *A Plantation Mistress on the Eve of the Civil War: The Diary of Keziah Goodwyn Hopkins Brevard July 1860 - April 1861.* Columbia: University of South Carolina Press, 1993.

Nash, Charles E. *Biographical Sketches of Gen. Pat Cleburne and Gen. T.C. Hindman, together with Humorous Anecdotes and Reminiscences of the Late Civil War.* Little Rock AR: Tunnah and Pittard, 1898.

New, C. B., to Pettus, 14 January 1861, Mississippi Archives, Jackson MS, series E, no. 56.

Reagan, John H. *Memoirs.* New York: Neale Publishing Company, 1906.

Ridley, B. L. *Journal of B. L. Ridley Lieut. General A.P. Stewart's Staff—C.S.A.* Mexico MO: Missouri Printing & Publishing Co., 1906.

Sherman, William T. *Memoirs of Gen. W. T. Sherman.* 2 volumes. New York: Charles L. Webster & Co., 1891.

———. Field orders, Atlanta campaign, 1864, Atlanta History Center, Atlanta, Georgia.

Smith, Robert D. *Diary of Robert D. Smith.* Columbus OH: self-published, 1916. Atlanta History Center, Atlanta, Georgia.

Columbus Sykes Letters. Kennesaw National Military Park, Kennesaw, Georgia.

Taylor, Richard. *Destruction and Reconstruction.* New York: Appleton & Co. 1879.

Marcus Joseph Wright Papers. Southern Historical Collection, University of North Carolina, Chapel Hill, North Carolina.

R. B. Young Letters. Carter House Archives, Franklin, Tennessee.

Newspapers

Arkansas State Gazette (Little Rock)
Baltimore Sun
Black Republican Bible
Boston Atlas and Bee
Boston Herald
Boston Transcript
Charleston (SC) *Daily Courier*
Chicago Times
Daily Evansville (IN) *Journal*
Dardanelle (AR) *Post Dispatch*
Helena (GA) *Weekly Note-Book*
Kennesaw (GA) *Gazette*
Mobile (AL) *Daily Advertiser and Register*
National Tribune (Washington, DC)
New Orleans Picayune
New York Herald
Vicksburg (MS) *Daily Whig*

Official Records and Published Collections

Confederate Military History. 12 volumes. Edited by Clement A. Evans. Atlanta: Confederate Publishing Company, 1899.

Confederate Reminiscences and Letters, 1861–1865. 22 volumes. Atlanta: Georgia Division of the United Daughters of the Confederacy, 1995.

Confederate Veteran. 41 volumes. Nashville: Blue and Gray Press, 1974.

Freeman, Douglas S., editor. *Lee's Dispatches.* New York: G. P. Putnam's Sons, 1957.

The Official Military Atlas of the Civil War. Edited by Calvin D. Cowles. 1891–1895.
    Reprint, New York: Barnes and Noble Publishing, 2003.
Preservation plan for the Ringgold Gap, Ga. Battlefield prepared by Keith S. Bohannon.
US Congress. *Congressional Globe.* 46 volumes. Washington, DC, 1834–1873.
Reed, D. W. *The Battle of Shiloh and the Organizations Engaged.* Washington, DC:
    Government Printing Office, 1913.
Southern Historical Society Papers. 52 volumes. Millwood NY: Kraus Reprint Co., 1977.
Stephens, Alexander H. *A Constitutional View of the Late War between the States.* 2 volumes
    Philadelphia: National Publishing Company, 1868–1870.
US War Department, compiler. *The War of the Rebellion: A Compilation of the Official
    Records of the Union and Confederate Armies.* 128 volumes. Washington, DC:
    Government Printing Office 1880–1901.

Secondary Sources

Dissertations
Clauss, Errol M. "The Atlanta Campaign 18 July–2 September, 1864." Ph.D. dissertation,
    Emory University, 1965.
Goforth, Robert. "Sherman and Cleburne at Tunnel Hill: The Myth of the Inevitability of
    Confederate Defeat at Chattanooga, November 23–25, 1863." Master's thesis, East
    Carolina University, 1992.
McMurry, Richard M. "The Atlanta Campaign December 23, 1863 to July 18, 1864."
    Ph.D. dissertation, Emory University, 1967.

Books
Alexander, E. Porter. *Fighting for the Confederacy.* Chapel Hill: University of North
    Carolina Press, 1989.
Angle, Paul M., and Miers, Earl S. *Tragic Years 1860–1865.* 2 volumes. New York: Simon
    and Schuster, 1960.
Austin, J. P. *The Blue and the Gray.* Atlanta: Franklin Printing and Publishing Co., 1899.
Bearss, Edwin C. *Forrest at Brice's Cross Roads.* Dayton OH: Morningside Bookshop,
    1997.
Bearss, Edwin C. *Fields of Honor.* Washington, DC: National Geographic, 2006.
Beatty, John. *The Citizen Soldier.* Cincinnati: Wilstach, Baldwin, 1879.
Bennett, L. G., and Haigh, William. *History of the 36th Illinois Volunteers.* Aurora IL:
    Knickerbocker & Hodder, 1876.
Bierce, Ambrose. *Ambrose Bierce's Civil War.* 1956. Reprint, New York: Regnery Gateway,
    1988.
Boritt, Gabor S. *Jefferson Davis's Generals.* New York: Oxford University Press, 1999.

Braley, Chad O. *The Battle of Gilgal Church.* Athens GA: Southeastern Archeological Services, Inc., 1987.

Brown, Norman D., editor. *One of Cleburne's Command.* Austin: University of Texas Press, 1980.

Brown, Russell K. *To the Manner Born: The Life of General William H. T. Walker.* Athens: University of Georgia Press, 1994.

Cantor, George. *Confederate Generals Life Portraits.* Dallas: Taylor Trade Publishing, 2000.

Castel, Albert. *Decision in the West.* Lawrence, KS: University of Kansas Press, 1992.

Catton, Bruce. *The American Heritage Picture History of the Civil War.* 1960. Reprint, New York: Bonanza Books, 1982.

Catton, Bruce. *Grant Moves South 1861–1863.* 1960. Reprint, Edison NJ: Castle Books, 2000.

Catton, Bruce. *The Coming Fury.* Garden City NY: Doubleday, 1961.

Catton, Bruce. *Terrible Swift Sword.* Garden City NY: Doubleday, 1963.

Catton, Bruce. *Never Call Retreat.* Garden City NY: Doubleday, 1965.

Catton, William and Bruce. *Two Roads to Sumter.* New York: McGraw-Hill, 1963.

Cisco, Walter Brian. *States Rights Gist A South Carolina General of the Civil War.* Shippensburg PA: White Mane Publishing Co., 1991.

Clark, William H.H. *History in Catoosa County.* Reprint, Ringgold GA: n.p., 1994.

Commager, Henry S. ed. *The Blue and the Gray.* 2 Volumes. New York: Bobbs-Merrill Company, 1950.

Connelly, Thomas L. *Army of the Heartland: The Army of Tennessee 1861–1862.* Baton Rouge: Louisiana State University Press, 1967.

Connelly, Thomas L. *Autumn of Glory: The Army of Tennessee 1862–1865.* Baton Rouge: Louisiana State University Press, 1971.

Connelly, T. W. *History of the 70th Ohio Regiment.* West Union OH: Adams County Historical Society, 1978.

Connolly, James. *Three Years in the Army of the Cumberland.* Bloomington: Indiana University Press, 1959.

Cope, Alexis. *The Fifteenth Ohio Volunteers and its Campaigns, 1861–1865.* Columbus OH: published by author, 1916.

Cooper, William J. Jr. *Liberty and Slavery Southern Policies in 1860.* New York: Alfred A. Knopf, 1983.

Coulter, E. Merton. *The Confederate States of America.* Baton Rouge: Louisiana State University Press, 1950.

Cox, Jacob D. *Atlanta.* 1882. Reprint Wilmington NC: Broadfoot Publishing, 1989.

Cox, Jacob D. *The Battle of Franklin.* 1897. Reprint Dayton OH: Morningside Bookshop, 1983.

Cozzens, Peter. *No Better Place to Die.* Urbana: University of Illinois Press, 1990.

————. *Shipwreck of Their Hopes.* Urbana: University of Illinois Press, 1994.

————. *This Terrible Sound.* Urbana: University of Illinois Press, 1992.

Crawford, Samuel W. *History of Fort Sumter.* New York: F.P. Harper, 1887.

Cullom, J.W. *Pastoral Sketches.* Nashville: M. E. Church, South, 1907.

Daniel, Larry J. *Shiloh.* New York: Simon & Schuster, 1997.

Davis, Stephen. *Atlanta Will Fall.* Wilmington DE: Scholarly Resources, 2001.

Davis, William C. *Breckinridge Statesman Soldier Symbol.* Baton Rouge: Louisiana State University Press, 1974.

————. *Jefferson Davis The Man and his Hour.* New York: HarperCollins, 1991.

Detzer, David. *Allegiance Fort Sumter, Charleston, and the Beginning of the Civil War.* New York: Harcourt, 2001.

Dodge, Grenville. *The Battle of Atlanta and Other Campaigns.* Council Bluffs IA: Monarch Printing Company, 1911.

Donald, David H. *Lincoln.* New York: Simon & Schuster, 1995.

Donnelly, James S. Jr. *The Land and People of Nineteenth-Century Cork.* London: Routledge & Keegan Paul, 1975.

Dougan, Michael B. *Confederate Arkansas.* Tuscaloosa: University of Alabama Press, 1976.

Douglas, Lucia R. *Douglas's Texas Battery, CSA.* Tyler TX: Smith County Historical Society, 1966.

Dowdey, Clifford. *Death of a Nation; the story of Lee and his men at Gettysburg.* New York: Alfred A. Knopf, 1958.

Dowdey, Clifford. *Lee.* Boston: Little Brown & Co., 1965.

————. *The Land They Fought for the Story of the South as the Confederacy 1832–1865.* Garden City NJ: Doubleday, Inc. 1955.

Drake, Edwin L. ed. *The Annals of the Army of Tennessee and Early Western History.* Nashville: A. D. Haynes, 1878.

Dumond, Dwight Lowell, editor. *Southern Editorials on Secession.* 1931; reprint, Gloucester MA: P. Smith, 1964.

Durden, Robert F. *The Gray and the Black.* Baton Rouge: Louisiana State University Press, 1972.

Dyer, John P. *The Gallant Hood.* New York: Bobbs-Merrill Company, 1950.

Eaton, Clement. *A History of the Southern Confederacy.* New York: The Macmillan Company, 1954.

Eckenrode, H. J. & Conrad, Bryan. *James Longstreet Lee's War Horse.* 1936. Reprint, Chapel Hill: University of North Carolina Press, 1986.

Eggleston, George Cary. *The History of the Confederate War.* New York: Sturgis & Walton Company, 1910.

Eisenschiml, Otto and Newman, Ralph. *The American Iliad.* New York: Bobbs-Merrill Company, 1947.

————. *The Story of Shiloh.* Chicago: Civil War Round Table, 1946.

Elliott, Sam D. *Soldier of Tennessee.* Baton Rouge: Louisiana State University Press, 1999.

————. *Doctor Quintard Chaplain C.S.A. and Second Bishop of Tennessee.* Baton Rouge: Louisiana State University Press, 2003.

Engle, Stephen D. *Struggle for the Heartland.* Lincoln: University of Nebraska Press, 2001.

Faust, Patricia. ed. *Historical Times Illustrated Encyclopedia of the Civil War.* New York: Harper & Row, 1986.

Fehrenbacher, Don E. *The Dred Scott Case.* New York: Oxford University Press, 1978.

Field, H.M. *Bright Skies and Dark Shadows.* New York: Charles Scribner's Sons, 1890.

Fiske, John. *The Mississippi Valley in the Civil War.* New York: Houghton Mifflin Company, 1900.

Force, M.F. *Fort Henry to Corinth.* New York: Charles Scribner's Sons, 1881.

Freeman, Douglas S. ed. *Lee's Dispatches to Jefferson Davis 1862–1865.* New York: G. P. Putnam's Sons, 1957.

————. *Lee's Lieutenants.* 3 volumes. New York: Charles Scribner's Sons, 1942–1944.

————. *R.E. Lee.* 4 volumes. New York: Charles Scribner's Sons, 1934–1936.

Furgurson, Ernest B. *Chancellorsville 1863.* New York: Alfred A. Knopf, 1992.

Gallagher, Gary. *Lee and his Generals in War and Memory.* Baton Rouge: Louisiana State University Press, 1998.

Govan, Gilbert & Livingwood, James. *Joseph E. Johnston "A Different Valor."* 1956. Reprint, New York: Smithmark, 1995.

Greeley, Horace. *The American Conflict.* 2 Volumes. Chicago: O.D. Case & Co., 1865.

Hafendorfer, Kenneth A. *Perryville.* Louisville KY: KH Press, 1991.

Halli Burton, W.H. *History of Arkansas County Arkansas 1541–1875.* Easley SC: Southern Historical Press, 1978.

Hallock, Judith Lee. *Braxton Bragg and Confederate Defeat.* Volume 2. Tuscaloosa: University of Alabama Press, 1991.

Hammock, John C. *With Honor Untarnished.* Little Rock AR: Pioneer Press, 1961.

Harwell, Richard B. ed. *The Civil War Reader.* New York: Mallard Press, 1958.

Hattaway, Herman. *General Stephen D. Lee.* Jackson: University Press of Mississippi, 1976.

Hay, Thomas Robson. *Pat Cleburne: Stonewall of the West.* In Irving A. Buck, *Cleburne and His Command.* 1908. Reprint, Wilmington NC: Broadfoot Publishing, 1995.

Hennessy, John J. *Return to Bull Run The Campaign and Battle of Second Manassas.* New York: Simon and Schuster, 1993.

Henry, Robert Selph. *The Story of the Confederacy.* New York: Grosset & Dunlap, 1931.

————. *As They Saw Forrest.* Jackson TN: McCowat-Mercer Press, 1956.

————. *Forrest First with the Most.* 1944. Reprint, Wilmington NC: Broadfoot Publishing, 1991.

Hess, Earl J. *Banners to the Breeze.* Lincoln: University of Nebraska Press, 2000.

Hewett, Janet B., editor. *The Roster of Confederate Soldiers, 1861–1865.* Wilmington NC: Broadfoot Publishing, 1999.

———, editor. *The Roster of Union Soldiers, 1861–1865.* Wilmington NC: Broadfoot Publishing, 1999.

Holland, Cecil F. *Morgan and his Raiders.* New York: MacMillan Company, 1943.

Horn, Stanley. *The Army of Tennessee.* Norman: University of Oklahoma Press, 1952.

Howell, H. Grady. *Going to Meet the Yankees.* Jackson MS: Chickasaw Bayou Press, 1981.

Hughes, Nathaniel C., Jr. *General William J. Hardee.* Baton Rouge: Louisiana State University Press, 1965.

Hurst, Jack. *Nathan Bedford Forrest: A Biography.* New York: Alfred A. Knopf, 1993.

Johnston, Robert Underwood, and Buel, Clarence Clough, editors. *Battles and Leaders of the Civil War.* 4 volumes. 1884–1887. Reprint, Secaucus NJ: Castle Books, n.d.

Johnston, William Preston. *The Life of Gen. Albert Sidney Johnston.* New York: D. Appleton and Company, 1879.

Jordan, Thomas, and Pryor, Roger. *The Campaigns of Lieut. Gen. Forrest.* New York: Blelock & Co., 1867.

Joslyn, Mauriel P., editor. *A Meteor Shining Brightly.* Macon GA: Mercer University Press, 2000.

Keegan, John. *The Mask of Command.* New York: Viking, 1987.

Kerksis, Sydney. "Action at Gilgal Church, June 15–16, 1864." In Sydney C. Kerksis *The Atlanta Papers* Dayton OH: Morningside Bookshop, 1970.

Key, William. *The Battle of Atlanta and the Georgia Campaign.* New York: Twayne Publishers, 1958.

King, Alvy L. *Louis T. Wigfall.* Baton Rouge: Louisiana State University Press, 1970.

Korn, Jerry. *The Fight for Chattanooga.* Chicago: Time-Life Books, 1985.

Lamers, William M. *The Edge of Glory.* New York: Harcourt, Brace & World, 1961.

Leech, Margaret. *Reveille in Washington.* New York: Harper & Brothers, 1941.

Logsdon, David R. *Eyewitnesses at the Battle of Franklin.* Nashville: Kettle Mills Press, 2000.

———. *Eyewitnesses at the Battle of Shiloh.* Nashville: Kettle Mills Press, 1994.

Lonn, Ella. *Foreigners in the Confederacy.* Chapel Hill: University of North Carolina Press, 1940.

Losson, Christopher. *Tennessee's Forgotten Warriors Frank Cheatham and His Confederate Division.* Knoxville: University of Tennessee Press, 1989.

Lytle, Andrew. *Bedford Forrest and His Critter Company.* New York: McDowell, Obolensky, 1960.

McCaffrey, James M. *This Band of Heroes.* Austin TX: Eakin Press, 1985.

McDonough, James Lee. *Chattanooga: A Death Grip on the Confederacy.* Knoxville: University of Tennessee Press, 1984.

————. *Shiloh: In Hell before Night.* Knoxville: University of Tennessee Press, 1977.

————. *War in Kentucky from Shiloh to Perryville.* Knoxville: University of Tennessee Press, 1994.

———— and Connelly, Thomas L. *Five Tragic Hours.* Knoxville: University of Tennessee Press, 1983.

McElroy, Robert. *Jefferson Davis.* 2 volumes. New York: Harper & Brothers, 1937.

McInvale, Morton E. *The Battle of Pickett's Mill: Foredoomed to Oblivion.* Atlanta: Georgia Department of Natural Resources, 1977.

McMurry, Richard M. *John Bell Hood.* Lexington: University Press of Kentucky, 1982.

McPherson, James M. *Battle Cry of Freedom.* New York: Oxford University Press, 1988.

————. *For Cause and Comrades.* New York: Oxford University Press, 1997.

McWhiney, Grady. *Braxton Bragg and the Confederate Defeat.* Volume 1. Tuscaloosa: University of Alabama Press, 1991.

————. *Attack and Die.* Tuscaloosa: University of Alabama Press, 1982.

Meredith, Roy. *Storm over Sumter.* New York: Simon & Schuster, 1957.

Milham, Charles C. *Gallant Pelham American Extraordinary.* Gaithersburg: Olde Soldier Books, 1987.

Miller, Francis T., editor. *The Photographic History of the Civil War.* 10 volumes. New York: Review of Reviews Co., 1911.

Moneyhon, Carl H. *The Impact of the Civil War and Reconstruction on Arkansas.* Baton Rouge: Louisiana State University Press, 1994.

Moore, Albert Burton. *Conscription and Conflict in the Confederacy.* 1924. Reprint, Columbia, SC: University of South Carolina Press, 1996.

Moore, Jerrold Northrop. *Confederate Commissary General.* Shippensburg PA: White Mane Publishing, 1996.

Neal, Diane, and Kremm, Thomas W. *Lion of the South General Thomas C. Hindman.* Macon GA: Mercer University Press, 1993.

Nevins, Allan. *The Emergence of Lincoln: Prologue to the Civil War 1859–1861.* 2 volumes. New York: Charles Scribner's Sons, 1950.

Nicolay, John G. *The Outbreak of Rebellion.* New York: Charles Scribner's Sons, 1881.

Noe, Kenneth. *Perryville: This Grand Havoc of Battle.* Lexington: University Press of Kentucky, 2001.

O'Connor, Richard. *Hood: Cavalier General.* New York: Prentice-Hall, 1949.

Osborne, Charles C. *Jubal.* Chapel Hill NC: Algonquin Books, 1992.

Parks, Joseph H. *General Edmund Kirby Smith, C.S.A.* Baton Rouge: Louisiana State University Press, 1954.

————. *General Leonidas Polk, C.S.A.: The Fighting Bishop.* Baton Rouge: Louisiana State University Press, 1962.

Perkins, Howard C., editor. *Northern Editorials on Secession.* 2 volumes. Gloucester MA: Peter Smith, 1964.

Peterson, Merrill D., editor. *Jefferson Writings.* New York: Literary Classics of the United States, 1984.

Polk, William M. *Leonidas Polk: Bishop and General.* 2 volumes. 1893. Reprint, New York, Sprinkle Publications, 2001.

Pollard, Edward A. *The First Year of the War.* New York: Charles B. Richardson, 1863.

————. *The Lost Cause.* New York: E. B. Treat, 1867.

Potter, David M. *The Impending Crisis, 1848–1861.* New York: Harper & Row, 1976.

Purdue, Howell and Elizabeth. *Pat Cleburne Confederate General.* 1973. Reprint, Gaithersburg MD: Olde Soldier Books, 1987.

Robertson, James I., Jr. *Stonewall Jackson.* New York: Macmillan Publishing, 1997.

Roland, Charles P. *Albert Sidney Johnston: Soldiers of Three Republics.* Austin: University of Texas Press, 1964.

Roman, Alfred. *Military Operations of General Beauregard.* 2 volumes. New York: Harper & Brothers, 1884.

Rowland, Dunbar, editor. *Jefferson Davis Constitutionalist: His Letters and Speeches.* 12 volumes. New York: J. J. Little & Ives Company, 1923.

Scaife, William R. *The Campaign for Atlanta.* Atlanta: Civil War Publications, 1993.

————. *The Campaign for Tennessee.* Atlanta: Civil War Publications, 2003.

————. *Civil War Atlas and Order of Battle.* Atlanta: Civil War Publications, 1997.

Sears, Stephen W. *Controversies & Commanders.* New York: Houghton Mifflin, 1999.

————. *To the Gates of Richmond.* New York: Ticknor & Fields, 1992.

Seitz, Don Carlos. *Braxton Bragg: General of the Confederacy.* New York: The State Company, 1924.

Shellenberger, John K. *The Battle of Spring Hill, Tennessee November 29, 1864.* Cleveland OH: Arthur H. Clark Company, 1913.

Sheppard, Eric W. *Bedford Forrest: The Confederacy's Greatest Cavalryman.* London: n.p., 1930.

Skinner, George W. *Pennsylvania at Chickamauga and Chattanooga.* Harrisburg PA: Wm. Stanley Ray, 1900.

Stampp, Kenneth M., editor. *The Causes of the Civil War.* New York: Touchstone Books, 1986.

Stevenson, Alexander F. *The Battle of Stone's River.* Boston: James R. Osgood and Company, 1884.

Strayer, Larry M. and Baumgartner, Richard A., editors. *Echoes of Battle.* Huntington WV: Blue Acorn Press, 1991.

Strode, Hudson. *Jefferson Davis: American Patriot 1808–1861.* New York: Harcourt, Brace and Company, 1955.

———. *Jefferson Davis: Confederate President.* New York: Harcourt, Brace and Company, 1959.

———. *Jefferson Davis: Tragic Hero.* New York: Harcourt Brace & World, 1964.

———. *Jefferson Davis Private Letters, 1823–1889.* New York: Harcourt Brace & World, 1966.

Sunderland, Glenn W. *Lightning at Hoover's Gap.* New York: Thomas Yoseloff, 1969.

Sword, Wiley. *Embrace an Angry Wind.* Columbus OH: General's Books, 1995.

———. *Shiloh, Bloody April.* New York: William Morrow & Co., 1974.

———. *Mountains Touched with Fire.* New York: St. Martin's, 1995.

Symonds, Craig L. *Stonewall of the West.* Lawrence: University of Kansas Press, 1997.

Thomason, Jr. John W. *Jeb Stuart.* New York: Charles Scribner's Sons, 1930.

Tucker, Glenn. *Chickamauga Bloody Battle of the West.* 1961. Reprint, New York: Smithmark, 1994.

Turchin, John B. *Chickamauga.* Chicago: Fergus Printing Co., 1888.

Warner, Ezra J. *Generals in Blue.* Baton Rouge: Louisiana State University Press, 1992.

———. *Generals in Gray.* Baton Rouge: Louisiana State University Press, 1992.

Watkins, Samuel R. *Co. Aytch.* 1882. Reprint, Dayton OH: Morningside Bookshop, 1982.

Wigginton, Thomas A. *Tennesseans in the Civil War.* 2 volumes. Knoxville: Civil War Centennial Commission, University of Tennessee Press, 1964.

Wiley, Bell I. *Southern Negroes, 1861–1865.* New Haven CT: Yale University Press, 1938.

Wills, Brian Steel. *A Battle from the Start: The Life of Nathan Bedford Forrest.* New York: HarperCollins, 1992.

Williams, T. Harry. *P. G. T. Beauregard.* Baton Rouge: Louisiana State University Press, 1954.

Wingfield, Marshall. *General A. P. Stewart: His Life and Letters.* Memphis: West Tennessee Historical Society, 1954.

Woods, James M. *Rebellion and Realignment.* Fayetteville: University of Arkansas Press, 1987.

Woodward, C. Vann. *Mary Chesnut's Civil War.* New Haven CT: Yale University Press, 1981.

Woodworth, Steven E. *Jefferson Davis and His Generals.* Lawrence: University of Kansas Press, 1990.

———. *Nothing but Victory.* New York: Alfred A. Knopf, 2005.

———. *Six Armies in Tennessee.* Lincoln: University of Nebraska Press, 1998

Wyeth, John A. *Life of General Nathan Bedford Forrest.* New York: Harper & Brothers, 1899.

Articles and Pamphlets

Ambrose, Stephen E. "By Enlisting Slaves, Could the South Still Win the War?" *Civil War Times Illustrated* 3/9 (January 1965): 16–21.

"Attention—Whitworth Rifles." *Confederate Veteran* 1/4 (April 1893): 117

Baylor, George. "With Gen. A. S. Johnston at Shiloh." *Confederate Veteran* 5/12 (December 1897): 609.

Brown, Campbell. "The Myth of the 5 Dead Rebel Generals." *Civil War Times Illustrated* 8/5 (August 1969): 14–15.

Claiborne, Thomas. "Battle of Perryville, Ky." *Confederate Veteran* 16/5 (May 1908): 227.

Clauss, Errol M. "The Battle of Jonesboro" *Civil War Times Illustrated* 7/7 (November 1968): 18–21.

Connor, Sam. "Cleburne and the Unthinkable." *Civil War Times Illustrated* 36/7 (February 1998): 45–47.

Cox, T. B. "Sixth Mississippi Regiment at Shiloh." *Confederate Veteran* 18/11 (November 1910): 509.

Crawford, W. T. "The Mystery of Spring Hill." *Civil War History* 1/2 (June 1955): 112.

Crownover, Sims. "The Battle of Franklin." *Tennessee Historical Quarterly* 14/1 (December 1955): 305.

Cunningham, S. A. "Events Leading to the Battle." *Confederate Veteran* 18/1 (January 1910): 17–20.

Davis, Steve. "That Extraordinary Document." *Civil War Times Illustrated* 16/8 (December 1977): 14–20.

Davis, Steve. "The General's Tour Atlanta Campaign: Hood Fights Desperately." *Blue & Gray* 6/6 (August 1989): 1–36, 38–55.

Dean, J. C. "The Battle of Franklin." *Confederate Veteran* 7/1 (January 1899): 27.

Dean, Jeff. "The Battle of Pickett's Mill." *Blue and Gray* 6/4 (April 1989): 28–34, 36–37.

Dillard, H. M. "Beauregard-Johnston-Shiloh." *Confederate Veteran* 5/3 (March 1897): 99–100.

Ellis, W. B. "Who Lost Shiloh to the Confederacy?" *Confederate Veteran* 22/7 (July 1914): 314.

Fessler, Paul R. "The Case of the Missing Promotion: Historians and the Military Career of Major General Patrick Ronayne Cleburne, C.S.A." *Arkansas Historical Quarterly* 53/2 (Summer 1994): 212–13.

Figuers, Hardin P. "A Boy's Impresssions of the Battle of Franklin." *Confederate Veteran* 23/1 (January 1915): 4–7.

Frierson, Robert M. "Gen. E. Kirby-Smith's Campaign in Kentucky." *Confederate Veteran* 1/9 (September 1893): 295.

Gilbert, C. C. "Bragg's Invasion of Kentucky." *Southern Bivouac* (September 1885): 296–301.

———. "Bragg's Invasion of Kentucky." *Southern Bivouac* (November 1885): 336–42.

———. "Bragg's Invasion of Kentucky." *Southern Bivouac* (December 1885): 430–36.

———. "Bragg's Invasion of Kentucky." *Southern Bivouac* (January 1886): 465–77.

Gibson, W. W. "Reminiscences of Ringgold Gap." *Confederate Veteran* 12/11 (November 1904): 526–27.

Gist, W. W. "The Other Side at Franklin." *Confederate Veteran* 24/1 (January 1916): 14.

Hafendorfer, Kenneth, editor. "The Kentucky Campaign Revisited: Major-General Simon B. Buckner's Unpublished After-Action Report on the Battle of Perryville." *Civil War Regiments: A Journal of the American Civil War* 4/3 (1995): 50–64.

Harley, Stan C. "Govan's Brigade at Pickett's Mill." *Confederate Veteran* 12/2 (February 1904): 74–76.

Hay, Thomas R. "The South and the Arming of the Slaves." *Mississippi Valley Historical Review* 6/1 (June 1919): 36–40.

———. "Campaign and Battle of Chickamauga." *Georgia Historical Quarterly* 7/3 (September 1923): 213–50.

———. "Battle of Chattanooga." *Georgia Historical Quarterly* 8/2 (June 1924): 121–41.

Head, Thomas A. "Thirty-Fifth Tennessee Infantry," 492–95. In *Military Annals of Tennessee* John B. Lindsley, editor. 1886; reprint, Nashville: J. M. Publisher Co. Publisher, 1995.

Horn, Stanley F. "The Battle of Perryville." *Civil War Times Illustrated* 10/4 (February 1966): 647.

Horn, Stanley F. "The Spring Hill Legend." *Civil War Times Illustrated* 11/1 (April 1969): 21–33.

Hyde, Anne B. "The Battle of Shiloh." *Confederate Veteran* 31/4 (April 1923): 129–32.

Jones, James A. "The Battle of Shiloh." *Confederate Veteran* 7/12 (December 1899): 556.

Kelly, Dennis. "The General's Tour Mountains to Pass, A River to Cross." *Blue & Gray* 6/5 (June 1989): 8–12, 16–30, 46–50.

Kelsey, Jasper. "The Battle of Shiloh." *Confederate Veteran* 25/2 (February 1917): 71–73.

Key, Thomas J. "Concerning Battle of Missionary Ridge." *Confederate Veteran* 12/8 (August 1904): 390.

LeMonnier, Y. R. "Gen. Leonidas Polk at Chickamauga." *Confederate Veteran* 24/1 (January 1916): 17–19.

M'Neilly, James H. "Franklin—Incidents of the Battle." *Confederate Veteran* 26/3 (March 1918): 116–18.

Mangum, L. H. "General P. R. Cleburne." *Kennesaw* (GA) *Gazette,* 15 June 1887, 2–6.

McDonough, James Lee. "The Mysteries of Spring Hill" *Blue & Gray* 11/1 (September 1984): 12–28, 33.

McKee, John Miller. "The Great Panic: Being Incidents Connected with Two Weeks of the War in Tennessee." In *Annals of Tennessee* 1 (Nashville: A. D. Haynes, 1878): 9.

McMurry, Richard M. "The General's Tour. The Atlanta Campaign: Rocky Face to the Dallas Line, the Battles of May 1864. " *Blue & Gray* 6/4 (April 1989): 10–23, 46–62.

———. "Patton Anderson: Major General C.S.A." *Blue & Gray* 1/2 (October/November 1983): 10–17.

———. "Kennesaw Mountain." *Civil War Times Illustrated* 11/8 (January 1970): 20–35.

———. "Cassville." *Civil War Times Illustrated* 10/8 (December 1971): 4–10.

———. "The Affair at Kolb's Farm." *Civil War Times Illustrated* 7/8 (December 1968): 20–27.

———. "Resaca: 'A Heap of Hard Fiten.'" *Civil War Times Illustrated* 9/7 (November 1970): 4–15, 44–48.

Milner, W. J. "Lieut. Gen. William J. Hardee." *Confederate Veteran* 22/8 (August 1914): 362.

Phillips, G. C. "Witness to the Battle of Franklin." *Confederate Veteran* 14/6 (June 1906): 261–62.

Pickett, W. D. "Reminiscences of Murfreesboro." *Confederate Veteran* 16/9 (September 1908): 449–54.

Porter, James D. "Spring Hill and Battle of Franklin." *Confederate Veteran* 12/7 (July 1904): 341–49.

Remington, J. D. "Cause of Hood's Failure at Spring Hill." *Confederate Veteran* 21/12 (December 1913): 569–70.

Ridley, B. L. "The Fifth and Sixteenth Tennessee." *Confederate Veteran* 8/3 (March 1900): 101–102.

Roth, David E. "The General's Tour: The Mysteries of Spring Hill, Tennessee." *Blue and Gray* 2/2 (November 1984): 12–28.

———. "The General's Tour The Battle of Perryville." *Blue and Gray* 1/2 (October/November 1983): 21–39.

Ryan, Frank T. "Address before Atlanta Camp." *Confederate Veteran* 26 (18 April 1894):158–59.

Scaife, William R. *The Battle of Pickett's Mill: A Criminal Blunder*. N.p., 2004.

Secrist, Philip L. "Scenes of Awful Carnage." *Civil War Times Illustrated* 10/3 (June 1971): 5–9, 45–48.

Shannon, Isaac N. "Sharpshooters with Hood's Army." *Confederate Veteran* 15/3 (March 1907): 124–25.

Shellenberger, John K. "The Fighting at Spring Hill, Tenn." *Confederate Veteran* 36/3–5 (March–May 1928): 100–103, 140–43, 188.

Shoup, Francis A. "How We Went to Shiloh." *Confederate Veteran* 2/5 (May 1894): 137–40.

Smith, William F. "An Historical Sketch of the Military Operations around Chattanooga, Tennessee, September 22 to November 27, 1863," 149–247. In *The Mississippi*

Valley: Tennessee, Georgia, Alabama, 1861–1864. Volume 8 of *The Papers of the Military Historical Society of Massachusetts.* Boston Military Historical Society of Massachusetts, 1910.

Stewart, Alexander P. "The Army of Tennessee," 67–78. In *Military Annals of Tennessee.* Edited by John B. Lindsley. Nashville: J. M. Lindsey and Company, 1886.

Stevens, Tillman H. "Other Side in Battle of Franklin." *Confederate Veteran* 11/4 (April 1903): 165–67.

Stiles, John C. "Confederate States Negro Troops." *Confederate Veteran* 23/6 (June 1915): 246–47.

Sword, Wiley. "The Other Stonewall." *Civil War Times Illustrated* 36/7 (February 1998): 36–45.

Thompson, William C. "From Shiloh to Port Gibson." *Civil War Times Illustrated* 3/6 (October 1964): 20–25.

Walker, James. "The Battles for Chattanooga." Civil War Times Illustrated 10/5 (August 1971).

Washburn, Wiley A. "Cleburne's Division at Franklin." *Confederate Veteran* 13/1 (January 1905): 27–28.

Watkins, Sam. "Dead Angle, on the Kennesaw Line." *Confederate Veteran* 25/4 (April 1917): 166–67.

Wheeler, J. A. "Cleburne's Brigade at Shiloh." *Confederate Veteran* 2/1 (January 1894): 13.

Young, J. P. "Hood's Failure at Spring Hill." *Confederate Veteran* 16/2 (January 1908): 25–41.

———. "Remington and Gen. Hood at Spring Hill." *Confederate Veteran* 22/3 (March 1914): 126–28.

INDEX

Gibson, Randall 97–98, 205
Gibson, William 269–70, 274
Gilgal Church 276
Gillespie, John 281
Gilmer, Jeremy 36
Gist, States Rights 168, 179, 229, 311, 313, 354
Glasgow, Kentucky 87
Glass's Mill 147
Goldthwaite, Richard W. 168, 190–91, 196–97, 199
Gordon, George 346, 348, 350–51, 354
Govan, Daniel C. 130–31, 148, 165, 168, 182, 189, 197, 199, 213, 252, 261, 264, 268, 272, 287–88, 293–95, 299–300, 302, 307, 312, 343–44, 346–47
Granbury, Hiram 165, 171, 174, 176, 178–80, 182, 189, 193, 199, 213, 252, 259, 261, 263–64, 268–69, 273, 299–300, 307, 312, 316–17, 347, 350–51, 353–54, 360–61
Grant, Hector 3
Grant, Ulysses S. 12, 24, 27, 32, 36–38, 40–42, 46, 65, 128, 166–68, 229, 285
Gravesend, Ireland 2
Graysville, Georgia 184–85
Green. Israel 7
Green, J. W. 110
Greenville, Missouri 25–26
Grenada, Mississippi 36
Griffin, Eli 277
Grigsby, Warren 187, 259, 261
Guibor, Henry 347
Guy's Gap 132

Hall, William 289, 293, 295
Halleck, Henry W. 72–73, 75, 166
Hamburg-Savannah Road 63
Hamlin, Hannibal 8
Hanly, Sylvanus 28, 108
Hanly, Thomas 4, 21
Hanson, Roger 113
Hardcastle, Aaron 53, 213
Hardee, William J. 22–28, 30, 32, 36, 39, 41, 48, 51, 62–63, 74, 76, 89–91,

100, 105–106, 109, 113–14, 116, 119–24, 127–28, 133–34, 136, 169–71, 177, 179, 182–83, 186, 197, 203, 205, 207–208, 212, 222, 224, 244, 247, 252–53, 257, 259, 264–66, 275–76, 278, 280, 285–89, 292, 298–99, 302–303
Harker, Charles G. 161
Harper, W. A. 58
Harper's Ferry, Virginia 6, 8, 215
Harpeth River 336, 353, 356
Harrisburg, Mississippi 241
Harris, Isham 33, 35
Harris, J. T. 59
Harrison's Landing 138–40
Harrodsburg, Kentucky 88–90, 99
Harrow, William 275
Hazen, William B. 156–57, 167, 269–70
Helena, Arkansas 3–4, 17, 19, 28
Helm, Benjamin H. 153–54
Henryville, Tennessee 306
Herron, W. P. 153
Heth, Henry 79–80, 87, 100
Hildebrand, Jesse 55, 61–62
Hill, Benjamin 59–60, 73–74, 83–87
Hill, Daniel Harvey 136, 142–43, 146, 149, 151, 153–54, 156, 162, 206
Hindman, Thomas C. 25, 28, 37, 39, 41, 52, 54, 141–42, 144, 155, 204, 207, 210, 212, 221, 235, 249, 257, 260, 262
Hiwassee River 138–39
Holly Tree Gap 342
Homestead Act 8
Hood, John B. 140, 154–55, 225, 229, 237–39, 244, 249, 252–53, 255, 260–61, 263, 265–67, 275, 278–80, 283, 288, 292, 297, 299, 303–305, 310–13, 315, 317, 319–23, 326–28, 336, 340–44, 350, 355, 357–58
Hooker, Joseph 166–69, 184–88, 190, 194–97, 201, 267, 279, 286, 290, 292
Hoover's Gap 123–24, 126, 128–29, 132
Hornet's Nest 64
Howard, Oliver Otis 181, 268, 273, 284